Test Prep
MCSE

Microsoft® Windows® 98

New
Riders

201 West 103rd Street, Indianapolis, Indiana 46290

Alain Guilbault

MCSE TestPrep: Windows 98

Copyright © 1999 by New Riders Publishing

International Standard Book Number: 1-56205-922-X

Library of Congress Catalog Card Number: 98-87246

Printed in the United States of America

First Printing: October, 1998

00 99 98   4 3 2 1

Trademarks

Warning and Disclaimer

EXECUTIVE EDITOR
Mary Foote

ACQUISITIONS EDITOR
Sean Angus

DEVELOPMENT EDITOR
Susan Brown Zahn

MANAGING EDITOR
Sarah Kearns

PROJECT EDITOR
Christopher Morris

COPY EDITORS
Daryl Kessler,
Jill D. Bond

COVER DESIGNER
Dan Armstrong

BOOK DESIGNER
Barb Kordesh

INDEXER
Chris Barrick

TECHNICAL EDITOR
Al Dyne

PROOFREADER
Jeanne Clark

PRODUCTION
Cheryl Lynch
Jeannie McKay

Contents at a Glance

Introduction *00*

1 Planning 1
2 Installation and Configuration, Part 1 43
3 Installation and Configuration, Part 2: Network Components 85
4 Configuring and Managing Resource Access, Part 1 139
5 Configuring and Managing Resource Access, Part 2 175
6 Integration and Interoperability 215
7 Monitoring and Optimization 257
8 Troubleshooting 301
   Practice Exam 1 365
   Practice Exam 2 387

Appendix A: Exam Strategies *413*
Appendix B: Glossary *431*
Appendix C: Fast Facts *443*
Index *461*

Table of Contents

1 Planning   **1**

Practice Questions: Develop an Appropriate Implementation Model for
Specific Requirements in a Microsoft Environment and Mixed Microsoft
and NetWare Environment 3

Answers & Explanations: Develop an Appropriate Implementation Model
for Specific Requirements in a Microsoft Environment and Mixed Microsoft
and NetWare Environment 7
    Taking a Current Inventory 7
    Choosing a File System 8
    Preparing to Support Long Filenames 9
    Installing and Distributing the Software 11
    Choosing a Workgroup Configuration or Logging On to an Existing
      Domain 13
    Planning for Success 15

Practice Questions: Develop a Security Strategy in a Microsoft Environment
and Mixed Microsoft and NetWare Environment 18

Answers & Explanations: Develop a Security Strategy in a Microsoft
Environment and Mixed Microsoft and NetWare Environment 23
    User Profiles 23
    User Profiles on a Network 26
    File and Printer Sharing 29
    System Policies 31
    Installation Overview of System Policy Editor 33
    Creating Policies for Users, Groups, and Computers 35
    Policy Template Files 36
    Remote Registry Editing and System Monitoring 37

Further Review: Develop a Security Strategy in a Microsoft Environment
and Mixed Microsoft and NetWare Environment 39
    Remote Administration 39

Chapter Summary 41

2 Installation and Configuration, Part 1   43

Practice Questions: Install Windows 98 45

Answers & Explanations: Install Windows 98 50

   System Requirements 50

   New Installations 51

   Automated Windows Setup 53

   Creating the Startup Disk 53

   Upgrade Installations 55

   Dual-booting with Microsoft Windows NT 55

   Setup Failure Detection and Recovery 58

   Uninstalling Windows 98 59

Practice Questions: Install and Configure Hardware Devices in a Microsoft
Environment and a Mixed Microsoft and NetWare Environment 61

Answers & Explanations: Install and Configure Hardware Devices in a
Microsoft Environment and a Mixed Microsoft and NetWare Environment 65

   Modems 65

   Installing a Local Printer 67

   Network Printer Setup 68

   USB Support 71

   Multiple Display Support 72

   IEEE 1394 Specification 73

Further Review: Install and Configure Hardware Devices in a Microsoft
Environment and a Mixed Microsoft and NetWare Environment 75

   Examining COM Ports 75

   Infrared Technology—IrDA 76

Practice Questions: Install and Configure the Backup Application 77

Answers & Explanations: Install and Configure the Backup Application 79

   The Backup Application 80

   Tape Drives 83

Chapter Summary 84

3 Installation and Configuration, Part 2: Network Components   85

Practice Questions: Configure Windows 98 Server Components 87

Answers & Explanations: Configure Windows 98 Server Components 89
  Peer Web Server (PWS) 89
  Dial-Up Server Networking 91

Practice Questions: Install and Configure the Network Components of
Windows 98 in a Microsoft Environment and a Mixed Microsoft and
NetWare Environment 92

Answers & Explanations: Install and Configure the Network Components
of Windows 98 in a Microsoft Environment and a Mixed Microsoft and
NetWare Environment 98
  Network Services 98
  Microsoft Networks 102
  Installing and Configuring Adapters 106
  NetWare Networks 111
  Windows 98 and ATM 114
  Point-to-Point Tunneling Protocol/Virtual Private Networks (PPTP/VPN) 115
  Browser Service 118

Further Review: Install and Configure the Network Components of
Windows 98 in a Microsoft Environment and a Mixed Microsoft and
NetWare Environment 122
  File and Printer Sharing 122
  Unified Logon 123

Practice Questions: Install and Configure Network Protocols in a Microsoft
Environment and a Mixed Microsoft and NetWare Environment 124

Answers & Explanations: Install and Configure Network Protocols in a
Microsoft Environment and a Mixed Microsoft and NetWare Environment 127
  Network Protocols 129

Chapter Summary 138

4 Configuring and Managing Resource Access, Part 1   139

Practice Questions: Assign Access Permissions for Shared Folders in a
Microsoft Environment and a Mixed Microsoft and NetWare Environment 141

Answers & Explanations: Assign Access Permissions for Shared Folders in a
Microsoft Environment and a Mixed Microsoft and NetWare Environment 145
  User-level vs. Share-level Security 148

Practice Questions: Create, Share, and Monitor Resources 152

Answers & Explanations: Create, Share, and Monitor Resources 156
  Remote File Shares...157
  Network Printers 159
  Printer Properties 162

Practice Questions: Back Up Data and the Registry and Restore Data and
the Registry 163

Answers & Explanations: Back Up Data and the Registry and Restore Data
and the Registry 167
  Backup Utility 170

Chapter Summary 173

5 Configuring and Managing Resource Access, Part 2   175

Practice Questions: Set Up User Environments by User Profiles and
System Policies 177

Answers & Explanations: Set Up User Environments by User Profiles and
System Policies 182
  User Profiles 183
  System Policies...187
  Applying Policies for Users, Groups, and Computers 190

Further Review: Set Up User Environments by User Profiles and
System Policies 191
  Windows Shell Restrictions 191
  Control Panel Restrictions 192

Practice Questions: Configure Hard Disks 198

Answers & Explanations: Configure Hard Disks 202
    Disk Compression 203
    Partitioning 205
    Converting to FAT32 208

Practice Questions: Create Hardware Profiles 210

Answers & Explanations: Create Hardware Profiles 212
    Hardware Profiles 213

Chapter Summary 214

6 Integration and Interoperability   215

Practice Questions: Configure a Windows 98 Computer as a Client
Computer in a Windows NT Network 217

Answers & Explanations: Configure a Windows 98 Computer as a Client
Computer in a Windows NT Network 221
    Microsoft Network Provider 224

Practice Questions: Configure a Windows 98 Computer as a Client
Computer in a NetWare Network 228

Answers & Explanations: Configure a Windows 98 Computer as a Client
Computer in a NetWare Network 232
    Novell NetWare Client 235

Practice Questions: Configure a Windows 98 Computer to Access
the Internet by Using Various Methods in a Microsoft Environment
and a Mixed Microsoft and NetWare Environment 238

Answers & Explanations: Configure a Windows 98 Computer to Access
the Internet by Using Various Methods in a Microsoft Environment
and a Mixed Microsoft and NetWare Environment 244
    TCP/IP 245
    Setting Up Dial-Up Networking 249
    Getting to the Internet through Proxy Server 254

Chapter Summary 255

7 Monitoring and Optimization   **257**

Practice Questions: Monitor System Performance 259

Answers & Explanations: Monitor System Performance 262
   Net Watcher 263
   Using the System Monitor 266

Practice Questions: Tune and Optimize the System in a Microsoft
   Environment and a Mixed Microsoft and NetWare Environment 269

Answers & Explanations: Tune and Optimize the System in a Microsoft
   Environment and a Mixed Microsoft and NetWare Environment 276
   Disk Defragmenter 277
   ScanDisk 280
   DriveSpace 285
   Updating Drivers and Service Pack 289
   Automating Tasks by Using the Maintenance Wizard 293
   Scheduling Tasks by Using the Task Scheduler 295
   Checking for Corrupt Files 298

Chapter Summary 300

8 Troubleshooting   **301**

Practice Questions: Diagnose and Resolve Installation Failures 303

Answers & Explanations: Diagnose and Resolve Installation Failures 305
   Resolving Installation Failures 306

Practice Questions: Diagnose and Resolve Boot Process Failures 308

Answers & Explanations: Diagnose and Resolve Boot Process Failures ... 311
   Resolving Boot Failures 313

Practice Questions: Diagnose and Resolve Connectivity Problems in a
   Microsoft Environment and a Mixed Microsoft and NetWare Environment ... 316

Answers & Explanations: Diagnose and Resolve Connectivity Problems
   in a Microsoft Environment and a Mixed Microsoft and NetWare
   Environment 319
   Connectivity Problems 321

Practice Questions: Diagnose and Resolve Printing Problems in a Microsoft Environment and a Mixed Microsoft and NetWare Environment 327

Answers & Explanations: Diagnose and Resolve Printing Problems in a Microsoft Environment and a Mixed Microsoft and NetWare Environment 330

   Printing 333

Practice Questions: Diagnose and Resolve File System Problems 336

Answers & Explanations: Diagnose and Resolve File System Problems 339

   File System Problems 341

Practice Questions: Diagnose and Resolve Resource Access Problems in a Microsoft Environment and a Mixed Microsoft and NetWare Environment 344

Answers & Explanations: Diagnose and Resolve Resource Access Problems in a Microsoft Environment and a Mixed Microsoft and NetWare Environment 346

   Resource Access Problems 347

Practice Questions: Diagnose and Resolve Hardware Device and Device Driver Problems 350

Answers & Explanations: Diagnose and Resolve Hardware Device and Device Driver Problems 353

   Hardware/Software Conflicts 354

   Modification of the Registry 357

Chapter Summary 363

Practice Exam 1   **365**

Exam Questions 365

Answers & Explanations 383

Practice Exam 2   **387**

Exam Questions 387

Answers & Explanations 407

Appendix A: Exam Strategies   413

Types of Certification 413

Certification Requirements 414

    How to Become a Microsoft Certified Professional 414

    How to Become a Microsoft Certified Professional+Internet 414

    How to Become a Microsoft Certified Professional+Site Building 414

    How to Become a Microsoft Certified Systems Engineer 415

    How to Become a Microsoft Certified Systems Engineer+Internet 416

    How to Become a Microsoft Certified Solution Developer 417

    Becoming a Microsoft Certified Trainer 419

Study and Exam Preparation Tips 420

    Study Tips 420

    Exam Prep Tips 422

    Putting It All Together 426

Final Considerations 428

Appendix B: Glossary   431

Appendix C: Fast Facts   443

Introduction 443

Planning 443

    Develop an appropriate implementation model for specific requirements in a Microsoft environment and a mixed Microsoft and NetWare environment 443

    Develop a security strategy in a Microsoft environment and a mixed Microsoft and NetWare environment. 444

Installation and Configuration 445

    Install Windows 98. 445

    Configure Windows 98 server components. 446

    Install and configure the network components of Windows 98 in a Microsoft environment and a mixed Microsoft and NetWare environment. 447

    Install and configure network protocols in a Microsoft environment and a mixed Microsoft and NetWare environment. 448

    Install and configure hardware devices in a Microsoft environment and a mixed Microsoft and NetWare environment. 450

    Install and configure the Microsoft Backup. 451

Configuring and Managing Resource Access 452

    Assign access permissions for shared folders in a Microsoft environment and a mixed Microsoft and NetWare environment. 452

    Create, share, and monitor resources. 452

    Set up user environments by using user profiles and system policies. 453

    Back up data and the Registry and restore data and the Registry. 453

    Configure hard disks. 453

    Create hardware profiles. 454

Integration and Interoperability 454

Configure a Windows 98 computer as a client computer in a network that
contains a Windows NT 4.0 domain. 454

Configure a Windows 98 computer as a client computer in a NetWare
network. 455

Configure a Windows 98 computer for remote access by using various
methods in a Microsoft environment or a mixed Microsoft and NetWare
environment. 455

Monitoring and Optimization 456

Monitor system performance by using Net Watcher, System Monitor, and
Resource Meter. 456

Tune and optimize the system in a Microsoft environment and a mixed
Microsoft and NetWare environment. 456

Troubleshooting 458

Diagnose and resolve installation failures. 458

Diagnose and resolve boot process failures. 458

Diagnose and resolve connectivity problems in a Microsoft environment
and a mixed Microsoft and NetWare environment. 459

Diagnose and resolve printing problems in a Microsoft environment
and a mixed Microsoft and NetWare environment. 460

Diagnose and resolve file system problems. 460

Diagnose and resolve resource access problems in a Microsoft environment
and a mixed Microsoft and NetWare environment. 460

Diagnose and resolve hardware device and device driver problems. 460

Summary 460

Index   **461**

About the Author

Alain Guilbault is a Microsoft Certified Systems Engineer (MCSE) and a Microsoft Certified Trainer (MCT). Alain obtained his certifications for NT 3.51 and NT 4.0 while working as a full-time technical instructor and IT coordinator for an international training company. He has been in the computer-training arena for the last six years. He currently lives with his wife, Sara, in Calgary, Alberta, Canada.

About the Technical Editor

Al Dyne is an electronic/computer technologist with 12 years related PC experience. He currently works as a technical analyst with PBSC Computer Training Centres in Winnipeg, Manitoba, Canada.

Acknowledgments

I would like to thank all the influences around me that have made the production of this book possible. Jason and Sean, thanks for giving me the opportunity to work with you. Gwen and Dena, thanks for giving a push when I needed it and for the confidence you placed in me allowing me to become the MCSE and MCT I am today. Thanks as well to all the students whom I have had the privilege to guide though new products in the Microsoft world; your questions and enthusiasm have given me the inspiration in writing this book.

Dedication

I would like to dedicate this book to my wonderful and supportive wife, Sara. Thank you for giving me the time and encouragement to complete this book. Your understanding of my deadlines and work schedule have made this endeavor possible.

Tell Us What You Think!

As the reader of this book, *you* are our most important critic and commentator. We value your opinion and want to know what we're doing right, what we could do better, what areas you'd like to see us publish in, and any other words of wisdom you're willing to pass our way.

As the Executive Editor for the Networking team at Macmillan Computer Publishing, I welcome your comments. You can fax, email, or write me directly to let me know what you did or didn't like about this book—as well as what we can do to make our books stronger.

Please note that I cannot help you with technical problems related to the topic of this book, and that due to the high volume of mail I receive, I might not be able to reply to every message.

When you write, please be sure to include this book's title and author, as well as your name and phone or fax number. I will carefully review your comments and share them with the author and editors who worked on the book.

Fax: 317-581-4663

Email: certification@mcp.com

Mail: Executive Editor
          Networking
          201 West 103rd Street
          Indianapolis, IN 46290 USA

Introduction

The *MCSE TestPrep* series was created to serve as a study aid for people preparing for Microsoft Certification exams. The series is intended to help reinforce and clarify information with which you are already familiar by providing sample questions and tests, as well as summary information relevant to each of the exam objectives. Note that this series is *not* intended to be the only source for your preparation, but is rather a review of information with a set of practice tests that can be used to increase your familiarity with the exam questions. Using books in this series with books from the complementary *MCSE: Training Guide* series can increase the likelihood of your success when taking an exam.

WHO SHOULD READ THIS BOOK

The *Windows 98* book in the *MCSE TestPrep* series is intended specifically for students preparing for Microsoft's Implementing and Supporting Microsoft Windows 98 (70-098) exam, which is one of the core exam electives in the MCSE Microsoft Windows NT 4.0 Track program.

HOW THIS BOOK HELPS YOU

This book provides a wealth of review questions similar to those you will encounter in the actual exam, categorized by the objectives published by Microsoft for the exam. Each answer is explained in detail in the "Answers & Explanations" section for each objective. The "Further Review" section provides additional information that is crucial for successfully passing the exam. The two full-length practice exams at the end of the book will help you determine whether you have mastered the skills necessary to successfully complete the Microsoft exam. The practice exams will also identify which areas you need to study further before taking the actual exam.

HOW TO USE THIS BOOK

When you feel as though you're fairly well prepared for the exam, use this book as a test of your knowledge. After you have taken the practice tests and feel confident in the material on which you were tested, you should be ready to schedule your exam. Use this book for a final quick review just before taking the test to make sure that all the important concepts are set in your mind. Appendix C, "Fast Facts," summarizes key information you need to know about each objective. This feature is excellent for the last-minute review before you take the exam.

HARDWARE AND SOFTWARE RECOMMENDATIONS

MCSE TestPrep: Windows 98 is meant to help you review concepts with which you already have training and experience. To make the most of this review, you should have as much background and experience as possible. The best way to do this is to complement your study with work on real networks using the products on which you will be tested. This section provides a description of the minimum computer requirements you need to build a good practice environment.

The minimum computer requirements to study everything on which you are tested include one workstation running Windows 98, and one server running Windows NT Server—both of which must be connected by a network.

The minimum Windows 98 requirements are as follows:

- Any computer on the Microsoft Hardware Compatibility List (HCL)

- 486DX 33MHz or better (Pentium recommended)

- A minimum of 12MB of RAM (32MB recommended)

- 200MB (or larger) hard disk

- 3.5-inch 1.4MB floppy drive

- VGA (or Super VGA) video adapter

- VGA (or Super VGA) monitor

- Mouse or equivalent pointing device

- Two-speed (or faster) CD-ROM drive

- A Windows NT–compatible Network Interface Card (NIC)

- Presence on an existing network, or use of a hub to create a test network

The minimum Windows NT Server requirements are as follows:

- Any computer on the Microsoft Hardware Compatibility List (HCL)

- 486DX2 66MHz or better (Pentium recommended)

- 16MB of RAM (64MB recommended)

- 340MB (or larger) hard disk

- 3.5-inch 1.44MB floppy drive

- VGA (or Super VGA) video adapter

- VGA (or Super VGA) monitor

- Mouse or equivalent pointing device

- Two-speed (or faster) CD-ROM drive

- A Windows NT–compatible Network Interface Card (NIC)

- Presence on an existing network, or use of a hub to create a test network

- Microsoft Windows NT Server

WHAT THE IMPLEMENTING AND SUPPORTING MICROSOFT WINDOWS 98 EXAM (70-098) COVERS

The Implementing and Supporting Microsoft Windows 98 certification exam measures your ability to implement, administer, and troubleshoot information systems that incorporate Windows 98. It focuses on determining your skill level in six major areas:

- Planning

- Installation and Configuration

- Configuring and Managing Resource Access

- Integration and Interoperability

- Monitoring and Optimization

- Troubleshooting

The Implementing and Supporting Microsoft Windows 98 certification exam uses these categories to measure your ability. Before taking this exam, you should be proficient in the job skills discussed in the following sections.

Planning

The Planning section is designed to ensure that you understand how to create an unattended installation of Windows 98, developing strategies for sharing and securing resources, as well as selecting the appropriate file system.

Objectives for Planning

- Develop an appropriate implementation model for specific requirements in a Microsoft environment and a mixed Microsoft and NetWare environment. Considerations include the following:

  Choosing the appropriate file system

  Planning a workgroup

- Develop a security strategy in a Microsoft environment and a mixed Microsoft and NetWare environment. Strategies include the following:

  System policies

  User profiles

  File and printer sharing

  Share-level access control or user-level access control

Installation and Configuration

The Installation and Configuration section of the Windows 98 exam measures your knowledge about installation, basic setup, and configuration of Windows 98. You are tested on various items such as removing existing Windows 98 installations, configuring automated server-based installations for Enterprise environments, installing hardware components, and using Control Panel to configure the machine.

Objectives for Installation and Configuration

- Install Windows 98. Installation options include the following:

  Automated Windows setup

  New

  Upgrade

  Uninstall

  Dual-boot combination with Microsoft Windows NT 4.0

- Configure Windows 98 server components. Server components include the following:

  Microsoft Personal Web Server 4.0

  Dial-Up Networking server

- Install and configure the network components of Windows 98 in a Microsoft environment and a mixed Microsoft and NetWare environment. Network components include the following:

  Client for Microsoft Networks

  Client for NetWare Networks

  Network adapters

  File and Printer Sharing for Microsoft Networks

  File and Printer Sharing for NetWare Networks

  Service for NetWare Directory Services (NDS)

  Asynchronous Transfer Mode (ATM)

  Virtual private networking (VPN) and PPTP

  Browse Master

- Install and configure network protocols in a Microsoft environment and a mixed Microsoft and NetWare environment. Protocols include the following:

  NetBEUI

  IPX/SPX-compatible Protocol

  TCP/IP

  Microsoft DLC

  Fast Infrared

- Install and configure hardware devices in a Microsoft environment and a mixed Microsoft and NetWare environment. Hardware devices include the following:

  Modems

  Printers

  Universal Serial Bus (USB)

  Multiple display support

  IEEE 1394 Firewire

  Infrared Data Association (IrDA)

  Multilink

  Power management scheme

- Install and configure the Microsoft Backup.

Configuring and Managing Resource Access

The Managing Resources section measures your skills in areas such as creating and managing shares, setting permissions on folders and files, and installing and configuring printers. This section also tests your knowledge about monitoring network shares through the use of Net Watcher.

Objectives for Configuring and Managing Resource Access

- Assign access permissions for shared folders in a Microsoft environment and a mixed Microsoft and NetWare environment. Methods include the following:

  Passwords

  User permissions

  Group permissions

- Create, share, and monitor resources. Resources include the following:

  Remote computers

  Network printers

- Set up user environments by using user profiles and system policies.

- Back up data and the Registry and restore data and the Registry.

- Configure hard disks. Tasks include the following:

  Disk compression

  Partitioning

  Enabling large disk support

  Converting to FAT32

- Create hardware profiles.

Integration and Interoperability

The integration and interoperability section deal with Windows 98 in a mixed environment with Novell, NT Server, and UNIX-based Internet services.

Objectives for Integration and Interoperability

- Configure a Windows 98 computer as a client computer in a network that contains a Windows NT 4.0 domain.

- Configure a Windows 98 computer as a client computer in a NetWare network.

- Configure a Windows 98 computer for remote access by using various methods in a Microsoft environment or a mixed Microsoft and NetWare environment. Methods include the following:

  Dial-Up Networking

  Proxy Server

Monitoring and Optimization

The Monitoring and Optimization section focuses on your abilities to use various Windows 98 tools to monitor system performance and utilization, as well as to modify the tunable parameters of Windows 98 for optimal performance.

Objective for Monitoring and Optimization

- Monitor system performance by using Net Watcher, System Monitor, and Resource Meter.

- Tune and optimize the system in a Microsoft environment and a mixed Microsoft and NetWare environment. Tasks include the following:

  Optimizing the hard disk by using Disk Defragmenter and ScanDisk

  Compressing data by using DriveSpace 3 and the Compression Agent

Updating drivers and applying service packs by using Windows Update and the Signature Verification Tool

Automating tasks by using Maintenance Wizard

Scheduling tasks by using Task Scheduler

Checking for corrupt files and extracting files from the installation media by using the System File Checker

Troubleshooting

The Troubleshooting section of the Windows 98 certification exam measures your knowledge of troubleshooting problems with Windows 98 such as, but not limited to, printing, installation, resource access, and the boot process.

Objectives for Troubleshooting

- Diagnose and resolve installation failures. Tasks include the following:

  Resolving file and driver version conflicts by using Version Conflict Manager and the Microsoft System Information utility

- Diagnose and resolve boot process failures. Tasks include the following:

  Editing configuration files by using System Configuration Utility

- Diagnose and resolve connectivity problems in a Microsoft environment and a mixed Microsoft and NetWare environment. Tools include the following:

  WinIPCfg

  Net Watcher

Ping

Tracert

- Diagnose and resolve printing problems in a Microsoft environment and a mixed Microsoft and NetWare environment.

- Diagnose and resolve file system problems.

- Diagnose and resolve resource access problems in a Microsoft environment and a mixed Microsoft and NetWare environment.

- Diagnose and resolve hardware device and device driver problems. Tasks include the following:

Checking for corrupt Registry files by using ScanReg and ScanRegW

Thank you for choosing *MCSE TestPrep: Windows 98*. We're sure you'll find this a valuable review tool. For more study aids, check your bookstore for the *MCSE Training Guide: Windows 98* or *MCSE Fast Track: Windows 98*, published by New Riders Publishing. Good luck with your exam!

Planning

Planning for a new or upgrade installation of Windows 98 will prove to be very effective. Windows 98 can be used to upgrade Windows 3.1 or Windows 95, as well as coexist in a dual-boot environment. This chapter offers an overview of basic planning and implementation issues.

OBJECTIVES

This chapter helps prepare you for the exam by reviewing the following objectives:

Develop an appropriate Implementation Model for specific requirements in a Microsoft and mixed Microsoft/NetWare environment. Considerations include the following:

- **Choosing the appropriate file system**
- **Planning a workgroup**

▶ This objective addresses the overall installation requirements for Windows 98. Choices made during installation can almost always be altered later.

Develop a security strategy in a Microsoft environment and mixed Microsoft and NetWare environment. Strategies include the following:

- **System policies**
- **User profiles**
- **File and printer sharing**
- **Share-level access control or user-level access control**

continues

▶ Windows 98 provides you with policies and profiles to help implement a secured environment. From the initial planning stages, the implementation of Windows 98 should follow a sound security model.

DEVELOP AN APPROPRIATE IMPLEMENTATION MODEL FOR SPECIFIC REQUIREMENTS IN A MICROSOFT ENVIRONMENT AND MIXED MICROSOFT AND NETWARE ENVIRONMENT

1. To know if existing hardware will work with Windows 98, which of the following must you check?

   A. Hardware Checklist

   B. Hardware Compatibility List

   C. Hardware Component List

   D. Hardware List

   E. Hardware Client List

2. What gives Windows 98 the capability to support large hard drive partitions?

   A. LPD

   B. NTFS

   C. FAT32

   D. NPFS

   E. HPFS

3. Which operating systems support FAT32? Select all that apply.

   A. Windows NT

   B. Windows 95 with the Plus Pack

   C. Windows 95 OSR2

   D. Windows 98

   E. Windows 3.1

4. Which of the following cannot be dual-booted in Windows 98? Select the best answer.

   A. DOS 6.x

   B. Windows 3.1

   C. Windows 3.11

   D. Windows 3.0

   E. Windows NT

5. How many characters does Windows 98 support in Long Filenames?

   A. 55

   B. 255

   C. 155

   D. 355

   E. 640

6. If a user wants to add options such as new drivers to her version of Windows 98, where would she find the tools to install these options on her system?

   A. Windows Drivers in the Control Panel

   B. Windows Update on the Start menu

   C. Add/Remove Hardware in the Control Panel

D. Add/Remove Software in the Control Panel

E. Add/Remove New Drivers in the Start menu

7. **What is the file extension used with Setup Information Files?**

   A. .INF

   B. .IFN

   C. .INB

   D. .ISF

   E. .IGA

8. **Which of the following does Microsoft *not* recommend as an option for the installation of Windows 98? Select the best answer.**

   A. Push

   B. Pull

   C. Disk Images

   D. Upgrade

   E. Automated

9. **You are a network administrator implementing Windows 98 on workstations in the network. What is the name of the Microsoft server application that enables you to automate installations in the network?**

   A. SSI

   B. SMS

   C. SDS

   D. SMI

   E. SSS

10. **What is the installation process that allows installation from a remote server and is sent to a workstation through a login script?**

   A. Push

   B. Pull

   C. Automatic

   D. Disk Images

   E. Upgrade

11. **Microsoft has published a White Paper for the Disk Images installation process. What is the title of this White Paper?**

   A. Disk Images on Microsoft Operating Systems

   B. Binary image copying of Microsoft Operating Systems

   C. On-demand installation with Microsoft Operating Systems

   D. Disk Images copying on Microsoft Operating Systems

   E. Direct installs

12. **A user asks which operating system can be part of a Windows NT domain. What is the correct answer?**

   A. Windows 98 and Windows NT

   B. Windows NT

   C. Windows NT and Windows 3.11

   D. Windows NT and DOS 6.x

   E. Windows for Workgroups

13. **What happens when you make a workgroup name the same as your domain name?**

   A. An error message is displayed, saying the workgroup does not exist.

B. Your workstation is the only system you can see in the Network Neighborhood.

C. Your workstation appears to have joined the domain in the Network Neighborhood.

D. An error message is displayed, saying the domain does not exist.

E. None of the above.

14. **Your workgroup name is different from your domain name. Also, you do not have File and Printer Sharing installed in the workgroup. What is the message you receive when you try to access the Entire Network in Network Neighborhood?**

A. File and Printer Sharing has not been installed.

B. No domain exists in the network.

C. You must specify a Domain name.

D. Unable to Browse the Network.

E. Unable to access server.

15. **You are developing an Implementation Model for upgrading to Windows 98. Which of the following does not need to be considered as part of the Implementation Model?**

A. Setting up a test lab

B. Taking an inventory of current equipment and software

C. Checking power sources

D. Assembling a distribution team

E. Purchasing software

16. **You have finished your deployment plans. Which of the following steps should you do next?**

A. Document the problems and solutions.

B. Set up a test lab.

C. Assemble an implementation team.

D. Develop a security strategy.

E. Purchase software.

17. **What is the final step in the Implementation Model?**

A. Set up a test lab.

B. Take a hardware and software inventory.

C. Conduct the Final Implementation Model.

D. Assemble an implementation team.

E. Purchase software.

18. **You are assembling your distribution team. What is the advantage of choosing people from each department?**

A. You have more people to help with installation.

B. You get to know the users.

C. You will know how Windows 98 will affect the way each department operates.

D. You manage the installation process remotely.

E. None of the above.

19. **Why is it important to keep a test implementation of Windows small?**

A. To get a feel for the time it will take to implement Windows 98.

B. To see if users will be able to use Windows 98.

C. To get the users accustomed to Windows 98.

D. If there is a problem, you will be able to revert the workstations back to their original state.

E. To monitor progress in the workgroup.

The following question is scenario-based. Please read all the requirements and proposed solution before answering.

20. **Scenario:**

    Patrick is the head of the R & D department and has asked you to help him through the preparations of the impending conversion to Windows 98.

    Required component:
    He needs to be able to follow a step-by-step plan and assign responsibility to his staff.

    Optional components:
    Patrick would like all information documented and to have a system in place to allow his staff to keep track of issues as they arise.

    Patrick would also like to get the planning done this afternoon so the roll out can start tonight.

    Proposed solution:
    You outline the planning steps for Patrick as follows:

    1. Take an inventory of current equipment and software and compare with Windows 98's Hardware Compatibility List.

    2. Choose a file system FAT or FAT32.

    3. Choose a software distribution method.

    4. Choose a workgroup name in Workgroup or log on to an existing domain.

    5. Use Long Filenames on Servers.

    6. Assemble a distribution team.

    7. Set up a test lab.

    8. Conduct a test Implementation Model.

    9. Document the problems and solutions.

    10. Conduct the Final Implementation Model.

    A. The proposed solution satisfies the required component and all of the optional components.

    B. The proposed solution satisfies the required component but only one of the optional components.

    C. The proposed solution satisfies the required component but none of the optional components.

    D. The proposed solution satisfies only one of the optional components and does not satisfy the required component.

    E. The proposed solution does not satisfy the required component or the optional components.

ANSWER KEY

1. B	6. B	11. B	16. D
2. C	7. A	12. B	17. C
3. C-D	8. C	13. C	18. C
4. D	9. B	14. D	19. D
5. B	10. A	15. C	20. B

DEVELOP AN APPROPRIATE IMPLEMENTATION MODEL FOR SPECIFIC REQUIREMENTS IN A MICROSOFT ENVIRONMENT AND MIXED MICROSOFT AND NETWARE ENVIRONMENT

1. To know if existing hardware will work with Windows 98, which of the following must you check?

    B. Hardware Compatibility List

1. CORRECT ANSWER: B

Microsoft publishes what is called a Hardware Compatibility List (HCL). This list is found with the Windows 98 CD source files and, eventually, at Microsoft's Web page `http://www.microsoft.com/windows98`. For more information, see the section "Taking a Current Inventory."

Taking a Current Inventory

This explanation supports question 1.

Prior to any other planning for the installation, you must take a thorough inventory of all hardware and software that your organization is currently using. From this you should cull any items that are excessively old or otherwise incompatible with Windows 98. You can also determine what upgrades are necessary. You will eventually be able to get a copy of the Windows 98 Hardware Compatibility List (HCL) from Microsoft's Web site (see `www.microsoft.com/windows98`). For the same reason, the software currently installed on the system should be identified, and a list of software can then be built, detailing items that should be replaced or upgraded. This process helps to determine applications that might be incompatible with Windows 98. Microsoft also provides software compatibility lists as well.

2. What gives Windows 98 the capability to support large hard drive partitions?

    C. FAT32

2. CORRECT ANSWER: C

Windows 98 supports FAT and FAT32. FAT32 supports large hard drive partitions using a smaller cluster size resulting in a savings of drive space. For more information, see "Choosing a File System."

3. Which operating systems support FAT32? Select all that apply.

   C. Windows 95 OSR2

   D. Windows 98

3. CORRECT ANSWER: C-D

FAT32 is available on Windows 95 OSR2 and Windows 98 to support large hard drives efficiently. The sizes of the clusters are reduced from 64KB to 4KB. If Windows NT or DOS is installed on the same computer, it will not be able to access the file system and may not run at all. Over the network, NT or DOS will be able to access shared files on a Windows 98 machine with FAT32. For more information, see "Choosing a File System."

4. Which of the following cannot be dual-booted in Windows 98?

   D. Windows 3.0

4. CORRECT ANSWER: D

Windows 98 can dual-boot with Windows 3.1, DOS 6.x, Windows 3.11, and Windows 95. Windows 3.0 is not compatible with Windows 98. Windows 98 can be installed on a Windows 3.0 system, but it will simply override the files and not perform an upgrade. For more information, see "Choosing a File System."

Choosing a File System

This explanation supports questions 2 through 4.

Microsoft has two file systems: FAT and FAT32. FAT is the same old file system that has been used for years in DOS, Windows 3.1, Windows NT, and OS/2. The new FAT32 file system offers a better allocation of data on the hard drive, resulting in more storage capacity without the need for disk compression. The smallest storage unit on a hard drive is a *cluster*. Data cannot use certain portions of a cluster. The typical size of cluster that FAT uses is 64KB; FAT32 uses only 4KB clusters. If 2KB of data needs to be stored in a 64KB cluster, there are 62KB lost on the hard drive, whereas the same 2KB of data in a 4KB cluster only wastes 2KB. Imagine this misuse of space repeated over the entire hard drive, and you understand how FAT32 stores more data.

The use of FAT32 must be considered carefully. A computer that will need to dual-boot with DOS or Windows NT cannot use FAT32. Only Windows 98 and Windows 95 OSR2 can use FAT32 on their local drives.

▼ **NOTE**

If you are on a network, earlier versions of Windows can still gain access to your FAT32 hard drive through the network.

Microsoft provides a conversion utility to change from FAT to FAT32, but cannot change FAT32 back to FAT. In the latter case, the partition must be reformatted.

The following list includes some of the reasons you might want to keep FAT:

- For dual-booting with Windows NT

- For dual-booting with DOS 6.x and Windows 3.1 or Windows for Workgroups 3.11

- Because older disk utilities are DOS-based and cannot read the FAT32 format

5. How many characters does Windows 98 support in Long Filenames?

B. 255

5. CORRECT ANSWER: B

Windows 98 supports Long Filenames up to 255 characters. Older applications may only be able to handle the convention of 8.3, which is an eight-character filename followed by a three-character extension. For this reason, Windows 98 always saves a file with two names: the full name (up to 255 characters) and a short name (8.3). For more information, see "Preparing to Support Long Filenames."

Preparing to Support Long Filenames

This explanation supports question 5.

Windows 98 supports filenames of up to 255 characters. For computers that are not running Windows 98, your filenames must conform to other standards. Some NetWare servers might not support Long Filenames. You must add Long Filenames support to your NetWare volumes to store files with longer filenames. Windows 3.x and DOS applications do not support Long Filenames, either. Windows 98 auto-generates short 8.3-compatible file- and folder names for such applications. Windows 98 uses the first six valid characters from the full name followed by ~1. If more than one file uses the first six characters, a ~2, and so on, are added. The extension is the first three characters after the first period (.) in the full name.

6. **If a user wants to add options such as new drivers to her version of Windows 98, where would she find the tools to install these options on her system?**

   B. **Windows Update on the Start menu**

6. CORRECT ANSWER: B

Windows 98 can connect to the Internet and download new drivers for the system. Microsoft keeps a Web site with the most current drivers. Your system can evaluate by comparing revision dates which current drivers need to be updated. Windows Update can also be found in the Start, Settings menu. For more information, see "Installing and Distributing the Software."

7. **What is the file extension used with Setup Information Files?**

   A. **.INF**

7. CORRECT ANSWER: A

All Windows 98 Setup Information Files have an extension of .INF, which is short for information file. An information file is used to automatically answer questions from the Setup program. For more information, see "Installing and Distributing the Software."

8. **Which of the following does Microsoft *not* recommend as an option for the installation of Windows 98?**

   C. **Disk Images**

8. CORRECT ANSWER: C

Disk Images is not recommended by Microsoft because it requires an exact duplicate of the system from which the Disk Image was created. With the improvements of Plug and Play, it has become easier to use. For more information, see "Installing and Distributing the Software."

9. **You are a network administrator implementing Windows 98 on workstations in the network. What is the name of the Microsoft server application that enables you to automate installations in the network?**

   B. **SMS**

9. CORRECT ANSWER: B

The System Management Server (SMS) from Microsoft copies source files to a location you specify and can initiate an installation automatically. The source files are used to install with the help of an *.INF file. The client machine may have this SMS package delivered at a specific time or at the next login. For more information, see "Installing and Distributing the Software."

10. What is the installation process that allows installation from a remote server and is sent to a workstation through a login script?

A. Push

11. Microsoft has published a White Paper for the Disk Images installation process. What is the title of this White Paper?

B. Binary image copying of Microsoft Operating Systems

10. CORRECT ANSWER: A

Push runs a standard scripted installation from the server to the workstation. The Push is not initiated by the user or the local system; rather, it is sent to the system. For more information, see "Installing and Distributing the Software."

11. CORRECT ANSWER: B

Microsoft does not recommend Disk Images on Windows 98 and has released White Paper 1.9 on this issue. For more information, see "Installing and Distributing the Software."

Installing and Distributing the Software

This explanation supports questions 6 through 11.

There are several options that you might want to consider when installing and distributing software. The three most important are Push installations with packages such as Microsoft's System Management Server (SMS), Pull or Automatic installation, and Disk Images. Push and Pull installations both run a standard scripted installation of Windows 98, which is the cleanest (and most recommended) way of deploying Windows 98.

Push installs are initiated at a remote server and sent to the workstation through a login script or other application. If you are using a network management package such as SMS, the server actually moves your source files to a location of your choice. SMS then sends the installation command to the workstation. The workstation starts the installation of Windows 98 by using a setup information (*.INF) file that ships with SMS or one that you have created.

Pull installations also use a setup .INF file that you have created, but the installation is initiated at the client workstation and pulled down from the server. You can use Netsetup, which comes with Windows 98. This utility enables you to place Windows 98 on a server for setup to desktop systems. This is different from copying files during an installation. You can also customize the setup .INF file for your organization.

Disk Images offers advantages over the previous two methods. The entire hard drive can be configured with multiple applications after the Windows 98 installation has been completed. This fully configured hard drive can now be copied to a single file through a special application. The process is then reversed to copy the contents of the file back to a hard drive. The destination hard drive should be in a computer that is similar in hardware configuration to the original, or source, computer. When the image is copied to another system, it is an identical copy. This means the computer name will conflict with the original. After the computer name is changed, this error is corrected. If the hardware is not identical, Windows 98 will use its Plug and Play to make the necessary adjustments.

Microsoft does not fully support or recommend the Disk Images method of installation of Windows 98. For more information, about this process, see the "Binary image copying of Microsoft Operating Systems" White Paper 1.9 from Microsoft.

Scripts (*.INF) are clean, but they often require several different scripts to get Windows 98 and all applications installed. Images are easier to install but are not as clean, because they are hardware-specific.

12. A user asks which operating system can be part of a Windows NT domain. What is the correct answer?

    B. Windows NT

12. CORRECT ANSWER: B

The only operating system that can be part of a Windows NT domain is Windows NT. All operating systems listed allow the user name to log in to the domain and participate as a user, but this is not the same as the computer being part of the domain. For more information, see "Choosing a Workgroup Configuration or Logging On to an Existing Domain."

13. What happens when you make a workgroup name the same as your domain name?

    C. Your workstation appears to have joined the domain in the Network Neighborhood.

13. CORRECT ANSWER: C

You are able to see the domain servers immediately when you open Network Neighborhood and get the same views as if your computer were part of the domain. In Windows NT Server Manager, the Windows 98 computer name is listed along with other computers that are in the domain.

The Windows 98 system is not able to administer remotely using the Server Manager, thus is not part of the domain. For more information, see "Choosing a Workgroup Configuration or Logging On to an Existing Domain."

14. Your workgroup name is different from your domain name. Also, you do not have File and Printer Sharing installed in the workgroup. What is the message you receive when you try to access the Entire Network in Network Neighborhood?

    D. Unable to Browse the Network.

14. CORRECT ANSWER: D

If you do not have at least one system in a workgroup with File and Printer Sharing enabled, you cannot see any other workstations or servers on the network. Each workgroup or domain must have a Master Browser. To even be considered to be a Master Browser, you must have File and Printer Sharing turned on. You can access the server though a drive mapping and a command line. Changing the name of the workgroup to match that of the domain allows the Windows 98 computers to use the domain's Master Browser. For more information, see "Choosing a Workgroup Configuration or Logging On to an Existing Domain."

Choosing a Workgroup Configuration or Logging On to an Existing Domain

This information supports questions 12 through 14.

When configuring a workgroup name for Windows 98, you should take some care in choosing the name. If the name is different from the workgroup names used by any servers on your network, then you are required to perform several additional steps to be able to browse network resources without knowing the names of the servers you want to access. The term *server* refers to any computer on your network that shares resources. This could be a NetWare server, but also it encompasses Windows for Workgroups, Windows 95, Windows 98, and Windows NT. If you decide to make your workgroup name the same as your domain name, then your computer appears to have joined the domain in the Network Neighborhood. The benefit of this is seeing the domain servers as soon as you open the Network Neighborhood (see Figure 1.1), which makes navigating your server's unmapped drives much easier.

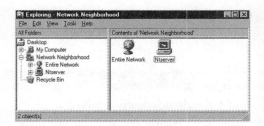

FIGURE 1.1
When you open the Network Neighborhood, you see the contents of your current workgroup.

▼ **NOTE**

Windows 98 can only be a part of a workgroup on your network. The only operating system that can be a part of a Windows NT domain is Windows NT. If you set a Windows 98 workgroup name to a Windows NT domain name currently in use, both computers share a list of resources. The Windows 98 computers also appear in Windows NT administration tools, such as Server Manager. This appearance is an illusion; the Windows 98 computers are not actually a part of the domain and therefore cannot be controlled by Windows NT.

If you choose a name for your workgroup that is different from your domain name, then you will have a shorter server list in that domain, but you will have to locate those servers through the Entire Network icon of the Network Neighborhood.

If you choose a workgroup name that differs from your domain name, then at least one computer in that workgroup must have File and Printer Sharing installed. By installing File and Printer Sharing, you ensure that the computer will maintain a list of servers in the workgroup, as well as a list of other workgroups or domains that exist on the network. If you do not have this list, you receive an "Unable to Browse the Network" error message when attempting to access the Entire Network icon of the Network Neighborhood. You can still access network resources through drive mappings for the Start Run menu. You just are not able to use the browsing tool.

15. **You are developing an Implementation Model for upgrading to Windows 98. Which of the following does not need to be considered as part of the Implementation Model?**

    C. Checking power sources

15. CORRECT ANSWER: C

Hopefully this issue would have already been resolved in an existing computing environment. For more information, see "Planning for Success."

16. **You have finished your deployment plans. Which of the following steps should you do next?**

    D. Develop a security strategy.

16. CORRECT ANSWER: D

Your deployment model should have covered all the steps in this objective. The next phase would be the beginning of a security strategy. For more information, see "Planning for Success."

17. What is the final step in the
Implementation Model?

    C. Conduct the Final Implementation
       Model.

Conducting the Final Implementation Model is the final step
and should be done in a logical order. Many administrators
jump right to this phase without proper planning. In some
cases, it works fine. In most cases, however, there are a lot of
revisions and repetition needed to get the setup just right.
Planning takes time initially, but can help save time in the
long run. For more information, see "Planning for Success."

18. You are assembling your distribution
team. What is the advantage of choosing people from each department?

    C. You will know how Windows 98 will
       affect the way each department
       operates.

You will see how the departments operate and how the
Windows 98 installation will affect each department. You will
be able to isolate individual problems on a departmental basis.
For more information, see "Planning for Success."

19. Why is it important to keep a test
implementation of Windows small?

    D. If there is a problem, you will be able
       to revert the workstations back to
       their original state.

If there are problems found in the test lab, you can revert a
small number of machines back to their original state. This
would not be a large disruption to business operations. For
more information, see "Planning for Success."

20. Proposed solution:

You outline the planning steps for
Patrick as follows:

    1. Take an inventory of current equip-
       ment and software and compare
       with Windows 98's Hardware
       Compatibility List.

    2. Choose a file system FAT or FAT32.

    3. Choose a software distribution
       method.

    4. Choose a workgroup name in
       Workgroup or log on to an existing
       domain.

    5. Use Long Filenames on servers.

    6. Assemble a distribution team.

    7. Set up a test lab.

The proposed solution provides Patrick with all the steps he
needs to follow to assure a successful roll out. Every item can
be assigned to a staff member of his team. The only problem
with Patrick's expectations is that he fails to understand the
time required to perform the testing in the lab before the roll
out. For more information, see "Planning for Success."

Planning for Success

This explanation supports questions 15 through 20.

After taking an inventory, steps should be taken to get a repre-
sentative sample of the various pieces of hardware and software
that are in use on the network. The computers in the test lab
are used to develop the installation script files (*.INF), as well
as the installation procedure.

20. **Proposed solution: continued**

    8. **Conduct a test Implementation Model.**

    9. **Document the problems and solutions.**

    10. **Conduct the Final Implementation Model.**

    B. **The proposed solution satisfies the required component but only one of the optional components.**

Windows 98 is compatible with a very wide range of hardware, but there are often times when certain pieces of hardware do not function properly together. Occasionally, you find information about incompatibilities listed in the installation documentation or the Web site for the hardware. You might also need updated drivers for the hardware before it will work properly with Windows 98. The importance of the test lab is similar to that of the distribution team. By choosing wisely, you limit the number of surprises that will occur during the actual deployment.

After performing thorough testing of the software and hardware, you are ready to conduct a test or pilot Implementation Model. This test should be limited in scope so problems can be given a proper amount of attention and time. A test Implementation Model might be made up of only one department or even just a handful of people in a department.

The test Implementation Model provides a shakedown test of the installation procedure you developed through testing. It also enables you to see what changes should be made to the installation procedure to keep problems from arising at the time of the entire installation. Because the number of computers in the test implementation has been kept relatively small, you may be able to revert them back to their original state if problems occur.

Documentation is one of the keys to a successful Implementation Model, but is often overlooked. Any problems you have should be documented and added to a database. This database can be referred to and updated during the Implementation Model. Document the steps required to perform the setup of each computer so that your distribution team will not have to perform ad hoc installs.

You should plan to perform upgrades in synchronization with a training schedule for the users. The training should cover the changes to their operating system, as well as any changes to the applications they use. Windows 98 enables users to be more productive, but productivity will drop during the orientation phase. By delivering timely training, this drop in productivity will be minimized.

The Final Implementation Model should be scheduled to convert users in a logical order. This order should be determined by how one upgraded user will affect the users who have not yet been upgraded. You might decide that upgrading by branch or department makes the most sense in your situation. On the other hand, you might decide that because sections of two departments communicate regularly, they should be upgraded at the same time. If you have to upgrade a number of branches, you will likely upgrade them one at a time; but you might start with the head office, because people in the head office need to communicate with all other branches.

Whatever order in which you decide to implement the upgrades, you should educate all of the users, upgraded or not, on how the temporary mixed environment will affect the way they work. Throughout this whole process, you should refer to the deployment database for solutions to previous problems, as well as for posting new problems and solutions.

Your deployment plan covers compatibility and logistics, but you have not yet created a secure network. The next major section prepares you to develop a security strategy.

Having other people with you as you implement Windows 98 will make the whole process move more smoothly. Choose people who can represent a number of departments or areas to enable your Implementation Model to address many of the concerns that are held in each of the departments.

By choosing people from each department, you will be aware of how the departments operate and how Windows 98 will affect both the way the department operates and the applications individuals within each department use.

DEVELOP A SECURITY STRATEGY IN A MICROSOFT ENVIRONMENT AND MIXED MICROSOFT AND NETWARE ENVIRONMENT

1. When enabling User Profiles, if you choose Include Desktop Icons and Network Neighborhood Contents, which of the following folders will not be duplicated for each user who logs on?

   A. Briefcase

   B. NetHood

   C. Desktop

   D. Recent

   E. Profile

2. What is the filename for default User Profiles?

   A. USER.BIN

   B. USER.EXE

   C. USER.MDF

   D. USER.DAT

   E. USER.DEF

3. When User Profiles are created, they are stored in which of the following directories? Select the best answer.

   A. C:\PROFILES

   B. C:\WINDOWS\PROFILES

   C. C:\WINDOWS\USERS

   D. C:\USERS

   E. C:\USERS\PROFILES

4. The location for enabling User Profiles can be under which icons in the Control Panel? Select all that apply.

   A. System Manager

   B. Network

   C. Passwords

   D. Users

   E. Profiles

5. What set of permissions is a user required to have in the home directory of the User Environment Profile on a Windows NT network?

   A. [RWX]

   B. [RXCG]

   C. [RWD]

   D. [RWXD]

   E. [RWCD]

6. Other than Microsoft's File and Printer Sharing for Microsoft Networks using user-level security, what is another way to implement File and Printer Sharing security?

A. Administration-level Access Control

B. Group-level Access Control

C. Share-level Access Control

D. Novel-level Access Control

E. Admin-level Access Control

7. **What is the only security option available when using Microsoft's File and Printer Sharing for NetWare?**

A. Group-level Access Control

B. Supervisor-level Access Control

C. Share-level Access Control

D. User-level Access Control

E. Admin-level Access Control

8. **Which of the following is considered to provide better security than Share-level Access Control?**

A. Workstation-level Access Control

B. Network-level Access Control

C. User-level Access Control

D. Group-level Access Control

E. Admin-level Access Control

9. **What is the single file referred to on a server processed when users log on to a network?**

A. Windows 98 policy

B. System policy

C. Network policy

D. Administration policy

E. User policy

10. **What sets up a user-specific customized environment maintained for each user by the user?**

A. User Profiles

B. User Policies

C. Group Policies

D. Group Profiles

E. None of the above

11. **The System Policy Editor is not installed by default. Where can the System Policy Editor be found on the Windows 98 CD-ROM?**

A. TOOLS\RESKIT\NETADMIN\POLEDIT

B. TOOLS\NETADMIN\POLEDIT

C. TOOLS\RESKIT\NETADMIN\POLICY

D. ADMIN\ADMINTOOLS\POLEDIT

E. ADMIN\TOOLS\POLEDIT

12. **What is the name of the Windows 98 Default Policy File?**

A. CONFIG.INF

B. CONFIG.DAT

C. CONFIG.POL

D. CONFIG.SYS

E. CONFIG.PLC

13. **Where does Windows 98 store the Default Policy File for a Novell NetWare network?**

A. SYS:SYSTEM

B. SYS:LOGIN

C. SYS:ETC

D. SYS:PUBLIC

E. SYS:POLICY

14. **You are using the System Policy Editor to create a new policy file. What two options are available?**

    A. LOCAL USER and DEFAULT COMPUTER

    B. LOCAL USER and LOCAL COMPUTER

    C. DEFAULT USER and LOCAL COMPUTER

    D. DEFAULT USER and DEFAULT COMPUTER

    E. LOCAL COMPUTER and DEFAULT USER

15. **Where are the changes stored when you alter the computer settings in the System Policy Editor?**

    A. SYSTEM.INI

    B. COMPUTER.DAT

    C. SYSTEM.DAT

    D. COMPUTER.INI

    E. POLICY.INI

16. **A new user logs on to a Windows 98 workstation. This user does not belong to a group and no policy has been set for this user. What policy entry does Windows 98 apply for this user?**

    A. DEFAULT COMPUTER

    B. LOCAL USER

    C. DEFAULT USER

    D. LOCAL COMPUTER

    E. No policy is applied

    The following question is scenario-based. Please read all the requirements and proposed solution before answering.

17. **Scenario:**

    Mike is a consultant hired to implement standards in a new Windows 98 environment. Mike will be moving on as soon as the job is done, so he wants to make sure the local administrators have some tools to control the environment.

    Required component:
    Mike is looking at a standard working environment for all Windows 98 systems in the network.

    Optional components:
    Mike needs to have the flexibility to let his users control their desktops a little and be mobile in the office.

    Mike would also like to have the ability to override any user preferences or configure any computer centrally.

    Proposed solution:
    Install all Windows 98 computers using one standard script.

    Activate User Profiles for all users.

    Set up a home directory on a Windows NT server for each user.

    Create a policy file and save it as Config.pol in the NETLOGON share of all the Domain Controllers.

    A. The proposed solution satisfies the required component and all of the optional components.

    B. The proposed solution satisfies the required component but only one of the optional components.

    C. The proposed solution satisfies the required component but none of the optional components.

    D. The proposed solution satisfies only one of the optional components and does not satisfy the required component.

E. The proposed solution satisfies neither
the required component nor the
optional components.

18. **Which of the following are default template files used by the System Policy
Editor? Select all that apply.**

A. COMMON.ADM

B. ADMIN.ADM

C. WINDOWS.ADM

D. WINDOWS98.ADM

E. POLICY98.ADM

**The following question is scenario-based.
Please read all the requirements and proposed solution before answering.**

19. **Scenario:**

Sara is implementing Remote Administration
for all Windows 98 computers in the office.
She asks you to help her through the preparations and configuration of the systems.

Required component:
Sara needs to be able use Remote
Administration to monitor network activity
and control shares.

Optional components:
Sara would like to make sure only Domain
Admins are allowed to perform any Remote
Administration.

Sara would also like to use the remote
Registry tool.

Proposed solution:
Install all Windows 98 computers to have the
following:

File and Printer Sharing

User-level security

Remote Administration enabled with only
the default Domain Admins group having
permission

A. The proposed solution satisfies the
required component and all of the
optional components.

B. The proposed solution satisfies the
required component but only one of
the optional components.

C. The proposed solution satisfies the
required component but none of the
optional components.

D. The proposed solution satisfies only one
of the optional components and does
not satisfy the required component.

E. The proposed solution satisfies neither
the required component nor the
optional components.

**The following question is scenario-based.
Please read all the requirements and proposed solution before answering.**

20. **Scenario:**

Carol would like to access all the hard drives
and Windows installation directories on
Windows 98 computers. Remote Administration
for all Windows 98 computers is already in
place. She asks you to help her through the
preparations and configuration of the systems.

Required component:
Carol needs to be able use Remote
Administration to access the local hard drives
and Windows directory of all Windows 98 computers on the network. Only Domain Admins
are allowed to perform any Remote
Administration on these drives.

Optional components:

Carol would like to access the CD-ROM on the remote systems.

Carol would also like to perform these tasks from her Windows NT workstation computer because she is a member of the Domain Admins global group.

Proposed solution:

Install all Windows 98 computers to have the following:

File and Printer Sharing

User-level security

Remote Administration enabled with only the default Domain Admins group having permission

A. The proposed solution satisfies the required component and all of the optional components.

B. The proposed solution satisfies the required component but only one of the optional components.

C. The proposed solution satisfies the required component but none of the optional components.

D. The proposed solution satisfies only one of the optional components and does not satisfy the required component.

E. The proposed solution satisfies neither the required component nor the optional components.

DEVELOP A SECURITY STRATEGY IN A MICROSOFT ENVIRONMENT AND MIXED MICROSOFT AND NETWARE ENVIRONMENT

1. When enabling User Profiles, if you choose Include Desktop Icons and Network Neighborhood Contents, which of the following folders will not be duplicated for each user who logs on?

A. Briefcase

1. CORRECT ANSWER: A

The Briefcase folder is user specific and is controlled by the user. Each user can create personal briefcases. By default, all users who log on see a common briefcase from Windows\ Desktop\My Briefcase. For more information, see "User Profiles."

2. What is the filename for default User Profiles?

D. USER.DAT

2. CORRECT ANSWER: D

Until User Profiles are established, everyone logging on to Windows 98 uses USER.DAT. After User Profiles are created, each user has his own copy of USER.DAT. For more information, see "User Profiles."

3. When User Profiles are created, they are stored in which of the following directories?

B. C:\WINDOWS\PROFILES

3. CORRECT ANSWER: B

A directory for each User Profile is created in the C:\WINDOWS\ PROFILES directory. A user named Mike would have a profile directory of C:\WINDOWS\PROFILES\MIKE. For more information, see "User Profiles."

4. The location for enabling User Profiles can be under which icons in the Control Panel?

C. Passwords

D. Users

4. CORRECT ANSWER: C-D

Under the Passwords icon you see a tab for User Profiles, or you can use the Users icon's Create a New User option to enable User Profiles. For more information, see "User Profiles."

User Profiles

This explanation supports questions 1 through 4.

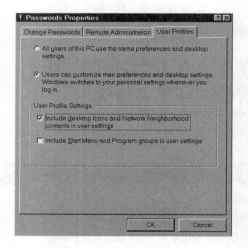

FIGURE 1.2
Use the Passwords Control Panel to enable
User Profiles.

User Profiles are customized settings for each user's environment. Until this option is enabled, every person who logs on to the computer uses the same USER.DAT file and shares the same subfolders in the Windows folder. After turning on this feature, each user gets her own settings or USER.DAT file and her own folder in the Windows folder. If the servers and workstations have all been properly configured, in a network environment, these settings will follow her from computer to computer.

To turn on User Profiles, you have to choose the User Profiles tab in the Passwords Control Panel (see Figure 1.2). Select the Users Can Customize Their Preferences and Desktop Settings option button. Windows switches to your personal settings whenever you log in. This enables User Profiles after your next reboot. When you reboot, Windows takes your username and creates a directory with your username in the C:\WINDOWS\ PROFILES directory (see Figure 1.3).

By enabling User Profiles, Windows now maintains a separate USER.DAT file for each user. The USER.DAT file contains all the personal Control Panel settings for a user.

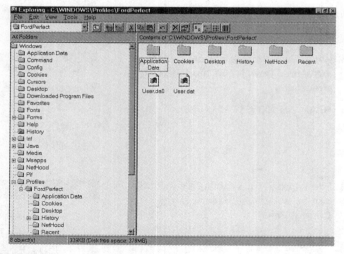

FIGURE 1.3
Windows 98 creates a directory for each user in the Profiles directory.

By choosing the Include Desktop icon and Network Neighborhood Contents in User Settings check box, you maintain additional settings for each user. The following folders from the Windows directory are also duplicated for each user who logs on:

- Desktop

- NetHood

- Recent

By also selecting the Include Start Menu and Program Groups in the User Settings check box, you maintain separate Start menus and Programs folders.

If a Local Profile becomes corrupt, you can escape the Logon dialog box and delete any or all of the profile in the Profiles directory. If the entire directory for a user is deleted, then fresh copies of the files and directories are taken from the Windows directory.

User Profiles are vital to security because System policies enforce their environment changes on the user by modifying each user's profile.

Windows 98 offers a new tool to create or customize Users Profiles. From the Control Panel, access the Users icon. This icon is very similar to the User Profiles tab in the Passwords icon. It offers more control over how a new User Profile is created. After a second profile has been generated, the system invokes User Profiles.

Creating a new user with the Users icon involves a wizard that the owner or administrator of the system can use to control usernames, passwords, and settings (see Figure 1.4). The items that can be customized include the following:

- Desktop folder and Documents menu

- Start menu

- Favorites folder

- Downloaded Web pages

- My Documents folder

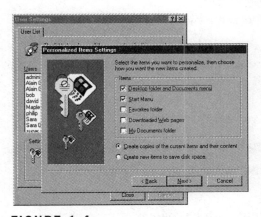

FIGURE 1.4

Each new user can be configured to maintain separate settings by using the Users icon in the Control Panel. The administrator can create profiles and let users maintain them.

Additional settings allow you to use a copy of the current uses settings or start from scratch. The wizard then creates the custom folder and settings for the new user. In this way you can control the usernames and settings initially.

The User Settings tool offers administrative options as well. A User Profile can be duplicated or deleted. When a profile is deleted, all the files and folders that were associated with the user are removed.

User passwords can be set or changed, and custom settings can be redefined if needed. Perhaps a user no longer wants a custom Start menu. It can be removed and the user reverts to using the default menu.

5. What set of permissions is a user required to have in the home directory of the User Environment Profile on a Windows NT network?

D. [RWXD]

5. CORRECT ANSWER: D

The user needs Read, Write, Execute, and Delete permissions to maintain the User Profiles. Every change made by the user must be saved back to the original location. For more information, see "User Profiles on a Network."

User Profiles on a Network

This information supports question 5.

If you are logging on to a Windows NT domain or a Novell NetWare 3.1x or 4.x server, your User Profile can follow you around the network, if certain conditions are met. The term for the ability of User Profiles to follow the user around the network is *Roving* (or *Roaming*) Profiles.

For Windows NT networks, the following conditions must be met:

- The Windows NT network must be configured as a domain.

- The user's account must be configured for a network directory in the Home Directory section of the User Environment Profile, as shown in Figure 1.5. The user must have at least Change [RWXD] permissions to the directory.

- The client computer must be configured to log on to the Windows NT domain. This is done through the properties of the Client for Microsoft Networks in the Network Control Panel, as shown in Figure 1.6.

- User Profiles must be enabled on the User Profiles tab of the Passwords Control Panel.

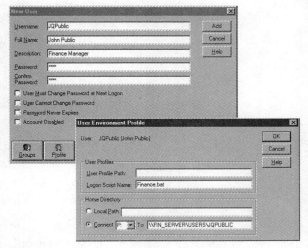

FIGURE 1.5

Setting a home directory for a user with User Manager for domains.

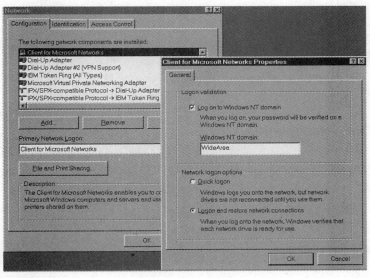

FIGURE 1.6

Domain logons are enabled in the Network Control Panel on the client.

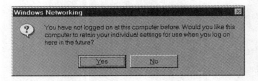

FIGURE 1.7
All new users are prompted to retain settings.

When the prior conditions are met, the User Profile is activated upon the next logon. During the logon process, the user is told that he has not logged on to this computer before and asked if he would like to retain his settings for the future (see Figure 1.7). If the answer is No, the default files found in the Windows directory are used; if the answer is Yes, these files are copied into the user's Local Profile directory. When the user logs out, the Local Profile directory is copied to the user's directory on the server—including any shortcuts that are on the desktop. Windows 98 does not copy the files (except for USER.DAT) as part of the profile.

When working with profiles, Windows 98 always checks in the network location to see if you already have a profile created. If it finds one, it copies it down to your Local Profile directory.

If you or your network administrator renames the USER.DAT file to USER.MAN, then any desktop changes that are made are not saved back to the network copy of your profile. These are referred to as Mandatory Profiles.

For NetWare 3.1x and NetWare 4.1 servers, the profile is automatically stored in the user's NetWare mail directory. If you are using a NetWare 4.11 server, then a Home directory must be configured in the user's account properties to store the User Profile.

6. **Other than Microsoft's File and Printer Sharing for Microsoft Networks using User-level security, what is another way to implement File and Printer Sharing security?**

   C. Share-level Access Control

6. CORRECT ANSWER: C

The Default System Security is Share-level Access Control. Without having a security provider, such as Windows NT or Novell, Windows 98 can share folders using only passwords. This type of security is not preferred because it requires users to maintain a list of passwords. Share-level security simply requires them to log in once with one password to have access to several shares on several Windows 98 systems. For more information, see "File and Printer Sharing."

7. **What is the only security option available when using Microsoft's File and Printer Sharing for NetWare?**

   D. User-level Access Control

For Microsoft's File and Printer Sharing for NetWare, the Windows 98 system must implement User-level Access Control. A Novell server is entered as the security provider. This assumes other clients on the network are logging in to the same Novell server. For more information, see "File and Printer Sharing."

8. **Which of the following is considered to provide better security than Share-level Access Control?**

   C. User-level Access Control

You must have a valid username and password with User-level Access Control. Users must be authenticated by a domain controller in the first place. With Share-level, all that is needed is a password. For more information, see "File and Printer Sharing."

File and Printer Sharing

This information supports questions 6 through 8.

File and Printer Sharing services can represent a major security problem on your network, and this is something you must consider before conducting your installations.

Many LAN administrators flinch at the mention of Personal File and Printer Sharing because it takes control away from the central security, which is usually the administrator. This section elaborates on the purpose and use of File and Printer Sharing services, as well as the differences in sharing methods between the two services that Microsoft supplies.

Files are kept safe, and information is kept hidden most effectively, if the files reside on a central server where a central security authority can control access to them. With the files in this central location, administrators can control who has access and the level of access each person has. On the point of safe files, most sites have implemented procedures to regularly back up the contents of the servers, daily or less often.

When files are kept on local hard drives, security is compromised. By ignoring the network login dialog box, users can gain access to all local files with total control. Local files are also usually not part of a regular and systematic backup procedure. If security and safety does not convince you to keep files on a central server, then the increased risk of enabling users to share local files with others should.

When you use NTFS in Windows NT, local files and directories can be protected with user-level security. Windows 98 can only use FAT or FAT32 and cannot be protected in the same manner.

When network users have access to, or are allowed to share files with other network users, they usually accomplish sharing through the Microsoft File and Printer Sharing for Microsoft Networks. It is also usually implemented with the default system security—Share-level Access Control. With Share-level Access Control, users are asked for a Read-Only password, a Full Access password, or both (see Figure 1.8). Either password can be left blank, which might leave the shared folder open to Full Access with no check in place. This security breach is impossible to control if each user is responsible for his or her own file sharing.

Rather than implement Share-level Access Control, you might choose to implement the other type of security: User-level Access Control (see Figure 1.9). This method provides substantially better security. You can log in by using a valid username and password on a Windows NT domain, a Windows NT Server, a Windows NT Workstation, or a Novell NetWare server (3.x or 4.x). When you choose User-level Access Security on the Access Control tab of the Network Control Panel, you must supply the name of the server or domain from which your account originates. This enables you to grant access to your system to users who are registered on a controlled server. It also means that you do not have to distribute a list of passwords to people accessing your computer because all they need are their usernames and passwords from the main server.

FIGURE 1.8
When implementing Share-level Access Control, your security is based on one or two passwords.

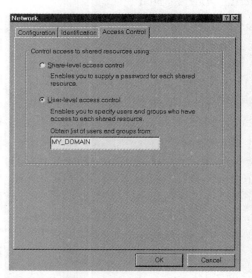

FIGURE 1.9
When using the File and Printer Sharing for Microsoft Networks, you have two security levels.

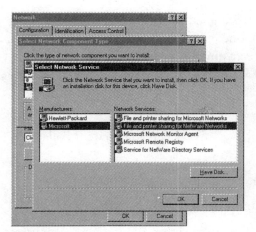

FIGURE 1.10
File and Printer Sharing services are available for both Microsoft and Novell Networks.

When using Microsoft's File and Printer Sharing service for NetWare (see Figure 1.10), the only security option is User-level Access Control, and the Security provider must be a Novell NetWare server.

9. What is the single file on a server processed referred to when users log on to a network?

    B. System policy

9. CORRECT ANSWER: B

System policy files contain the settings and restrictions applied to users, groups, or computers at log on. A single policy file can contain information and restrictions for all users on the network. The policy file also contains default user and default computer entries that can be applied to all users or computers not mentioned specifically. For more information, see "System Policies."

10. What sets up a user-specific customized environment maintained for each user by the user?

    A. User Profiles

10. CORRECT ANSWER: A

User Profiles are used to store a working environment for the user. Although User Profiles can override these settings or impose restrictions, they are not controlled by the user. For more information, see "System Policies."

System Policies

This information supports questions 9 through 10.

A *System policy* is a single file on a server that is processed when users log on to your network. This file contains a list of settings or restrictions that are to be applied to the users at logon. System policies work in conjunction with User Profiles (customized settings maintained for each user) to restrict or control access to components of the Windows 98 operating system or to configure an environment for the user. Much of the security of which Windows 98 is capable can be implemented through System policies, which are created with the System Policy Editor. In this section you will do the following:

- Read the installation overview of the System Policy Editor.

- Examine the user settings of a policy file.

- Examine the computer settings of a policy file.

- Create policies for specific users, groups, and computers.

- Create policy template files.

11. The System Policy Editor is not installed by default. Where can the System Policy Editor be found on the Windows 98 CD-ROM?

A. TOOLS\RESKIT\NETADMIN\POLEDIT

11. CORRECT ANSWER: A

The Policy Editor is found on the Windows 98 CD in the folder TOOLS\RESKIT\NETADMIN\POLEDIT. From this location you can install both the System Policy Editor and group policies. The System Policy Editor need only be installed on an administrator's computer. The group policy .DLLs must be installed on all systems that will be implementing user group policies. For more information, see "Installation Overview of System Policy Editor."

12. What is the name of the Windows 98 Default Policy File?

C. CONFIG.POL

12. CORRECT ANSWER: C

The Default Policy File Windows 98 looks for is called CONFIG.POL in %SYSTEMROOT%\SYSTEM32\REPL\IMPORT\SCRIPTS. This folder is shared as NETLOGON and exists as the default on every domain controller. For Windows 98 clients to look on the Windows NT domain controller, Microsoft must be the primary logon and configured with the domain name. Other filenames could be used and the file could be stored elsewhere as long as all systems are configured as such. For more information, see "Installation Overview of System Policy Editor."

13. Where does Windows 98 store the Default Policy File for a Novell NetWare network?

D. `SYS:PUBLIC`

13. CORRECT ANSWER: D

Windows 98 looks for the `CONFIG.POL` file on a NetWare network on the `SYS:` volume in the `Public` directory. For Windows 98 clients to look on the Novell server, Novell must be the primary logon and configured with the server name. Other filenames could be used and the file could be stored elsewhere as long as all systems are configured as such. For more information, see "Installation Overview of System Policy Editor."

Installation Overview of System Policy Editor

This information supports questions 11 through 13.

System Policy Editor is not installed as one of the default applications with Windows 98. The application must be installed through the Have Disk button on the Windows Setup tab of the Add/Remove Programs icon, pointing to the `\TOOLS\RESKIT\NETADMIN\POLEDIT` directory of the Windows 98 CD-ROM. From this location, you are able to install both the System Policy Editor and group policies on your computer. You must install the System Policy Editor only on the machine that you will be using to create the System policy. If you plan to assign the policy to users based on the server groups to which they belong, you must install the group policies on every machine on your network.

After the System Policy Editor is installed, you can create a policy file (*.POL). The default policy file that Windows 98 looks for is `CONFIG.POL`, which is expected to be in one of the following locations:

- Windows NT Domain, in the `NetLogon` directory of domain controllers, which is `<win_root>\SYSTEM32\REPL\IMPORT\SCRIPTS\`

- Novell NetWare 3.x or 4.x server on the `SYS:` volume in the `PUBLIC` directory

To work with the Policy Editor, select it from the Start menu, under Programs, Accessories, System Tools, System Policy Editor.

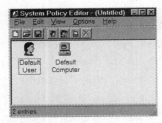

FIGURE 1.11
System Policy Editor working on a policy file.

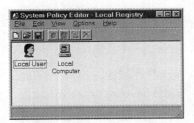

FIGURE 1.12
System Policy Editor working on a local Registry.

FIGURE 1.13
Each check box in the Policy Editor has three settings; the gray box is a neutral setting.

To create a policy file, select New from the File menu. This leaves you with a two icons: DEFAULT USER and DEFAULT COMPUTER (see Figure 1.11). You also have the capability to use the System Policy Editor to edit the local Registry by choosing Open Registry from the File menu. If you open the Registry by mistake, the two icons in the Policy Editor will read LOCAL USER and LOCAL COMPUTER (see Figure 1.12).

When using the Policy Editor to make a policy file, each check box in the settings windows has three settings: On, Off, and Neutral (see Figure 1.13). When you use the Policy Editor to edit the local Registry, there are only two settings: On and Off.

Each setting gives you the ability to create the policy file you require. An On setting means the policy will be implemented. An Off setting means the policy will not be implemented. A Neutral setting means the previous policy will be maintained if one previously existed. The Neutral setting is represented by a gray check box. The gray check box indicates that two or more policies will be enforced, one after another, such as when group policies are used.

14. You are using the System Policy Editor to create a new policy file. What two options are available?

    D. DEFAULT USER **and** DEFAULT COMPUTER

14. CORRECT ANSWER: D

The two options you have are DEFAULT USER and DEFAULT COMPUTER. These settings are only implemented if a specific entry cannot be found for the username or computer name.

You can also edit the Registry directly from here using LOCAL USER and LOCAL COMPUTER. For more information, see "Creating Policies for Users, Groups, and Computers."

15. **Where are the changes stored when you alter the computer settings in the System Policy Editor?**

   C. SYSTEM.DAT

15. CORRECT ANSWER: C

SYSTEM.DAT contains the changes made to computer settings and applies them to the system no matter who is logged on. For the most part, the settings in the Default Computer or any specific computer are hardware- or general software-related and apply equally to all users. For more information, see "Creating Policies for Users, Groups, and Computers."

16. **A new user logs on to a Windows 98 workstation. This user does not belong to a group and no policy has been set for this user. What policy entry does Windows 98 apply for this user?**

   C. DEFAULT USER

16. CORRECT ANSWER: C

When a user does not have a policy specifically set up and is not a member of a group that has a policy, Windows 98 uses the DEFAULT USER. For more information, see "Creating Policies for Users, Groups, and Computers."

17. **Proposed solution:**

- **Install all Windows 98 computers using one standard script.**
- **Activate User Profiles for all users.**
- **Set up a home directory on a Windows NT server for each user.**
- **Create a policy file and save it as** Config.pol **in the NETLOGON share of all the Domain Controllers.**

   A. **The proposed solution satisfies the required component and all of the optional components.**

17. CORRECT ANSWER: A

Mike has achieved these goals by using a common script to set the standards initially. Using a policy file, he can offer the local administrators a tool to control the environment. With the profiles and the home directory, he gives the users a little flexibility and mobility. For more information, see "Creating Policies for Users, Groups, and Computers."

Creating Policies for Users, Groups, and Computers

This information supports questions 14 through 17.

When creating a policy file for a server, you have the additional option of adding individual icons for each user or group of users from your server, as well as icons for each computer on your network (see Figure 1.14). To add entries to your policy, choose Add User, Add Computer, or Add Group from the Edit menu. If you have configured your system for User-level Access Control, you can browse a list of users, groups, and computers; otherwise, you must type the name of the user, group, or computer.

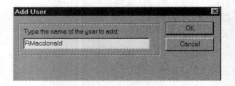

FIGURE 1.14
Individual policy entries can be created for users or groups from your server, as well as for computers on your network.

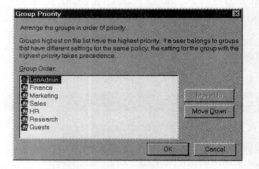

FIGURE 1.15
Groups are processed from the bottom up, making the items higher in the list override lower settings.

18. **Which of the following are default template files used by the System Policy Editor? Select all that apply.**

   A. COMMON.ADM

   C. WINDOWS.ADM

When applying the policies, Windows 98 first determines whether there is an entry for the user logging in, and then applies the changes for the user. If there are no entries for that user, Windows 98 then checks to see whether the user is a member of any the groups that it has entries for. If the user is not a member of any of the groups, then the entry for DEFAULT USER is applied. After applying the user policy, Windows 98 then applies a computer policy. If there is an entry for your current computer name, it is applied; otherwise, the entry for DEFAULT COMPUTER is applied.

When working with groups in the Policy Editor, the client computers need to have group policies installed on their computers. The groups listed in the policy file are applied in a particular order, which can be seen by choosing Group Priority from the Options menu (see Figure 1.15). The policy entries are applied for each group that the user is a member of, starting from the bottom of the list and working up. This means that if any of the entries conflict with one other, the entry that is higher in the list takes precedence.

18. CORRECT ANSWERS: A-C

WINDOWS.ADM and COMMON.ADM are located in the C:\WINDOWS\INF directory and are the default template files. WINDOWS.ADM has entries that are specific to Windows 98, whereas COMMON.ADM has entries that could be used for Windows 98 or Windows NT clients. For more information, see "Policy Template Files."

Policy Template Files

This explanation supports question 18.

The Policy Editor is an alternative shell to enable editing of the Windows 98 Registry. It does not know anything about the structure or form of the Registry. Everything that the Policy Editor displays and changes is a result of the Policy Template file that is in use. The default template file is C:\WINDOWS\INF\COMMON.ADM. Windows 98 uses two basic templates: COMMON.ADM and WINDOWS.ADM. WINDOWS.ADM applies

Registry settings just for Windows 98, whereas COMMON.ADM can set values for Windows 98 and Windows NT 4.0. To change the template file, choose Template from the Options menu. The template file is a text file with a particular structure.

19. Proposed solution:

Install all Windows 98 computers to have the following:

- **File and Printer Sharing**

- **User-level security**

- **Remote Administration enabled with only the default Domain Admins group having permission**

  B. The proposed solution satisfies the required component but only one of the optional components.

20. Proposed solution:

Install all Windows 98 computers to have the following:

- **File and Printer Sharing**

- **User-level security**

- **Remote Administration enabled with only the default Domain Admins group having permission**

  C. The proposed solution satisfies the required component but none of the optional components.

19. CORRECT ANSWER: B

Remote Administration, including Net Watcher and share administration, requires simply that Remote Administration be active. For remote Registry administration, additional remote Registry editing services must be installed. For more information, see "Remote Registry Editing and System Monitoring."

20. CORRECT ANSWER: C

Remote Administration allows Carol to use the Administer button from the properties of a remote Windows 98 system to access the hidden share C$ for the local hard drive and Admin$ for the Windows directory.

Carol must perform these tasks from a Windows 98 computer only. It cannot be done from a Windows NT workstation even if Carol is a member of the Domain Admins group. Carol cannot access the CD-ROM drives because Windows 98 does not create hidden shared files for floppy disks or CD-ROMs. For more information, see "Remote Registry Editing and System Monitoring."

Remote Registry Editing and System Monitoring

This explanation supports questions 19 through 20.

From the planning side, if you wish to use either of these tools, there are some things you must take into consideration. To perform remote Registry editing, you must meet the following criteria:

- File and Printer Sharing must be installed.

- User-level security should be installed.

- Remote Administration must be enabled, and the person attempting remote Registry editing must have Administration rights.

- The remote Registry editing service must be installed. This can be done through Add, Service in the Network Control Panel. You must choose the Have Disk button and specify the path `<Windows_98_cd>\TOOLS\RESKIT\NETADMIN\REMOTREG`.

When System Monitor runs, it requires access to Registry key `HKEY_DYN_DATA\PERFSTATS` and its subkeys, as shown in Figure 1.16. To perform remote system monitoring, you require access to the same Registry keys on the remote machine. It is for this reason that all of the requirements for remote Registry editing must also be met for remote system monitoring.

This is a planning issue because it requires that extra services be installed on all machines, and, as discussed earlier, the File and Printer Sharing service can be a potential security hole. You do have the option of disabling the sharing controls for all users through a System policy, which helps the situation.

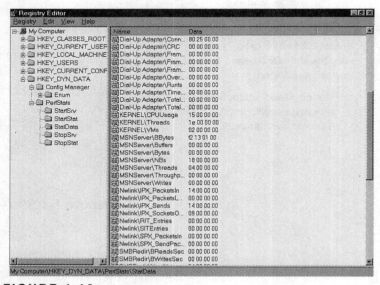

FIGURE 1.16
System Monitor retrieves its information from the Registry.

DEVELOP A SECURITY STRATEGY IN A MICROSOFT ENVIRONMENT AND MIXED MICROSOFT AND NETWARE ENVIRONMENT

Remote Administration

Remote Administration is enabled in the Passwords Control Panel. The goal of Remote Administration is to give someone on the network full access to your local file system and to allow remote changes to your File and Printer Sharing settings. This enables a network administrator to control the local shared resources on your computer, as well as to update any files that might be corrupted or out-of-date.

Files and Printer Sharing must be installed to implement Remote Administration. When enabling Remote Administration, the settings look different depending on the type of access control that you are using. If you are using Share-level Access Control, then the Remote Administration tab has a check box to enable Remote Administration and two text boxes for a password and confirmation. Anyone who knows your password can perform Remote Administration on your computer. If you are using User-level Access Control, then user- or group names from your security provider are granted administration rights on your computer (see Figure 1.17).

If you are logging on to a Windows NT domain or a Novell NetWare server, have installed File and Printer Sharing, and are using User-level Access Control, Remote Administration rights are automatically granted to Domain Admins, Supervisor, or Admin, depending on the type of security

provider you are using. Other users can be granted the right to perform Remote Administration by adding their network account names to the list on the Remote Administration tab of the Passwords Control Panel.

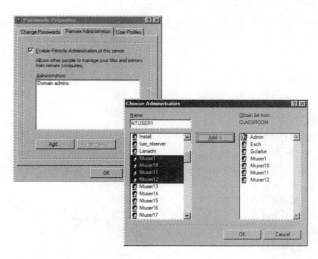

FIGURE 1.17
Users and groups from your security provider can be assigned administration privileges on your computer.

To perform Remote Administration on a network computer that you have Remote Administration rights on, you can browse the Network Neighborhood for a target computer and obtain its properties (see Figure 1.18). Choose the Administer button on the Tools tab to gain access to the local file system. You will see all fixed hard drives with dollar signs after the drive letters.

These represent the hidden drive shares on the target machine. When Remote Administration is enabled, each fixed drive is automatically shared with Full Control rights for the people who have administration rights. This enables the administrator to navigate the entire directory structure and add, modify, or delete any files that are necessary (see Figure 1.19).

FIGURE 1.18
Properties of remote computers can give you access to the Remote Administration tools.

FIGURE 1.19
Remote Administration of a remote file system gives you full control to the drives on the target computer.

There is one additional share that is not listed when using the Administer button: ADMIN$ (see Figure 1.20). ADMIN$ is the hidden share for the current Windows directory.

FIGURE 1.20
The ADMIN$ share is a direct link to the target computer's Windows directory.

In addition to the Administer button, the Tools tab also has buttons to launch System Monitor and Net Watcher. System Monitor enables you to view utilization of system resources, whereas Net Watcher enables you to view and share resources, connect users, and open files; you are also able to modify the shared resources on the target computer. Both System Monitor and Net Watcher require that File and Printer Sharing be installed on the target computer. When File and Printer Sharing has been installed on a computer, care should be taken if giving that computer access to the Internet, which will be the next topic you consider.

CHAPTER SUMMARY

Windows 98 has been set up to upgrade Windows 95 systems and Windows 3.x. A whole new set of wizards is included to simplify the upgrade process. Microsoft has maintained the same distribution methods for larger rollouts.

A successful roll out can be assured with proper planning and testing. A suggested path has been described in the previous sections to offer a solid guideline. As most planning sessions do, it requires a fair amount of time to implement, but usually helps avoid costly mistakes and reduces overall time and effort during an actual roll out.

A Windows 98 computer environment can be controlled in many ways. Each user can set up his own User Profiles and carry them to each system on the network though his login.

Administrators can control or customize a systems environment through user, group, or computer policies that take effect each time a user logs in to a Windows NT domain or Novell server. These settings override the User Profile preference and the settings are merged into the user's Registry.

Finally, the administrators can administer each Windows 98 system remotely through Remote Administration and remote Registry.

The Installation and Configuration section of Windows 98 explores almost every topic in Windows 98. For this reason this objective is covered over two chapters. This chapter looks at the installation of basic components in Windows 98, whereas Chapter 3, "Installation and Configuration, Part 2: Network Components," covers configuration of additional optional components.

Installation and Configuration, Part 1

This chapter helps you prepare for the exam by covering the following objectives:

Install Windows 98. Installation options include the following:

- **Automated Windows Setup**
- **New**
- **Upgrade**
- **Uninstall**
- **Dual-boot combination with Microsoft Windows NT 4.0**

▶ Windows 98 is an easy upgrade from Windows 95, 3.1, and 3.11. Basic planning and automated installs can make the transition smooth. The Installation section focuses on planning for a successful installation or upgrade.

Install and configure hardware devices in a Microsoft environment and a mixed Microsoft and NetWare environment. Hardware devices include the following:

continues

- **Modems**
- **Printers**
- **Universal Serial Bus (USB)**
- **Multiple Display Support**
- **IEEE 1394 Firewire**
- **Infrared Data Association (IrDA)**
- **Multilink**
- **Power Management Scheme**

▶ Windows 98 is a modular operating system able to interact with numerous other operating systems as well as technologies. The list of objectives includes components used to enhance Windows 98's capabilities.

Install and configure the Microsoft Backup.

▶ The backup system should be in place from the beginning in order to establish good working habits. Windows 98 provides a basic Backup program with a very intuitive graphical interface.

INSTALL WINDOWS 98

1. **A typical installation of Windows 98, without any optional components, requires approximately how much hard disk space?**

   A. 60–80MB

   B. 80–100MB

   C. 100–150MB

   D. 150–200MB

   E. 200–250MB

2. **Which of the following are disadvantages of a shared installation of Windows 98?**

   A. You lose your network connection when you shut down.

   B. More space is required on the hard drive for network files.

   C. You cannot log off and log on as another user.

   D. Network performance is degraded.

   E. The system is more efficient.

3. **From where can you run the Windows 98 installation program?**

   A. CD-ROM

   B. Floppy disk

   C. Across a network

   D. All of the above

   E. None of the above

4. **What must you do before you can install Windows 98 across a network?**

   A. Copy the installation CD-ROM to a network drive.

   B. Run NETSETUP to create the network setup files or copy the CD to a network share.

   C. Place the Windows 98 CD-ROM in your drive and share that drive with other users.

   D. Run the installation but specify the name of the computer on which you want to install Windows 98.

   E. Run an SMS installation of Windows 98.

5. **Which program(s) can you use to create custom scripts for automated Windows 98 installation?**

   A. NOTEPAD.EXE

   B. BATCH.EXE

   C. SETUP.EXE

   D. SCRIPT.EXE

   E. AUTOSETUP.BAT

6. **Batch setup scripts can be used in which environments to automate Windows 98 installation?**

   A. CD-ROM

   B. Floppy disk

   C. Across a network

   D. From the hard drive

   E. All of the above

7. **What extension is used for batch script files that are needed with Windows 98 automated setup?**

   A. .BAT

   B. .SCR

   C. .DAT

   D. .INF

   E. .AUT

8. **How can you create a Windows 98 emergency startup disk?**

   A. By manually copying the necessary files to a floppy disk

   B. By allowing the installation process to create the disk for you

   C. By formatting a floppy disk and selecting the Copy System Files option

   D. From the Add/Remove Programs icon in the Control Panel

   E. From the CD's Recovery folder

9. **If you choose to install Windows 98 in the same directory as a previous installation of Windows 3.x or Windows 95, what happens?**

   A. A dual-boot configuration between the two operating systems is created.

   B. The old operating system is replaced and all settings are lost.

   C. The old operating system is replaced, and all settings are copied to the Windows 98 Registry.

   D. An error occurs, halting installation.

   E. The installation fails and Windows 98 prompts you for a new path.

10. **If you choose to keep Windows 3.x and create a dual-boot with Windows 98, what happens to applications installed under Windows 3.x?**

    A. Applications are available in either operating system.

    B. Applications are available only in Windows 3.x.

    C. Applications are moved from Windows 3.x and made available only in Windows 98.

    D. The Windows 98 installation resets all Registry settings, so applications must be reinstalled in both operating systems.

    E. None of the above.

11. **You have installed Windows 98 over a Windows 3.1 operating system, replacing Windows 3.1. When can you uninstall Windows 98 and revert back to a Windows 3.1 operating system?**

    A. Any time you install Windows 98 over Windows 3.1

    B. When you install Windows 98 and select the Save System Files option

    C. When you install Windows 98 in a directory other than the one used by Windows 3.1

    D. When you use the Restore command in the Backup utility

    E. Never

12. **When you upgrade from Windows for Workgroups to Windows 98, Windows 98 copies settings from which of the following files?**

A. `PROTOCOL.INI`

B. `SYSTEM.INI`

C. `WIN.INI`

D. `WFW.INI`

E. `WINDOWS.INI`

13. **If you are creating a dual-boot between Windows 98 and Windows NT, which of the following files contains the necessary dual-boot settings?**

A. `MSDOS.SYS`

B. `SYSTEM.DAT`

C. `SYSTEM.INI`

D. `CONFIG.SYS`

E. `DUALBOOT.DAT`

14. **On which type of machine can you run the NETSETUP program?**

A. MS-DOS

B. Windows 95

C. Windows 98

D. OS/2

E. NT Server

15. **Which utility runs as part of the Windows 98 installation process?**

A. ScanDisk

B. Disk Defragmenter

C. Backup

D. System Monitor

E. System updates

16. **If Windows 98 fails during the hardware detection phase of installation, which file is used to restart the detection phase?**

A. `SETUPLOG.TXT`

B. `DETLOG.TXT`

C. `SETUP.LOG`

D. `DETCRASH.LOG`

E. `RESTART.LOG`

17. **What is the most likely point of failure for the Windows 98 Setup program?**

A. Startup and Information Gathering

B. File Copy

C. Hardware Detection

D. Final System Configuration

E. Corrupted disks

18. **Under which circumstance can Windows 98 be uninstalled?**

A. When Windows 98 is set up as a dual-boot with the previous version of Windows

B. When the previous system files are saved

C. When the `BOOT.INI` file contains the `BootMulti=1` entry

D. When the `MSDOS.SYS` file contains the `BootMulti=1` entry

E. Never—the drive must be reformatted

The following two questions are based on the same scenario, required components, and optional components. Read the full question and proposed solutions before answering.

19. Scenario:

Sara is a network administrator who has been given the task to upgrade her department to Windows 98. The department currently has 25 Windows 95 computers, 30 Windows for Workgroups 3.11 computers, and three NT servers organized in a single domain. Sara understands the need for a fast migration with little disruption to her clients.

All systems are compatible with Windows 98 and need to have the same settings. The department feels strongly about standards.

Required components:
All systems must be upgraded over a weekend and Sara is the only resource to do the work.

All systems must have the same options installed.

Optional components:
All applications that were running on the older platform must run in the new Windows 98 platform.

Users should be comfortable using Windows 98 systems.

Proposed solution:
Sara will set up a small test lab with a few Windows 95 and Windows for Workgroups computers and test out Batch installation files she created with the BATCH.EXE program. Sara will also place the source Windows 98 files on a share on one of the Windows NT servers.

After all the issues have been resolved with the final *.INF file, Sara sets aside a weekend to perform the upgrades. All systems are to be upgraded with the same *.INF file.

The installation path is to be the same as the current operating system. Windows 98 installation is to have all the bells and whistles Windows 98 has to offer, including the new interface.

A. The proposed solution satisfies all the required components and all of the optional components.

B. The proposed solution satisfies all the required components but only one of the optional components.

C. The proposed solution satisfies all the required components but none of the optional components.

D. The proposed solution satisfies none of the required components but one of the optional components.

E. The proposed solution satisfies none the required components and none of the optional components.

20. Scenario:

Sara is a network administrator who has been given the task to upgrade her department to Windows 98. The department currently has 25 Windows 95 computers, 30 Windows for Workgroups 3.11 computers, and three NT servers organized in a single domain. Sara understands the need for a fast migration with little disruption to her clients.

All systems are compatible with Windows 98 and need to have the same settings. The department feels strongly about standards.

Required components:
All systems must be upgraded over a weekend and Sara is the only resource to do the work.

All systems must have the same options installed.

Optional components:
All applications that were running on the older platform must run in the new Windows 98 platform.

Users should be comfortable using Windows 98 systems.

Proposed solution:

Sara will set up a small test lab with a few Windows 95 and Windows for Workgroups computers and test out Batch installation files she created with the BATCH.EXE program. Sara will also place the source Windows 98 files on a share on one of the Windows NT servers.

After all the issues have been resolved with the final *.INF file, Sara will set aside a week-end to perform the upgrades. All systems will be upgraded with the same *.INF file.

The installation path will be the same as the current operating system. Windows 98 installation will have all the bells and whistles Windows 98 has to offer, including the new interface.

Finally, Sara will arrange for a day of training for each user just prior to the system updates that will focus only on the changes and the basics of Windows 98.

A. The proposed solution satisfies all the required components and all of the optional components.

B. The proposed solution satisfies all the required components but only one of the optional components.

C. The proposed solution satisfies all the required components but none of the optional components.

D. The proposed solution satisfies none of the required components but one of the optional components.

E. The proposed solution satisfies none of the required components and none of the optional components.

ANSWER KEY

1. D	6. E	11. B	16. D
2. A-C-D	7. D	12. A-B-C	17. C
3. D	8. A-B-D	13. A	18. B
4. B-C	9. C	14. C	19. C
5. A-B	10. B	15. A	20. A

ANSWERS & EXPLANATIONS

INSTALL WINDOWS 98

1. A typical installation of Windows 98, without any optional components, requires approximately how much hard disk space?

D. 150–200MB

1. CORRECT ANSWER: D

An installation, without any optional components, takes up between 150 and 200MB depending on your hardware settings. For more information, see "System Requirements."

System Requirements

This explanation supports question 1.

Windows 98 is designed to be flexible on many types of systems. Faster and more powerful computers will always allow Windows 98 to perform better. Some of the higher-end components will not run properly on lower-end systems.

Microsoft provides a minimum system requirement guideline to help you initially decide which equipment should be upgraded to Windows 98 and which should simply be replaced.

The following lists the minimum system requirements:

- 486DX/66 MHz or higher processor
- 16MB of memory
- A minimum 195MB of free hard disk space (between 120–295)
- CD-ROM or DVD-ROM drive
- VGA or higher-resolution monitor
- Microsoft mouse or compatible pointing device

2. Which of the following are disadvantages of a shared installation of Windows 98?

A. You lose your network connection when you shut down.

C. You cannot log off and log on as another user.

D. Network performance is degraded.

2. CORRECT ANSWERS: A-C-D

Because a shared installation requires the network to run Windows 98, you lose network support when you shut down Windows 98, and network performance is degraded because of the file transfer between client and server. In addition, you cannot log off and log on as a different user. You must completely restart Windows.

3. From where can you run the Windows 98 installation program?

    D. All of the above

Windows 98 installation can be run from floppy disks, a CD-ROM, or over a network. When a large group of computers are to be upgraded, usually the "across a network" method is used. The floppy-disk method does not contain all the tools that Windows 98 is shipped with, such as the Windows 98 Resource Kit and its tools. For more information, see "New Installations."

4. What must you do before you can install Windows 98 across a network?

    B. Run NETSETUP to create the network setup files or copy the CD to a network share.

    C. Place the Windows 98 CD-ROM in your drive and share that drive with other users.

Before you can install Windows 98 from a network, you must run the NETSETUP program, which creates the required Windows 98 setup files on a network drive. An alternate method is simply to copy all the .CAB files to a network share. Sharing the CD off a Windows 98 computer will work, but it is a very slow process. For more information, see "New Installations."

New Installations

This explanation supports questions 2 through 4.

The Windows 98 installation process is modular. The Windows 98 Setup program steps through this process, running only those modules that are either requested or needed. For example, the hardware detection phase identifies specific components on the computer, and the Windows 98 Setup program runs only those installation modules that match. Some of the modules used by the Windows 98 Setup program are standard wizards, such as those for setting up network components, modems, printers, and display monitors.

Windows 98 installation consists of four logical phases:

- Startup and Information Gathering
- Hardware Detection
- File Copy
- Final System Configuration

The Windows Setup program offers several switches that can be used to alter processing during installation.

Another thing to consider when you're installing from Windows 98 is the media from which you are installing. You can install in the conventional way:

- Floppy disks

- CD-ROM

- Across a network

The least favorable media to use for installing Windows 98 is probably the floppy disk because it requires several disks. Another disadvantage to installing from disks is that the disks do not include all the files and utilities that come packaged on the CD-ROM. Items found on the CD-ROM, such as the Windows 98 Online Help, the network administration tools, and the Windows 98 Resource Kit, are omitted from the floppy disk version due to the size limitations.

A third option for Windows 98 installation is to install over a network. To use this option, you would place all the required setup files on a network server that can be accessed by all the clients that will be installing Windows 98.

5. Which program(s) can you use to create custom scripts for automated Windows 98 installation?

   A. NOTEPAD.EXE

   B. BATCH.EXE

5. CORRECT ANSWERS: A-B

Custom scripts can be created either manually with an editor such as Notepad or with the BATCH.EXE utility. The BATCH.EXE program offers suggestions to include in a script file, whereas the Notepad option requires you to know all the commands. Most administrators use BATCH.EXE to create a basic script and add to it with Notepad. For more information, see "Automated Windows Setup."

6. Batch setup scripts can be used in which environments to automate Windows 98 installation?

   E. All of the above

6. CORRECT ANSWER: E

Batch setup scripts can be run when installing Windows 98 from floppy disk, CD-ROM, or across a network. All the setup scripts do is answer the questions the setup program asks. The same questions are asked regardless of the media format used. For more information, see "Automated Windows Setup."

7. What extension is used for batch script files that are needed with Windows 98 automated setup?

D. .INF

Batch script files used in automated Windows 98 installations have the .INF extension. .INF is short for Information file. This file is a basic text file that can be viewed or edited with any text editor. For more information, see "Automated Windows Setup."

Automated Windows Setup

This explanation supports questions 5 through 7.

If you have to install Windows 98 on a number of machines, you can simplify the installation process and reduce the amount of user intervention that is required. Install from a network source while using *batch scripting* to remove some of the manual effort of the setup process.

Batch scripting can be used with any of the installation media—floppy disks, CD-ROM, or network Setup files. These scripts can be created with the BATCH.EXE utility. With this utility, you can specify various options and parameters required by the setup process. BATCH.EXE creates a script file (.INF) for you to use when you run Setup.

8. How can you create a Windows 98 emergency startup disk?

A. By manually copying the necessary files to a floppy disk

B. By allowing the installation process to create the disk for you

D. From the Add/Remove Programs icon in the Control Panel

A Windows 98 startup disk can be created during installation or from the Add/Remove dialog box in the Control Panel. It can also be created manually, although this method is not recommended because there is more of a chance to forget files and make the disk a system disk. For more information, see "Creating the Startup Disk."

Creating the Startup Disk

This explanation supports question 8.

A startup disk is a Windows 98 bootable floppy disk that contains utilities you can use to troubleshoot a malfunctioning system. The startup disk loads the operating system and presents an MS-DOS command line. You can create a Windows 98 startup disk during the file copy phase of Windows 98 Setup. You can also create or update a disk after the Windows 98 installation by using the Add/Remove Programs option in Control Panel.

▼ **NOTE**

For recovery purposes, you might also want to copy the following files into a subdirectory on the startup disk: SYSTEM.DAT, CONFIG.SYS, AUTOEXEC.BAT, WIN.INI, SYSTEM.INI, and any CD-ROM or other device drivers. If you do not place these files in a subdirectory, you'll have to rename them to prevent problems with the startup disk.

9. **If you choose to install Windows 98 in the same directory as a previous installation of Windows 3.x or Windows 95, what happens?**

   C. **The old operating system is replaced, and all settings are copied to the Windows 98 Registry.**

9. CORRECT ANSWER: C

When you install Windows 98 over an existing copy of Windows 95, Windows 3.x, or Windows for Workgroups, all settings from the prior operating system are copied to Windows 98's Registry. This is an upgrade, not a dual-boot. For more information, see "Upgrade Installations."

10. **If you choose to keep Windows 3.x and create a dual-boot with Windows 98, what happens to applications installed under Windows 3.x?**

   B. **Applications will be available only in Windows 3.x.**

10. CORRECT ANSWER: B

If you create a dual-boot with Windows 3.x and Windows 98, you must reinstall all your applications under Windows 98. Some DOS applications do not have any entries in the operating system's configuration files and might be functional under both platforms. For more information, see "Upgrade Installations."

11. **You have installed Windows 98 over a Windows 3.1 operating system, replacing Windows 3.1. When can you uninstall Windows 98 and revert back to a Windows 3.1 operating system?**

   B. **When you install Windows 98 and select the Save System Files option.**

11. CORRECT ANSWER: B

Selecting the Save System Files option allows you to uninstall Windows 98 and revert to a prior operating system. This is not a dual-boot—it is an upgrade. For a dual-boot you simply need to SYS the C: drive using SYS C: and delete all the Windows 98 files manually. For more information, see "Upgrade Installations."

12. **When you upgrade from Windows for Workgroups to Windows 98, Windows 98 copies settings from which of the following files?**

   A. PROTOCOL.INI

   B. SYSTEM.INI

   C. WIN.INI

12. CORRECT ANSWERS: A-B-C

When upgrading from Windows for Workgroups, Windows 98 reads settings from PROTOCOL.INI, SYSTEM.INI, and WIN.INI, as well as other system files such as AUTOEXEC.BAT and CONFIG.SYS. All these settings, if needed, are incorporated into Windows 98's Registry. For more information, see "Upgrade Installations."

Upgrade Installations

This explanation supports questions 9 through 12.

The upgrade version of Windows 98 requires that Windows 3.x, Windows for Workgroups, Windows 95, or OS/2 be installed on your computer previously. The setup program checks for the existence of these files: WINVER.EXE, USER.EXE, WIN.COM, SYSTEM.INI, and (in Windows for Workgroups only) PROTOCOL.INI.

If the Windows 98 Setup program detects an earlier version of Windows on the computer, it gives you the choice of installing Windows 98 in the same directory. This is an important choice. If you decide to install Windows 98 in the same directory as Windows 3.x, Windows 95, or Windows for Workgroups, you will save a lot of time setting up applications under Windows 98. When you use the same directory as a previous version of Windows, Windows 98 reads through your settings and copies all the information from your program groups into Windows 98. You will not have to reinstall your older applications in Windows 98.

Should you decide to install Windows 98 in a directory other than the one used for Windows 3.x, Windows 95, or Windows for Workgroups, you will have to reinstall your applications under Windows 98 and create groups and icons for those applications. On the other hand, by using a different directory, you preserve your older operating system, whereas if you install to the same directory, you lose access to the earlier installation of Windows.

13. If you are creating a dual-boot between Windows 98 and Windows NT, which of the following files contains the necessary dual-boot settings?

　A. MSDOS.SYS

13. CORRECT ANSWER: A

Information about a dual-boot between Windows 98 and Windows NT is kept in the MSDOS.SYS file for Windows 98. For more information, see "Dual-booting with Microsoft Windows NT."

Dual-booting with Microsoft Windows NT

This explanation supports question 13.

The file that makes dual-booting with Windows NT possible is the Windows 98 version of MSDOS.SYS. In MSDOS.SYS, you must make sure the entry BootMulti=1 is set properly. If it is set to 1, the ability to run multiple operating systems is enabled. If it is set to 0, dual-booting is disabled. To set up a dual-boot with Windows NT after Windows 98 has been installed, use the following process:

1. Start up Windows 98.

2. Exit to a command prompt.

3. Switch to the directory holding the Windows NT source files and type **WINNT** /w (this allows Windows NT Setup to run under Windows). Windows NT creates a BOOT.INI file that lists the location of the WINNT directory, the Windows directory, and the default boot operating system.

If Windows NT is already installed, the procedure is a bit more complex. These are the steps to take:

1. Ensure that the Windows NT machine will already dual-boot between MS-DOS and Windows NT.

2. Start the computer under MS-DOS.

3. Run Windows 98 Setup.

4. If you run MS-DOS from a floppy disk when you install Windows 98, you will have to run the Windows NT Emergency Recovery Disk (ERD) in order to be able to start Windows NT.

   If you want to run MS-DOS after you have installed Windows 98 in a dual-boot configuration, you will have to select MS-DOS from the boot menu and then select Previous Version from the Windows 98 menu.

Keep the following things in mind when dual-booting with Windows NT and Windows 98:

- Windows 98 can read FAT16 and FAT32 partitions. Windows NT can read FAT16 and NTFS partitions.

- If your Windows NT machine has an NTFS file system but does not have a FAT partition, you cannot dual-boot Windows 98.

- If you have Windows 98 installed and you install Windows NT on the same partition, and in the process you convert your FAT partition to NTFS, Windows 98 will no longer work.

- It works best if you have two partitions: one FAT and one NTFS; that way you can take advantage of the strengths of both operating systems.

- If you want to share an application (such as Microsoft Office), you must install it twice in order to affect the appropriate Registry entries for both operating systems. (However, you can install to the same directory as long as you select the same options.)

Make sure you have a good backup before you try any of this! (Refer to the section on Windows 98 Backup for assistance in this area.)

---

14. On which type of machine can you run the NETSETUP program?

  C. Windows 98

14. CORRECT ANSWER: C

The NETSETUP program can be run only on a computer running Windows 98. The setup program checks whether the current software is licensed properly and uses this license on the network copy of the software. For more information, see "Setup Failure Detection and Recovery."

---

15. Which utility runs as part of the Windows 98 installation process?

  A. ScanDisk

15. CORRECT ANSWER: A

When you install Windows 98, ScanDisk is automatically run to check the integrity of the hard drive before any upgrade or installation can be done. If an error is encountered, Windows 98 prompts you to fix it before continuing with the installation. You may choose to skip the ScanDisk by using the /is switch. The switch /iq will not check for cross-linked files. It is not recommended to skip these checks on existing systems that are being upgraded. On a newly formatted drive, however, this may save time. For more information, see "Setup Failure Detection and Recovery."

16. **If Windows 98 fails during the hardware detection phase of installation, which file is used to restart the detection phase?**

    D. DETCRASH.LOG

16. CORRECT ANSWER: D

If the Windows 98 installation fails during the hardware detection phase, the DETCRASH.LOG file is used to restart the process. On subsequent boots and detection Windows 98 has learned from its mistakes and will not crash again due to the same error. If you delete the DETCRASH.LOG file from the root of the C: drive, it may cause Windows 98 to crash next time it detects hardware. In this case, Windows 98 must perform the same learning steps as it did during the installation. All conflicts are eventually ironed out and a new DETCRASH.LOG is stored on the C: drive. For more information, see "Setup Failure Detection and Recovery."

17. **What is the most likely point of failure for the Windows 98 Setup program?**

    C. Hardware Detection

17. CORRECT ANSWER: C

If Windows 98 installation fails, it is usually during the hardware detection phase. Because Windows 98 has a built-in recovery tool in the DETCRASH.LOG file, simply reboot the computer and let Windows 98 work out its conflicts. You may need to reboot the system several times before all the conflicts are recorded in the DETCRASH.LOG file. For more information, see "Setup Failure Detection and Recovery."

Setup Failure Detection and Recovery

This explanation supports questions 14 through 17.

The Windows 98 Setup program maintains a setup log (SETUPLOG.TXT) during the installation and can determine where failures occur. The most likely place for failure is during hardware detection. A detection log (DETLOG.TXT) keeps track of what the Windows 98 Setup program discovers during the hardware detection phase.

If any previous attempt to install Windows 98 has failed, Windows 98 Setup lets you choose whether to use the Safe Recovery feature or to run a full new Setup. If the Safe Recovery dialog box appears when you start the Windows 98 Setup program, you should always select the Use Safe Recovery option. When you select this option, Windows 98 Setup can use various built-in methods to avoid the problems that occurred previously.

You should know the following basic Safe Recovery rules in case a failure occurs: Your most likely point of failure will occur during the hardware detection phase. Only a limited number of Interrupts (IRQs), DMA channels, I/O address assignments, and upper memory space allocations are available. Conflicts are especially common if you add multimedia capability, CD-ROMs, network interface cards, SCSI adapters, or other hardware devices to your computer.

18. Under which circumstance can Windows 98 be uninstalled?

B. When the previous system files are saved

18. CORRECT ANSWER: B

The system files must be saved during the installation if a successful uninstall is to take place. Windows 98 removes itself from the system and returns the previous version of Windows. For more information, see "Uninstalling Windows 98."

Uninstalling Windows 98

This information supports question 18.

If you upgrade to Windows 98 from Windows 3.x or Windows for Workgroups, you are presented with the option Save System Files. Selecting this option causes the Windows 98 Setup program to save the existing MS-DOS–based and Windows-based system files and enables you to easily uninstall Windows 98 from the computer if necessary.

To remove Windows 98, use the Windows 98 startup disk's Uninstall program (UNINSTAL.EXE). Use the following steps to uninstall Windows 98:

1. Place your Windows 98 startup disk in the floppy drive (or the CD-ROM in the CD-ROM drive).

2. From the Start menu, choose Run. Type **a:\uninstal.exe** and press Enter.

3. In the Windows 98 Uninstall dialog box, click Yes to begin the uninstall process. Windows 98 shuts down, and the uninstall process continues automatically.

4. Your previous configuration is restored. When prompted, remove the Windows 98 startup disk or the CD-ROM from the drive and press Enter to reboot your computer.

19. **Proposed solution:**

    Sara will set up a small test lab with a few Windows 95 and Windows for Workgroups computers and test out Batch installation files she created with the BATCH.EXE program. Sara will also place the source Windows 98 files on a share on one of the Windows NT servers.

    After all the issues have been resolved with the final *.INF file, Sara will set aside a weekend to perform the upgrades. All systems will be upgraded with the same *.INF file. The installation path will be the same as the current operating system.

    Windows 98 installation will have all the bells and whistles Windows 98 has to offer, including the new interface.

    C. The proposed solution satisfies all the required components but none of the optional components.

19. CORRECT ANSWER: C

The upgrade will be fast and consistent because Sara is using a network share for the source files and one *.INF file common to all systems.

The new interface, as well as all the bells and whistles, will limit users who have been using Windows for Workgroups. The interface is different enough that the users may not feel comfortable locating applications or tools.

Applications that are compatible with Windows for Workgroups may be compatible with Windows 98, but there is no guarantee. Sara would have had to test them in the lab before rolling out Windows 98.

20. **Proposed Solution:**

    Sara will set up a small test lab with a few Windows 95 and Windows for Workgroups computers and test out Batch installation files she created with the BATCH.EXE program. Sara will also place the source Windows 98 files on a share on one of the Windows NT servers.

    After all the issues have been resolved with the final *.INF file Sara will set aside a weekend to perform the upgrades. All systems will be upgraded with the same *.INF file.

    The installation path will be the same as the current operating system. Windows 98 installation will have all the bells and whistles Windows 98 has to offer, including the new interface.

    Finally, Sara will arrange for a day of training for each of the users just prior to their systems being updated that will focus only on the changes and the basics of Windows 98.

    A. The proposed solution satisfies all the required components and all of the optional components.

20. CORRECT ANSWER: A

The upgrade will be fast and consistent because Sara is using a network share for the source files and one *.INF file common to all systems.

The new interface, as well as all the bells and whistles, will be covered in the training for users who have been using Windows for Workgroups.

INSTALL AND CONFIGURE HARDWARE DEVICES IN A MICROSOFT ENVIRONMENT AND A MIXED MICROSOFT AND NETWARE ENVIRONMENT

1. **Which of the following statements are true?**

   A. Modulation is the translation of signals from a phone line into data your computer can read.

   B. Modulation is the translation of data from your computer into a signal that can be sent over the phone line.

   C. Demodulation is the translation of data from your computer into signals that can be sent over the phone line.

   D. Demodulation is the translation of signals from a phone line into data your computer can read.

   E. None of the above are true.

2. **What information does Windows 98 get from a Plug and Play printer?**

   A. Manufacturer and model

   B. Paper size

   C. Amount of memory installed

   D. Font cartridges installed

   E. Amount of ink left in cartridge

3. **Windows 98 always attempts to select a driver for a printer it detects. What happens if Windows 98 doesn't find a driver?**

   A. You are given a chance to install the driver from a floppy disk.

   B. You can select any driver that is compatible.

   C. Windows uses a standard driver to give you basic printer capabilities.

   D. The printer cannot be used.

   E. You can print, but only text.

4. **Which of the following tasks can you perform from the Printers folder (in the Control Panel)?**

   A. Connect to a network printer.

   B. Share a printer on a network.

   C. Set permissions for a printer.

   D. Uninstall a printer.

   E. Print.

5. **In order to be able to change the priority of print jobs, which of the following must be true?**

   A. Network software must support the feature.

   B. User-level security must be in effect.

   C. You must have administrator privileges.

   D. Share-level security must be in effect.

   E. None of the above; changing priority after the print job has been sent cannot be done.

6. **What is the most significant improvement of the USB port?**

   A. It is a standard plug type for different devices.

   B. It incorporates Plug and Play.

   C. USB devices do not require IRQs or any other specific resources.

   D. USB devices automatically assign IRQs and any other resources required.

   E. USB can be used by all types of computers.

7. **How many devices can a single USB port support?**

   A. 8

   B. 15

   C. 127

   D. 255

   E. 640

8. **Windows 98 can support multiple display adapters at once. What type of adapter card(s) must be used? Select all that apply.**

   A. ISA cards

   B. PCI cards

   C. SCSI cards

   D. AGP cards

   E. EISA

9. **How many separate monitors can Windows 98's Multiple Display Support handle?**

   A. 2

   B. 7

   C. 9

   D. 12

   E. Unlimited, if using USB

10. **What additional feature does IEEE 1394 offer a Windows 98 user?**

    A. IEEE 1394 is the support for USB.

    B. IEEE 1394 is the support for Multiple Display.

    C. IEEE 1394 is the support for DVD CD-ROMs.

    D. IEEE 1394 is the support for Demanding Digital Devices.

    E. IEEE 1394 is the support for Infrared protocol.

11. **What are the speeds of the IEEE 1394 BUS?**

    A. Transfer rates the same as a PCI BUS

    B. Transfer rates from 100–400MB/s

    C. Transfer rates the same as a USB BUS—about 12MB/s

    D. Transfer rates from 12–25MB/s

    E. Transfer rates the same as RAM

12. **While using RAS, what is the name of the component that allows Windows 98 to use more than one phone line to establish a single connection?**

    A. Multilink

    B. Multiline

    C. MultiRas

D. Multiconnect

E. MultiModem

13. **A client calls to ask why, when he uses Multilink with his server using Call Back, the multilink seems to fail. What could be the problem?**

A. Multilink must have two numbers configured in the Call Back as well as the client.

B. Call Back does not support Multilink at this time.

C. Multilink must have the Call Back option enabled.

D. The client must use Call Back to a user-specified number and enter both numbers for Multilink to work.

E. Multilink requires special modems.

The following question is scenario based. Please read all the requirements and proposed solution before answering.

14. **Scenario:**

Carol is researching new technologies for her company. She needs to make an informed decision about which operating system to use to support this new technology.

Required component:
Carol's company needs to make use of new technology and be able to quickly configure hardware and software to make everything work together without conflict.

Optional components:
Carol would like to make use of digital editing technology on the company's PCs to produce small promotional videos.

Carol would also like to add and remove devices as she needs them. There are only so many devices that can be purchased and they must be shared in the office.

Proposed solution:
Install Windows 98 on all the systems in the office. Make sure all new equipment uses the USB connectors. Install an Adaptec 1394 adapter to handle all the digital equipment.

A. The proposed solution satisfies the required component and all of the optional components.

B. The proposed solution satisfies the required component and only one of the optional components.

C. The proposed solution satisfies the required component and none of the optional components.

D. The proposed solution satisfies one of the optional components and does not satisfy the required component.

E. The proposed solution satisfies none of the optional components and does not satisfy the required component.

The following question is scenario based. Please read all the requirements and proposed solution before answering.

15. **Scenario:**

Walter has decided to connect all of the printers in the office to the same print server. He needs to keep control over who can manage the print jobs.

Required component:
There can only be certain designated administrators who control the print queue.

Optional components:

All clients must be able to connect to the printers and have the drivers downloaded automatically from the server.

All clients must be able to use DOS applications and print.

Proposed Solution:

Install a Windows 98 system as a print server. Share all the printers off the system and grant permissions to everyone. Have each user connect via the UNC name for each printer.

A. The proposed solution satisfies the required component and all of the optional components.

B. The proposed solution satisfies the required component and only one of the optional components.

C. The proposed solution satisfies the required component and none of the optional components.

D. The proposed solution satisfies one of the optional components and does not satisfy the required component.

E. The proposed solution satisfies none of the optional components and does not satisfy the required component.

ANSWER KEY

1. B-D	6. C	11. B
2. A-C-D	7. C	12. A
3. A-B	8. B-D	13. B
4. A-B-C	9. C	14. A
5. A-B-C	10. D	15. B

INSTALL AND CONFIGURE HARDWARE DEVICES IN A MICROSOFT ENVIRONMENT AND A MIXED MICROSOFT AND NETWARE ENVIRONMENT

1. Which of the following statements are true?

B. Modulation is the translation of data from your computer into a signal that can be sent over the phone line.

D. Demodulation is the translation of signals from a phone line into data your computer can read.

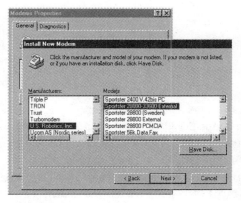

FIGURE 2.1
All modems supported at release date are listed in the Install New Modem dialog box.

---

1. CORRECT ANSWERS: B-D

Modulation is the translation of data from your computer into a signal that can be transmitted over telephone lines; demodulation is the reverse process. A computer uses a digital signal, whereas the standard phone line uses an analog signal. For more information, see "Modems."

Modems

This explanation supports question 1.

A *modem* is a special piece of computer hardware that converts the data from your computer into a signal that can be transmitted through normal telephone lines. This process is called *modulation*. The modem also converts signals from the phone line into data that your computer can understand through a process called *demodulation*. Most modems fall into one of these main categories: internal, external, PCMCIA format (for notebook computers), or portable.

To find out if Windows 98 supports a modem you have or intend to purchase, look in the Windows 98 Drivers List located on the Windows 98 CD-ROM in the \DRIVERS folder. The filename is DRIVERS98.CHM. You can obtain the most recent version of the Windows 98 Drivers List online at the Microsoft Web site. To install a new modem, use the Modem icon in the Control Panel. The Install New Modem dialog box appears (see Figure 2.1).

Windows 98 makes installing and configuring your modem a simple process. If you have a modem installed in your computer, for example, the Windows 98 Setup program attempts to detect the modem's brand and speed, and then it installs the proper driver files.

If you want to change your modem or install a new modem while you are running Windows 98, you can install and configure the modem yourself from the Windows 98 Control Panel. You also can reconfigure an existing modem. To display the Modems Properties sheet, which you use to add, remove, or modify a modem, use the following steps:

1. From the Start menu, choose Settings, Control Panel.

2. Double-click on the Modems icon to display a general Modems Properties sheet.

3. Click on the Add button on the Modems Properties sheet. A Windows 98 wizard guides you through the process of installing the new modem.

4. Specify the manufacturer and name of the modem (in order to install the proper modem drivers).

5. Select the port number and enter other required information. When you finish, click OK.

After installing the new modem, you can, if necessary, change its properties.

▼ **NOTE**

Although Windows 98 can control all the system settings, the computer's CMOS will still override the COM port assignment to the port. For example, suppose you have a laptop with only one COM port and an infrared port. You can use the CMOS to tell the system or Windows 98 that the external port will be COM2 and the infrared will be COM1. The infrared port is not truly COM1, but it will use the system resources of COM1. The end result is that CMOS will override any settings that Windows tries to set. A COM port is not Plug and Play.

2. What information does Windows 98 get from a Plug and Play printer?

A. Manufacturer and model

C. Amount of memory installed

D. Font cartridges installed

2. CORRECT ANSWERS: A-C-D

Windows 98 can get the manufacturer, model, memory, and font settings from a Plug and Play printer. For more information, see "Installing a Local Printer."

Installing a Local Printer

This explanation supports question 2.

There are two ways to install a local printer under Windows 98: by using Plug and Play and by using the Add Printer Wizard. Using Plug and Play is the simplest way to install a printer that is Plug and Play–compliant. You simply connect the printer to the computer, and Windows 98 detects and installs it the next time you start the system. Occasionally, Windows 98 can't find a printer driver for the printer, in which case it prompts you to insert a disk or CD-ROM containing the driver.

You can also install a printer by using the Add Printer Wizard, which can be found in the Printers folder, accessible from the Start menu's Settings option or from the Control Panel (see Figure 2.2).

To install a printer with the Add Printer Wizard, use the following procedure:

1. Open the Printers folder.

2. Double-click on the Add Printer Wizard and choose Next. You are asked whether the printer is attached directly to the computer or is accessed from the network.

3. Select Local Printer and choose Next.

4. Select the printer manufacturer from the Manufacturers list and select the printer model from the Printers list. If you do not have an actual local printer, you can select Generic as the manufacturer and choose the Generic/Text Only driver.

5. From the list of available ports, select the port to which the printer is connected. For example, for a parallel port, you might select LPT1:. If you do not have a local printer attached, select FILE:.

6. Choose Next and assign the printer a printer name. You can accept the default name, or you can use a more descriptive name such as "LaserJet IV in Room 312."

7. If you want print jobs to be sent to this printer by default, choose Yes and then choose Next. Otherwise, choose No and then Next.

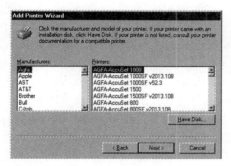

FIGURE 2.2
The Add Printer Wizard provides a list of printers supported when Windows 98 was released.

8. The Add Printer Wizard then asks you whether you want to print a test page. If you do, the wizard copies the files from the Windows 98 distribution media. If Windows 98 cannot find the files, you are prompted for the path. An icon for the printer is created in the Printers folder.

A local printer can then be shared to the rest of the network. A network printer refers to a printer located remotely from the user. A local printer can be shared but is still referred to as a local printer for the user who installed it.

3. **Windows 98 always attempts to select a driver for a printer it detects. What happens if Windows 98 doesn't find a driver?**

   A. **You are given a chance to install the driver from a floppy disk.**

   B. **You can select any driver that is compatible.**

3. CORRECT ANSWERS: A-B

If Windows cannot find a driver for a printer, you are prompted to insert a disk with the driver, or you are given the opportunity to select from a list of compatible drivers. Incorrect drivers are the most common source of problems with peripherals. Make sure the drivers are correct or are at least compatible. For more information, see "Network Printer Setup."

4. **Which of the following tasks can you perform from the Printers folder (in the Control Panel)?**

   A. **Connect to a network printer.**

   B. **Share a printer on a network.**

   C. **Set permissions for the printer.**

4. CORRECT ANSWERS: A-B-C

From the Printers icon in the Control Panel, you can connect to a network printer, share a printer on a network, set permissions, and change various printer settings. For more information, see "Network Printer Setup."

5. **In order to be able to change the priority of print jobs, which of the following must be true?**

   A. **Network software must support the feature.**

   B. **User-level security must be in effect.**

   C. **You must have administrator privileges.**

5. CORRECT ANSWERS: A-B-C

In order to be able to change the priority of print jobs, you must have administrator rights, user-level security must be in effect, and the network software must support priority changes. For more information, see "Network Printer Setup."

Network Printer Setup

This explanation supports questions 3 through 5.

To connect to a network printer, you must first install, configure, and share the printer on the network server. For information about installing and configuring the driver on the network server, refer to the preceding sections on local printer installation and configuration.

After the Windows 98 printer driver has been configured on the network print server attached to the printer, the printer must be shared to allow other users to access it. In order for a printer to be shared in Windows 98, the network print server must be running a 32-bit protected-mode client, and a File and Printer Sharing service must be enabled. The following steps demonstrate how to share a network printer:

1. Open the Properties sheet for the printer.

2. Select the Sharing tab to display the Sharing configuration settings.

3. Select Shared As, and then enter a share name and an optional descriptive comment for the printer.

4. Grant permissions to access this printer. If share-level permissions are used, you must assign a password to the printer, and to access the print queue, users must supply the correct password. If user-level permissions are used, you must add the users who will be granted access to this print queue.

5. Choose OK to share the printer. The printer icon now appears as a hand holding, or sharing, printer with others. Remote users with the correct permissions can now access the print queue after setting up the correct printer driver on their computers.

When the printer has been configured and shared on the network print server, a Windows 98 client can be configured to connect to the print server and print to the printer over the network. You can set up this configuration either manually with the Add Printer Wizard or by configuring the network printer for Point and Print setup.

To manually configure a Windows 98 client to print to the network printer using the Add Printer Wizard, perform the following steps:

1. Start the Add Printer Wizard from the Printers folder.

2. In the Printer Type field, select Network Printer and choose Next.

3. Enter the Universal Naming Convention (UNC) path for the network printer, such as \\SERVER\HP4.

4. If you will not be using MS-DOS applications to print to this printer, select No under Do You Print from MS-DOS Based Programs?. To have the printer associated with a printer port, such as LPT1:, you should select Yes for that option. Choose Next.

5. If you specified that you will print to the printer using MS-DOS–based applications, you are prompted to select the desired port from the Capture Printer Port dialog box. Choose OK to continue.

6. Choose Next, and then select the printer manufacturer and model from the Manufacturers and Printers lists, respectively.

7. Enter a descriptive name for the printer.

8. If you want to test your ability to print properly to the network printer, select Send Test Page.

9. Choose Finish to have Windows 98 begin copying the printer driver files to the hard drive if the latest drivers are not already on the hard drive. If Windows 98 cannot find the files, you are prompted to enter the path to the Windows 98 distribution files.

10. An icon for the network printer is created in the Printers folder. If desired, you can drag a copy of this icon to the desktop to create a shortcut.

A network printer can then be accessed from any Windows 98 system on the network without being prompted for drivers. Any other system must have the drivers loaded locally.

6. What is the most significant improvement of the USB port?

    C. USB devices do not require IRQs or any other specific resources.

USB allows several devices to be daisy-chained on a single standard plug and makes use of Plug and Play to determine the device. The biggest improvement, however, is the removal of individual IRQs and DMA or I/O addresses being assigned to each device. This allows for the elimination of conflicts. For more information, see "USB Support."

7. How many devices can a single USB port support?

    C. 127

A single USB port can have up to 127 devices. This removes the problem faced by users with several devices all trying to use the same parallel or serial port. For more information, see "USB Support."

USB Support

This explanation supports questions 6 through 7.

Windows 98 supports a new standard of expansion BUS and ports. A USB (short for Universal Serial Bus) supports up to 127 devices.

USB removes the need for IRQ, DMA, I/O addresses, and Memory. The USB deals with all devices, automatically alleviating the configuration issues encountered in the past.

USB also uses a new connector type that has been designated as a standard for new devices; most devices no longer require power cords and these devices support hot swapping. USB ports are about 10 times faster (around the 12MB/s range) than traditional ports, even when shared among several devices.

For more information, on USB, connect to WWW.USB.NET and WWW.USB.ORG.

8. Windows 98 can support multiple display adapters at once. What type of adapter cards must be used? Select all that apply.

    B. PCI cards

    D. AGP cards

Each video card must be a PCI (Peripheral Component Interconnect) or AGP (Accelerated Graphics Port) to be used with Windows 98's Multiple Display Support. Each monitor must be connected to its own video adapter card. After two monitors are connected properly, the size of the screen has, in effect, doubled. For more information, see "Multiple Display Support."

9. How many separate monitors can Windows 98's Multiple Display Support handle?

C. 9

9. CORRECT ANSWER: C

Windows 98's Multiple Display Support can handle up to nine separate monitors, as long as the supporting hardware is present. One monitor is always set up as a primary display. The primary display cannot be a video card that is on the motherboard. For more information, see "Multiple Display Support."

Multiple Display Support

This explanation supports questions 8 through 9.

Windows 98 now supports multiple video adapters on the same system. Each monitor can be used to display a separate section of an application or a separate application. In effect, the size of the desktop will be as large as the number of monitors.

Video resolution on each of the monitors does not have to be the same. Some monitors might be running in SVGA, while others are simply VGA. All monitors must be connected to their own PCIs or AGP controllers. Windows 98 supports up to nine external PCI or AGP adapter cards. The primary adapter will control the rest of the screen.

Each adapter can be set up using different resolutions while being used together. All are available as long as they are at least VGA.

10. What additional feature does IEEE 1394 offer a Windows 98 user?

D. IEEE 1394 is the support for Demanding Digital Devices.

10. CORRECT ANSWER: D

IEEE 1394 is the foundation for Digital Demanding Devices. IEEE 1394 defines a new type of BUS to carry large amounts of information at very high speeds. Devices such as video recorders, photo scanners, and videodisk players require data to be transferred very fast. For more information, see "IEEE 1394 Specification."

11. **What are the speeds of the IEEE 1394 BUS?**

    B. **Transfer rates from 100–400MB/s**

IEEE 1394 has transfer rates from 100–400MB/s, depending on the number of devices attached. IEEE 1394 can support up to 63 devices simultaneously. For more information, see "IEEE 1394 Specification."

IEEE 1394 Specification

This explanation supports questions 10 through 11.

Microsoft has incorporated the IEEE 1394 specification to handle devices that demand greater bandwidth. IEEE 1394 offers transmission rates from 100–400MB/s for up to 63 devices on the same BUS.

The intent was for Demanding Digital Devices to be able to function properly under Windows 98. Devices such as video recorders, video cameras, photo scanners, and videodisc players can be used with Windows 98.

At this time there are few devices on the market that will support IEEE 1394 devices. Microsoft offers a list of Adaptec adapters that are already IEEE 1394–compliant.

12. **While using RAS, what is the name of the component that allows Windows 98 to use more than one phone line to establish a single connection?**

    A. **Multilink**

Multilink allows a RAS client to dial out on two or more lines; after the connections have been established, the lines act as one.

13. **A client calls to ask why, when he uses Multilink with his server using Call Back, the Multilink seems to fail. What could be the problem?**

    B. **Call Back does not support Multilink at this time.**

Multilink can only use multiple connections when it is established by a user. Call Back is initiated by the Remote Access Server and at this time does not support multiple connections. If a client wants to use Multilink, he must give up using Call Back.

14. Proposed solution:

Install Windows 98 on all the systems in the office. Make sure all new equipment uses USB connectors. Install an Adaptec 1394 adapter to handle all the digital equipment.

A. The proposed solution satisfies the required component and all of the optional components.

14. CORRECT ANSWER: A

By using USB devices, Carol and her coworkers can share devices easily. When a new USB device is connected to the Windows 98 system, Plug and Play takes over and loads the appropriate drivers. An IEEE 1394 adapter offers high bandwidth for digital video.

15. Proposed solution:

Install a Windows 98 system as a print server.

Share all the printers off the system and grant permissions to everyone.

Have each user connect via the UNC name for each printer.

B. The proposed solution satisfies the required component and only one of the optional components.

15. CORRECT ANSWER: B

Clients using Windows 98 will have the drivers loaded from the Windows 98 server. Plug and Play will make sure configuration is completed properly.

Only administrators and owners will be able to control the print queue.

DOS applications cannot be printed with a UNC. They must have a port captured.

FURTHER REVIEW

INSTALL AND CONFIGURE HARDWARE DEVICES IN A MICROSOFT ENVIRONMENT AND A MIXED MICROSOFT AND NETWARE ENVIRONMENT

Windows 98 supports several new technologies that are explained further in each of the following sections.

Examining COM Ports

Modems are configured to transfer data to and from your computer through connections called *COM ports* (communication ports). COM ports are connected to your computer's main motherboard and allow communications devices to pass data into and out of the computer.

Windows 98 Setup checks all COM ports during installation. If a modem is detected, Windows 98 installs the drivers needed to configure it. COM ports can be configured either with or without a modem attached. A COM port is not the modem itself; it is simply the connector being used. A COM port can be used for devices other than modems. Printers and other PCs can be connected through the COM port. The COM port has its own icon in the Control Panel.

The Windows 98 Setup program automatically detects your COM ports and attempts to configure any devices (such as modems) attached to those ports. Alternatively, you can select a specific COM port for your modem from the Connections tab of the Modems Properties sheet. Windows 98 attempts to communicate with the COM port and creates the computer files and connections necessary to allow data to flow from the computer to the device.

To manually configure a COM port (without a modem attached), follow these steps:

1. Open the Control Panel and double-click on the System icon. Then select the Device Manager tab to see a list of all the computer devices in your computer.

2. Double-click on the COM port you want to configure; a Communications Port Properties sheet with several tabs appears.

3. From this Properties sheet, you can configure the port to meet whatever specifications you need. These settings include port settings, device driver setup, and resource allocation information.

4. When you finish, click OK.

After the COM port is configured, any new device can make use of it (see Figure 2.3).

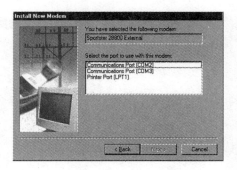

FIGURE 2.3
Adding a new modem will list all available ports.

Infrared Technology—IrDA

Windows 98, like its predecessor Windows 95, supports infrared communication. Under Windows 95, it was an additional component, whereas Windows 98 provides support out of the box.

Infrared communication allows computers and peripherals to connect without cables of any type.

As a Plug and Play system enters a room with an Infrared Plug and Play printer present, Windows 98 will load the necessary drivers.

With the latest IrDA specifications, a Windows 98 system with Infrared can connect to a LAN through an access point device in the room.

INSTALL AND CONFIGURE THE BACKUP APPLICATION

1. **The Windows 98 Backup utility can be used to create backups of compressed drives. True or False?**

   A. True, because compressed files are read by the operating system, then passed to the Backup utility.

   B. False, because compressed files have a different format that Backup cannot read.

   C. True, because compressed files are not really compressed—they are placed on a separate drive.

   D. False, unless you enable support for compressed files in the Backup utility.

   E. True, but only if the files have been backed up at least once prior to having been compressed.

2. **To which of the following can a backup of data be written?**

   A. Floppy disk

   B. Tape drive

   C. Network drive

   D. Local hard drives

   E. All of the above

3. **Suppose you run a full backup on Monday and an incremental backup on Tuesday. When you run another incremental backup on Wednesday, what happens?**

   A. All files that have changed since the full backup are backed up again.

   B. All files that have changed since the incremental backup are backed up again.

   C. All files are backed up.

   D. An error occurs because you can't run two incremental backups consecutively.

   E. Nothing, because all the files are already backed up.

4. **Suppose you run a full backup on Monday and incremental backups each day Tuesday through Friday. How would you restore Friday's files if necessary?**

   A. By restoring the incremental backups backward from last to first, followed by the full backup

   B. By restoring the full backup and then the last incremental

   C. By restoring the full backup and each of the incremental backups in order

   D. By restoring the incremental backups in order and then restoring the full backup

   E. None of the above

5. **What is included in a backup set?**

   A. Data that has been backed up

   B. Parameters used for the backup

   C. Information about all incremental backups needed to restore a drive

   D. Instructions for restoring data

   E. The number of tapes used for the backup

6. **Long Filenames are fully supported by the Backup utility. True or False?**

   A. True, because Backup is fully Windows 98–compatible.

   B. False, because Backup is an older 16-bit application.

   C. True, if you enable Long Filename support.

   D. False, because Backup was developed before Long Filenames were introduced.

   E. True, if you use the LFNBK utility.

7. **MS-DOS and Windows 3.1 backup sets can be restored using the Windows 98 Backup utility. True or False?**

   A. True, because Backup is backward compatible.

   B. False, because Backup has been redesigned.

   C. True, because Backup is a 32-bit application.

   D. False, because Backup is a 32-bit application.

   E. True, but only if support for DOS and WIN 3.1 is enabled.

8. **Where does the Windows 98 Backup utility store the settings used to create a backup?**

   A. In the `BACKUP.INI` file

   B. In the backup set

   C. In the file set

   D. In the system Registry

   E. In the `WINDOWS.INI` file

9. **You created a backup last week, and now you need to restore that data. The Backup utility will let you restore the files to which of the following locations?**

   A. To the same directories on the machine from which they were backed up

   B. To a different directory structure on the same machine

   C. To the same directory structure on a different machine

   D. To a different directory structure on a different machine

   E. All of the above

10. **Which types of tape media can be used with the Backup utility?**

    A. QIC 40

    B. QIC 80

    C. QIC 3010

    D. SCSI Tape drives

    E. All of the above

ANSWER KEY

1. A	5. A-D	9. E
2. E	6. A	10. E
3. B	7. B	
4. C	8. B	

INSTALL AND CONFIGURE THE BACKUP APPLICATION

1. The Windows 98 Backup utility can be used to create backups of compressed drives. True or False?

    A. True, because compressed files are read by the operating system, then passed to the Backup utility.

1. CORRECT ANSWER: A

With the Windows 98 Backup utility, you can back up compressed files just as you would uncompressed files. For more information, see "The Backup Application."

2. To which of the following can a backup of data be written?

    E. All of the above

2. CORRECT ANSWER: E

Backed up data can be written to floppy disks, tapes, or network drives. However, because of the limited room on a floppy disk, you would most likely use a tape or network drive. For more information, see "The Backup Application."

3. Suppose you run a full backup on Monday and an incremental backup on Tuesday. When you run another incremental backup on Wednesday, what happens?

    B. All files that have changed since the incremental backup are backed up again.

3. CORRECT ANSWER: B

An incremental backup backs up only files that have changed since the last backup, whether that backup was full or incremental. For more information, see "The Backup Application."

4. Suppose you run a full backup on Monday and incremental backups each day Tuesday through Friday. How would you restore Friday's files if necessary?

    C. By restoring the full backup and each of the incremental backups in order

4. CORRECT ANSWER: C

To restore from both full and incremental backups, you must first restore the full backup and then restore the incremental backups in the order in which they were made. For more information, see "The Backup Application."

5. What is included in a backup set?

    A. Data that has been backed up

    D. Instructions for restoring data

5. CORRECT ANSWERS: A-D

Backup sets include data that has been backed up, as well as parameters that were used to create the backup. For more information, see "The Backup Application."

6. Long Filenames are fully supported by the Backup utility. True or False?

   A. True, because Backup is fully Windows 98–compatible.

Long Filenames are fully supported by the Windows 98 Backup utility. For more information, see "The Backup Application."

7. MS-DOS and Windows 3.1 backup sets can be restored using the Windows 98 Backup utility. True or False?

   B. False, because Backup has been redesigned.

Because they lacked support for Long Filenames, backup sets created by MS-DOS and Windows 3.x cannot be used by the Windows 98 Backup utility. For more information, see "The Backup Application."

8. Where does the Windows 98 Backup utility store the settings used to create a backup?

   B. In the backup set

When a backup is created, the parameters used to create that backup are stored in the backup set. For more information, see "The Backup Application."

9. You created a backup last week, and now you need to restore that data. The Backup utility will let you restore the files to which of the following locations?

   E. All of the above

The Backup utility can be used to restore files to either the same directories or different directories on either the same computer or a different computer. For more information, see "The Backup Application."

The Backup Application

This explanation supports questions 1 through 9.

The Windows 98 Backup utility is a useful, easy-to-use tool for creating backups of data. By default, Backup is not installed with Windows 98. You can check to see whether it is installed on your computer by opening Programs, Accessories, System Tools. The Microsoft Backup utility is shown in Figure 2.4.

If Backup cannot be found in that location, you can install it easily by using the following steps:

   1. Open the Control Panel and double-click the Add/Remove Programs icon.

2. When the Add/Remove Programs dialog box appears, click the Windows Setup tab.

3. You are presented with a list of Windows 98 components. Select Disk Tools, and then click the Details button.

4. Select Backup, and then click OK to close the open dialog boxes.

5. Windows will most likely prompt you for the installation disks or CD-ROM so it can find the necessary program files. If it does, insert the disk or CD. It then installs the Backup utility for you.

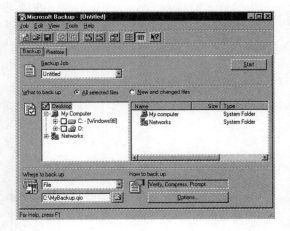

FIGURE 2.4
The new look of the Backup utility offers a wizard to guide you through the steps.

The Backup program creates two types of backups:

- All Selected Files makes backups of all the files you have selected.

- New and Changed Files backs up only files that have changed since the last All Selected Files backup. After the files are backed up, the archive bit is changed; therefore, on the next New or changed backup, those files are not included.

You probably want to perform a mix of both types of backups. Then if you need to restore files, you will restore the All Selected Files backup first, followed by each of the New and Changed Files backups you have made since. If you have a large number of changed backups, this can be a long process. On the other hand, if you use only All Selected Files backups, you will need a lot of storage space. It is a good practice to perform an All Selected Files backup on a weekly basis and perform New and Changed Files backups daily if you use your computer heavily.

When you create backups, you can save data on floppy disks, a tape drive, or a network drive. Most likely, you will not want to use floppy disks because of the volume of data you will need to back up. Later in this section, backup tape drives are discussed.

You should remember a few other important things about the Backup utility:

- It is possible to perform a comparison between a backup set and the directories from which it was backed up to find any differences between the two.

- Long Filenames (LFNs) are fully supported.

- It is possible to drag and drop backup sets onto a Backup icon to restore the set.

- During a full system backup, Windows 98 also backs up the Registry by copying it to a temporary file. If you restore the backup set later, the Registry files are merged back into the existing Registry.

- Backup allows the filtering of file types for inclusion or exclusion from a file set.

- MS-DOS 6.2 and Windows 3.1 backup sets cannot be restored using the Windows 98 Backup utility because of incompatibility issues with LFNs in MS-DOS 6.2 and earlier.

10. Which types of tape media can be used with the Backup utility?

E. All of the above

Windows 98 Backup now supports SCSI as well as QIC (quarter-inch cartridge) 40, 80, and 3010 tape drives. For more information, see "Tape Drives."

Tape Drives

This explanation supports question 10.

After you have installed Backup, you must tell it what kind of tape drive you have. This is easily done by selecting Tools, Re-Detect Tape Drive.

The capability to back up to a tape drive is new to the Windows 98 version of Backup (previous MS-DOS versions supported only floppy disk backups). The type of tape media that is supported is called *Quarter-Inch Cartridge* (QIC), and it comes in various specifications. The following tape drive specifications are supported:

- QIC 40, QIC 80, and QIC 3010 tape drives connected through the primary floppy disk controller (various manufacturers)

- QIC 40, QIC 80, and QIC 3010 tape drives connected to a parallel port (Colorado Memory Systems only)

▼ **NOTE**

SCSI tape backup units are now supported by Windows 98 Backup.

Windows 98 should be able to detect any supported tape drives automatically. If it cannot detect the tape drive, a message to that effect appears when you start Backup, and a number of troubleshooting suggestions appear. You can cancel the error and perform your backups to floppy or hard drive.

CHAPTER SUMMARY

Windows 98 can be installed as an upgrade to Windows 3.x or Windows 95. The upgrade path can vary depending on the current system configuration and installation method.

An OEM version of the Windows 98 software is available on a new PC. This version is not an upgrade and cannot be purchased. Windows 98 offers more flexibility in its installation component by opening the Add/Remove Programs icon in the Control Panel.

Windows 98 is very modular. As more hardware is added to the system, more software and drivers are added. All the tools added in Windows 98 can take up nearly 300MB of drive space. It is important therefore to understand how much software needs to be added.

New technology is not lost on Windows 98: It can take advantage of the new USB ports, IEEE 1394 specifications, and Infrared.

Windows 98 also provides a solid backup and restore program to maintain a safe and reliable working environment. Complete and partial backups are available to satisfy everyone's needs.

CHAPTER 3

In this chapter, the questions address the installation of the four major components of the network subsystem: protocols, adapters, client services, and server services. You will be examining protocols and adapters in depth. There will also be an examination of the computer browser service, Personal Web Server, and Dial-Up Networking.

Installation and Configuration, Part 2: Network Components

OBJECTIVES

This chapter helps prepare you for the exam by covering the following objectives:

Configuring Windows 98 Server components. Server components include the following:

- **Microsoft Personal Web Server 4.0**

- **Dial-Up Networking Server**

▶ Windows 98 offers complete integration into a Microsoft or Novell network. This section reviews the components and their configuration.

Installing and configuring the network components of Windows 98 in a Microsoft environment and a mixed Microsoft and NetWare environment. Network components include the following:

- **Client for Microsoft Networks**

- **Client for NetWare Networks**

- **Network Adapters**

- **File and Printer Sharing for Microsoft Networks**

continues

- **File and Printer Sharing for NetWare Networks**

- **Service for NetWare Directory Services (NDS)**

- **Asynchronous Transfer Mode (ATM)**

- **Virtual Private Network (VPN) and PPTP**

- **Browse Master**

▶ The network configuration within Windows 98 is broken into four major component types: clients to access resources, server service to provide resources, protocols to exchange data, and adapters to offer the physical hardware as the foundation of all previous components.

Installing and configuring network protocols in a Microsoft and a mixed Microsoft and NetWare environment. Protocols include the following:

- **NetBIOS Enhanced User Interface (NetBEUI)**

- **Internet Packet eXchange/Sequenced Packet eXchange (IPX/SPX)**

- **Transmission Control Protocol/Internet Protocol (TCP/IP)**

- **Microsoft Data Link Control (DLC)**

- **Fast Infrared**

▶ Windows 98 supports a variety of protocols that enable systems of different type to be able to exchange data with Windows 98. Microsoft provides a core set of common protocols that are widely in use in the industry. Third-party manufacturers may also offer Windows 98 systems additional protocols more specific to their products.

CONFIGURE WINDOWS 98 SERVER COMPONENTS

1. **What version of Peer Web Server ships with Windows 98?**

   A. Version 1.0

   B. Version 3.0

   C. Version 4.0

   D. Version 5.0

   E. Version 6.0

2. **Which operating system can run PWS?**

   A. Windows 3.1

   B. Windows 95

   C. Windows 98

   D. Windows NT Workstation

   E. Windows NT Server

3. **What is the difference between PWS and IIS? Select all that apply.**

   A. PWS does not support ISAPI and CGI scripts.

   B. IIS supports an unlimited number of clients while PWS only supports one client at a time.

   C. PWS and IIS are the same. IIS is just faster because it runs on a Windows NT server.

   D. PWS is a peer Web server intended for small groups while IIS is a full Internet-ready Web solution.

   E. None of the above.

4. **What Internet protocols are supported on PWS 4.0? Select all that apply.**

   A. HTTP

   B. FTP

   C. Gopher

   D. News

   E. POP

5. **How do you install a Dial-Up Networking Server?**

   A. Select Dial-Up Networking icon in the Control Panel and turn on server.

   B. Using Add/Remove, Windows components, select Communications and Dial-Up Networking Server.

   C. From the Dial-Up Networking icon, select Connections and Dial-Up Server.

   D. From the Network icon in the Control Panel, select Dial-Up Adapter's properties and turn on Dial-Up Server.

   E. None of the above.

6. **How many connections can be made to a Dial-Up Server running on Windows 98?**

   A. One.

   B. One per modem/adapter.

   C. As many as the share permits.

   D. As many as the license permits.

   E. None. Windows 98 does not support Dial-Up Server.

7. **What are the server types that Windows 98's Dial-Up Networking can emulate? Select all that apply.**

    A. Windows for Workgroups and Windows NT 3.1

    B. PPP, Windows NT

    C. PPTP, Windows NT, and Windows 98

    D. Windows 3.1

    E. DOS

    The following question is scenario-based. Please read all the requirements and proposed solution before answering.

8. **Scenario:**

    A small company wants to use the Internet as a means of connecting its branch offices.

    Required components:
    You want to enable PPTP support on the Dial-Up client.

    You want to enable PPTP support on the Dial-Up server.

    Optional components:
    Only PPTP clients should be allowed to connect.

    Allow users to choose between using PPTP and standard dial-up.

Proposed solution:
Enable the PPTP filter in the Dial-Up Server item of the Connections menu in the Dial-Up Networking.

    A. The proposed solution satisfies all the required components and all the optional components.

    B. The proposed solution satisfies all the required components but only one of the optional components.

    C. The proposed solution satisfies all the required components but none of the optional components.

    D. The proposed solution satisfies none of the required components but one of the optional components.

    E. The proposed solution satisfies none of the required components and none of the optional components.

9. **What are the two security methods with Dial-Up Server? Select two.**

    A. User level

    B. Share level

    C. Password

    D. Windows NT challenge

    E. Windows 98 challenge

ANSWER KEY

1. C	4. A-B	7. A-C
2. B-C-D	5. C	8. E
3. D	6. A	9. A-B

ANSWERS & EXPLANATIONS

CONFIGURE WINDOWS 98 SERVER COMPONENTS

1. What version of Peer Web Server ships with Windows 98?

C. Version 4.0.

1.   CORRECT ANSWER: C

Windows 98 ships with version 4.0 of the Peer Web Server. For more information, see "Peer Web Server (PWS)."

2. Which operating system can run PWS?

B. Windows 95

C. Windows 98

D. Windows NT Workstation

2.   CORRECT ANSWER: B-C-D

Windows 98 ships with PWS, while Windows 95 and Windows NT Workstation must download the software from Microsoft or the Windows NT 4.0 Option pack. For more information, see "Peer Web Server (PWS)."

3. What is the difference between PWS and IIS? Select all that apply.

D. PWS is a peer Web server intended for small groups while IIS is a full Internet-ready Web solution.

3.   CORRECT ANSWER: D

PWS could service the Internet, but the system resources are not enough to be efficient in a large deployment. IIS is designed to work on a Windows NT server. For more information, see "Peer Web Server (PWS)."

4. What Internet protocols are supported on PWS 4.0? Select all that apply.

A. HTTP

B. FTP

4.   CORRECT ANSWER: A-B

HTTP is supported for Web page access and management while FTP service is in place for file transfers. PWS does not support Gopher or News. IIS is used for these protocols. For more information, see "Peer Web Server (PWS)."

Peer Web Server (PWS)

This explanation supports questions 1 through 4.

Windows 98 ships with version 4.0 of Peer Web Server. Peer Web Server is a scaled-down version of the Internet Information Server that is designed to work off a Windows NT server. PWS and IIS are very similar in functionality, but PWS was designed for a small workgroup while IIS is for Internet publishing.

PWS is available for Windows 95 and 98 and Windows NT 4.0. The latest version of the software 4.0 is included with Windows 98 but can be downloaded from Microsoft Web page for Windows 95 and Windows NT 4.0.

PWS will only support a limited set of publishing protocols—HTTP for Web page publishing and FTP for file transfer. Applications will be able to make use of ISAPI and CGI.

5. How do you install a Dial-Up Networking Server?

C. From the Dial-Up Networking icon, select Connections and Dial-Up Server.

5. CORRECT ANSWER: C

Dial-Up Server is installed at the same time as Dial-Up Networking. By default, the service is off. From the Connections menu in Dial-Up Networking, select Dial-Up Server. For more information, see "Dial-Up Server Networking."

6. How many connections can be made to a Dial-Up Server running on Windows 98?

A. One.

6. CORRECT ANSWER: A

Windows 98's Dial-Up Server can only handle one dial-up connection at a time, even if there are multiple modems. For more information, see "Dial-Up Server Networking."

7. What are the server types that Windows 98's Dial-Up Networking can emulate? Select all that apply.

A. Windows for Workgroups and Windows NT 3.1

C. PPTP, Windows NT, and Windows 98

7. CORRECT ANSWER: A-C

Windows for Workgroups and Windows NT 3.1 are available for compatibility with older systems and the default choice is the PPP, Windows NT, and Windows 98 option. PPTP uses PPP to communicate. For more information, see "Dial-Up Server Networking."

8. Proposed solution:

Enable the PPTP filter in the Dial-Up Server item of the Connections menu in Dial-Up Networking.

E. The proposed solution satisfies none the required components and none of the optional components.

8. CORRECT ANSWER: E

There are no options to set PPTP filtering or access from the Dial-Up Server. PPTP is used only on outgoing calls using a VPN adapter. For more information, see "Dial-Up Server Networking."

9. What are the two security methods with Dial-Up Server? Select two.

A. User level

B. Share level

User level is the same as Windows NT challenge, but you won't find any Windows NT challenge menu anywhere for this. From the Access Control tab of the Network icon, select User level or Share level. Password is an option on the Dial-Up Server but is put in place by share-level security. For more information, see "Dial-Up Server Networking."

Dial-Up Server Networking

This explanation supports questions 5 through 9.

Windows 98 contains the tools to act as a Dial-Up Networking Server. The Dial-Up software contains a menu that will enable Windows 98 to receive data calls (see Figure 3.1). This feature is not new to Windows, as Windows 95 and the Windows Plus pack offered Dial-Up Server.

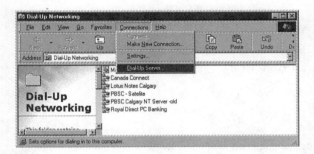

FIGURE 3.1
Dial-Up Server is enabled from the Dial-Up Networking menu system.

The Dial-Up server can act as a PPP, Windows NT, and Windows 98 server, as well as a Windows NT 3.1–Windows for Workgroups–compatible server. Only one dial-up connection at a time is supported (see Figure 3.2).

Windows 98's implementation of Dial-Up Server must rely on share-level or user-level security for user authentication and does not support call back security or PPTP filtering.

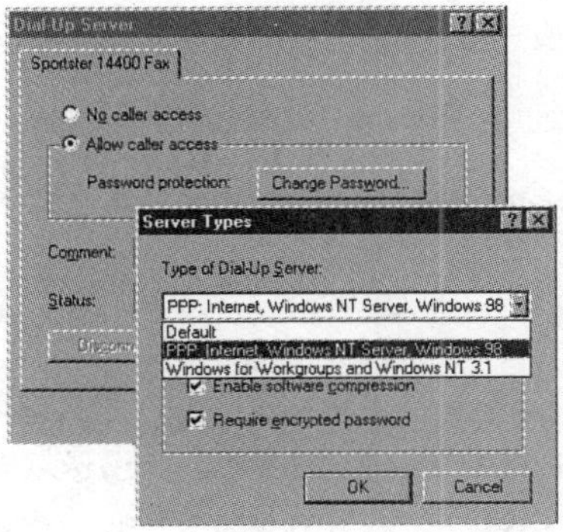

FIGURE 3.2
The Dial-Up Server offers a list of compatible server types.

INSTALL AND CONFIGURE THE NETWORK COMPONENTS OF WINDOWS 98 IN A MICROSOFT ENVIRONMENT AND A MIXED MICROSOFT AND NETWARE ENVIRONMENT

1. **How do you start a network service?**

   A. Log on

   B. Do nothing

   C. Start -> Programs -> <choose *service*>

   D. Start -> Programs -> NET START

   E. Start server service

2. **Windows 98 includes support for which of the following types of networks? Select all that apply.**

   A. Novell NetWare 1.1

   B. Windows NT

   C. Banyan VINES 4.2

   D. Windows 95

   E. OS/2 Peer

3. **Where would you change the name of your computer?**

   A. Right-click My Computer -> Properties

   B. Start -> Run -> NETCONFIG.EXE

   C. The Identification tab of the Network icon in the Control Panel

   D. The Identification tab of the System icon in the Control Panel

   E. The TCP/IP properties

4. **Sara did not install or configure any networking settings while performing the Windows 98 install. Where must she do this after installing Windows 98?**

   A. System icon in the Control Panel

   B. Network icon in the Control Panel

   C. Start -> Run -> NETCONFIG.EXE

   D. Right-click My Computer -> Properties

   E. Run Setup again

5. **How can you edit network service settings in Windows 98? Select all that apply.**

   A. Network icon in the Control Panel

   B. System icon in the Control Panel

   C. Start -> Run -> NETCONFIG.EXE

   D. During the installation of Windows 98

   E. Run Setup and use the Add/Remove option

The following two questions are based on the same scenario, required components, and optional components. Please read all the requirements and proposed solutions before answering.

6. Scenario:

You have a mixed network environment running Windows 98 systems with Novell and NT servers.

Required components:
Offer a single logon name for both networks.

Offer a single password for all networks.

Optional components:
Do not allow blank passwords.

Keep all passwords synchronized when changing passwords.

Proposed solution:
Set your primary logon to Client for Microsoft Networks, which will dictate which password to use.

Have the same username on Novell and NT.

A. The proposed solution satisfies all the required components and all the optional components.

B. The proposed solution satisfies all the required components but only one of the optional components.

C. The proposed solution satisfies all the required components but none of the optional components.

D. The proposed solution satisfies none of the required components but one of the optional components.

E. The proposed solution satisfies one the required components and none of the optional components.

7. Scenario:

You have a mixed network environment running Windows 98 systems with Novell and NT servers.

Required components:
Offer a single logon name for both networks.

Offer a single password for all networks.

Optional components:
Do not allow blank passwords.

Keep all passwords synchronized when changing passwords.

Proposed solution:
Have the same username on Novell and NT.

Have the same password on Novell, NT, and Windows 98.

Set the password option to synchronize all passwords when changing passwords.

A. The proposed solution satisfies all the required components and all the optional components.

B. The proposed solution satisfies all the required components but only one of the optional components.

C. The proposed solution satisfies all the required components but none of the optional components.

D. The proposed solution satisfies none of the required components but one of the optional components.

E. The proposed solution satisfies one the required components and none of the optional components.

8. Sara is running Windows 95 and wants to connect to a share on your Windows 98 computer. Both computers are using the NetBEUI protocol. What must you enable for Sara to connect to your share?

A. Install File and Printer Sharing for Microsoft Networks

B. Install the Microsoft Client for Microsoft Networks

C. Install File and Printer Sharing for Windows 95

D. Install user-level security

E. Enable Sharing for Windows 98

9. **What must you do to set up a Windows 98 computer so that it can operate as a print server on a NetWare network? Select all that apply.**

A. Install File and Printer Sharing for NetWare

B. Install Client for Microsoft Networks

C. Install Client for NetWare Networks

D. Set up a user account in the NetWare server

E. Set up a group account in the NetWare server

10. **Which type of device, in most cases, does not support Plug and Play?**

A. 24× CD-ROM drive

B. 17-inch Super VGA monitor

C. PCI video card

D. Legacy network card

E. ISA PNP network card

11. **Where can you change the resource settings for a network interface card? Select all that apply.**

A. Network icon in the Control Panel

B. Start -> Run -> NETCONFIG.EXE

C. Device Manager tab of the System icon in the Control Panel

D. During installation of Windows 98

E. None of the above

12. **You install a Plug and Play network card into an appropriate slot and start Windows 98. What further action is necessary to complete the installation of the network card? Select all that apply.**

A. Insert the driver disk supplied by manufacturer (if required).

B. Specify an IRQ (interrupt) for the card.

C. Specify an IO (input/output) port for the card.

D. No further action is necessary.

E. Specify a home directory for the drivers.

13. **What three driver types may be used with Windows 98? (Choose three options.)**

A. Enhanced-mode NDIS

B. Enhanced-mode ODI

C. Real-mode NDIS

D. Real-mode ODI

E. Safe mode NDIS

14. **You are installing a NetWare server for use by a Windows 98 workgroup. What must you do to ensure that Windows 98 Long Filenames are preserved on the NetWare server? Select all that apply.**

A. Install the NetWare LONG.NAM namespace option on the Windows 98 system.

B. Choose Long Filenames during installation of Client for NetWare Networks on the Windows 98 system.

C. Install the NetWare OS/2 namespace option on the NetWare server.

D. Do nothing; no further action is required.

E. Install the Novell 32-bit client.

15. **What must you have installed to enable directories and printers to be shared with NetWare users? Select all that apply.**

A. User-level security

B. File and Printer Sharing for NetWare Networks

C. NetBEUI protocol

D. Computer name of the NetWare server with the list of user accounts

E. ODI-compliant network card

16. **To set up user-level security, what type of system must be present in the network? Select all that apply.**

A. Windows 98 computer

B. Windows NT Workstation

C. Windows NT Server

D. NetWare 3.12 Server

E. Windows 95

17. **What is the purpose of installing NDS for Windows 98? Select all that apply.**

A. NDS will allow access to Novell 3.x servers.

B. NDS will run Novell utilities, such as NWAdmin.

C. NDS will allow full login script variables and parameters.

D. NDS will allow access to Windows 98 systems set up as file and printer servers for NetWare.

E. NDS does not provide any extra benefits to Windows 98.

18. **Where will Windows 98 store user profiles on a Novell server if NDS is implemented? Select the best answer.**

A. In the user's Mail directory

B. In the user's name folder under the Public folder

C. In the user's Profile folder

D. In the user's home folder

E. In the NetLogon share

19. **What does the acronym ATM represent?**

A. Analog Terminal Modulator

B. Asynchronous Terminal Modulator

C. Asynchronous Transfer Mode

D. Analog Transfer Mode

E. Analog Terminal Mode

20. **When is ATM implemented in a network configuration?**

A. When connecting a PC to a local network.

B. When connecting a PC to a WAN.

C. When using an analog phone line.

D. ATM is not a network device.

E. When connecting to a mainframe.

21. **Where in Windows 98 do you install support for Virtual Private Networks?**

    A. From the Network icon in the Control Panel

    B. From the System icon in the Control Panel

    C. From the Communication option in the Windows Components

    D. From the Internet option in the Windows Components

    E. From the VPN icon in the Control Panel

22. **After support for Virtual Private Networks is installed in Windows 98, which additional components are found in the Network icon of the Control Panel? Select all that apply.**

    A. A dial-up adapter with VPN support.

    B. Each protocol to which the VPN adapter is bound.

    C. NDISWAN for Microsoft VPN is bound.

    D. Microsoft Virtual Private Networking adapter.

    E. VPN dialer.

23. **What compiles a list of all computers with shared resources in a domain or workgroup?**

A. Backup browser

B. Master browser

C. Each computer

D. Router

E. None of the above

24. **Organize the following list of operating systems in the order in which they would appear to be the Master browser in a browser election.**

    A. Windows NT Workstation

    B. Primary domain controller

    C. Windows NT Server

    D. Windows 98 computer

    E. Windows for Workgroups

25. **Where would you change the browser master settings on a Windows 98 computer?**

    A. Network icon in the Control Panel

    B. System icon in the Control Panel

    C. Start -> Run -> NETCONFIG.EXE

    D. In the CONFIG.SYS file under SET MASTERBROWSE=yes/no

    E. In the Registry

26. **How many minutes are the intervals at which a Master browser will update a Backup browser?**

    A. 12 minutes

    B. 15 minutes

    C. 18 minutes

    D. 25 minutes

    E. Only at startup

27. **What problems might be encountered if a user turns off his or her computer without properly shutting down the computer through Start -> Shutdown?**

    A. The system will be corrupt and will not function properly.

    B. The browsing will stop and recover when the system is back on line.

    C. The Master browser will continue to offer the computer name in the list but no other system will be able to access the downed Windows 98 computer.

    D. The clients will remove the server from their list as soon as they try to access and fail.

    E. None of the above.

28. **What must you do to enable browsing on your network?**

    A. Change a setting in the Registry

    B. Change a setting in File and Printer Sharing

    C. Do nothing

    D. Change the Properties of the client

    E. Change the role of the system to be a Master browser

ANSWER KEY

1. B	8. A	15. A-B-D	22. A-B-C-D
2. B-D	9. A-C-D	16. B-C-D	23. B
3. C	10. D	17. B-C	24. B-C-A-D-E
4. B	11. A-C-D	18. D	25. A
5. A	12. A	19. C	26. B
6. E	13. A-C-D	20. B	27. C
7. C	14. C	21. C	28. C

ANSWERS & EXPLANATIONS

INSTALL AND CONFIGURE THE NETWORK COMPONENTS OF WINDOWS 98 IN A MICROSOFT ENVIRONMENT AND A MIXED MICROSOFT AND NETWARE ENVIRONMENT

1. How do you start a network service?

    B. Do nothing

1. CORRECT ANSWER: B

Network services are automatically started when Windows 98 is booted. They do not require you to log on. A Windows 98 computer will offer all its network services to remote systems. For more information, see "Network Services."

Network Services

This explanation supports question 1.

Services are applications that execute in the background. Services load after Windows 98 boots. They often tend to give additional network functionality in the form of a server application, but can provide other capabilities such as the Hewlett-Packard JetAdmin tool. The most frequently used service is File and Printer Sharing for Microsoft Networks. To install a network service, follow these steps:

1. Open the Network icon in the Control Panel and choose the Configuration tab.

2. Click the Add button and choose Service.

3. Click the Add button.

4. Choose the Manufacturer and Service you want to install (see Figure 3.3). If it is an updated or unlisted service, click the Have Disk button and provide the path to the OEMSETUP.INF file and choose the service you want. Click OK.

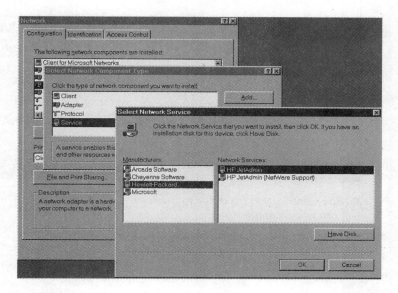

FIGURE 3.3
Microsoft includes a variety of services from different manufacturers.

5. Click the OK button to close the Network icon in the Control Panel. You might be prompted for the Windows 98 CD during the time in which the service files are copied to your hard drive.

▼ **NOTE**

Services are applications that are automatically started after your network software is loaded and your Logon screen is displayed. You do not have to log on for the services to start.

Only one file and print sharing service can be installed on a computer at a time. If you install File and Printer Sharing for NetWare Networks, you will receive file and print sharing capabilities for both NetWare and Microsoft networks.

Now that you have examined installing all the network components, it is time to take a look at the configuration of network adapters and protocols.

2. Windows 98 includes support for which of the following types of networks? Select all that apply.

   B. Windows NT

   D. Windows 95

2. CORRECT ANSWER: B-D

Windows 98 does not include support for Novell NetWare before version 2.15, or Banyan VINES before version 5.52. Windows NT and Windows 95, being Microsoft operating systems, are fully supported. For more information, see "Microsoft Networks."

3. Where would you change the name of your computer?

   C. The Identification tab of the Network icon in the Control Panel.

3. CORRECT ANSWER: C

You can only change your computer name in the Network icon in the Control Panel. After you change the name, you must restart the computer for the change to take effect. All computers on the network must have a unique computer name. If the name is not unique, Windows 98 will generate an error number 38 duplicate name on the network when it starts up. For more information, see "Microsoft Networks."

4. Sara did not install or configure any networking settings while performing the Windows 98 install. Where must she do this after installing Windows 98?

   B. Network icon in the Control Panel

4. CORRECT ANSWER: B

Sara must use the Network icon in the Control Panel to install and configure new network settings. All configurations can be done from the Network icon. For components not shipped standard with Windows 98, the Network icon will also supply a Have Disk button to load from alternate sources. For more information, see "Microsoft Networks."

5. How can you edit network service settings in Windows 98? Select all that apply.

   A. Network icon in the Control Panel

5. CORRECT ANSWER: A

The network icon will offer all configuration settings and a dialog box in which to edit them. The System icon will only enable you to change the resource settings for the network adapter. NETCONFIG.EXE is not an executable file. For more information, see "Microsoft Networks."

6. Proposed solution:

Set your primary logon to Client for Microsoft Networks, which will dictate which password to use.

Have the same username on Novell and NT.

E. The proposed solution satisfies one the required components and none of the optional components.

Primary logons only determine which password is first expected but does not synchronize passwords. The usernames and passwords must be the same to prevent multiple logon screens. For more information, see "Microsoft Networks."

7. Proposed solution:

Have the same username on Novell and NT.

Have the same password on Novell, NT, and Windows 98.

Set the password option to synchronize all passwords when changing passwords.

C. The proposed solution satisfies all the required components but none of the optional components.

With the same username and password, users initially will only get one logon screen. There is no control in Windows 98 to prevent blank passwords or to ensure that passwords are always synchronized. For more information, see "Microsoft Networks."

8. Sara is running Windows 95 and wants to connect to a share on your Windows 98 computer. Both computers are using the NetBEUI protocol. What must you enable for Sara to connect to your share?

A. Install File and Printer Sharing for Microsoft Networks.

Only File and Printer Sharing for Microsoft Networks is required. There is no difference between sharing with a Windows 95 or 98 system. Although user-level security would work in this situation, it is not necessary. For more information, see "Microsoft Networks."

9. What must you do to set up a Windows 98 computer so that it can operate as a print server on a NetWare network? Select all that apply.

A. Install File and Printer Sharing for NetWare.

C. Install Client for NetWare Networks.

D. Set up a user account in the NetWare server.

Both the Client for NetWare Networks and File and Printer Sharing for NetWare must be used to share a printer to NetWare clients. NetWare requires the use of user-level security, which in turn requires the client for NetWare on the 98 system. The Windows 98 client also should have an account on the Novell server that it is using as a security provider. For more information, see "Microsoft Networks."

Microsoft Networks

This explanation supports questions 2 through 9.

The first time you are given access to the installation of network components is during the Windows 98 installation. After the Hardware Detection phase, you receive a prompt to complete the network information. The Windows 98 installation will collect that information during two Windows 98 Setup Wizard steps. You first will be prompted for the installation of other network components through the dialog box shown in Figure 3.4. After choosing the proper components, you receive a prompt for the computer and workgroup names. After installation of Windows 98, you may access all these network settings through the Network icon in the Control Panel.

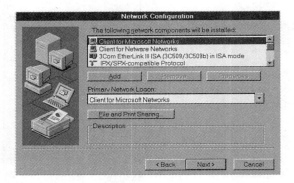

FIGURE 3.4
All network components can be installed during installation.

Much of the configuration of the network settings will be performed after the initial installation of Windows 98, because of the changing network environment in most workplaces. Because most of the configuration will be accomplished after the installation of Windows 98, this chapter deals with the configuration of the network components through the Network icon in the Control Panel. The Configuration tab of the Network icon in the Control Panel enables you to add, remove, and modify your network components. On this screen, you can modify the following four components:

- Clients

- Adapters

- Protocols
- Services

You also can configure which client will be your Primary Network Logon and enable File and Printer Sharing from the Configuration tab.

The networking functionality built in to Windows 98 enables a Windows 98 computer to be a client on a wide variety of networks. A Windows 98 client can run multiple network protocols, services, and clients simultaneously, and thus can be a client on many different networks at the same time.

Windows 98 includes software to support the following networks:

- Microsoft Windows NT
- Microsoft Windows 95, 98
- Microsoft Windows for Workgroups 3.x
- Microsoft LAN Manager
- Novell NetWare version 2.15 and later
- Banyan VINES version 5.52 and later
- DEC Pathworks version 4.1 and later
- SunSoft PC-NFS version 5.0 and later

Microsoft does not include the client files for several 16-bit network clients. These files will have to be installed from the disk supplied from each of the third-party companies. The 16-bit network clients are from Banyan, Novell, DEC, and SunSoft.

For most of these third-party clients, Windows 98 does not support installation after the installation of Windows 98. These clients should be installed before the installation of Windows 98. This will not be a problem for any computers upgraded to Windows 98 from either MS-DOS or Windows for Workgroups, because the 16-bit network software will already be installed. This may require the installation of MS-DOS and the network software prior to the installation of Windows 98, if you were planning to install Windows 98 to a freshly formatted hard drive. If you want to install the client after the installation of Windows 98, you must manually install the client software from the third-party client installation disks.

▼ **NOTE**

Windows 98 can have only one 16-bit network client installed at a time, but can run multiple 32-bit clients. The 32-bit clients that come with Windows 98 are the Microsoft Client for Windows Networks and Microsoft Client for NetWare Networks.

Many of the network vendors, whose 16-bit network clients Windows 98 supports, now have 32-bit network clients that can function in conjunction with the network components that ship with Windows 98.

To add a new network client, follow these steps:

1. Open the Network icon in the Control Panel and choose the Configuration tab.

2. Click on the Add button, and then select Client (see Figure 3.5).

3. Click on the Add button.

4. Select the Manufacturer and Client you want to install (see Figure 3.6). If it is an updated or unlisted client, select the Have Disk button and provide the path to the OEMSETUP.INF file and choose the client. Click the OK button.

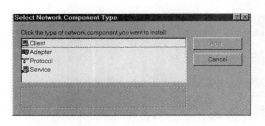

FIGURE 3.5
This Select Network Component Type dialog box enables you to choose which component to add.

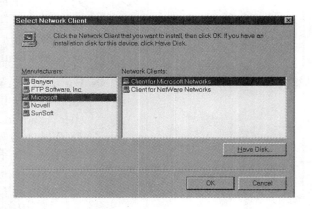

FIGURE 3.6
The Select Network Client dialog box enables you to choose which type of client you want to install. Microsoft supplies two 32-bit clients.

5. Click the OK button to close the Network icon in the Control Panel. You may be prompted for the Windows 98 CD while the client files are copied to your hard drive.

6. At the prompt, restart your computer.

The Client for Microsoft Networks may be used if your network is made up of any of the following:

- Windows NT
- Windows 95, 98
- Windows for Workgroups
- LAN Manager

To communicate with another computer, both computers must run a proper client for the other computer, and must be using the same network protocol. For security implementation with Microsoft networks, Windows 98 can implement share-level and user-level security.

10. **Which type of device, in most cases, does not support Plug and Play?**

   D. Legacy network card

10. CORRECT ANSWER: D

Most legacy cards (older cards) were produced before the advent of Plug and Play and, therefore, cannot take advantage of the new technology. For more information, see "Installing and Configuring Adapters."

11. **Where can you change the resource settings for a network interface card? Select all that apply.**

   A. Network icon in the Control Panel

   C. Device Manager tab of the System icon in the Control Panel

   D. During installation of Windows 98

11. CORRECT ANSWER: A-C-D

There is no executable called NETCONFIG.EXE. The resource settings (IRQ, IO port) may be changed from the Network icon or the Device Manager in the Control Panel. During Setup, limited options are available for configuration. For more information, see "Installing and Configuring Adapters."

12. **You install a Plug and Play network card into an appropriate slot and start Windows 98. What further action is necessary to complete the installation of the network card? Select all that apply.**

    A. **Insert the driver disk supplied by manufacturer (if required)**

You will have to supply a driver disk for the network card. If the driver is included with Windows 98, you will most likely be asked for the Windows 98 installation disks/CD. There also may be a few confirmation prompts that need to be answered. For more information, see "Installing and Configuring Adapters."

13. **What three driver types may be used with Windows 98? (Choose three options.)**

    A. **Enhanced-mode NDIS**

    C. **Real-mode NDIS**

    D. **Real-mode ODI**

The three driver types you can use are enhanced-mode (32- and 16-bit) NDIS, real-mode (16-bit) NDIS, and real-mode (16-bit) ODI. By viewing the properties of any network card in the Network icon of the Control Panel, you will see these three choices. For more information, see "Installing and Configuring Adapters."

Installing and Configuring Adapters

This explanation supports questions 10 through 13.

Windows 98 includes drivers for many of the most popular network adapters. Additional network adapter drivers may be supplied by the network adapter vendor for use with Windows 98. Before you can install any other Windows 98 networking components, you first must install a network adapter driver through the Network icon in the Control Panel. If you do not have an actual network card in the computer, you can use the Microsoft Dial-Up Adapter driver, along with a compatible modem for network connectivity. You also can add drivers and adapters through the Add New Hardware option in the Control Panel.

Network adapter card drivers are configured by selecting the adapter in the Network icon in the Control Panel and then choosing Properties. If the network card supports the Plug and Play standard, Windows 98 can automatically configure the driver according to information the card provides to the Windows 98 operating system. Otherwise, the card should be configured according to the manufacturer's documentation.

To install a network adapter, follow these steps:

1. Open the Network icon in the Control Panel and choose the Configuration tab.

2. Click the Add button, and then choose Adapter.

3. Click the Add button.

4. Choose the Manufacturer and Adapter you want to install (see Figure 3.7). If it is an updated or unlisted adapter, click the Have Disk button and provide the path to the OEMSETUP.INF file and choose the adapter you want. Click OK.

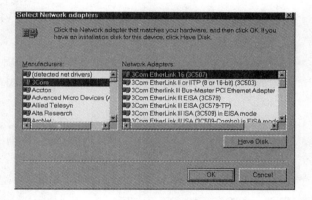

FIGURE 3.7
Microsoft provides drivers for a wide range of network cards from most major card manufactures.

5. Click the OK button to close the Network Control Panel. You may be required to specify resource settings (IRQ, IO) for the adapter, and may be prompted for the Windows 98 CD during the time in which the adapter files are copied to your hard drive.

Proper configuration of network adapters is required to create and maintain network connectivity, which is a major concern for most people running Windows 98. Network adapters can have some or all of their settings changed in two locations—either the Network icon in the Control Panel or the Device Manager. These settings or properties usually include the following:

- Driver type
- Bindings
- Advanced configuration
- Resources (in some cases)

All the settings are accessible through the Network icon in the Control Panel. You also can access the Resources settings for the network card through the Device Manager tab of the System icon in the Control Panel.

If you choose to access the settings on the network card through the Network icon in the Control Panel, you will want to select the installed network card and click on the Properties button.

Three driver types can be used: enhanced-mode (32-bit and 16-bit) NDIS, real-mode (16-bit) NDIS, and real-mode (16-bit) ODI drivers.

Whenever they are available, you should use the enhanced-mode (32-bit and 16-bit) NDIS drivers because they will load in protected memory, which frees up conventional memory for DOS sessions. If the drivers are 32-bit, they will also give you the added advantage of increased speed.

16-bit drivers are a second choice. Two versions of 16-bit drivers are available. NDIS is a network driver specification developed by consortium of Microsoft, Intel, and other vendors in the computer industry. It allows multiple protocols to be used independently on a network card. ODI is a similar network driver specification that was developed by Novell.

Binding involves attaching two items together. The Bindings tab lists the connections to an adapter by various protocols (see Figure 3.8). The Bindings tab always lists the items on the next level up in the Windows 98 network model. Bindings list all the protocols that are connected or "bound" to the adapter you are viewing. You can unbind the protocols by clearing the check boxes. To improve the overall speed of your computer's network access, you should unbind all unneeded network protocols. If a protocol is installed on your computer, but not bound to any adapters, you will not actually be using the protocol.

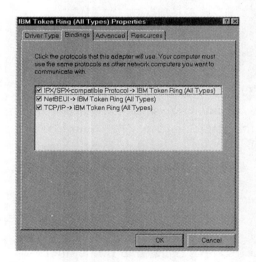

FIGURE 3.8

By only making necessary bindings, you can decrease the amount of time that it takes for your computer to establish a connection with a server.

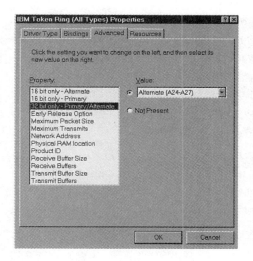

FIGURE 3.9
Many network adapters have advanced settings that can be modified to provide support for specific features of the adapter.

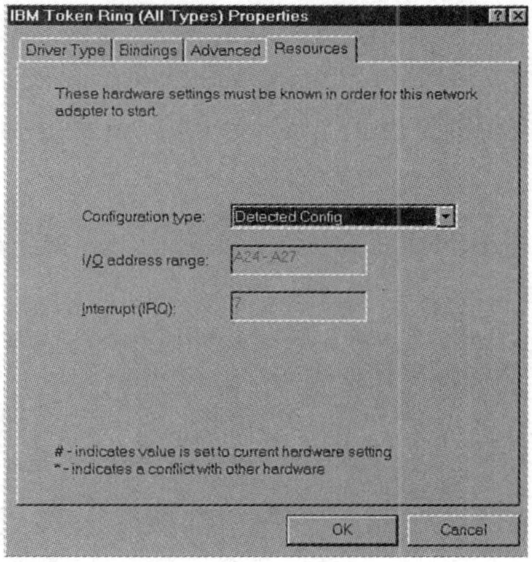

FIGURE 3.10
Hardware resources that Windows 98 reserves for the adapter may be modified. They may still have to be modified on the adapter itself.

The Advanced tab lists a series of advanced settings for the network card (see Figure 3.9). The list of settings varies from one network card driver to another. This tab often includes settings such as the maximum transmission size for network packets, and buffer settings for the network card. You should not change the default values without consulting your network administrator or the card manufacturer to find out how changing the settings will affect your network.

Every network card occupies specific hardware resources on a computer. The Resources tab enables you to see—and depending on your network card, change—the resources in use by the network card (see Figure 3.10). The resources used by the card include the IRQ and Input/Output (I/O) address.

Changes made to the network card's resources might alter the actual settings on the network card itself. Not all network cards support these alterations by Windows 98. If you are using a network card that does not allow Windows 98 to make the modifications to the card's resources, the settings on the Resources tab will only affect the resources that Windows 98 expects the network card to have. You will still have to change the settings on the card, using whatever method is suggested by the manufacturer.

If the card does not allow you to change the settings in the Network icon in the Control Panel, you may be able to change the settings on the Device Manager tab of the System icon in the Control Panel. Your network card should be located under the Network Adapters section, and the settings can be changed in the Resources tab of the properties of the card. Not all network cards can be changed this way.

When a network interface card is Plug and Play–compliant, it can be automatically detected and configured by Windows 98. Just plug the network card into the appropriate expansion slot and start Windows 98. The model of the card will be detected, and the appropriate Windows 98 driver will be installed. Windows 98 then assigns an available interrupt request (IRQ) line and memory or I/O address range to the network card as appropriate and configures the card to use these settings.

The term *legacy* refers to older cards (not only network cards, but all expansion cards) that are not Plug and Play. Some legacy cards support software configuration for IRQ and I/O addresses, but many in this class only allow configuration changes by changing jumpers or dip switches. Legacy cards do not always have support with 32-bit drivers; 16-bit (possibly real-mode) drivers may have to be used.

When working with very new network cards, or very old legacy network cards, you may find that the cards are not listed in the default distribution files that ship with Windows 98. Rather than choosing a network card, click the Have Disk button, and then provide the path to the unlisted drivers.

Some Plug and Play cards may require you to supply a path to the drivers if they are not included in the Windows 98 distribution.

One of the best tools to view and modify the resource settings such as IRQs, DMAs, I/O, and memory is the Device Manager. The Device Manager will list all components and display their current settings. Not all components, however, can be modified through this tool.

14. You are installing a NetWare server for use by a Windows 98 workgroup. What must you do to ensure that Windows 98 Long Filenames are preserved on the NetWare server? Select all that apply.

C. Install the NetWare OS/2 namespace option on the NetWare server.

14. CORRECT ANSWER: C

The NetWare server is responsible for preserving Long Filenames. The OS/2 namespace and LONG.NAM options on the NetWare server will mimic the Windows 98 Long Filename format. There is no configuration required on the Windows 98 system for Long Filename support on the NetWare server. For more information, see "NetWare Networks."

15. What must you have installed to enable directories and printers to be shared with NetWare users? Select all that apply.

A. User-level security

B. File and Printer Sharing for NetWare Networks

D. Computer name of the NetWare server with the list of user accounts

15. CORRECT ANSWER: A-B-D

All these are necessary to enable directories and print queues to be shared with NetWare users. The user-level security is mandatory with File and Printer Sharing for NetWare. The computer name of the NetWare server is to be entered as the security provider for user-level security. For more information, see "NetWare Networks."

16. **To set up user-level security, what type of system must be present in the network? Select all that apply.**

B. Windows NT Workstation

C. Windows NT Server

D. NetWare 3.12 Server

16. CORRECT ANSWER: B-C-D

You must have one of these operating systems installed on your network to use user-level security. All these are capable of maintaining a list of users that Windows 98 will use when applying access permissions. Windows 98 does not contain an account database of its own and, therefore, cannot be a security provider for another 98 system. For more information, see "NetWare Networks."

17. **What is the purpose of installing NDS for Windows 98? Select all that apply.**

B. NDS will run Novell utilities, such as NWAdmin.

C. NDS will allow full login script variables and parameters.

17. CORRECT ANSWER: B-C

NDS will offer a Windows 98 client full login to a Novell 4.x server, as well as the capability to run NetWare utilities. Only a Novell 4.x server will make use of NDS. A Windows 98 system running as File and Printer Sharing for Novell is emulating a Novell 3.x server. For more information, see "NetWare Networks."

18. **Where will Windows 98 store user profiles on a Novell server if NDS is implemented? Select the best answer.**

D. In the user's home folder

18. CORRECT ANSWER: D

Each user must now have a home folder to store roaming profiles on system running NDS. When a user logs on a bindery-compatible system (non-NDS), the profiles will be stored in the user's Mail directory on the Novell server. For more information, see "NetWare Networks."

NetWare Networks

This explanation supports questions 14 through 18.

Windows 98 integrates well into a NetWare network running Novell NetWare version 3.11 or higher. With Windows 98, Microsoft includes the following three options for communicating on a Novell network:

- Microsoft's 32-bit Client for NetWare Networks

- Novell NetWare Workstation Shell 3.x (NETX)

- Novell NetWare Workstation Shell 4.x (VLM)

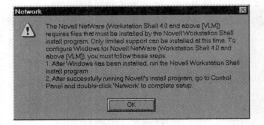

FIGURE 3.11
To install the VLM client, you must manually
run the install the Workstation Shell.

If you choose either of the clients supplied by Novell, you receive a prompt to insert the NETX or VLM client disk from your server client disks that shipped with your original server software. If you install the VLM client, you receive a prompt to manually install the Workstation Shell 4.x software after completing the Windows 98 portion of the setup (see Figure 3.11). Windows 98 requires that the VLM client be installed, but will not perform the complete installation from within the Windows 98 client installation. For mixed NetWare 4.x (non-bindery mode) and Windows NT environments, Microsoft has a 32-bit Microsoft Service for NetWare Directory Services (NDS) available for Windows 98 that will allow a better integration with Novell 4.x.

▼ NOTE

There are some disadvantages or limitations when running Windows 98 on a NetWare network, such as the following:

- Long Filenames are not supported natively by NetWare. You must load the OS/2 Name Space (OS2.NAM) NetWare Loadable Module (NLM) in NetWare, which supports 254 characters, or LONG.NAM in IntranetWare 4.11, which in turn supports 255 characters.

- If running the real-mode ODI and VLM or NETX real-mode shell, performance may suffer because it (the real-mode NetWare driver) uses RAM that MS-DOS applications could use.

- Users of Windows 98 can direct jobs to print queues without capturing a printer port.

- Users of Windows 98 can see whichever print queues the bindery or NDS provides them access to use.

The Client for NetWare Networks can be used to access NetWare servers running NetWare 2.15 and above and NetWare 4.x servers using bindery emulation. The Client for NetWare Networks requires the IPX/SPX-compatible protocol, which is installed by default when the client is installed.

Although the 16-bit Novell NetWare clients do not provide all the advantages of the 32-bit client, a 16-bit NETX or VLM client is required if any of the following are used:

- NCP packet signature security (requires VLM).

- NetWare IP protocol (which does not use Microsoft's TCP/IP as it tunnels IPX/SPX through the IP protocol).

- Helper Terminate-and-Stay-Resident (TSR) applications loaded from DOS (such as 3270 emulators).

- Custom Virtual Loadable Modules (VLMs) with functionality not provided by the Windows 98 components, such as Personal NetWare (PNW.VLM).

- Novell utilities, such as NWADMIN or NETADMIN. Most of the DOS-based 3.x utilities, such as SYSCON, RCONSOLE, and PCONSOLE, will still work.

- NetWare Directory Services (NDSes), although a separate Microsoft Service for NetWare Directory Services (NDS) is now available.

- IPX ODI protocol.

- Monolithic IPX (IPX.COM) or ARCnet protocols.

In addition to the listed clients, Novell has released a 32-bit NetWare client called *IntranetWare Client 2.2 for Windows 95-98*, or *Client 32*. This client has been optimized to communicate with Novell IntranetWare 4.11 servers and NDS. The IntranetWare client can utilize either NDIS (Network Device Interface Specification) network card drivers, which are a cross-industry standard, or ODI (Open Data-Link Interface) network card drivers, which are Novell-specific. By using the NDIS drivers, you guarantee compatibility with other network clients.

▼ **NOTE**

OS/2 Namespace in this context has no relationship with IBM operating system OS/2.

19. What does the acronym ATM represent?

    C. Asynchronous Transfer Mode

19. CORRECT ANSWER: C

Windows 98 supports Asynchronous Transfer Mode communication. For more information, see "Windows 98 and ATM."

20. When is ATM implemented in a network configuration?

    B. When connecting a PC to a WAN.

20. CORRECT ANSWER: B

ATM is used as a high-speed connection over a WAN. Windows 98 will support ATM when connecting to another LAN through a WAN. For more information, see "Windows 98 and ATM."

Windows 98 and ATM

This explanation supports questions 19 through 20.

Windows 98 now supports ATM as a Wide Area Network connection. Its implementation is limited at the moment, but as more ATM network connections and software packages are developed, Windows 98 will support fast connection from LAN to LAN.

21. Where in Windows 98 do you install support for Virtual Private Networks?

    C. From the Communication option in the Windows Components

21. CORRECT ANSWER: C

Windows 98 offers support for PPTP and VPN as a Windows component. It is installed from the Communication option in the Add/Remove programs' Windows Components tab. For more information, see "Point-to-Point Tunneling Protocol/Virtual Private Networks (PPTP/VPN)."

22. After support for Virtual Private Networks is installed in Windows 98, which additional components are found in the Network icon of the Control Panel? Select all that apply.

    A. A dial-up adapter with VPN support.

    B. Each protocol to which the VPN adapter is bound.

    C. NDISWAN for Microsoft VPN is bound.

    D. Microsoft Virtual Private Networking adapter.

22. CORRECT ANSWER: A-B-C-D

The virtual private network software will load a separate dial-up adapter to be used with RAS and bind it to the Microsoft Virtual Private Networking adapter software with NDISWAN. As well, each existing protocol, such as NetBEUI, IPX, and TCP/IP, also will be bound to the new VPN adapter. For more information, see "Point-to-Point Tunneling Protocol/Virtual Private Networks (PPTP/VPN)."

Point-to-Point Tunneling Protocol/Virtual Private Networks (PPTP/VPN)

This explanation supports questions 21 through 22.

Point-to-Point Tunneling Protocol is a secure wide area network (WAN) protocol that is starting to receive wide acceptance as a secure protocol over the Internet. PPTP enables you to make a secure connection to your network from a remote location on the Internet. If you will have Internet connectivity on your network, you should consider installing PPTP on both your network servers and remote workstations. The protocol (NDISWAN) is a virtual protocol, and does not actually exist. It instead is a modified version of TCP/IP that allows for carrying of other packets in the data section of the IP packet. This virtual protocol receives a binding with an equally virtual local area network (LAN) adapter—the Microsoft Virtual Private Networking (VPN) adapter (see Figure 3.12).

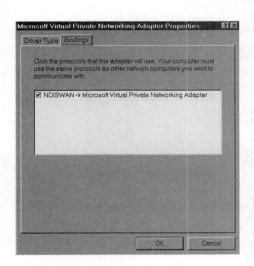

FIGURE 3.12
The Microsoft Virtual Private Networking adapter is bound to the NDISWAN protocol, and both use TCP/IP for communication.

The Advanced settings tab on the Dial-Up Adapter #2 (VPN Support) Properties dialog box allows for a log file (similar to the PPP or modem log files) to track and troubleshoot connections to remote servers (see Figure 3.13). The Advanced settings also enable you to identify the physical media that you will be running the PPTP connection over.

To effectively use PPTP and VPN, you need some or all of the following components installed (see Figure 3.14):

- Client for Microsoft Networks.

- Optional second client for use on remote LAN.

- Dial-up adapter if making the VPN connection through an Internet service provider (ISP).

- NDISWAN protocol installed for packet encapsulation.

- TCP/IP to act as a transport for the NDISWAN protocol.

- Optional second protocol to be used on the remote LAN. This would include NetBEUI or IPX/SPX if you will not be using TCP/IP on the remote LAN.

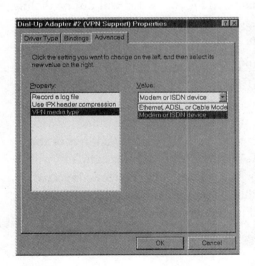

FIGURE 3.13
Dial-Up Adapter #2 (VPN Support) Advanced Properties enables you to specify the log file creation and PPTP media types.

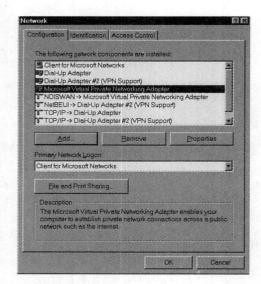

FIGURE 3.14
The components that make up a PPTP client configuration.

When creating the Dial-Up Networking document to connect to your Remote Access Services server running PPTP, you will not be specifying a modem as a connection device, but rather the Microsoft VPN adapter. This connector will not be dialing a phone number; instead, it will require the IP address of the network adapter on the RAS server.

Before establishing a PPTP connection, you will first establish a connection to a TCP/IP network. This may be a LAN connection or a dial-up connection to an ISP. After that connection is in place, you will open up the PPTP dial-up connection (see Figure 3.15). This connection will have the IP address of the PPTP adapter on the RAS server as the destination. You will dial this virtual call, but it will keep your modem connected. Once dialed, you have all the transactional security that you would have had by dialing the server directly.

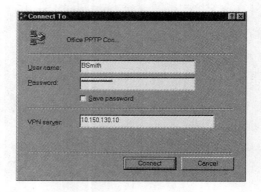

FIGURE 3.15
The dial-up connection leaves previous connections open.

23. What compiles a list of all computers with shared resources in domain or workgroup?

    B. Master browser

23. CORRECT ANSWER: B

The Master browser is responsible for compiling a list of all computers with shared resources. It passes that list periodically to the Backup browser. The computers on the network contact the Master browser for a list of Backup browsers and then contact the Backup browsers for the browse list. An individual server will provide the list of shared resources it has to offer. A router does not participate in compiling a browse list. By default, browsing does not work across a router. For more information, see "Browser Service."

24. Organize the following list of operating systems in the order in which they would appear to be the Master browser in a browser election.

    B. Primary domain controller

    C. Windows NT Server

    A. Windows NT Workstation

    D. Windows 98 computer

    E. Windows for Workgroups

24. CORRECT ANSWER: B-C-A-D-E

A primary domain controller will always be Master browser if one is present. The others will be given priority based on their operating system. A Windows NT Server will always win over a Windows NT Workstation, which in turn will always win over a Windows 98 computer if they are all in the same domain and the Windows 98 computers have their workgroup name the same as the domain. A Windows 95 and Windows 98 machine will have the same value. For more information, see "Browser Service."

25. Where would you change the browser master settings on a Windows 98 computer?

    A. Network icon in the Control Panel

25. CORRECT ANSWER: A

The settings to determine whether a Windows 98 computer is preferred to be, will be, or will not be a Master browser are set in the Network icon of the Control Panel under File and Printer Sharing for Microsoft Networks properties. For more information, see "Browser Service."

26. How many minutes are the intervals at which a Master browser will update a Backup browser?

    B. 15 minutes

26. CORRECT ANSWER: B

A Master browser will update a Backup browser every 15 minutes. Each server in the network will announce itself to the Master browser on startup and every 12 minutes thereafter. For more information, see "Browser Service."

27. **What problems might be encountered if a user turns off his or her computer without properly shutting down the computer through Start -> Shutdown?**

   C. The Master browser will continue to offer the computer name in the list but no other system will be able to access the downed Windows 98 computer.

28. **What must you do to enable browsing on your network?**

   C. Do nothing

---

27. CORRECT ANSWER: C

If a computer is shut down improperly, it does not have a chance to notify the Master browser. It then must fail at three of its 12-minute announcements before the Master browser will remove the computer from the browse list. This will result in the computer being visible in the browse list, even though the computer is not online. Clients that attempt to access any the server will receive an error message. For more information, see "Browser Service."

28. CORRECT ANSWER: C

Browsing is automatically enabled. Changes are only required if you do not want a specific computer to participate in the browse list compiling process, or prefer that certain computers do participate. For more information, see "Browser Service."

Browser Service

This explanation supports questions 24 through 28.

Windows 98 features *unified browsing*—all computers that can be accessed by Windows 98 are displayed together in the Network Neighborhood. NetWare servers appear along with Windows-based computers in the Network Neighborhood, for example, if both the Client for Microsoft Networks and Client for NetWare Networks are installed.

When users access the Network Neighborhood, they are viewing a list of computers on the network known as a *browse list*.

Microsoft and NetWare networks can use NetBIOS to distribute browse lists throughout a domain. The browse list contains all NetBIOS computers that have shared resources in the domain; it is compiled by the Master browser of the domain.

When the Master browser has compiled the browse list, it distributes the list to the Backup browsers. When a client requires access to the browse list, it obtains it from a Backup browser; thus the Master browser does not become overloaded with requests from all the computers.

The decision of which computers are Master and Backup browsers is determined through browse elections. If a primary domain controller is present, that controller will always be the Master browser. Each type of operating system in the network has a different potential to be a browser. Windows NT computers are more favored to be browsers than Windows 98 computers. If a computer is a preferred browser, it can be elected to be a browser depending on the operating system it is running and whether it has been manually configured to be a preferred browser.

When a network client needs to consult a browse list to browse the network, it contacts one of the Backup browsers for a copy of the current browse list. The Backup browsers periodically (every 15 minutes) receive updated browse lists from the Master browser to make sure the browse lists remain current.

A Windows 98 computer can be configured to maintain or to not maintain browse lists by configuring the File and Printer Sharing service for either Microsoft or NetWare networks.

Normally, you let the browser elections automatically determine which computers are the browsers. If you do not want the potential performance load on the Windows 98 computer that can result from browsing, however, you can configure the computer to *never* be a browser. In addition, you can set a particular computer, on which an extra network load would have little effect, to be a preferred browser.

▼ NOTE

Be careful when removing a potential Master browser as there must be at least one Master browser on every segment of every domain or workgroup. Clients will not be able to browse the network if there is no Master browser.

The browser configuration is performed using the properties for the File and Printer Sharing for Microsoft Networks service or the File and Printer Sharing for NetWare Networks service.

To access the browser configuration options for a computer running File and Printer Sharing for Microsoft Networks, follow these steps:

1. Click on the Network icon in the Control Panel and select the File and Printer Sharing for Microsoft Networks service.

2. Choose Properties and select the Browse Master property.

3. Choose one of the following options from the Value drop-down list (see Figure 3.16):

   • Select Automatic as the value to have Windows 98 automatically determine whether the computer is needed as a browse server.

   • Select Disabled as the value to prevent the computer from maintaining browse lists for the network.

   • To give the computer a higher weighting for the browse elections, select Enabled for the value. This computer then will be preferred over other Windows 98 computers that have Automatic set for the Browse Master value for the browse elections.

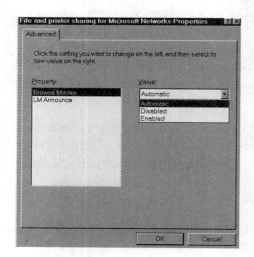

FIGURE 3.16
Browser options for File and Printer Sharing for Microsoft Networks.

4. Double-click OK and restart the computer.

To access the browser configuration options for a computer running File and Printer Sharing for NetWare Networks, follow these steps:

1. Click on the Network icon in the Control Panel applet and select the File and Printer Sharing for NetWare Networks service.

2. Choose Properties and select the Workgroup Advertising property.

3. Choose one of the following options from the drop-down list (see Figure 3.17):

   • To have Windows 98 automatically determine whether the computer is needed as a browse server, select Enabled: May Be Master for the value.

   • To prevent the computer from maintaining browse lists for the network, select Enabled: Will Not Be Master for the value.

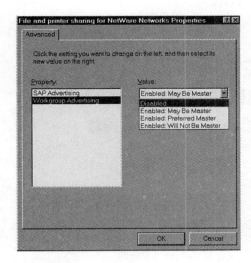

FIGURE 3.17
Browser options for File and Printer Sharing for
NetWare Networks.

- To give the computer a higher weighting for the browse elections, select Enabled: Preferred Master for the value. This computer will then be preferred over other Windows 98 computers that have Automatic set for the Browse Master value for the browse elections.

- To prevent the computer from using the browser service to browse network resources, select Disabled for the value.

- To allow the computer to send SAP broadcasts announcing its presence to real-mode NetWare clients, select the SAP Advertising property and change the value to Enabled.

4. Double-click OK and restart the computer.

FURTHER REVIEW

INSTALL AND CONFIGURE THE NETWORK COMPONENTS OF WINDOWS 98 IN A MICROSOFT ENVIRONMENT AND A MIXED MICROSOFT AND NETWARE ENVIRONMENT

The following information is especially important to review before taking the exam.

File and Printer Sharing

To set up Windows 98 to use user-level security, you must have at least one Windows NT computer on your network. The Windows NT computer can be either a Windows NT Server, a Windows NT Domain Controller, or a Windows NT Workstation. All these computers maintain a list of users that Windows 98 will use when applying access permissions. You also need to have Client for Microsoft Networks enabled.

You now can set up folders and printers to be shared on the Windows 98 client computers. You can share a folder, for example, by opening Explorer in Windows 98, locating the folder you want to share, and right-clicking. Choose Sharing from the context-sensitive menu and set up access rights as explained in Chapter 4, "Configuring and Managing Resource Access, Part 1."

To enable directories and print queues to be shared with NetWare users, add the File and Printer Sharing for NetWare Networks service in the Network Control Panel. If the File and Printer Sharing for Microsoft Networks service is already installed, remove that service first.

After File and Printer Sharing for NetWare Networks is installed, enable sharing by choosing the appropriate File and Printer Sharing options from the Network Control Panel.

▼ **NOTE**

File and Printer Sharing for NetWare Networks must use the User-level Access Control security model.

The computer name of the NetWare server that maintains the list of user accounts must be specified in the Access Control tab of the Network Control Panel.

You must use user-level security when running Windows 98 on a NetWare network and want to have peer services enabled for the Windows 98 clients. When using user-level security with NetWare networks, security authentication requests are handled using the pass-through security method. This type of security method passes the authentication requests to a NetWare server for authentication.

User-level security on NetWare is used to protect shared network resources by storing a list of users and groups who have access to a network resource. To gain access to a resource, a user must be on the access account list stored on the NetWare server bindery and also have the proper access rights for that resource. Administrators can set up access rights on a per-user or per-group basis. The rights that can be assigned to a user for a specific resource include read, write, create, delete, change attribute, directory search, and access control.

Specifying the specific folders and printers to be shared on a client computer is accomplished at a user level. To set up a folder as a shared resource, for example, a user opens Explorer, locates the folder to share, and right-clicks on it. From the context-sensitive menu, the Sharing command is selected and the Sharing tab is filled out. You can learn more about sharing a folder in Chapter 4.

Unified Logon

As mentioned previously, a Windows 98 computer can have more than one network client installed at a time. If a network contains both Windows NT and Novell NetWare servers, for example, the Windows 98 computer can run both the Client

for Microsoft Networks and the Client for NetWare Networks. If the passwords are the same for the two networks, the Unified Logon feature of Windows 98 requires that the password be entered only once for both networks. Similarly, if the Windows password is the same as the network password, the password needs to be entered only once. If the passwords are not the same, they need to be entered individually.

▼ **NOTE**

The password list file (PWL) is secured by each user's Windows 98 password. To cut down the number of different passwords a user must track and maintain, some network administrators advocate the use of a blank Windows 98 password. However, the use of a blank Windows 98 password along with password caching can expose your user's network resources to unauthorized use. Using a blank Windows 98 password is not recommended.

INSTALL AND CONFIGURE NETWORK PROTOCOLS IN A MICROSOFT ENVIRONMENT AND A MIXED MICROSOFT AND NETWARE ENVIRONMENT

1. Which of the following protocols are routable? Select all that apply.

   A. IPX/SPX

   B. NetBEUI

   C. TCP/IP

   D. Microsoft DLC

   E. NDIS and ODI

2. Which frame type is automatically used if no frame type is detected when using Autodetect with IPX/SPX?

   A. 802.1

   B. 802.2

   C. 802.3

   D. 802.5

   E. Ethernet II

3. Every computer on a TCP/IP network must be assigned a unique IP address comprised of how many bits?

   A. 4

   B. 8

   C. 16

   D. 32

   E. 128

4. What configuration settings are available for the NetBEUI protocol? Select all that apply.

   A. Computer Name

   B. Maximum Sessions

   C. Maximum Sockets

   D. Network Address

   E. Session Name

5. Which TCP/IP feature will resolve NetBIOS names to IP addresses?

   A. IPS

   B. DHCP

   C. DNS

   D. WINS

   E. ARP

6. When is the DLC protocol most widely used? Select all that apply.

   A. Small local area networks (LANs)

   B. Network printing

   C. Wide area networks (WANs)

   D. Connecting to mainframe computers

   E. Connecting to Apple Macintosh systems

7. **Which of the following items do not have to be unique on a network? Select all that apply.**

    A. Computer name

    B. IP address

    C. Workgroup name

    D. Domain name

    E. Server name

8. **Which of the following protocols are shipped with Windows 98? Select all that apply.**

    A. NetBEUI

    B. TCP/IP

    C. AppleTalk

    D. DLC

    E. Fast Infrared

9. **Which protocol is required for the Client for NetWare Networks?**

    A. NetBEUI

    B. TCP/IP

    C. IPX/SPX

    D. DLC

    E. NWLink

10. **Which protocols does Windows 98 install by default when installing an adapter? Select all that apply.**

    A. NetBEUI

    B. TCP/IP

    C. IPX/SPX

    D. DLC

    E. AppleTalk

The following two questions are based on the same scenario, required components, and optional components. Please read the full question and proposed solutions before answering.

11. **Scenario:**

    The Anderson Pipeline Company is setting up two small locations and have common resources at the Head Office. Each location is connected to the H.O. through a router.

    Required components:
    Connect all the system with a single protocol.

    Browse the WAN through the Network Neighborhood.

    Optional components:
    Central configuration of the protocol for all systems.

    Dynamic updates to names in the Network Neighborhood.

    Proposed solution:
    Set up each Windows 98 system with TCP/IP and have the protocol obtain an address automatically.

    Set up and configure a DHCP server at each location to hand out TCP/IP addresses automatically.

    A. The proposed solution satisfies all the required components and all the optional components.

    B. The proposed solution satisfies all the required components but only one of the optional components.

    C. The proposed solution satisfies all the required components but none of the optional components.

D. The proposed solution satisfies one of the required components and one of the optional components.

E. The proposed solution satisfies none of the required components and none of the optional components.

12. **Scenario:**

The Anderson Pipeline Company is setting up two small locations and have common resources at the Head Office. Each location is connected to the H.O. through a router.

Required components:
Connect all the system with a single protocol.

Browse the WAN through the Network Neighborhood.

Optional components:
Central configuration of the protocol for all systems.

Dynamic updates to names in the Network Neighborhood.

Proposed solution:
Set up each Windows 98 system with TCP/IP and have the protocol obtain an address automatically.

Set up and configure a DHCP server at each location to hand out TCP/IP addresses automatically.

Set up a single WINS server at H.O. and have DHCP assign the address to each client.

A. The proposed solution satisfies all the required components and all the optional components.

B. The proposed solution satisfies all the required components but only one of the optional components.

C. The proposed solution satisfies all the required components but none of the optional components.

D. The proposed solution satisfies one of the required components and one of the optional components.

E. The proposed solution satisfies none of the required components and none of the optional components.

INSTALL AND CONFIGURE NETWORK PROTOCOLS IN A MICROSOFT ENVIRONMENT AND A MIXED MICROSOFT AND NETWARE ENVIRONMENT

1. Which of the following protocols are routable? Select all that apply.

A. IPX/SPX

C. TCP/IP

1. CORRECT ANSWER: A-C

If you have multiple network segments on your network, you will need a routable protocol to communicate between them. IPX/SPX and TCP/IP packets can be routed over multiple segments. Additional hardware and software configuration is required to properly route data over a WAN. For more information, see "Network Protocols."

2. Which frame type is automatically used if no frame type is detected when using Autodetect with IPX/SPX?

C. 802.3

2. CORRECT ANSWER: C

802.3 is used when no other frame type is detected on the network. 802.3 is an older frame type. This standard is used by most systems running Ethernet networks. If the frame type does not match, there is no communication. For more information, see "Network Protocols."

3. Every computer on a TCP/IP network must be assigned a unique IP address comprised of how many bits?

D. 32

3. CORRECT ANSWER: D

A TCP/IP IP address is comprised of 32 bits split up into 4 octets (8 bits each). Each octet is usually presented in a decimal format. For more information, see "Network Protocols."

4. What configuration settings are available for the NetBEUI protocol? Select all that apply.

A. Computer Name

B. Maximum Sessions

4. CORRECT ANSWER: A-B

Only the Computer Name and Maximum Sessions from this list are correct. The other configurable settings for NetBEUI are Workgroup Name and Network Control Block Size. Maximum Sockets and Network Address are settings for the IPX/SPX protocol. For more information, see "Network Protocols."

5. Which TCP/IP feature will resolve NetBIOS names to IP addresses?

D. WINS

5. CORRECT ANSWER: D

WINS (Windows Internet Naming Service) will resolve a NetBIOS name into an IP address. This enables the client to use a Windows computer name to connect to another computer in a solely TCP/IP network. For more information, see "Network Protocols."

6. When is the DLC protocol most widely used? Select all that apply.

B. Network printing

D. Connecting to mainframe computers

6. CORRECT ANSWER: B-D

DLC is most widely used for network printing and connecting to mainframe computers. For more information, see "Network Protocols."

7. Which of the following items do not have to be unique on a network? Select all that apply.

C. Workgroup name

D. Domain name

7. CORRECT ANSWER: C-D

A workgroup name or domain name must be the same for every computer that is participating in that workgroup or domain. An IP address and computer name must be different from every computer on the network. For more information, see "Network Protocols."

8. Which of the following protocols are shipped with Windows 98? Select all that apply.

A. NetBEUI

B. TCP/IP

D. DLC

E. Fast Infrared

8. CORRECT ANSWER: A-B-D-E

NetBEUI, TCP/IP, DLC, and Fast Infrared are shipped with Windows 98. IPX/SPX and ATM are also standard protocols. Microsoft also lists in the Control Panel variations of these protocols provided by IBM, Novell 3COM, and Banyan VINES. For more information, see "Network Protocols."

9. Which protocol is required for the Client for NetWare Networks?

C. IPX/SPX

9. CORRECT ANSWER: C

IPX/SPX is the only required protocol when installing Client for NetWare Networks. This will enable a connection with any Novell server running IPX as well. Novell server may also run TCP/IP, in which case TCP/IP would be needed. For more information, see "Network Protocols."

10. Which protocols does Windows 98 install by default when installing an adapter? Select all that apply.

    A. NetBEUI

    C. IPX/SPX

TCP/IP is installed by default on Windows NT, DLC is not installed by default, and AppleTalk is not shipped with Windows 98. For more information, see "Network Protocols."

11. Proposed solution:

Set up each Windows 98 system with TCP/IP and have the protocol obtain an address automatically.

Set up and configure a DHCP server at each location to hand out TCP/IP addresses automatically.

    D. The proposed solution satisfies one of the required components and one of the optional components.

TCP/IP is a routable protocol that can be assigned automatically through a DHCP server. Browsing the network from Network Neighborhood will only list local servers since browsing does not pass through routers. For more information, see "Network Protocols."

12. Proposed solution:

Set up each Windows 98 system with TCP/IP and have the protocol obtain an address automatically.

Set up and configure a DHCP server at each location to hand out TCP/IP addresses automatically.

Set up a single WINS server at H.O. and have DHCP assign the address to each client.

    A. The proposed solution satisfies all the required components and all the optional components.

TCP/IP is a routable protocol that can be assigned automatically through a DHCP server. Browsing the network from Network Neighborhood will now offer a list of local and remote servers since browsing using the WINS server will exchange browse lists. For more information, see "Network Protocols."

Network Protocols

This explanation supports questions 1 through 12.

Windows 98 supports many major protocols and ships with four protocols. Some protocols have specific purposes, but others can be chosen by administrators for basic communication on your network. The following protocols ship with the Windows 98 operating system:

- NetBEUI
- IPX/SPX-compatible
- TCP/IP
- Microsoft DLC
- Fast Infrared

If you want to install any protocol other than these four, you will need software from the manufacturer of the protocol. To install a network protocol, follow these steps:

1. Open the Network icon in the Control Panel and choose the Configuration tab.

2. Click the Add button and choose Protocol.

3. Click the Add button.

4. Choose the Manufacturer and Protocol you want to install (see Figure 3.18). If it is an updated or unlisted protocol, click the Have Disk button and provide the path to the `OEMSETUP.INF` file and choose the protocol you want. Click OK.

5. Click the OK button to close the Network icon in the Control Panel. You may be prompted for the Windows 98 CD while the protocol files are copied to your hard drive.

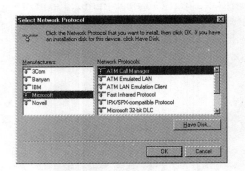

FIGURE 3.18
Support is included for other protocols, but the only protocols that ship with Windows 98 are found under the Microsoft section.

The NetBEUI and IPX/SPX-compatible protocols install by default when a network adapter driver is installed. If the Windows 98 computer needs to communicate with other computers, it must have the same protocol installed as the other computers.

The following sections highlight the configuration options for each protocol.

▼ **NOTE**

Unless you are required to use a third-party protocol to communicate with other computers, use one of the Microsoft protocols to take full advantage of the Windows 98 networking features. As a further consideration, be aware that the third-party protocols provided often require extra components, licenses, and configuration.

The NetBIOS Extended User Interface (NetBEUI) protocol is relatively easy to implement because it does not require the configuration of additional network settings for each computer other than the computer name and domain or workgroup name.

The advantages of the NetBEUI protocol include the following:

- Communication is fast on smaller networks.

- Performance is dynamically self-tuned.

- The only configuration required is a NetBIOS computer name and workgroup or domain name.

The disadvantages of the NetBEUI protocol include the following:

- Not routable

- Broadcast based, causing more network traffic

Other than the computer name and workgroup name, only two settings can be changed. You can find these two settings on the Advanced tab of the Protocol to Adapter properties. The two settings are as follows:

- Maximum Sessions identifies the maximum number of network sessions that your computer is capable of keeping track of. These include both inbound and outbound sessions.

- NCBS (Network Control Block Size) identifies the size or number of network control blocks that Windows 98 will use. These blocks are used to transfer or carry NetBIOS information for the NetBEUI protocol.

Because these are the only two configuration settings that may be changed, it makes NetBEUI an easy protocol to configure. Bindings, as with adapters, can be configured for each protocol. Protocols are bound to items on the next layer up in the Windows 98 network model. The next major layer above the protocols includes both clients and services (see Figure 3.19).

Bindings are listed on the Bindings tab for any clients or services that can work using NetBEUI. Because the NetWare client requires the IPX/SPX-compatible protocol, it is not listed on the Bindings tab for NetBEUI. As with bindings on the network card, any that are not used should be disabled.

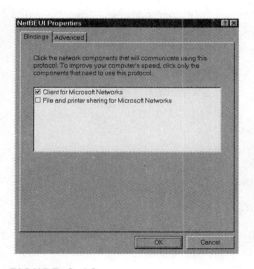

FIGURE 3.19
NetBEUI bindings enable you to disable clients or services for the protocol.

The IPX/SPX protocol is a routable network protocol developed by Novell. IPX/SPX is a more complex protocol than NetBEUI. If you have multiple network segments on your network, you will require a routable protocol. The IPX/SPX protocol is required for communication with NetWare servers, and has now become an industry standard protocol (used by many network operating systems). IPX/SPX must be installed if the Client for NetWare Networks is used, although other protocols may also be installed at the same time. If IPX/SPX is used with the Client for Microsoft Networks, the optional NetBIOS support should be enabled.

IPX/SPX has a number of settings that you can adjust on the Advanced tab of the IPX/SPX protocol, including the following:

- Force Even Length Packets is used for compatibility with older NetWare Ethernet drivers with monolithic protocol stacks, and on some older IPX routers.

- Frame Type: IPX supports several variations on standard network packets. The different frame specifications are referred to by the term *frame type*. You can only talk to servers or clients that are using the same frame type as you. If a frame type is not specified, Windows 98 will go with the detected frame type, or 802.2. You can choose from these other frame types:

  - 802.2
  - 802.3
  - ETHERNET II
  - ETHERNET_SNAP
  - Token_Ring
  - Token_Ring_Snap

- Maximum Connections enables you to set the maximum number of network sessions that Windows 98 will support.

- Maximum Sockets specifies the number of IPX Socket connections that may be made to or from the server. This is excluded from NetBIOS traffic.

- Network Address enables you to change the network, hardware, or MAC address of your network card. This address is the basis of all communication on your network. Not all addresses typed in will be valid, and invalid addresses will prevent you from communicating with other computers on your network. You should change this only with extreme caution.

- Source Routing specifies the cache size to use with source routing.

With the number of settings that can be modified, and the loss of network connectivity if the settings are configured incorrectly, IPX/SPX is a more difficult protocol to work with on a network than NetBEUI.

NetBIOS is required for Microsoft network clients to communicate with Microsoft servers. NetBIOS is also used to create and maintain lists of servers on the network. By default, IPX/SPX does not use NetBIOS—although you can enable NetBIOS on the NetBIOS tab of the IPX/SPX protocol properties (see Figure 3.20).

Windows 98 comes with the Microsoft 32-bit TCP/IP protocol, related connectivity utilities, and an SNMP client.

To install the TCP/IP protocol on a Windows 98 computer, follow these steps:

1. From the Start menu, choose Settings, Control Panel.

2. Double-click on the Network icon and select the Configuration tab.

3. Click Add to open the Select Network Component Type dialog box.

4. Select Protocol and choose Add to open the Select Network Protocol dialog box.

5. Select Microsoft from the Manufacturers list and TCP/IP from the Network Protocols list.

6. Click OK to return to the Network dialog box.

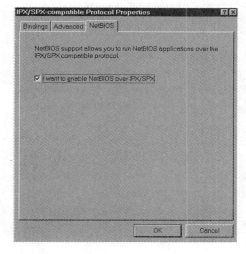

FIGURE 3.20

You can either enable or disable IPX/SPX-compatible protocol NetBIOS settings.

After installing TCP/IP on a Windows 98 computer, the tabbed TCP/IP Properties dialog box appears. From this dialog box, you can configure the appropriate values. To reconfigure TCP/IP, click the Network icon from the Control Panel to open the Network dialog box again.

To configure TCP/IP for Windows 98, follow these steps:

1. From the Network dialog box Configuration tab, select TCP/IP and click on Properties.

2. From the TCP/IP Properties sheet, select the IP Address tab. Select Obtain an IP Address Automatically if there is a Dynamic Host Configuration Protocol (DHCP) server on the network configured to supply this machine with an IP address. Otherwise, type the IP address and subnet mask in the spaces provided.

▼ **NOTE**

An incorrect IP address or subnet mask can cause communication problems with other TCP/IP nodes on the network. If an IP address is the same as another already on the network, it also can cause either machine to hang.

3. Each of the other tabs in the TCP/IP Properties sheet contains optional configuration information. For each of these tabs, enter the appropriate values as required. Click OK when you finish to restart the computer and initialize TCP/IP.

The other tabs of the TCP/IP Properties sheet, discussed in the following sections, contain optional TCP/IP configuration parameters.

▼ **NOTE**

It is highly recommended that a default gateway be configured for the Windows 98 client using the Gateway tab. The default gateway can help route TCP/IP messages to remote destinations.

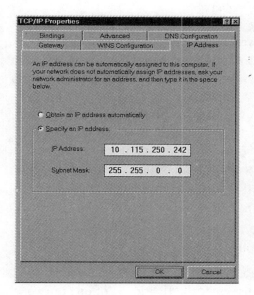

FIGURE 3.21
Every computer on your network requires a network-specific IP address.

Every computer on a TCP/IP network is individually identified by a unique 32-bit address. Currently this address is written using dotted decimal notation (see Figure 3.21). In addition to the IP address, you also require a subnet mask. The subnet mask is used to determine whether the other people whom you are contacting are on your network segment or elsewhere.

These numbers should be received from your network administrator. If your network administrator has created a server to host Dynamic Host Configuration Protocol (DHCP) service, all you have to do is select Obtain an IP Address Automatically and you will receive complete IP configuration from the server.

When the route needed for an IP message to reach a destination is not known, the message is forwarded to the default gateway. The default gateway is a router connected to other TCP/IP network segments. Messages are sent to this gateway when it is not known on which segment the destination is. The Gateway tab contains the IP addresses of default gateways that can be used in the order they appear on the list.

If the subnet mask determines that the address you are trying to reach is remote, your computer will send it to a gateway.

▼ **NOTE**

Only one gateway is used to route messages. If a gateway is unavailable (because of hardware problems, for example), the next gateway on the list is used. If that gateway does not respond, the next gateway is used. A second gateway is never used if the first one is available, even if the destination computer is unavailable or the message is undeliverable.

A Windows Internet Naming Service (WINS) server can be used to register and resolve NetBIOS names to IP addresses. If the Windows 98 computer wants to map a drive to the computer name SERVER3 on a remote TCP/IP network, for example, it can query the WINS server to find out the IP address of SERVER3.

Communication using TCP/IP must always use IP addresses; therefore, a WINS server or some other form of NetBIOS name-to-IP-address-resolution must be used if communication using NetBIOS names is required. An alternative to using a WINS server is to use a static LMHOSTS file in the `<system-root>` directory, which contains NetBIOS name-to-IP-address mappings. A WINS server is preferred, however, because NetBIOS names can be automatically and dynamically registered with the WINS server, which is much more flexible and accurate than an LMHOSTS file or other method. All the WINS configuration is completed on the WINS tab.

The three choices of WINS configuration for a Windows 98 TCP/IP client are as follows:

- Enable WINS Resolution. If WINS Resolution is enabled, you must enter the IP address of one or two WINS servers in the appropriate fields. If the primary WINS server is unavailable for some reason, TCP/IP accesses the secondary WINS server if one is configured.

- Disable WINS Resolution. If WINS is disabled, an alternative form of NetBIOS name resolution is required to resolve NetBIOS names to computer names for destinations on remote networks.

- Use DHCP for WINS Resolution. If DHCP has been enabled in the IP Address tab, you can select the Use DHCP for WINS Resolution option to use the WINS servers specified by the DHCP Server options(s).

▼ **NOTE**

This last option on the list, Use DHCP for WINS Resolution, does not mean that a DHCP server provides name resolution. The option is used when a DHCP server has been configured to advise the DHCP clients of the IP address(es) of the WINS server(s).

The *domain name service* (DNS) provides address resolution for DNS host and domain names. Host names are used with Windows Sockets applications. The host name for a Windows-based computer is often the same as the computer name, but the domain name is usually something like `domain.company.com`. World Wide Web addresses often consist of DNS host names appended to the DNS domain name to form a Fully Qualified Domain Name, such as `www.microsoft.com`, where `www` is the host (computer) name, and `microsoft.com` is the domain name. You configure DNS options on the DNS tab.

To access a computer using a DNS name over TCP/IP, the DNS name must be resolved to an IP address. This can be done using a static HOSTS file in the `<systemroot>` directory, or by accessing a DNS server. The DNS server contains a database that is distributed over an internetwork. If a DNS server cannot fully resolve a domain name to an IP address, it can pass the request on to another DNS server until the name is found and resolved.

The DNS Server Search Order list in the TCP/IP Properties sheet lists the order in which DNS servers will be queried for DNS name resolution. The Domain Suffix Search Order list shows the order in which domain names can be appended to a host name to try to resolve the resulting Fully Qualified Domain Name. If the Domain Suffix Search Order list contains `ACME.COM`, and if the host name `FRED` cannot be resolved, DNS then attempts to resolve the name `FRED.ACME.COM`. If that fails, DNS attempts to resolve the host name with the next suffix on the list.

Use the Advanced tab to specify whether you want the TCP/IP protocol to be the default or preferred protocol. The default protocol is the first protocol used when attempting to connect to network resources. If the NetBEUI protocol is installed, it will be the default protocol. If most of the network resources you will be connecting to are using TCP/IP, you can improve performance by setting TCP/IP as the default protocol.

The Bindings tab shows network components that can use the TCP/IP protocol. If a component has a check mark next to it, it will bind to TCP/IP and then can use the TCP/IP protocol for communication. To improve performance, remove the check marks from any components that do not require TCP/IP.

The other Microsoft-written network protocol included with Windows 98 is Microsoft DLC. This protocol is used only for communicating with certain network interface printers and mainframe systems. DLC is not used for peer-to-peer networking of Windows 98 computers. Due to DLC's limited use, you should consult the documentation for the items you are connecting to with DLC to determine the best settings for items listed on the Advanced configuration tab.

CHAPTER SUMMARY

Windows 98 offers intranet resources to local and remote clients. Windows 98 will offer basic HTTP and FTP services to any Web browser in the network. Using Dial-Up Server, remote clients can access the same Web services remotely.

Windows 98 also will integrate into existing networks with the use of its multiple clients. Windows 98 may also participate in a distributed resource sharing environment with its File and Printer Sharing capabilities for Microsoft and NetWare.

All components are subject to proper configuration and implementation. Each network may be different, and Windows 98 has the tools to adjust.

And finally, Windows 98's networking is completed by the choice of supported protocols. Each protocol has a role to play in an enterprise's network. Routable protocols enable Windows 98 to span a wide area network and even the Internet.

CHAPTER 4

Windows 98 offers users the capability to share folders and printers in a Microsoft and Novell environment. Each share offers its own permissions and controls. As the owner of the share, you can monitor activity. As an administrator, you are able to monitor, control, and remotely administer shared resources on the network.

Configuring and Managing Resource Access, Part 1

OBJECTIVES

This chapter helps prepare you for the exam by reviewing the following objectives:

Assign access permissions for shared folders in a Microsoft environment and a mixed Microsoft and NetWare environment. Methods include the following:

- **Passwords**

- **User permissions**

- **Group permissions**

▶ Windows 98 creates shares on the hard drive for remote users to access. This chapter examines in detail the steps and concepts needed to perform sharing tasks.

Create, share, and monitor resources. Resources include the following:

- **Remote computers**

- **Network printers**

continues

▶ Several types of resources on your Windows 98 computer can be shared with other people on your network. Although these are local resources (on your computer) to you, to other people on your network they are remote resources (on the network). Most resources are monitored with different tools, depending on the resource.

▶ Before sharing folders or printers, you must enable the File and Printer Sharing services on your Windows 98 computer. Because each resource is different, you will now examine how to create, share, and monitor each type of resource.

Back up data and the Registry and restore data and the Registry.

▶ Windows 98 offers file backups as well as Registry backup. In the event of a system failure, information can be restored on a new system. The Registry facilitates the restoration of Windows 98's configuration.

ASSIGN ACCESS PERMISSIONS FOR SHARED FOLDERS IN A MICROSOFT ENVIRONMENT AND A MIXED MICROSOFT AND NETWARE ENVIRONMENT

1. **Where do you enable passwords for access to shared folders in Windows 98?**

   A. Passwords Control Panel

   B. Network Control Panel

   C. Users Control Panel

   D. System Control Panel

   E. Security icon in the Control Panel

2. **You want to share resources on your Windows 98 system. You have decided to use user-level access control. Which of the following cannot be a security provider for user-level access control?**

   A. Windows NT Domain

   B. NetWare 3.x or 4.x server

   C. Windows 98 Workgroup

   D. Windows NT Server

   E. Microsoft LAN Manager

3. **Which one of the following pieces of information must you provide when configuring user-level access control?**

   A. Usernames

   B. Workgroup name

   C. Security provider name

   D. User passwords

   E. Server names

4. **What permissions are assigned to users for a folder called Data? Select the best answer.**

   A. Implicit

   B. Inherited

   C. Implied

   D. Explicit

   E. Overwritten

5. **From the preceding question, after you have the permissions for Data, you create a subfolder called Private. This folder should contain information that only you can access, yet you realize other users can access it also. Why can other users access this subfolder?**

   A. The permissions are implicit to the subfolder.

   B. The permissions are explicit to the subfolder.

   C. The permissions are implied to the subfolder.

   D. The permissions are implicated to the subfolder.

   E. The permissions are overwritten on the subfolder.

6. Susan is attaching her Windows 98 computer to another Windows 98 computer using the Microsoft Network. She wants to provide access from one computer to the other so that each computer has access to files and printers on either machine. What must she do to enable this in Windows 98? Select the best answer.

   A. Set up user-level security.

   B. Disable File and Printer Sharing for Microsoft Networks.

   C. Set up share-level security.

   D. Enable the Windows 98 Firewall program.

   E. Set up admin-level security.

7. Your computer is running Windows 98 and you would like to share your printer on the Windows NT network. You want only valid Windows NT users to access the printer. Which access control should you select in the network properties?

   A. Share-level

   B. User-level

   C. Domain-level

   D. Admin-level

   E. Workgroup-level

8. Your computer has share-level security enabled, and you are switching to user-level security. What must you do to your existing shared folders so that they are accessible to other users after you change security levels? Select the best answer.

   A. Nothing.

   B. You must remove the shared status of the folders and re-share the folders after you switch to user-level security.

   C. You must re-share the folders after you switch to user-level security.

   D. You must change the attributes of the folders.

   E. You must re-create the folder and shares.

9. Which level of security is used by default when Microsoft File and Printer Sharing is installed?

   A. Group-level

   B. User-level

   C. Share-level

   D. Resource-level

   E. Admin-level

10. With which type of security are passwords assigned to resources?

    A. Group-level

    B. User-level

    C. Share-level

    D. Password-level

    E. Admin-level

11. If no password is assigned a resource in share-level security, what rights will a remote user have to the directory?

    A. Full

    B. Read-only

C. Depends on which option was specified when the directory was shared

D. Modify

E. Change

12. **When creating a shared directory by using share-level security, which three types of access can be granted?**

A. Read

B. Full

C. Depends on password

D. Modify

E. Change

13. **What is the primary benefit of using user-level security with a NetWare server in a File and Printer Sharing for NetWare network?**

A. Further protection of shared resources.

B. You have no choice; it must be user-level security when using File and Printer Sharing for NetWare.

C. More enforced password changes.

D. Stronger algorithms.

E. Faster access time.

14. **With a NetWare network, administrators can set up rights based on which two criteria?**

A. Resource name

B. Username

C. Group name

D. Time of day

E. Computer name

15. **When running Windows 98 on a NetWare network, which level of security must be implemented?**

A. Share-level

B. User-level

C. NDS-level

D. Bindery-based

E. Admin-level

The following two questions are based on the same scenario, required components, and optional components. Please read all the requirements and proposed solution before answering.

16. **Scenario:**

Users in a small workgroup would like to share folders with one another. They are not set up in an environment that uses a Novell or NT server.

Required components:

Share folders among the workgroup members.

Assign passwords to users, granting some full access and some read only.

Optional components:

Maintain separate passwords for each user.

Share to DOS clients, Novell clients, and other Windows 98 systems.

Proposed solution:

Enable File and Printer Sharing for Microsoft on all Windows 98 systems that will have folders to share.

Create share names of 15 characters or fewer.

A. The proposed solution satisfies all the required components and all of the optional components.

B. The proposed solution satisfies all the required components but only one of the optional components.

C. The proposed solution satisfies all the required components but none of the optional components.

D. The proposed solution satisfies none of the required components but one of the optional components.

E. The proposed solution satisfies none of the required components and none of the optional components.

17. **Scenario:**

Users in a small workgroup would like to share folders with one another. They are not set up in an environment that uses a Novell or NT server.

Required components:
Share folders among the workgroup members.

Assign passwords to users, granting some full access and some read only.

Optional components:
Maintain separate passwords for each user.

Share to DOS clients, Novell clients, and other Windows 98 systems.

Proposed solution:
Enable File and Printer Sharing for Microsoft on all Windows 98 systems that will have folders to share.

Create share names of 12 characters or fewer.

Enable File and Printer Sharing for Novell on all Windows 98 systems that will have folders for Novell clients.

A. The proposed solution satisfies all the required components and all of the optional components.

B. The proposed solution satisfies all the required components but only one of the optional components.

C. The proposed solution satisfies all the required components but none of the optional components.

D. The proposed solution satisfies none of the required components but one of the optional components.

E. The proposed solution satisfies none the required components and none of the optional components.

ANSWER KEY

1. B	6. C	11. C	16. E
2. C	7. B	12. A-B-C	17. C
3. C	8. C	13. B	
4. D	9. C	14. B-C	
5. A	10. C	15. B	

ASSIGN ACCESS PERMISSIONS FOR SHARED FOLDERS IN A MICROSOFT ENVIRONMENT AND A MIXED MICROSOFT AND NETWARE ENVIRONMENT

1. Where do you enable passwords for access to shared folders in Windows 98?

    B. Network Control Panel

1. CORRECT ANSWER: B

You enable passwords for access to shared folders under the Access Control tab in the Network Control Panel. For more information, see "User-level vs. Share-level Security."

2. You want to share resources on your Windows 98 system. You have decided to use user-level access control. Which of the following cannot be a security provider for user-level access control?

    C. Windows 98 Workgroup

2. CORRECT ANSWER: C

The other security provider available to you is Windows NT Workstation. A security provider must have an account database. Windows 95 and Windows 98 do not maintain an account database of their own. For more information, see "User-level vs. Share-level Security."

3. Which of the following pieces of information must you provide when configuring user-level access control?

    C. Security provider name

3. CORRECT ANSWER: C

The security provider is responsible for verifying usernames and passwords for Windows 98. For more information, see "User-level vs. Share-level Security."

4. What permissions are assigned to users for a folder called Data?

    D. Explicit

4. CORRECT ANSWER: D

The term is explicit because the permissions are made at the folder and nowhere else to the given user. For more information, see "User-level vs. Share-level Security."

5. From the preceding question, after you have the permissions for Data, you create a subfolder called Private. This folder should contain information that only you can access, yet you realize other users can access it also. Why can other users access this subfolder?

   A. The permissions are implicit to the subfolder.

5. CORRECT ANSWER: A

Their permissions are considered to be implicit to the subfolder if they are explicit to the Data folder. For more information, see "User-level vs. Share-level Security."

6. Susan is attaching her Windows 98 computer to another Windows 98 computer using the Microsoft Network. She wants to provide access from one computer to the other so that each computer has access to files and printers on either machine. What must she do to enable this in Windows 98?

   C. Set up share-level security.

6. CORRECT ANSWER: C

Share-level security allows other Windows 98 systems to access shared resources on a Windows 98 network without the need for a security provider. For more information, see "User-level vs. Share-level Security."

7. Your computer is running Windows 98 and you would like to share your printer on the Windows NT network. You want only valid Windows NT users to access the printer. Which access control should you select in the network properties?

   B. User-level

7. CORRECT ANSWER: B

User-level security enables the user to select valid users from the Windows NT domain. The domain of which the users are members must be the security provider. For more information, see "User-level vs. Share-level Security."

8. Your computer has share-level security enabled, and you are switching to user-level security. What must you do to your existing shared folders so that they are accessible to other users after you change security levels?

   C. You must re-share the folders after you switch to user-level security.

8. CORRECT ANSWER: C

Share-level security and user-level security have different access configurations to shared resources. If you switch from share level to user level or vice versa, you must re-create all the shares. For more information, see "User-level vs. Share-level Security."

9. Which level of security is used by default when Microsoft File and Printer Sharing is installed?

   C. Share-level

9. CORRECT ANSWER: C

Share-level security is used by default when File and Printer Sharing for Microsoft Networks is installed. For more information, see "User-level vs. Share-level Security."

10. With which type of security are passwords assigned to resources?

    C. Share-level

With share-level security, passwords are assigned to each share to permit access to a directory or printer share. To access the share, a user must supply the correct password. For more information, see "User-level vs. Share-level Security."

11. If no password is assigned a resource in share-level security, what rights will a remote user have to the directory?

    C. Depends on which option was specified when the directory was shared

If no password is used, any user will have full or read-only access to the directory, depending on which option was specified when the shared directory was created. For more information, see "User-level vs. Share-level Security."

12. When creating a shared directory by using share-level security, which three types of access can be granted?

    A. Read

    B. Full

    C. Depends on password

When creating a shared directory using share-level security, one of three types of access can be granted: read, full, or depends on password. For more information, see "User-level vs. Share-level Security."

13. What is the primary benefit of using user-level security with a NetWare server in a File and Printer Sharing for NetWare network?

    B. You have no choice; it must be user-level security when using File and Printer Sharing for NetWare.

File and Printer Sharing for NetWare requires user-level security. User-level security on NetWare is used to protect shared network resources by storing a list of users and groups who have access to a network resource. To gain access to a resource, a user must be on the access account list stored on the NetWare server bindery and then have the proper access rights for that resource. For more information, see "User-level vs. Share-level Security."

14. With a NetWare network, administrators can set up rights based on which two criteria?

    B. Username

    C. Group name

Administrators can set up access rights on a per-user or per-group basis. For more information, see "User-level vs. Share-level Security."

15. **When running Windows 98 on a NetWare network, what level of security must be implemented?**

   B. User-level

15.   CORRECT ANSWER: B

User-level security is the only available option when you are running File and Print sharing in Windows 98 on a NetWare network. For more information, see "User-level vs. Share-level Security."

16. **Proposed solution:**

   Enable File and Printer Sharing for Microsoft on all Windows 98 systems that will have folders to share.

   Create share names of 15 characters or fewer.

   E. The proposed solution satisfies none of the required components and none of the optional components.

16.   CORRECT ANSWER: E

Windows 98 can share folders to other Windows 98 systems with share names up to 12 characters. Novell clients cannot access shares if File and Printer Sharing for Microsoft is used. For more information, see "User-level vs. Share-level Security."

17. **Proposed solution:**

   Enable File and Printer Sharing for Microsoft on all Windows 98 systems that will have folders to share.

   Create share names of 12 characters or fewer.

   Enable File and Printer Sharing for Novell on all Windows 98 systems that will have folders for Novell clients.

   C. The proposed solution satisfies all the required components but none of the optional components.

17.   CORRECT ANSWER: C

Each folder can be shared with up to 12 characters for a share-name. DOS, Novell, and Windows 98 clients can read up to 12 characters. Share-level security allows for two levels of access: read only and full control, depending on the password. Each user cannot have his own password. File and Printer Sharing for Novell cannot co-exist with File and Printer Sharing for Microsoft. For more information, see "User-level vs. Share-level Security."

User-level vs. Share-level Security

This explanation supports questions 1 through 17.

To enable passwords as a security method, you must enable Share-Level Access Control in the Network Control Panel (see Figure 4.1).

This is the default setting for Windows 98. After Share-Level Access Control has been enabled, any resource that you wish to present to the network will provide you with an option for typing in a password for the resource (see Figure 4.2). To allow others to access this resource, you must somehow distribute the password to them.

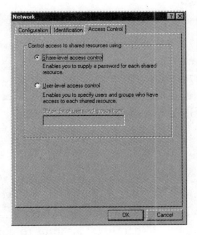

FIGURE 4.1
The default setting is share-level security.

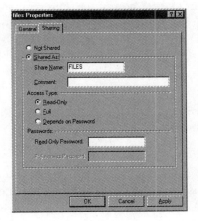

FIGURE 4.2
When implementing share-level security, passwords are assigned to resources as a method of security.

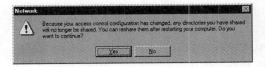

FIGURE 4.3
This warning message appears when changing from user-level to share-level or vice versa. All existing shares will no longer be shared.

The major advantage of this method of security is that it requires no other support devices elsewhere on the network. This security method has the following two major flaws, however:

- Distribution of passwords
- Maintaining control of passwords

The first major drawback of this system is the distribution of the passwords after they have been assigned. If you want other people to use this resource, you must have some method of notifying all the potential users.

The second major drawback is having to maintain control of passwords, or rather having to maintain control of access to the resource. Even on a small network, the number of passwords that must be remembered can quickly climb to an unmanageable limit.

User permissions and group permissions can be implemented on your network, offering easier password distribution and greater security.

▼ NOTE

User-level security and share-level security use very different methods of authenticating users. If you change from one method to the other you must re-share all the existing shared folders (see Figure 4.3).

User Permissions

To implement user permissions, you must enable user-level security on your Windows 98 system. You can share resources with individuals on your network by the user's network name. This requires access to additional network services.

To enable user-level security, open the Network Control Panel and choose the Access Control tab. When choosing user-level access control, you must provide the name of a security provider. The security provider may be any of the following:

- Microsoft Windows NT domain
- Microsoft Windows NT Server

- Microsoft Windows NT Workstation
- Novell NetWare 3.x or 4.x server

The security provider is responsible for providing a list of users when you want to share a resource (see Figure 4.4). The security provider is also responsible for verifying usernames and passwords for Windows 98 when users attempt to access resources.

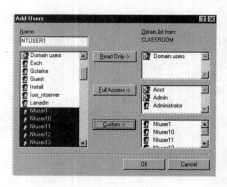

FIGURE 4.4
The security provider is responsible for supplying a list of users when you attempt to share a resource.

When you share resources, Windows 98 can provide you with a list of users to whom you might grant access. The users you select from the list need no additional information before being able to access the resource. When users attempt to connect to the resource, their network client passes their network usernames and passwords to the Windows 98 computer they are connecting to. The Windows 98 computer then connects to its security provider and verifies each client's username and password.

▼ **NOTE**

When using File and Printer Sharing for NetWare, the Windows 98 system must be running user-level security.

Group Permissions

Implementing group permissions is similar to implementing user permissions. The first step is to enable user-level security on your Windows 98 system. After user-level security has been enabled, you can share information with users on the network based on their group membership on your security provider.

The security providers listed in the "User Permissions" section support the creation of groups of users also. In the same fashion as sharing with users, you can share your resources and assign permissions with groups. The Windows 98 computer connects to its security provider and checks whether each user's name and password are valid, and then checks to see which groups the user is a member of. If the user is a member of any groups that have been granted access to the resource, the user is granted access to the resource.

▼ **NOTE**

When you assign permissions for users to a directory, these permissions are termed *explicit*. Each subdirectory automatically has the same list of permissions applied to it. For the subdirectories, the permissions are *implicit*, or *inherited*.

These explicit and implicit permissions enable you to control access to your directory structure on a folder-by-folder basis.

CREATE, SHARE, AND MONITOR RESOURCES

1. Which services must you enable before you can share folders or printers on your Windows 98 system? Select the best answer.

   A. Server service

   B. Workstation service

   C. Folder and Print Sharing

   D. File and Printer Sharing

   E. Computer sharing

2. Which is the command to create a new folder from the command prompt?

   A. MC

   B. MCD

   C. MD

   D. CD

   E. MK

3. Which Windows 98 utility enables you to see who is currently connected to your computer?

   A. Net Searcher

   B. Network Neighborhood

   C. Explorer

   D. Net Watcher

   E. Network Viewer

4. Which menu in the preceding utility enables you to disconnect users from your system?

   A. User Maintenance

   B. Administer

   C. Tools

   D. View

   E. Net Use

5. Susan uses Net Watcher to view connections to her local computer. Which toolbar button does she click to see the users connected to her computer?

   A. View Users

   B. Show Connected Users

   C. View Connected Users

   D. Show Users

   E. View Connected Computers

6. Which option of Add Printer do you choose from when you connect a new printer to your Windows 98 system printer port?

   A. Local Printer

   B. New Printer

   C. Select Printer

   D. Configure Printer

   E. Install Printer

7. **If the new printer you are installing is not listed as a printer model selection, what is the name of the file you must provide to Windows 98 to continue installation?**

    A. `PRINTER.INF`

    B. `WIN98.INF`

    C. `OEMSETUP.INF`

    D. `SETUP.INF`

    E. `INSTALL.INF`

8. **A Windows NT client connects to your Windows 98 system and tries to set up a connection to your shared printer. Where are the drivers loaded from?**

    A. The Hidden share on the Windows 98 system

    B. The Windows 98 source files

    C. The Windows NT hidden share

    D. The Windows NT source files

    E. The printer

9. **You want to optimize all printers connected to your Windows 98 computers. From what you know about Windows 98 printer support, what is the main factor in ensuring print performance?**

    A. Spool settings

    B. Driver compatibility

    C. Queue management

    D. Font management

    E. Printer preferences

10. **To enable people to install printer drivers from your Windows 98 system using Point and Print, what steps must you take? Select the best answer.**

    A. Copy the files to `C:\` and create a share called `PRINTER$`.

    B. Copy the files to `C:\WINDOWS` and create a share called `DRIVER$`.

    C. Copy the files to `C:\WINDOWS\ PRINTERS` and create a share called `PRINTERS$`.

    D. Just share the printer; the hidden share is automatically created where the files are located.

    E. None of the above.

11. **A Windows 98 system is set up as a print server. Michael wants to connect to the shared printer from his Windows 98 system. The printer drivers on the server are newer than the driver he has installed on his computer. What should he do?**

    A. Remove his printer first, and then install the newer drivers from the print server.

    B. Upgrade his print drivers before trying to connect to the shared printer.

    C. Allow the newer files to be copied to his computer from the print server.

    D. Refuse to copy the files to his computer because there may be a virus on the print server.

    E. None of the above.

12. **How do you remove a print job that some-one else has sent to a network printer?**

    A. Pause the printer and purge the print queue.

    B. Select the job in the queue and press Delete.

    C. You cannot remove it. Only the creator or a print manager can remove someone else's print jobs.

    D. Power off the printer and then power it back on.

    E. Take ownership of the print job then delete it.

13. **When can you pause a network printer? Select the best answer.**

    A. When you are a normal user

    B. When you are the administrator

    C. When you are viewing the print queue

    D. When the printer is in your office

    E. Any time by anyone

14. **As you instruct a user on how to configure a peer-to-peer network with five Windows 98 computers connected together, you use the term *Windows 98 server* several times. After you finish, he asks you what a Windows 98 server is. What do you tell him?**

    A. A computer that is the primary domain controller on the LAN

    B. A computer running Windows 98 that has the Enable Windows 98 Server Registry option turned on

    C. A Windows 98 computer that has the File and Printer Sharing Service enabled

    D. A computer running Windows 98 that performs as an application and database server for the LAN

    E. None of the above

The following question is scenario based. Please read all the requirements and proposed solution before answering.

15. **Scenario:**

    Several new printers have been purchased for the office. The new models do not show up on the list of printers when users try to install them.

    Required components:
    Install a printer driver to get the printers into operation.

    User should be able to print test pages.

    Optional component:
    Make full use of all the features the printer offers.

    Proposed solution:
    From Add Printer, select an earlier model of the same printer manufacturer.

    A. The proposed solution satisfies all the required components and the optional components.

    B. The proposed solution satisfies one of the required components and the optional component.

    C. The proposed solution satisfies all the required components but does not satisfy the optional component.

D. The proposed solution satisfies one of the required components but does not satisfy the optional component.

E. The proposed solution satisfies none of the required components and does not satisfy the optional component.

ANSWER KEY

1. D	6. A	11. C
2. C	7. C	12. C
3. D	8. D	13. B
4. B	9. A	14. C
5. D	10. D	15. C

ANSWERS & EXPLANATIONS

CREATE, SHARE, AND MONITOR RESOURCES

1. Which services must you enable before you can share folders or printers on your Windows 98 system? Select the best answer.

D. File and Printer Sharing

1. CORRECT ANSWER: D

File and Printer Sharing must be enabled from the Network Control Panel before the Sharing menu will appear. File and Printer Sharing for Microsoft or File and Printer Sharing for NetWare can be used. For more information, see "Remote File Shares."

2. Which is the command to create a new folder from the command prompt?

C. MD

2. CORRECT ANSWER: C

Use the MD command or the MKDIR command. The command md data would create a directory in the current directory. md \data would create a directory at the root of the current drive. For more information, see "Remote File Shares."

3. Which Windows 98 utility enables you to see who is currently connected to your computer?

D. Net Watcher

3. CORRECT ANSWER: D

The Net Watcher utility enables you to see who is currently connected to your computer, and can also provide a list of shared folders. It also provides you with tools that permit you to Share, Stop Sharing, or Modify the properties of Shared Folders. For more information, see "Remote File Shares."

4. Which menu in the preceding utility enables you to disconnect users from your system?

B. Administer

4. CORRECT ANSWER: B

The Administer menu enables you to disconnect users when you use the View by Connections option. There is also a tool-bar button to disconnect users. This does not prevent a user from reconnecting immediately. It is only effective if permissions are removed from the user before the disconnection. For more information, see "Remote File Shares."

5. Susan uses Net Watcher to view connections to her local computer. Which
toolbar button does she click to see
the users connected to her computer?

    D. Show Users

---

5. CORRECT ANSWER: D

The Show Users option in Net Watcher enables you to see who is connected to your system. For more information, see "Remote File Shares."

Remote File Shares

This explanation supports questions 1 threough 5.

Although it is called remote file sharing, Windows 98 allows sharing of only folders, not individual files. You can employ three basics methods to create a new directory or folder on your computer. Two methods use the graphical Windows environment, and one uses the command prompt. In the Windows 98 GUI, open the folder where you wish to create your new folder and either choose File, New, Folder from the menus, or right-click in a white area of the folder and choose New, Folder. The folder name will be selected. To give the folder a new name, type the name and press the Enter key to save it. If you create a new folder from a command prompt, you have a choice of two commands that do the same thing: MKDIR and the shorter MD.

▼ **NOTE**

When using Windows Explorer to work with folders, menus at the top of the window are context-sensitive. They change depending on which folder is selected in the left, or *navigation*, frame of the Explorer window. The folder is created inside the folder selected in the navigation frame.

You can share a created folder by viewing the shared folder properties through any of the following methods:

- Select the folder and choose Sharing from the File menu.

- Right-click on the folder and choose Sharing from the context menu.

- Select the folder and choose Properties from the File menu. Then select the Sharing tab.

- Right-click on the folder and choose Properties from the context menu. Then select the Sharing tab.

FIGURE 4.5

Net Watcher enables you to view users and see the shared folders to which they are connected or view shares and see which users are accessing them.

The Sharing tab enables you to assign a share name for the folder. This name may differ from the actual name of the folder. Depending on the type of access control that has been implemented on your system, you will either be asked to provide a password for the resource, or to provide a list of users that will be allowed access to the resource. For more information, see "User-level vs. Share-level Security" earlier in this chapter.

To enable you to see who is currently connected to your shared folders, Microsoft provides Net Watcher with Windows 98. Net Watcher can provide you with information about who is currently connected to your computer, and what they are connected to (see Figure 4.5). The View by Connections option enables you to disconnect users by selecting Disconnect User from the Administer menu. Net Watcher can also provide you with a list of shared folders and can tell who is connected to each one. The last feature of Net Watcher is to allow you to Share, Stop Sharing, or Modify the properties of Shared Folders.

6. **Which option of Add Printer do you choose from when you connect a new printer to your Windows 98 system printer port?**

   A. **Local Printer**

6. CORRECT ANSWER: A

You have two options at this point: Local Printer or Network Printer. To install a printer attached directly to your system, choose Local Printer. To install printer drivers for a printer situated out on the network, choose Network Printer. For more information, see "Network Printers."

7. **If the new printer you are installing is not listed as a printer model selection, what is the name of the file you must provide to Windows 98 to continue installation?**

   C. **OEMSETUP.INF**

7. CORRECT ANSWER: C

OEMSETUP.INF is the file required to continue the installation of a new printer Windows 98 does not recognize. This file is provided by the manufacturer of the printer on floppy disk, CD-ROM, or over the Internet. For more information, see "Network Printers."

8. **A Windows NT client connects to your Windows 98 system and tries to set up a connection to your shared printer. Where are the drivers loaded from?**

   D. **The Windows NT source files**

8. CORRECT ANSWER: D

Windows NT and Windows 98 do not share the same printer drivers. Windows NT will read printer make and model off the share, but will need to refer to its own source files. For more information, see "Network Printers."

9. You want to optimize all printers connected to your Windows 98 computers. From what you know about Windows 98 printer support, what is the main factor in ensuring print performance?

   A. Spool settings

Configuring spool settings affects how fast your printer starts to print on your Windows 98 system. For more information, see "Network Printers."

10. To enable people to install printer drivers from your Windows 98 system using Point and Print, you need to:

    D. Just share the printer; the hidden share is automatically created where the files are located.

The files are copied to the SYSTEM folder and the PRINTER$ share is created automatically when a printer is installed and shared. These drivers are only valid for other Windows 98 and Windows 95 systems. For more information, see "Network Printers."

11. A Windows 98 system is set up as a print server. Michael wants to connect to the shared printer from his Windows 98 system. The printer drivers on the server are newer than the driver he has installed on his computer. What should he do?

    C. Allow the newer files to be copied to his computer from the print server.

Windows 98, recognizing that Michael's driver files are older, prompts him to upgrade his files at that time. For more information, see "Network Printers."

12. How do you remove a print job that someone else has sent to a network printer?

    C. You cannot remove it. Only the creator or a print manager can remove someone else's print jobs.

Only a print manager or administrator can manage other person's print jobs. For more information, see "Network Printers."

13. When can you pause a network printer?

    B. When you are the administrator

The administrator can manage a network printer. For more information, see "Network Printers."

Network Printers

This explanation supports questions 6 through 13.

Shared printers are like shared directories on Windows 98 computers.

The easiest way to install a printer in Windows 98 is to plug it in and reboot. Windows 98 scans the printer port at every boot, and if the printer can provide enough information to Windows 98, Windows 98 automatically installs the printer driver for the printer. Windows 98 is looking for `OEMSETUP.INF` to install the drivers. If the printer is not identified by Windows 98, you can manually add the printer if you point to `OEMSETUP.INF` files by following these steps:

1. Choose Printers from Settings in the Start menu.

2. From the `Printers` folder, open the Add Printer icon.

3. Choose Local Printer and select the Next button.

4. Choose your printer from the list provided, which includes most printer manufacturers and types. If your printer model is not listed, you can click on the Have Disk button and locate the `OEMSETUP.INF` or equivalent INF file for your new printer driver (see Figure 4.6). Click the Next button to continue the installation.

5. Choose the printer port that you want to use. Click the Next button.

6. Choose a name for your printer. This name will be the default name used when the printer is shared, but does not have to be the name used to share the printer. Choose whether you want Windows 98 to use this printer as the default Windows printer. Click the Next button to continue.

7. Windows 98 will then finish the installation of the printer and ask you whether the test page printed properly.

After the printer is installed, it may be shared by doing any of the following:

- Select the printer and choose Sharing from the File menu.

- Right-click on the printer and choose Sharing from the context menu.

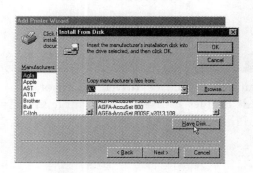

FIGURE 4.6
All known printers are listed in the Add Printer Wizard dialog box. To add an unlisted printer, click the Have Disk button.

- Select the printer and choose Properties from the File menu. Then select the Sharing tab.

- Right-click on the printer and choose Properties from the context menu. Then select the Sharing tab.

When the Share Printer window opens, it will look like one of the two shared folders windows (for user-level or share-level access control), with the exception that it is geared to sharing printers (see Figure 4.7). You still have the option of adding users or groups from the server to grant them access, or to assign a password to the printer. In this window, you can also assign a share or network name for your printer; it will default to the local name you gave to it.

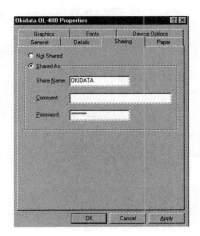

FIGURE 4.7
A share-level security screen will have an option to use a password.

▼ **NOTE**

When other computers first connect to your shared printer, they are required to install the drivers for it. The files are copied from a hidden folder on your computer. If the files are not compatible, the local system's source files will be needed.

Management of the printer is done through the Printer icon in the Printers folder. When you open the Printer icon, it lists all the jobs that have been spooled and are waiting to be printed on the printer. You have the option of changing the order of the print jobs, pausing them, or canceling them.

14. As you instruct a user on how to configure a peer-to-peer network with five Windows 98 computers connected together, you use the term *Windows 98 server* several times. After you finish, he asks you what a Windows 98 server is. What do you tell him?

C. A Windows 98 computer that has the File and Printer Sharing Service enabled

14. CORRECT ANSWER: C

With File and Printer Sharing enabled, the Windows 98 system appears as a server to other systems on the network. The only difference is the Windows 98 system does not validate logons or maintain an account database as most servers do. For more information, see "Printer Properties."

15. Proposed solution:

From Add Printer, select an earlier model of the same printer manufacturer.

C. **The proposed solution satisfies all the required components but does not satisfy the optional component.**

FIGURE 4.8
Proper spool settings can greatly improve the performance on your computer.

The printer might work with an older compatible driver, but none of the new features will be enabled. The drivers should be provided on disk with the new printer from the manufacturer. For more information, see "Printer Properties."

Printer Properties

This explanation supports questions 14 through 15.

Settings in the Printer Property sheets also affect printing performance. To view the properties of your printer, right-click on the printer and select Properties. The Details Properties page has the Spool Settings button—click it to see the dialog box shown in Figure 4.8. Table 4.1 summarizes the options that can be configured in the Spool Settings dialog box.

TABLE 4.1 PRINTER SPOOL SETTINGS

Item	Description
Spool Print Jobs so Program Finishes Printing Faster	If you disable print spooling, you will find that your printer takes longer to print.
Start Printing After Last Page is Spooled	If you choose this setting, the total print time may be increased.
Start Printing After First Page is Spooled	If this option is chosen, a large print job will tie up the printer after the first page is spooled, until the job has finished printing.
Spool Data Format	If your network is composed of only Windows 98 computers, you might want to implement Enhanced Metafile (EMF) spooling. It takes less time for the application to generate this file than it takes to generate a RAW file.

BACK UP DATA AND THE REGISTRY AND RESTORE DATA AND THE REGISTRY

1. **As system administrator, you draft a purchase order to acquire tape backup devices. Windows 98 supports QIC tape systems, but not universally. Which of the following tape backup systems is not supported by Windows 98?**

   A. QIC 3010 through parallel port.

   B. QIC 3010 through floppy disk controller.

   C. QIC 3010 through SCSI port.

   D. QIC 80 through floppy disk controller.

   E. All are supported in Windows 98.

2. **As the system administrator, you want to protect your users' data and enable for restoration from a central location. How can you accomplish this? Select the best answer.**

   A. Instruct your users to back up to a predetermined network location.

   B. Ask your users to email their most recent backup sets to you.

   C. Visit all of your users' workstations and back up their drives to floppy disks.

   D. Back up your users' hard drives to CD-ROM.

3. **A backup set that includes only files that have changed since the last full backup is called what?**

   A. A partial backup

   B. An incremental backup

   C. An incomplete backup

   D. An archive backup

4. **Sara is concerned that she will not be able to reproduce certain data files if she should have a hard drive failure. Which disk-management tool would you recommend to her?**

   A. Disk Defragmenter

   B. ScanDisk

   C. DriveSpace

   D. Backup

5. **Why can't Windows 98 Backup restore MS-DOS backup sets? Select the best answer.**

   A. Windows 98 Backup cannot mount MS-DOS drives.

   B. There are incompatibility issues with Long Filenames in MS-DOS drives.

   C. Windows 98 and MS-DOS use different file allocation tables.

   D. MS-DOS backup sets do not contain the Windows 98 Registry.

6. **You find that you often back up the same files each time you run Windows 98**

Backup. How can you avoid selecting the individual files each time you run Backup? Select the best answer.

A. Save the list of files in a file set.

B. Save the list of files in a text file, and specify that text file on Backup's command line.

C. Run Backup from a batch file.

D. Re-select the files each time you run Backup.

7. **What information is contained in every backup set, in addition to the files that were backed up? Select the best answer.**

A. The patch to the Windows 98 Backup program

B. The Windows 98 Registry

C. The parameters that were set for the backup session

D. The name of the last full backup set

8. **Carol is running Windows 98 Backup. She wants to select an appropriate backup destination. Which of the following can she choose? Select all that apply.**

A Windows NT Server share

B. Novell NetWare volume

C. A 1.44MB floppy drive

D. SCSI tape backup unit

9. **Which is not a feature of Windows 98 Backup?**

A. LFNs are fully supported.

B. Backup sets can be compared to source directories to determine differences.

C. Backup sets can be dragged and dropped on to a Backup icon to perform a restore operation.

D. Backup sets can be used by the MS-DOS 6.2 Backup utility.

10. **Susan wants to know what will happen to her Registry files when she restores from a full backup. What do you tell her?**

A. The backup copies of the Registry files will be merged into the existing Registry.

B. The current Registry files will be overwritten by those from the backup set.

C. The date/time stamps on the Registry files will be compared, and she will be prompted to select the ones she wants to use.

D. Nothing will happen to her Registry files.

11. **Patrick runs incremental backups on his system twice a week. Why would he do this? Select all that apply.**

A. He wants to conserve space on his backup media.

B. He has only floppy disks as backup media.

C. He does not want to spend time backing up files that have not changed since the last full backup.

D. He wants to maintain an archive of his personal data.

12. **How can a Windows 98 user best maximize available disk space?**

A. Run the Disk Defragmenter.

B. Run the DriveSpace utility.

C. Select all BMP files.

D. Create a RAM drive.

13. **Which of the following is *not* a new feature on Windows 98 Backup?**

    A. It is possible to perform a comparison between a backup set and the directories from which it was backed up to in order to determine any differences between the two.

    B. LFNs are not supported.

    C. During a full system backup, Windows 98 also backs up the Registry by copying it to a temporary file.

    D. Backup allows the filtering of file types for inclusion or exclusion from a file set.

14. **Which of the following contains parameters for a backup session?**

    A. Registry set

    B. File set

    C. Backup set

    D. Time/date stamp

15. **How does Windows 98 Backup restore the Registry?**

    A. It uses filtering to determine which entries should be restored.

    B. It merges the backed-up Registry into the existing Registry.

    C. It replaces the existing Registry with the backed-up Registry.

    D. It cannot restore the Registry.

    The following two questions are based on the same scenario, required components, and optional components. Please read all the requirements and proposed solution before answering.

16. **Scenario:**

    Sara is implementing a new backup routine on all Windows 98 systems in a small workgroup.

    Required components:
    Backups need to be done weekly using existing tools.

    Sara wants to minimize the time it takes to perform weekly backups.

    Optional components:
    The Registry needs to be included in all backups.

    All backups should be run from a central location.

    Proposed solution:
    Make sure Windows 98's Backup utility is installed from Add/Remove Programs in the Control Panel.

    Perform a full backup each week on all systems using local backup software.

    A. The proposed solution satisfies all the required components and all of the optional components.

    B. The proposed solution satisfies all the required components but only one of the optional components.

    C. The proposed solution satisfies all the required components but none of the optional components.

    D. The proposed solution satisfies none of the required components but one of the optional components.

    E. The proposed solution satisfies one the required components and none of the optional components.

17. **Proposed solution:**

Make sure Windows 98's Backup utility is installed from Add/Remove Programs in the Control Panel.

Perform a full backup the first week on all systems using local backup software.

Perform only changed and new file backups on subsequent weeks to reduce backup times.

Include the Registry through the Advanced tab of the Backup Job parameters.

A. The proposed solution satisfies all the required components and all of the optional components.

B. The proposed solution satisfies all the required components but only one of the optional components.

C. The proposed solution satisfies all the required components but none of the optional components.

D. The proposed solution satisfies none of the required components but one of the optional components.

E. The proposed solution satisfies one of the required components and none of the optional components.

ANSWER KEY

1. E	6. A	11. A-C-D	16. E
2. A	7. C	12. B	17. D
3. B	8. A-B-C-D	13. B	
4. D	9. D	14. C	
5. B	10. A	15. B	

BACK UP DATA AND THE REGISTRY AND RESTORE DATA AND THE REGISTRY

1. As system administrator, you draft a purchase order to acquire tape backup devices. Windows 98 supports QIC tape systems, but not universally. Which of the following tape backup systems is *not* supported by Windows 98?

   E. All are supported in Windows 98.

1. CORRECT ANSWER: E

Windows 98 now supports SCSI tape drives. Earlier versions of Windows did not. For more information, see "Backup Utility."

2. As the system administrator, you want to protect your users' data and enable for restoration from a central location. How can you accomplish this?

   A. Instruct your users to back up to a predetermined network location.

2. CORRECT ANSWER: A

Backing up to a predetermined network location allows for data protection and restoration from a central location. For more information, see "Backup Utility."

3. A backup set that includes only files that have changed since the last full backup is called what?

   B. An incremental backup

3. CORRECT ANSWER: B

Incremental backups contain only files that have changed since the last full backup. Windows 98's backup program uses an option button that identifies New and Changed Files instead of the older term Incremental. For more information, see "Backup Utility."

4. Sara is concerned that she will not be able to reproduce certain data files if she should have a hard drive failure. Which disk-management tool would you recommend to her?

   D. Backup

4. CORRECT ANSWER: D

She should run Backup to make a copy of her files that can be restored if the hard drive fails. For more information, see "Backup Utility."

5. Why can't Windows 98 Backup restore MS-DOS backup sets? Select the best answer.

   B. There are incompatibility issues with Long Filenames in MS-DOS drives.

5. CORRECT ANSWER: B

Windows 98 Backup is not compatible with the MS-DOS Backup program. Long Filenames are just one issue. For more information, see "Backup Utility."

6. You find that you often back up the same files each time you run Windows 98 Backup. How can you avoid selecting the individual files each time you run Backup?

   A. Save the list of files in a file set.

6. CORRECT ANSWER: A

A file set is a reusable list of files you want backed up. Each time a backup is performed, the file set can be opened and all the drives, folders, or files will be selected again. For more information, see "Backup Utility."

7. What information is contained in every backup set, in addition to the files that were backed up?

   C. The parameters that were set for the backup session

7. CORRECT ANSWER: C

A backup set contains the parameters in effect for that backup session, as well as the data files that were backed up. The Registry is not backed up unless it is specifically requested. For more information, see "Backup Utility."

8. Carol is running Windows 98 Backup. She wants to select an appropriate backup destination. Which of the following can she choose? Select all that apply.

   A. Windows NT Server share

   B. Novell NetWare volume

   C. A 1.44MB floppy drive

   D. SCSI tape backup unit

8. CORRECT ANSWER: A-B-C-D

Network locations and floppy disks are valid backup locations. Windows 98 Backup now supports SCSI tape drives. Additional locations could be other hard drives. For more information, see "Backup Utility."

9. Which is not a feature of Windows 98 Backup?

   D. Backup sets can be used by the MS-DOS 6.2 Backup utility.

9. CORRECT ANSWER: D

Windows 98 Backup is not compatible with the MS-DOS Backup program. For more information, see "Backup Utility."

10. Susan wants to know what will happen to her Registry files when she restores from a full backup. What do you tell her?

   A. The backup copies of the Registry files will be merged into the existing Registry.

10. CORRECT ANSWER: A

When it restores from a full backup, Windows 98 Backup merges the old Registry files into the existing Registry if the Restore Registry option is selected. Any duplicate entries have no effect on a restore. For more information, see "Backup Utility."

11. Patrick runs incremental backups on his system twice a week. Why would he do this? Select all that apply.

   A. He wants to conserve space on his backup media.

   C. He does not want to spend time backing up files that have not changed since the last full backup.

   D. He wants to maintain an archive of his personal data.

11. CORRECT ANSWER: A-C-D

Incremental backups allow for archiving of data files while saving time and conserving backup media space by only backing up files that have changed since the last full backup. For more information, see "Backup Utility."

12. How can a Windows 98 user maximize available disk space?

   B. Run the DriveSpace utility.

12. CORRECT ANSWER: B

The DriveSpace utility compresses data on disk, thereby making more space available. For more information, see "Backup Utility."

13. Which of the following is *not* a new feature on Windows 98 Backup?

   B. LFNs are not supported.

13. CORRECT ANSWER: B

In Windows 98, Long Filenames are fully supported. For more information, see "Backup Utility."

14. Which of the following contains parameters for a backup session?

   C. Backup set

14. CORRECT ANSWER: C

A backup set contains the parameters in effect for that backup session, as well as the data files that were backed up. For more information, see "Backup Utility."

15. How does Windows 98 Backup restore the Registry?

   B. It merges the backed-up Registry into the existing Registry.

15. CORRECT ANSWER: B

When restoring Registry files, Windows 98 Backup merges the old Registry files into the existing Registry. For more information, see "Backup Utility."

16. Proposed solution:

Make sure Windows 98's backup utility is installed from Add/Remove Programs in the Control Panel.

Perform a full backup each week on all systems using local backup software.

E. The proposed solution satisfies one the required components and none of the optional components.

17. Proposed solution:

Make sure Windows 98's backup utility is installed from Add/Remove Programs in the Control Panel.

Perform a full backup the first week on all systems using local backup software.

Perform only changed and new file backup on subsequent weeks to reduce backup times.

Include the Registry through the Advanced tab of the Backup Job parameters.

D. The proposed solution satisfies none of the required components but one of the optional components.

16. CORRECT ANSWER: E

Windows 98 ships with its own backup utility that can be used to perform full weekly backup. Each full backup, however, includes all files even if they were not modified in the past week. The Registry is not included by default in the backup program. For more information, see "Backup Utility."

17. CORRECT ANSWER: D

Windows 98 ships with its own backup utility that can be used to perform full weekly backup. A full backup at the beginning will include all files while in subsequent weeks you need to back up only the files that have been modified or added since the last backup. The Registry can be included from the Advanced tab of the backup job. Backups cannot be performed remotely with Windows 98's version of Backup. For more information, see "Backup Utility."

Backup Utility

This explanation supports questions 1 through 17.

If you have installed the Backup utility, it will be located in the Start menu under Programs, Accessories, System Tools, Backup (see Figure 4.9).

To install the Backup utility, use Add/Remove Programs and select the Windows Setup tab in the Control Panel. You will find the Backup program under the System Tools.

The Windows 98 Backup program supports four backup methods:

- Back up to a tape drive
- Back up to floppy disks
- Back up to hard drive
- Back up to a network location

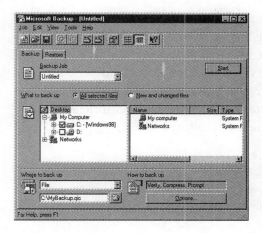

FIGURE 4.9

The Backup utility provided with Windows 98 is capable of maintaining complete backups of your system.

Windows 98 has now expanded to include SCSI tape drives. The `Driver98.chm` file in the `Drivers` folder of the Windows 98 CD lists all compatible drives.

Windows 98 should be able to detect any supported tape drives automatically. If it cannot detect the tape drive, a message appears upon starting Backup, and a number of troubleshooting suggestions are listed.

Floppy disks are the standard backup destination for both the MS-DOS and Windows 3.1 versions of Backup. Files are transferred from the local hard drive to a number of floppy disks. Windows 98 will support backup to floppy. Considering the size of most hard drives, however, backups on floppy tend to be very tedious.

If you have a second hard drive in your computer, a folder on this drive can be a backup destination. The destination could be on the same drive, but this does not provide any safety if the drive seizes or becomes corrupted. This method does, however, eliminate the need for dozens, or even hundreds, of floppy disks.

This backup destination enables the user to back up files to a remote location on the network. Backing up to a remote network location can be useful if, for example, a network administrator wants all users to back up their files to one central location on the network to simplify the administrator's management tasks. If you are going to use a network location, ensure that you have received permission from your network administrator.

Learning the Backup Types

Files can be backed up in two ways: by a full backup and by an incremental backup. In a full backup scenario, all selected files are backed up. An incremental backup copies only those files that have changed since the last backup (full or incremental). Windows 98's backup tools offer the options All Selected Files for a full backup and New and Changed Files for an incremental backup. In both cases, files that are to be backed up must be selected. Even if all the files on the hard drive are selected, New and Changed Files will only back up the files that have been changed.

FIGURE 4.10
Only files with the A attribute are backed up during an incremental backup. Using the `Attrib` command in any directory will list all the archive attributes.

Files required to be backed up are determined by the archive attribute on the file. Each new file and modified file has the A attribute added to the filename. Windows 98's backup tool looks for all files with the A attribute and includes them in the backup. When the files are backed up, the A attribute is removed. The attribute is only added back on if the file is modified and therefore needs to be backed up again. See Figure 4.10.

An example of a full backup is your complete hard disk including the operating system. An incremental backup would back up only files with the archive bit turned on.

Learning the Backup Sets and Jobs

A *backup set* is a collection of files that have been backed up. A backup set is created during each backup procedure and contains not only the actual files, but also the parameters that were set for the backup (for example, which file types to include in the backup).

Jobs is a list of files you want to back up and the configuration choices made for the current backup. You can save Jobs so that you don't have to re-select the files for backup every time you perform the backup.

Other Features of Windows 98 Backup

Windows 98 Backup contains a number of additional features, including the following:

- It is possible to perform a comparison between a backup set and the directories from which it was backed up to determine any differences between the two.

- Long Filenames (LFNs) are fully supported.

- It is possible to drag and drop backup sets onto a Backup icon to restore the set, or to double-click on the Backup Set icon to start the backup procedure.

- During a full system backup, Windows 98 also backs up the Registry by copying it to a temporary file. When the backup set is restored, the Registry files are merged back into the existing Registry. See Figure 4.11.

FIGURE 4.11
The Registry is only backed up if the Advanced setting in the job is selected.

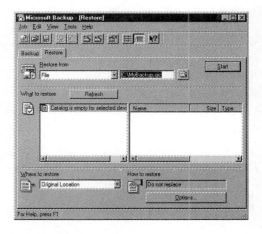

FIGURE 4.12
The Backup utility offers a Restore tab to rebuild lost hard drives. File types for backup sets are .QIC.

- Backup allows the filtering of file types for inclusion or exclusion from a file set.

- Backup will compress data onto the backup media to save space.

▼ **NOTE**

MS-DOS 6.2 and Windows 3.1 backup sets cannot be restored using the Windows 98 Backup utility due to incompatibility issues with LFNs in MS-DOS 6.2 and earlier.

Restoring Files from Backup

To restore files on your computer, you first launch the backup application. Choose the Restore tab, and locate your backup file (*.QIC). The Next Step button brings you to a screen that enables you to select the individual files you want to restore. To select a file or folder to restore, place a check mark in front of the file or folder. To start the restore procedure, press the Start Restore button (see Figure 4.12).

The Registry can be exported as an alternate to backups, then imported to restore a damaged system. More information about Registry backups is presented in Chapter 8, "Troubleshooting."

CHAPTER SUMMARY

Windows 98 can share files by using two security methods. Share-level security simply uses passwords that are given to any and all users who need access to the shared resource. User-level security relies on an account database such as Windows NT Server or a Novell server. Each user is listed by name or group membership. As long as the user has logged on with the security provider, Windows 98 can confirm a valid name and password. User-level security is seen as a better solution than share-level because changes are easier to make and each user only needs to remember his logon password.

Windows 98 also offers peer network printer sharing and continues to use EMF (Enhanced MetaFile) to speed up and improve printing standards.

Windows 98 also ships with a Backup utility that can back up files, folders, and the Registry to several backup media such as SCSI tapes, floppy disks, or other hard drives (local or network). The new Graphical User Interface and wizard make it easier to use.

R eview of configuring and managing resource
access continues in this chapter.
Configuration of the user's environment and hard
disk management will be the main focus.

Configuring and Managing Resource Access, Part 2

OBJECTIVES

This chapter helps prepare you for the exam by
covering the following objectives:

**Set up user environments by using user profiles
and system policies.**

▶ User profiles enable users to keep personalized
settings on a computer. If the computer is
accessed by multiple users, each user may have
his own settings saved. With user profiles, one
user's settings do not interfere in any way with
anyone else's.

Configure hard disks. Tasks include the following:

- **Disk compression**

- **Partitioning**

- **Enabling large disk support**

- **Converting to FAT32**

▶ Windows 98 runs more efficiently when the
hard drives are properly maintained. One of
the most important factors when using a computer is making sure data files are safe. Properly
maintained hard drives will be less likely to fail.

continues

Create hardware profiles.

▶ Hardware profiles can be used in two situations: to test new configurations and to set up a system to function with multiple hardware configurations.

SET UP USER ENVIRONMENTS BY USER PROFILES AND SYSTEM POLICIES

1. Brenda modifies her user profile so that each time she starts Windows 98, a shortcut to her finance spreadsheet displays on the desktop. Which of the following cannot be done by setting user profiles? Select the best answer.

   A. Display specific applications in the Start menu.

   B. Customize desktop settings, such as colors and wallpaper.

   C. Install an application for a specific user only.

   D. Display recently used documents in the Start menu's Documents folder.

   E. Customize network drives.

2. A user complains that the settings she made to her desktop are not saved each time she logs on to the network and starts Windows 98. You have her computer set up to download a user profile from the server and enable her to save changes to it. What might be one of the causes for her settings not being saved properly?

   A. Her version of Windows 98 needs to be updated.

   B. Her workstation's time is not synchronized with the server's time.

   C. She does not have the Remote Administration feature enabled.

   D. Windows 98 must have remote profiles enabled.

   E. All the above.

3. In a training class you conduct for system administrators, you are asked why the Registry comprises two files. From the following list, what is the best answer to this question?

   A. Makes editing configuration settings safer.

   B. Separates user and system information so that system policies and user profiles can be created.

   C. Allows dynamic information from the hardware tree to be updated while user settings are idle.

   D. Enables a user to copy his USER.DAT from a floppy disk to a laptop and maintain the same look and feel as his desktop computer.

   E. Enables easier backup of the Registry as each file fits on a single disk.

4. You are storing user profiles on a Windows NT server. You want to enable users to access the same desktop settings anywhere on the network; however, you do not want users to have the ability to change the settings from session to session. Where must you store the user

profile information on the Windows NT server, and what name should the file be given?

A. NETLOGON directory, USER.DAT

B. NETLOGON directory, USER.MAN

C. User's home directory, USER.MAN

D. User's home directory, USER.DAT

E. User's mail directory

5. **The computers on your network are configured with a 16-bit network client. What must you do so that the users of these computers can use system policies?**

A. Enable system policies on each of the workstations individually.

B. Ensure that each of the workstations has user-level security enabled to use system policies when using a 16-bit network client.

C. Upgrade each workstation to a 32-bit network client so that the users can use system policies.

D. These workstations can use system policies without changes.

E. Configure each client to use profiles in a legacy environment.

6. **What would be the result of implementing system policies and not enabling user profiles on each of the target workstations?**

A. None of the system policies will be implemented at the workstations.

B. Only the user settings will be written to the Registries of the workstations.

C. Only the computer-specific settings will be written to the Registries of the workstations.

D. The system policy will be downloaded and written to the Registries as normal. User profiles need only be enabled for use with user profiles and mandatory user profiles.

E. The system policy file will not download.

7. **As system administrator, you want to set up each user's computer so that the user cannot start an MS-DOS prompt from within Windows 98. How can this be done?**

A. Use the System Policy Editor. Open the Default User Properties sheet, click on System, click on Restrictions, and select the Disable MS-DOS Prompt check box.

B. Use the System Policy Editor. Open the Default User Properties sheet, click on System, click on Restrictions, and deselect the Enable MS-DOS Prompt check box.

C. Use the System Policy Editor. Open the Default User Properties sheet, click on System, and select the MS-DOS Prompt check box.

D. Use the System Policy Editor. Open the Default User Properties sheet, click on System, click on Restrictions, and select the Disable Single-Mode MS-DOS Applications check box.

E. None of the above.

8. Jack asks why the System Policy Editor is useful. Name two System Policy Editor features that help you administer Windows 98 workstations.

   A. It enables you to edit the Registry without using the Registry Editor.

   B. It enables you to set default settings on a user's group or user's computer by using a template file.

   C. It enables you to edit the Registry with the Registry Editor.

   D. It enables you to set only user-related settings.

   E. It enables you to set a username and computer name for each system.

9. You have implemented system policies on your network; however, a number of computers do not reflect the policy settings that you have instituted. Which of the following best describes why the computers in question do not reflect the changes?

   A. User profiles are not enabled on the computers.

   B. The computers have not been restarted since the policy file was instituted.

   C. The users of the computers already have user profiles defined.

   D. The system policy was already in effect on those computers.

   E. The Policy file is corrupted.

10. A user logs on while the server that contains the user's profile is offline. The user continues to log on and make changes to the user profile contained on the local workstation. Later that afternoon, the server is brought back online and the user logs off and back on. After logging on, which user profile will be used on the local workstation? Select the best answer.

    A. The default profile contained on the local workstation.

    B. The user profile contained on the server.

    C. The user profile on the local workstation will be loaded and, upon logging off, the profile information on the server will then be updated to reflect the changes made to the workstation.

    D. The user will log on using the most current user profile.

    E. The profile that was used from the server last.

11. The Windows 98 System Policy Editor can be opened in one of two modes. Select the modes that apply.

    A. User mode

    B. Policy File mode

    C. Computer mode

    D. Registry mode

    E. System mode

12. Kim wants to install the Policy Editor on several machines. On which directory on the Windows 98 CD can the System Policy Editor be found?

    A. \TOOLS\RESKIT\ADMIN\NETTOOLS\ POLEDIT directory

    B. \TOOLS\RESKIT\NETADMIN\POLEDIT directory

C. \ADMIN\TOOLS\APPTOOLS\POLEDIT
    directory

D. \ADMIN\TOOLS\POLEDIT directory

E. \ADMIN\TOOLS\NETAPPS\POLEDIT
    directory

13. **The company wants to implement a better user logon security system. What can
be done in using System Policy Editor to
improve security? Select all that apply.**

A. Use the password item in the user set-
    tings to require alphanumeric pass-
    words.

B. Use the password item in the system
    settings to require alphanumeric pass-
    words.

C. Use the logon item in the system set-
    tings to hide the last logged-on user.

D. Use the logon item in the user settings
    to hide the last logged-on user.

E. Use the network item in the Policy
    Editor to secure the logon screen.

**The following two questions are based
on the same scenario, required components, and optional components. Please
read all the requirements and proposed
solution before answering.**

14. **Scenario:**

The administrator has enabled user profiles and
used the Policy Editor to create a policy file.

Required component:
Prevent users from disabling remote administration and locking out administrators.

Optional components:
Prevent users from deleting the policy file.

Prevent users from disabling profiles.

Proposed solution:
Modify the policy file to hide the Remote
Administration tab in the Password icon in the
Control Panel.

Change the permissions on the Config.pol file
to no access on each user's local hard drive.

A. The proposed solution satisfies the
    required component and all of the
    optional components.

B. The proposed solution satisfies the
    required component and only one of
    the optional components.

C. The proposed solution satisfies the
    required component and none of the
    optional components.

D. The proposed solution satisfies one of
    the optional components but does not
    satisfy the required component.

E. The proposed solution satisfies none
    of the optional components and does
    not satisfy the required component.

15. **Scenario:**

The administrator has enabled user profiles and
used the Policy Editor to create a policy file.

Required component:
Prevent users from disabling remote administration and locking out administrators.

Optional components:
Prevent users from deleting the policy file.

Prevent users from disabling profiles.

Proposed solution:

Modify the policy file to hide the Remote Administration tab in the Password icon in the Control Panel.

Modify the policy file to hide the Profiles tab in the Password icon in the Control Panel.

Make sure the server share is still read only.

A. The proposed solution satisfies the required component and all of the optional components.

B. The proposed solution satisfies the required component and only one of the optional components.

C. The proposed solution satisfies the required component and none of the optional components.

D. The proposed solution satisfies one of the optional components and does not satisfy the required component.

E. The proposed solution satisfies none of the optional components and does not satisfy the required component.

16. **A user policy, group policy, and computer policy are in place for Sara on her Windows 98 system. In what order will the policy files be implemented? Select in order.**

A. User policy

B. Group policy

C. Computer policy

D. Default user

E. Default computer

ANSWER KEY

1. C	5. C	9. B	13. B-C
2. B	6. C	10. C	14. C
3. B	7. A	11. B-D	15. A
4. C	8. A-B	12. B	16. A-C

SET UP USER ENVIRONMENTS BY USER PROFILES AND SYSTEM POLICIES

1. Brenda modifies her user profile so that each time she starts Windows 98, a shortcut to her finance spreadsheet displays on the desktop. Which of the following cannot be done by setting user profiles?

   C. Install an application for a specific user only.

1. CORRECT ANSWER: C

User profiles allow users to maintain their personal settings (such as wallpaper settings), custom Start menu settings, and desktop items, but not applications. For more information, see "User Profiles."

2. A user complains that the settings she made to her desktop are not saved each time she logs on to the network and starts Windows 98. You have her computer set up to download a user profile from the server and enable her to save changes to it. What might be one of the causes for her settings not being saved properly?

   B. Her workstation's time is not synchronized with the server's time.

2. CORRECT ANSWER: B

Windows 98 checks the date stamp on the user profile and treats all profiles that were created after that time as invalid, and ignores them. For more information, see "User Profiles."

3. In a training class you conduct for system administrators, you are asked why the Registry comprises two files. From the following list, what is the best answer to this question?

   B. Separates user and system information so that system policies and user profiles can be created.

3. CORRECT ANSWER: B

Keeping the files separate allows for an easier implementation of user profiles (just replacing the USER.DAT file) and system policies. For more information, see "User Profiles."

4. You are storing user profiles on a Windows NT server. You want to enable users to access the same desktop settings anywhere on the network; however, you do not want users to have the ability to change the settings from session to session. Where must you store the user profile information on the Windows NT server, and what name should the file be given?

C. User's home directory, USER.MAN

In Windows NT, a user's profile is pulled from his home directory. The .man extension stands for Mandatory and prevents changes from being written to the profile. For more information, see "User Profiles."

User Profiles

This explanation supports questions 1 through 4.

The Registry in Windows 98 is stored in two files on your local hard drive: SYSTEM.DAT and USER.DAT. SYSTEM.DAT stores all the hardware-specific information about your computer, and USER.DAT stores all the user-specific information for the computer. If you create a generic USER.DAT file on one computer, you can move that file to all other computers in your organization. Users can still make modifications to their settings, which is beneficial because it places all users at the same starting point. User profiles will maintain individual USER.DAT files for each user on your computer.

User profiles are enabled through the User Profiles tab of the Password Control Panel. To enable user profiles, the proper choice is Users Can Customize Their Preferences and Desktop Settings. This option alone will keep a separate USER.DAT file for each user who logs on to the computer. The USER.DAT file for each user is initially copied from the USER.DAT file in the Windows directory. Two additional settings can be included in each user profile: Include Desktop Icons and Network Neighborhood Contents in User Settings, and Include Start Menu and Program Groups in User Settings.

When working in a network environment, user profiles are copied to and from your servers as you log on and log off. These profiles are referred to as *roaming* user profiles. The following criteria must be met to implement roaming user profiles:

- For Windows NT networks, your Windows 98 computer must be configured to Log On to Windows NT Domain as the primary network. This is configured in the Client for Microsoft Networks, on the Configuration tab of the Network Control Panel.

• Your Windows NT domain controller must have a home directory configured for the user to be stored on a server.

The Windows 98 user profile is automatically copied from the local hard drive to the user's home directory when the user logs off. When the user logs on, profile existence is checked in the following order:

1. If there is a server copy, it is copied to the local hard drive.

2. If there is not a server copy, the local copy is used.

3. If there is not a local copy, a new copy is created from the default files in the Windows directory. This new local profile is copied to the server when the user logs off.

If you are implementing user profiles on a Novell NetWare network, the user profile is stored in the user's NetWare `Mail` directory. This is a directory in the `SYS:MAIL` directory. For more information, see "System Policies."

---

5. **The computers on your network are configured with a 16-bit network client. What must you do so that the users of these computers can use system policies?**

   C. Upgrade each workstation to a 32-bit network client so that the users can use system policies.

5. CORRECT ANSWER: C

System policies require the 32-bit network client. A 16-bit client must be upgraded if policies are run remotely. The administrator can use system policy on the local Registry to make the changes to the users' systems. For more information, see "System Policies."

---

6. **What would be the result of implementing system policies and not enabling user profiles on each of the target workstations?**

   C. Only the computer-specific settings will be written to the Registries of the workstations.

6. CORRECT ANSWER: C

User profiles must be enabled on the workstations for user- and group-specific policies to be downloaded to the Registries. For more information, see "System Policies."

7. **As system administrator, you want to set up each user's computer so that the user cannot start an MS-DOS prompt from within Windows 98. How can this be done?**

   A. Use the System Policy Editor. Open the Default User Properties sheet, click on System, click on Restrictions, and select the Disable MS-DOS Prompt check box.

7. CORRECT ANSWER: A

Selecting Disable MS-DOS Prompt prevents access to the MS-DOS prompt. For more information, see "System Policies."

8. **Jack asks why the System Policy Editor is useful. Name two System Policy Editor features that help you administer Windows 98 workstations.**

   A. It enables you to edit the Registry without using the Registry Editor.

   B. It enables you to set default settings on a user's group or user's computer by using a template file.

8. CORRECT ANSWERS: A-B

Using the Registry Editor is always a last resort to change a system's settings. Default settings on a group of users' computers makes administration easier because they represent a consistent environment. For more information, see "System Policies."

9. **You have implemented system policies on your network; however, a number of computers do not reflect the policy settings that you have instituted. Which best describes the reason why the computers in question do not reflect the changes?**

   B. The computers have not been restarted since the policy file was instituted.

9. CORRECT ANSWER: B

The user must log off and log back on for the policies to be downloaded and enforced. For more information, see "System Policies."

10. **A user logs on while the server that contains the user's profile is offline. The user continues to log on and make changes to the user profile contained on the local workstation. Later that afternoon, the server is brought back online and the user logs off and back on. After logging on, which user profile will be used on the local workstation? Select the best answer.**

    C. The user profile on the local workstation will be loaded and, upon logging off, the profile information on the server will then be updated to reflect the changes made to the workstation.

10. CORRECT ANSWER: C

The date and time on the workstation was more current, so that profile was used. When logging off, the workstation profile overwrote the information on the server. For more information, see "System Policies."

11. **The Windows 98 System Policy Editor can be opened in one of two modes. Select the modes that apply.**

    B. Policy File mode

    D. Registry mode

Policy File mode and Registry mode are available in the Policy Editor. For more information, see "System Policies."

12. **Kim wants to install the Policy Editor on several machines. On which directory on the Windows 98 CD can the System Policy Editor be found?**

    B. \TOOLS\RESKIT\NETADMIN\POLEDIT directory

The \TOOLS\RESKIT\NETADMIN\POLEDIT directory on the Windows 98 CD contains the file to set up the System Policy Editor. For more information, see "System Policies."

13. **The company wants to implement a better user logon security system. What can be done in using System Policy Editor to improve security? Select all that apply.**

    B. Use the password item in the system settings to require alphanumeric passwords.

    C. Use the logon item in the system settings to hide the last logged-on user.

User policies do not control logon features for the system. The system policies offer a logon and password category to help improve overall logon security. For more information, see "System Policies."

14. **Proposed solution:**

    Modify the policy file to hide the Remote Administration tab in the Password icon in the Control Panel.

    Change the permissions on the Config.pol **file to no access on each user's local hard drive.**

    C. The proposed solution satisfies the required component and none of the optional components.

The policy file in most cases resides on a server and has a shared permission of read only. Profiles and policies are controlled separately. For more information, see "System Policies."

15. **Proposed solution:**

Modify the policy file to hide the Remote Administration tab in the Password icon in the Control Panel.

Modify the policy file to hide the Profiles tab in the Password icon in the Control Panel.

Make sure the server share is still read only.

A. **The proposed solution satisfies the required component and all of the optional components.**

---

15. CORRECT ANSWER: A

The policy file in most cases resides on a server and has a shared permission of read only. Profiles and policies are controlled separately. If profiles are disabled, a user might log on to a new system and not be affected by policies. After a policy has run, it is merged into the Registry and a user cannot make changes to the policy file. For more information, see "System Policies."

System Policies

This explanation supports questions 5 through 15.

System policies can be used to create and enforce a custom environment for users. It allows restrictions to be set on system usage, such as Control Panels.

System policies enable you to modify the USER.DAT and SYSTEM.DAT files on a destination computer automatically when the user logs on to the network. Policies are implemented based on usernames, group membership, and computer names. If you wish to create a new policy configuration file for your server, you must use the System Policy Editor. To install the System Policy Editor, follow these steps:

1. Click on the Start button and choose Settings, Control Panel.

2. Open the Add/Remove Programs Control Panel.

3. Select the Windows Setup tab, and click the Have Disk button.

4. Select the following path from the Windows 98 CD: <Windows_98_CD>\TOOLS\RESKIT\NETADMIN\POLEDIT.

5. Select both the System Policy Editor and Group Policies check boxes, and then click the Install button.

You only have to install the System Policy Editor on the machine you will be using to create the system policy. If you plan to assign the policy to users based on which server groups they belong to, you must install the group policies on every machine on your network.

You can install the group policy files on any computer by following these steps on each workstation that requires them:

1. Click the Start button and choose Settings, Control Panel.

2. Open the Add/Remove Programs Control Panel.

3. Select the Windows Setup tab, and click the Have Disk button.

4. Select the following path from the Windows 98 CD: `<Windows_98_CD>\TOOLS\RESKIT\NETADMIN\POLEDIT`.

5. Select the check box for Group Policies, and click the Install button.

With group policies installed, your computer will import policy settings from the configuration file based on the server groups to which you belong.

Depending on the type of network you are working on, Windows 98 expects the policy configuration file to be in certain locations. The locations are as follows:

- Windows NT Domain, in the `NetLogon` directory of domain controllers, which is `<win_root>\SYSTEM32\REPL\IMPORT\SCRIPTS\`

- Novell NetWare 3.x or 4.x server, on the `SYS` volume in the `PUBLIC` directory

▼ **NOTE**

By default, the name of the configuration file is `CONFIG.POL`. If you are creating policy files to be used with Windows NT 4.0 as well, the Windows NT default policy filename would be `NTCONFIG.POL`. You can use other filenames as long as the local computer is set up to find the other filenames.

To launch the System Policy Editor, choose it from the Start menu under Programs, Accessories, System Tools. It opens with a blank window. To create a new policy file, choose New from the File menu. If you are working on a policy file, you should have at least two icons visible: Default User and Default Computer.

When working with the Policy Editor to make a policy file, you will notice that each check box in the Settings windows has three states: on (checked), off (clear), and neutral (gray).

▼ **NOTE**

The three states of the check boxes in the System Policy Editor (checked, clear, and gray) can be interpreted the following ways:

Checked is a value that you are setting to the On position. This turns the setting on for all computers processing this policy.

Clear is a value that you are setting to the Off position. This turns the setting off for all computers processing this policy.

Gray is a value that you are leaving alone. These values are neutral, and will not change the settings. This is the default for all values in Default User and Default Computer.

File and Printer Sharing Restrictions

File and Printer Sharing is necessary on workstations to make remote administration possible. The following two policy entries enable you to leave the service installed, but remove all the controls from the users (see Figure 5.1).

- Disable File Sharing Controls
- Disable Print Sharing Controls

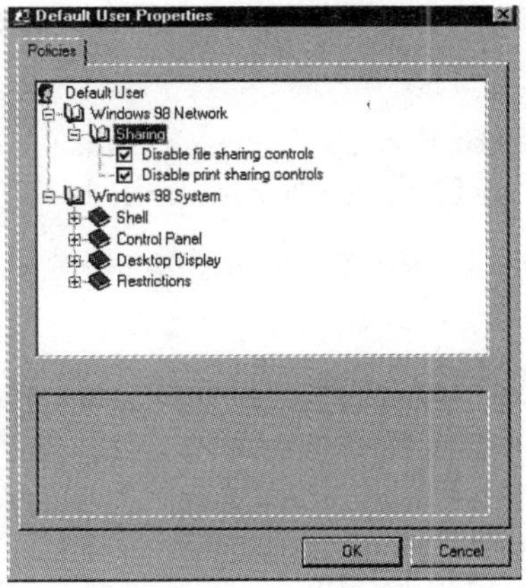

FIGURE 5.1
Windows 98 Network sharing restrictions remove a user's ability to turn file or printer sharing on or off.

16. **A user policy, group policy, and computer policy are in place for Sara on her Windows 98 system. In what order will the policy files be implemented? Select in order.**

A. User policy

C. Computer policy

16. CORRECT ANSWERS: A-C

Group policy, default user, and default computer are not implemented if a user policy exists. For more information, see "Applying Policies for Users, Groups, and Computers."

Applying Policies for Users, Groups, and Computers

This explanation supports question 16.

When you create a policy file for a server, you have the additional option of adding individual icons for each user or group of users from your server, as well as icons for each computer on your network. To add additional entries to your policy, choose Add User, Add Computer, or Add Group from the Edit menu.

Windows 98 follows a particular order when reading the policy file:

1. Windows 98 checks to see whether there is an entry for the user logging on. If there is an entry for the user, Windows 98 then applies the policy for that user.

2. If a user-specific policy is not in use, Windows 98 checks for entries to determine whether the user is a member of any of the groups. Groups are processed in the order prescribed by the administrator at the time of adding a new group to the policy file.

3. If there are no entries for that user or no groups processed, the entry for Default User is applied.

4. After applying the user policy, Windows 98 applies a computer-specific policy if one exists.

5. If there is no entry for your current computer name, the entry for Default Computer is applied.

For group policies to be implemented at a system, the Grouppol.dll file must be loaded locally.

SET UP USER ENVIRONMENTS BY USER PROFILES AND SYSTEM POLICIES

Windows shell restrictions are important to review before you set up the working environment for users. Your decisions about access and control features will be guided by your knowledge of user profiles and system policies.

Windows Shell Restrictions

Windows Explorer is the default shell used by Windows 98. A *shell* is the program that sets up the working environment in which applications and other services run. In Windows 3.1, for example, the shell was referred to as Program Manager. Policy Editor provides several security features regarding Windows Explorer, which can be found in the form of custom folders and shell restrictions (see Figure 5.2).

You can find the settings for both of these security features in the following lists. These are the custom folders that you can configure:

- **Custom Programs Folder.** Enables you to specify an alternative location for a folder that has the contents of the Programs directory. The folder can be stored locally on the workstation, or can be located on a network drive and accessed through a UNC path such as this: \\server\share\folder.

- **Custom Desktop Icons.** Enables you to specify an alternative location for a folder that has the contents of the Desktop directory.

- **Hide Start Menu Subfolders.** Enables you to hide the default Start menu folders.

- **Custom Startup Folder.** Enables you to specify an alternative location for a folder that has the contents of the Startup directory.

- **Custom Network Neighborhood.** Enables you to specify an alternative location for a folder that has the contents of the Network Neighborhood.

- **Custom Start Menu.** Enables you to specify an alternative location for a folder that has the contents of the Start menu directory.

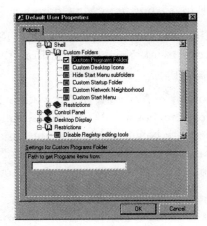

FIGURE 5.2
Custom folders force users to have a common set of menu items and desktop items each time they log on.

In addition to the custom folders, you can apply several restrictions to the users' desktop shells (see Figure 5.3). The various shell restrictions are as follows:

- **Remove Run Command.** Removes the Run command from the Start menu, which helps to prevent users from running executables that you have not provided shortcuts for in the Start menu.

- **Remove Folders from Settings on Start Menu.** Hides the Printers and Control Panel folders in the Settings folder in the Start menu.

- **Remove Taskbar from Settings on Start Menu.** Hides Taskbar in the Settings folder in the Start menu.

- **Remove Find Command.** Removes the Find command from the Start menu.

- **Hide Drives in My Computer.** Removes all drive icons from My Computer.

- **Hide Network Neighborhood.** Removes the Network Neighborhood from the desktop.

- **No Entire Network in Network Neighborhood.** If you choose to leave the Network Neighborhood on the desktop, you may choose to hide the Entire Network icon to prevent network browsing outside of the current workgroup.

- **No Workgroup Contents in Network Neighborhood.** If you choose to leave the Network Neighborhood on the desktop, you may choose to hide the current workgroup contents. This forces browsing resources through the Entire Network icon.

- **Hide All Items on Desktop.** Removes all icons—both user- and OS-created—from the desktop.

- **Disable Shut Down Command.** Removes the Shutdown command from the Start menu.

- **Don't Save Settings at Exit.** Prevents desktop changes from being saved when users are exiting Windows.

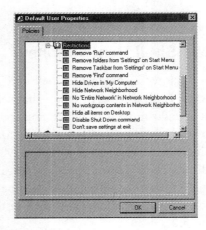

FIGURE 5.3
Shell restrictions remove or hide basic navigation components like the Run command or the Entire Network icon.

Control Panel Restrictions

The Control Panel settings enable you to control or restrict access to most of the Control Panel applets.

You can apply restrictions to the following Control Panel applets:

- Display
- Network
- Passwords
- Printers
- System

Restricting the Display Control Panel

Figure 5.4 shows the Display Control Panel. The restrictions for the Display Control Panel are as follows:

- **Disable Display Control Panel.** Disables all access to the Display Control Panel.

- **Hide Background Page.** Removes the Background tab from the Display Control Panel.

- **Hide Screen Saver Page.** Removes the Screen Saver tab from the Display Control Panel.

- **Hide Appearance Page.** Removes the Appearance tab from the Display Control Panel.

- **Hide Settings Page.** Removes the Settings tab from the Display Control Panel.

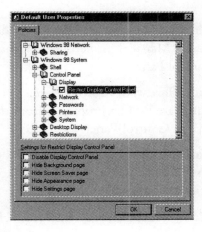

FIGURE 5.4
Control Panel display restrictions prevent users from changing display settings and appearances.

Restricting the Network Control Panel

The Network icon in the Control Panel restricts network configuration (see Figure 5.5). The following settings enable you to modify the restrictions to the Network Control Panel:

- **Disable Network Control Panel.** Prevents all access to the Network Control Panel.

- **Hide Identification Page.** Hides the Identification properties of the Network Control Panel.

- **Hide Access Control Page.** Hides the Access Control (user-level versus share-level) properties of the Network Control Panel.

FIGURE 5.5
Control Panel network restrictions prevent users from changing the NetBios name or access control.

Restricting the Passwords Control Panel

For most users, some access to the Passwords Control Panel is required. You can, however, apply restrictions from the following list (see Figure 5.6):

- **Disable Passwords Control Panel.** Prevents all access to the Passwords Control Panel.

- **Hide Change Passwords Page.**   Hides the Change Passwords properties of the Passwords Control Panel.

- **Hide Remote Administration Page.** Hides the Remote Administration properties of the Passwords Control Panel.

- **Hide User Profiles Page.**   Hides the Profiles properties of the Passwords Control Panel.

FIGURE 5.7
Control Panel printer restrictions prevent users from changing any settings on local printers.

FIGURE 5.6
Control Panel password restrictions prevent users from disabling remote administration.

Restricting Printer Configuration

Figure 5.7 displays printer settings. You can place the following restrictions on printers:

- **Hide General and Details Pages.**   Hides the General and Details properties for the Printer icons in the Printers folder.

- **Disable Deletion of Printers.**   Prevents the deletion of installed printers.

- **Disable Addition of Printers.**   Prevents the installation of printers.

Restricting the System Control Panel

See Figure 5.8 for System icon settings. You can apply the following restrictions to the System Control Panel:

- **Hide Device Manager Page.**   Hides the Device Manager properties from the System Control Panel.

- **Hide Hardware Profiles Page.**   Hides the Hardware Profiles properties from the System Control Panel.

- **Hide File System Button.**   Hides the File System button from the Performance properties in the System Control Panel.

- **Hide Virtual Memory Button.**   Hides the Virtual Memory button from the Performance properties in the System Control Panel.

FIGURE 5.8
Administrators will want to restrict most users from the System icon in the Control Panel.

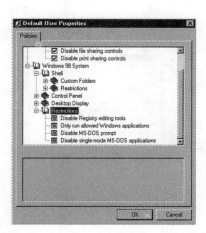

FIGURE 5.9
System restrictions are aimed at controlling the application types that are executed.

System Restrictions

System restrictions are in place to prevent the user from getting away from the Windows 98 graphical user interface (GUI) and the controlled environment (see Figure 5.9). If a user is allowed to close the Windows 98 GUI, none of the policy changes that you have implemented will have any effect on the user.

The system restrictions are not limited to the shell itself, but rather to the operating system:

- **Disable Registry Editing Tools.**

- **Only Run Allowed Windows Applications.**   Allows only the applications listed under the Show dialog box to be run on the system.

- **Disable MS-DOS Prompt.**

- **Disable Single-mode MS-DOS Applications.**

These are all the user settings that can be modified based on Microsoft's default template.

Computer Policies

Computer policies are based on the computer name. When a specific computer name is not defined in the policy file, the default computer settings apply.

Regardless of the user logged on, including administrators, the PC can be restricted.

General Network Settings

The Network Settings section of the computer policy covers configuration options for most of the network interface of Windows 98 (see Figure 5.10). These are not seen so much as restrictions to, but rather as standardizations of, the users' environments. Descriptions of these options appear in the list that follows.

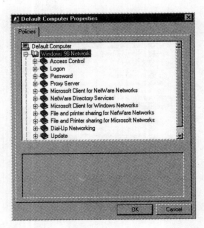

FIGURE 5.10
Network configuration settings can be configured remotely
with System policies.

- **Access Control.**   Enables you to specify
  user-level access control. When checked, it
  enables user-level access control with security provider list in options section.

- **Logon.**   Enables you to set additional
  warnings and security on Windows 98, such
  as not displaying the last logged-on user.

- **Password.**   Alters the way that Windows
  98 works with passwords. You can hide
  passwords with asterisks or require alphanu-
  meric passwords for Windows.

- **Proxy Server.**   Enables you to remotely
  configure the settings for each system.

- **Microsoft Client for NetWare Networks.**
  Includes information such as preferred
  servers.

- **NetWare Directory Services.**   Offers
  more detail about clients running directory
  services for Novell 4.x.

- **Microsoft Client for Windows Networks.**
  Lets you configure Domain logons and
  workgroup memberships.

- **File and Printer Sharing for NetWare
  Networks.**   Enables you to disable SAP
  advertising. This stops the Server
  Advertising Protocol from being used for file
  and printer sharing for NetWare networks.

- **Dial-Up Networking.**   Enables you to disable dial-in. This stops Dial-Up Server from
  working on the computer.

- **Update.**   Helps configure the locations
  and names of custom policy files.

Windows 98 System Configuration

Windows 98 system configuration changes the settings on all or selected Windows 98 machines (see
Figure 5.11). General settings can be made to all
systems. The list following describes the Windows
98 system configuration settings.

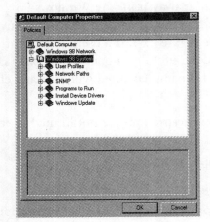

FIGURE 5.11
Windows 98 system configuration is based on computer
names rather than usernames.

- **User Profiles.**   Enable profiles on a
  system.

- **Network Paths.**   Used to determine the
  locations of Windows setup files and Help
  Tour files.

- **SNMP.**   Configures community names and permissions.

- **Program to Run.**   Sets application as start up once each boot up only once only.

- **Install Device Drivers.**   Adds only a new digital signature feature.

- **Windows Update.**   Enable use of the Web-based configuration and driver update tools.

PRACTICE QUESTIONS

CONFIGURE HARD DISKS

1. **A client asks how he can fit more data on his existing hard drive without adding another hard drive or storing files on a network. What Windows 98 disk utility should he use to compress the data on his hard drive?**

   A. DoubleSpace

   B. DriveSpace

   C. Disk Defragmenter

   D. ScanDisk

   E. Disk Clean up

2. **When John runs Disk Compression under Windows 98, he calls asking you how files are compressed. Which two of the following do you tell him are ways in which disk compression maximizes disk space?**

   A. Cluster conversion

   B. Token conversion

   C. ASCII collapse

   D. Sector allocation conversion

   E. Cluster compression

3. **Windows 98 implements which form of disk compression?**

   A. On-the-fly compression

   B. Read/write compression

   C. Token conversion

   D. LIZ compression

   E. ZIPs

4. **Rhone wants to compress his 1.5GB hard drive into one compressed volume. Which of the following should he use?**

   A. DriveSpace 2.0

   B. DriveSpace 3.0

   C. DoubleSpace

   D. Stacker

   E. ZIP

5. **Which of the following is not a benefit of DriveSpace compression?**

   A. DriveSpace is integrated into the operating system.

   B. DriveSpace uses no conventional memory.

   C. DriveSpace uses all 32-bit code.

   D. DriveSpace drivers stay loaded at all times.

   E. DriveSpace 3.0 is compatible with Stacker.

6. **Susan uses DriveSpace 3.0 to compress her hard disk. She wants to know where her files have been stored. What do you tell her?**

A. They are stored in a hidden file called a compressed volume file (CVF).

B. They have been moved to another disk, called a CFI disk.

C. They have been moved to the H: drive.

D. They have been replaced by tokens.

E. They have been renamed to the CVF file.

7. **What is the name of the utility used in Windows 98 to manage partitions?**

   A. Partition Manager

   B. FDISK

   C. Disk Partition

   D. PDISK

   E. Partition Magic

8. **What size drive will trigger the partition utility to prompt for large disk support?**

   A. 255MB

   B. 512MB

   C. 1024MB

   D. 2GB

   E. 4GB

9. **How many partitions can Windows 98's FDISK support per drive?**

   A. 4

   B. 3

   C. 2

   D. 1

   E. Unlimited, depending on space

The following two questions are based on the same scenario, required components, and optional components. Please read all the requirements and proposed solution before answering.

10. **Scenario:**

    Sara is rebuilding a system that had Windows 98 on Drive C: and NT loaded with an NTFS partition on Drive D: in a dual-boot.

    Required component:
    Remove the NTFS partition and NT from the Windows 98 system.

    Optional components:
    Keep the existing Windows 98 operating system.

    Remove the dual-boot menu.

    Proposed solution:
    Boot in Windows 98 and use FDISK to delete the NTFS partition and reboot the system.

    A. The proposed solution satisfies the required component and all of the optional components.

    B. The proposed solution satisfies the required component and only one of the optional components.

    C. The proposed solution satisfies the required component and none of the optional components.

    D. The proposed solution satisfies only one of the optional components but does not satisfy the required component.

    E. The proposed solution satisfies none of the optional components and does not satisfy the required component.

11. **Scenario:**

Sara is rebuilding a system that had Windows 98 on Drive C: and NT loaded with an NTFS partition on Drive D: in a dual-boot.

Required component:
Remove the NTFS partition and NT from the Windows 98 system.

Optional components:
Keep the existing Windows 98 operating system.

Remove the dual-boot menu.

Proposed solution:
Boot in Windows 98 and use FDISK to delete the NTFS partition.

Reboot using a Windows 98 system disk by running the SYS C: command.

A. The proposed solution satisfies the required component and all of the optional components.

B. The proposed solution satisfies the required component and only one of the optional components.

C. The proposed solution satisfies the required component and none of the optional components.

D. The proposed solution satisfies one of the optional components but does not satisfy the required component.

E. The proposed solution satisfies none of the optional components and does not satisfy the required component.

12. **How many entries can be stored on the root directory of a FAT32 partition?**

A. 255.

B. 512.

C. 2048.

D. 4GB.

E. There is no limit.

13. **What is the default cluster size for a FAT32 partition?**

A. 4KB

B. 16KB

C. 64KB

D. 254KB

E. 255KB

14. **How can you format a drive as FAT32?**

A. Use the Format menu with the FAT32 option.

B. Use Format c: /fs:FAT32 from a command line.

C. Use FDISK and enable support for large disks.

D. Use FDISK and enable FAT32 formatting.

E. A specific command for format as FAT32 does not exist.

The following question is scenario-based. Please read all the requirements and proposed solution before answering.

15. **Scenario:**

Your system is running out of hard drive space. The 1GB drive is currently formatted as FAT.

Required component:
Create more free space on the 1GB hard drive.

Optional components:
Do not use disk compression.

Do not slow down the average disk access time.

Proposed solution:
Run Disk Defragmenter and convert the drive to FAT32 by using Windows 98's conversion utility.

A. The proposed solution satisfies the required component and all of the optional components.

B. The proposed solution satisfies the required component and only one of the optional components.

C. The proposed solution satisfies the required component and none of the optional components.

D. The proposed solution satisfies one of the optional components but does not satisfy the required component.

E. The proposed solution satisfies none of the optional components and does not satisfy the required component.

ANSWER KEY

1. B	6. A	11. A
2. B-D	7. B	12. E
3. A	8. B	13. A
4. B	9. C	14. E
5. D	10. D	15. A

ANSWERS & EXPLANATIONS

CONFIGURE HARD DISKS

1. A client asks how he can fit more data on his existing hard drive without adding another hard drive or storing files on a network. What Windows 98 disk utility should he use to compress the data on his hard drive?

   B. DriveSpace

1. CORRECT ANSWER: B

DriveSpace 3.0 is the compression program included in Windows 98. For more information, see "Disk Compression."

2. When John runs Disk Compression under Windows 98, he calls asking you how files are compressed. Which two of the following do you tell him are ways in which disk compression maximizes disk space?

   B. Token conversion

   D. Sector allocation conversion

2. CORRECT ANSWER: B-D

Token conversion and sector allocation conversion are the two ways that space is saved. For more information, see "Disk Compression."

3. Windows 98 implements which form of disk compression?

   A. On-the-fly compression

3. CORRECT ANSWER: A

DriveSpace performs compression on-the-fly (transparently and in the background). For more information, see "Disk Compression."

4. Rhone wants to compress his 1.5GB hard drive into one compressed volume. Which of the following should he use?

   B. DriveSpace 3.0

4. CORRECT ANSWER: B

The maximum size of a compressed volume with DriveSpace 2.0 is 512MB (Windows 95). DriveSpace 3.0, included with Windows 98, can compress volumes up to 2GB. For more information, see "Disk Compression."

5. Which of the following is not a benefit of DriveSpace compression?

   D. DriveSpace drivers stay loaded at all times.

5. CORRECT ANSWER: D

DriveSpace drivers are loaded only when compressed media is detected and mounted. For more information, see "Disk Compression."

6. Susan uses DriveSpace 3.0 to compress her hard disk. She wants to know where her files have been stored. What do you tell her?

A. They are stored in a hidden file called a compressed volume file (CVF).

A CVF is a single file that contains the data files that have been compressed by DriveSpace. For more information, see "Disk Compression."

Disk Compression

This explanation supports questions 1 through 6.

Windows 98 implements a form of disk compression known as on-the-fly compression. On-the-fly compression is so named because the compression/decompression process occurs automatically in the background and is transparent to the user. On-the-fly compression is the process of intercepting normal MS-DOS read/write calls and compressing the data before writing it to the hard disk.

Disk compression as implemented in Windows 98 (and in the versions released with MS-DOS 6.x) consists of two processes. The first, called *token conversion*, replaces repetitive patterns that occur in a given piece of data with a token, which takes up less space.

The second, called *sector allocation granularity*, involves changing the way data is stored on a hard drive by circumventing the often large amounts of wasted space created under a normal FAT file system.

After disk compression is installed and the files are initially compressed, the files are stored in the compressed volume file (CVF), which is actually a large hidden file that sits on the physical C: drive. When the system boots up, however, the CVF is assigned the drive letter *C*. The physical C: drive, which now contains only a few files because everything else is in a compressed state inside the CVF, is assigned a higher drive letter, typically *H*. This higher-lettered drive is called a *host* drive and, by default, is hidden from normal view. The process of switching the drive letters and making the CVF available for viewing in MS-DOS and Windows is called *mounting*.

The main advantages to using Windows 98 disk compression are as follows:

- Disk compression is implemented with 32-bit code for better performance.

- It does not use any conventional memory.

- It is integrated with the operating system for ease of use and better performance.

▼ **NOTE**

When a floppy is compressed, the DriveSpace drivers load only when the floppy disk is in the drive. In general, the DriveSpace drivers load only when compressed media (hard drive or floppy disk) is detected.

The following information should be noted whenever a user is considering Windows 98 disk compression:

- Windows 98 is compatible with many third-party compression software such as Stacker versions 2.x, 3.x, and 4.x, and with all versions of SuperStor, another disk compression utility.

- The maximum size of a compressed volume is 2GB, using DriveSpace 3.0 that ships with Windows 98. This size refers to the compressed size.

- There are four compression ratios within DriveSpace 3.0; the average (or normal) is 2.4:1. DriveSpace 3.0 can use a High pack, Standard, Compress Only if X% Full, or No Compression settings. More compression results in slower access time. Less compression does not slow down the system.

▼ **NOTE**

With DriveSpace 3.0, Windows 98 is able to compress files on FAT partitions only. DriveSpace 3.0 does not function on a drive using FAT32. See "Converting to FAT32" later in this chapter for more information.

7. What is the name of the utility used in Windows 98 to manage partitions?

B. FDISK

7. CORRECT ANSWER: B

FDISK is a revised version of FDISK for DOS. It displays the same menu as the DOS version but supports larger drives. For more information, see "Partitioning."

8. What size drive will trigger the partition utility to prompt for large disk support?

B. 512MB

8. CORRECT ANSWER: B

When a drive larger than 512MB is detected, Windows 98's partition utility prompts for large drive support. For more information, see "Partitioning."

9. How many partitions can Window's 98's FDISK support per drive?

C. 2

9. CORRECT ANSWER: C

FDISK can create no more than two partitions in Windows 98. A primary and an extended partition. For more information, see "Partitioning."

10. Proposed solution:

Boot in Windows 98 and use FDISK to delete the NTFS partition and reboot the system.

D. The proposed solution satisfies only one of the optional components but does not satisfy the required component.

10. CORRECT ANSWER: D

Windows 98 and Windows NT will share drive C: as a bootable drive. The NT BOOT.INI menu will remain even if NT is deleted. The C: drive must have the Windows 98 system files reloaded. For more information, see "Partitioning."

11. Proposed solution:

Boot in Windows 98 and use FDISK to delete the NTFS partition.

Reboot using a Windows 98 system disk by running the SYS C: command.

A. The proposed solution satisfies the required component and all of the optional components.

11. CORRECT ANSWER: A

Windows 98 and Windows NT will share drive C: as a bootable drive. The NT BOOT.INI menu will not be used if the drive has been made a Windows 98 system drive. For more information, see "Partitioning."

Partitioning

This explanation supports questions 7 through 11.

All hard disks must be partitioned before they can be formatted and used. A partition is a section of the hard drive set aside to store information. A hard drive can have up to two partitions in Windows 98. The Windows 98 partitioning utility is FDISK.EXE, as shown in Figure 5.12.

FIGURE 5.12
FDISK is used to view, create, and delete partitions in Windows 98.

Windows 98 supports two types of files systems: FAT16 and FAT32. In most cases, FAT16 is referred to as simply FAT. The disk partitioning utility can create partitions to support large drives with FAT32. When the utility is first started, it checks the size of the hard drives on the system. If a drive is larger than 512MB, FDISK prompts the user to enable support for FAT32 (see Figure 5.13). For more information on FAT32, see "Converting to FAT32" later in this chapter.

FIGURE 5.13
Windows 98's FDISK has detected a hard drive larger than 512MB.

Partitions between 512MB and 2GB can be formatted as FAT or FAT32. Partitions above 2GB must be FAT32. See Table 5.1 for details and differences between FAT16 and FAT32.

TABLE 5.1   COMPARISON BETWEEN FAT16 AND FAT32

Description	FAT16	FAT32
Maximum partition size	2 GB	2 TB
Cluster size on a 2GB partition	32KB	4KB
Support for DriveSpace compression	Yes	No

▼ **NOTE**

In addition to these differences, after FAT32 is installed, the only operating systems that can read FAT32 partitions are Windows 98 and Windows 95 OSR2. The only way to remove a FAT32 partition is to delete it and create a new partition, which can result in lost data.

FDISK knows how to identify primary partitions that are FAT16, FAT32, and OS/2's HPFS. FDISK identifies NTFS partitions (Windows NT's own partition format) as HPFS. Windows 98 cannot read information from either NTFS or HPFS partitions.

▼ **NOTE**

FDISK cannot delete an NTFS partition if it is an extended partition. You can delete either NTFS or HPFS partitions by choosing option 3—Delete Partition, and then choosing to delete the non-DOS partition. HPFS can also use Delete Logical Drive.

12. How many entries can be stored on the root directory of a FAT32 partition?

　E.　There is no limit.

12. CORRECT ANSWER: E

FAT32 handles the File Allocation Table's location and removes the 512-entry limit that exists for FAT. For more information, see "Converting to FAT32."

13. What is the default cluster size for a FAT32 partition?

   A. 4KB

13. CORRECT ANSWER: A

FAT32 can use a 4KB cluster for drives up to 8GB. For more information, see "Converting to FAT32."

14. How can you format a drive as FAT32?

   E. A specific command for format as FAT32 does not exist.

14. CORRECT ANSWER: E

At this time Windows 98 cannot format a drive. A new partition can be created with support and then a regular format can take place. The system will use FAT32 on all partitions larger than 512MB. For more information, see "Converting to FAT32."

15. Proposed solution:

Run Disk Defragmenter and convert the drive to FAT32 by using Windows 98's conversion utility.

   A. The proposed solution satisfies the required component and all of the optional components.

15. CORRECT ANSWER: A

FAT32 will reduce the size of each cluster, resulting in less wasted space on the drive. For more information, see "Converting to FAT32."

Converting to FAT32

This explanation supports questions 12 through 15.

Windows 98 provides you with tools to help maintain the proper system stability. The hard drives are most vulnerable to difficulties because data is added, moved, and deleted constantly. Windows 98 supports two types of partition formats: FAT16 (also known simply as FAT) and FAT32. FAT stands for File Allocation Table.

FAT16 is used in DOS, Windows 3.1, Windows 95, and Windows NT. Microsoft introduced FAT32 with the release of Windows 95's OS/R2 and continues to support it in Windows 98.

FAT32 offers several advantages over basic FAT. FAT32 uses a smaller cluster size to store data, which results in more overall storage space on the drive. FAT32 can use a 4KB cluster size for partitions up to 8GB.

Depending on the size of the partition, FAT must increase the size of the clusters. A larger cluster leads to more wasted space.

Suppose a file needs 12KB of hard drive space and FAT has determined the smallest cluster size is 64KB. This would result in a wasting of 52KB of disk space. The same file stored under FAT32's 4KB cluster would take up three clusters but would not waste any space.

FAT32 was designed for larger hard drives and is not recommended for drives with fewer than 512MB . After a partition reaches this size, it becomes beneficial to convert to FAT32. FAT must contend with a maximum partition size of 2GB, whereas FAT32 can be used on drives up to 2TB.

Each FAT drive is currently limited to 512 entries on the root of the hard drive. Using Long Filenames (one entry for each 13 characters and one for the alias), the drive's root limitations can be reached quickly. FAT32 allows the file allocation table to be stored anywhere on the drive, thus removing this limitation.

To use the FAT32 converted you can choose a DOS or command-line utility, or a GUI version. To run the DOS version type CVT *Drive:* /CVT32; for the GUI version use the Windows 98 menu Start, Programs, Accessories, System Tools, Drive Converter FAT32.

After a drive has been converted to FAT32, it cannot be converted back to FAT. The partition would have to be deleted. Systems that run other operating systems in a dual-boot with Windows 98 cannot access the FAT32 partition. FAT32 also cannot be compressed using DriveSpace.

CREATE HARDWARE PROFILES

1. **A local administrator is perplexed by a new type of network card. It seems two drivers can be used for the card and the administrator is not sure which one is best. Presently an older driver is present and functions. What can the administrator do to test both card drivers without risking messing up the current settings?**

   A. Enable dual driver mode.

   B. Install the card a second time with new drivers.

   C. Update the drivers of the current card.

   D. Create a hardware profile and disable one card on each profile.

   E. None of the above since Windows 98 cannot support more than one card of the same type.

2. **Where can you go in Windows 98 to create hardware profiles?**

   A. Select Hardware Profiles from the Start menu.

   B. Select Hardware Profiles from the Task Manager.

   C. Select the Hardware Profiles icon from the Control Panel.

   D. Select the Hardware Profiles tab from the Hardware icon in the Control Panel.

   E. Select the Hardware Profiles tab from the System icon in the Control Panel.

3. **Once hardware profiles are created, how can changes to the system be made?**

   A. Boot up into the hardware profile of choice and all changes made to the system affect only the current profile.

   B. Boot up into an alternate hardware profile and make changes to the profile's properties from the Hardware Profile tab of the system icon.

   C. Boot up into any profile and make changes in the Device Manager, making sure to identify which profile is to be affected.

   D. The only way is to boot up in any profile and use the Registry Editor to make changes in the HKEY_Local_Machine under Hardware Profiles.

   E. The only way is to disable any profile that you do not want to change and then perform modifications to the system.

4. **An administrator has clients complaining they cannot use the sound card on their systems. The corporate mandate was to disable all sound cards to cut down on noise in the office. The clients promise just to use the sound card when at home or on the road. What can be done to allow the clients to use their sound cards when on the road? Select the best answer.**

A. Create a hardware profile with the sound card enabled at the office and disabled at home.

B. Create two hardware profiles: One for the office with the sound card on and a second for home use with the sound card off.

C. Create two hardware profiles: One for the office with the sound card off and a second for home use with the sound card on.

D. Create a single hardware profile with the sound card turned on, but with a low volume.

E. Create a hardware profile for the sound card that can be enabled by the user when needed.

5. **The administrator is worried about clients making changes to their hardware profiles and circumventing the configuration put in place. How can you help the administrator prevent users from making changes to their hardware profiles?**

A. You cannot. Profiles are personal choices and must be controlled by the user.

B. You cannot. Hardware profiles are selected and changes prior to starting Windows 98. There are not security items that can take effect until Windows 98 is started.

C. You can create a local or network policy that disables the system icon for the default user.

D. You can create a local or network profile that can disable the system icon for all users, but not the administrator account.

E. You can create a local or network policy that can disable the System icon for all users, but not the administrator account.

ANSWER KEY

1. D	3. C	5. E
2. E	4. C	

CREATE HARDWARE PROFILES

1. A local administrator is perplexed by a new type of network card. It seems two drivers can be used for the card and the administrator is not sure which one is best. Presently an older driver is present and functions. What can the administrator do to test both card drivers without risking messing up the current settings?

D. Create a hardware profile and disable one card on each profile.

1. CORRECT ANSWER: D

Hardware profiles can be used to create two entries for the card, each using a driver. Testing the system is done by rebooting the system in each configuration and deleting the one that is not as good. For more information, see "Hardware Profiles."

2. Where can you go in Windows 98 to create hardware profiles?

E. Select the Hardware Profiles tab from the System icon in the Control Panel.

2. CORRECT ANSWER: E

Hardware profiles are created in the Hardware Profiles tab by selecting an existing profile and clicking on the copy button. The new profile is exactly the same as the original until changes are made. For more information, see "Hardware Profiles."

3. Once hardware profiles are created, how can changes to the system be made?

C. Boot up into any profile and make changes in the Device Manager, making sure to identify which profile is to be affected.

3. CORRECT ANSWER: C

Any hardware profiles can be used to boot up. Once in the system, the Device Manager will show a list of hardware profiles available on the system. Changes can be made to all profiles or a single one can be identified. For more information, see "Hardware Profiles."

4. An administrator has clients complaining they cannot use the sound card on their systems. The corporate mandate was to disable all sound cards to cut down on noise in the office. The clients promise just to use the sound card when at home or on the road. What can be done to allow the clients to use their sound cards when on the road? Select the best answer.

C. Create two hardware profiles: One for the office with the sound card off and a second for home use with the sound card on.

4. CORRECT ANSWER: C

Any hardware profiles can be set up with the sound card enabled and a second with the sound disabled. You are still relying on each client to use the profile with sound only when they are out of the office. For more information, see "Hardware Profiles."

5. The administrator is worried about clients making changes to their hardware profiles and circumventing the configuration put in place. How can you help the administrator prevent users from making changes to their hardware profiles?

E. You can create a local or network policy that can disable the System icon for all users, but not the administrator account.

Hardware profiles can be changed by any user initially. By setting up a policy to restrict users from the Control Panel System icon and leaving access for administrators you can control who can make changes. The Device Manager is also in the System icon and must be protected. For more information, see "Hardware Profiles."

Hardware Profiles

Windows 98 uses Plug and Play along with the administrator's settings to configure the hardware in the best possible way. There are situations, however, when more than one configuration is required. Windows 98 will support all settings simultaneously, but would not be as efficient.

Laptops are the most common systems using hardware profiles since they will be in at least two environments. A laptop at the office connected to a docking station may have different needs than the same laptop at home connecting via a modem.

A hardware profile allows the administrator to create a proper configuration for the system by enabling or disabling devices and their associated drivers. Upon startup the user is presented with a menu listing all configurations and they must choose one.

A hardware profile can also be used while troubleshooting a system—take, for example, a system with a defective sound card. To make sure the changes will be beneficial, the administrator can create a test profile by making a copy of the original, make all changes to the test profile, and evaluate the solution before implementing it for real. This type of safety net will allow the administrator to return the system to its original state simply by deleting the copy profile.

Hardware profiles can be created in the System icon of the Control Panel. Once a profile is created you must reboot and select the profile. All changes can be made using the Device Manager, regardless of which profile is current. Disabling a device will now offer a choice of which hardware profile will be affected. Disabling a device may be better than deleting it if you need to change your mind.

Users can circumvent these hardware profiles if they have access to the Control Panel's System icon, which contains the Device Manager and the Hardware Profile tab. To restrict users, consider using a local or network policy file and grant access only to administrators.

CHAPTER SUMMARY

In this chapter, you're concluding your review of the objectives associated with configuring and managing resource access. Your review has covered user environments, managing hard disks, and creating hardware profiles.

An administrator can control the user's environment and the systems configuration remotely through user and computer policies. A client system must have profiles enabled for user policies to be applied.

A policy editor is used to create policy files for remote administration or to modify the local Registry. After a policy is merged into the Registry either locally or remotely, it cannot be undone simply by deleting the policy file. A reverse entry must be created and merged.

Windows 98 offers several disk management tools, such as Backup, DriveSpace, and disk compression. DriveSpace 3.0, which ships with Windows 98, is not to be used with FAT32. FAT32 stores data in a very different format and stores the data very efficiently anyway.

DriveSpace 3.0 supports partitions up to 2GB. FAT32 supports clusters of 4KB up to 8GB partitions.

Finally, hardware profiles offer the flexibility to run multiple configurations on the same system.

CHAPTER 6

Integration and Interoperability

Windows 98 is very well-suited to integrate into a Microsoft and Novell network. Microsoft has provided built-in configuration tools to connect within a LAN or through a Dial-Up Network access a LAN or the Internet.

OBJECTIVES

This chapter helps you prepare for the exam by covering the following objectives:

Configure a Windows 98 computer as a client computer in a network that contains a Windows NT 4.0 domain.

▶ The Windows 98 modular architecture allows concurrent communications with several different networks using multiple protocols. A Windows 98 computer can have concurrent connections to a NetBEUI-based Windows NT network, an IPX/SPX NetWare network, and the TCP/IP-based Internet.

Configure a Windows 98 computer as a client computer in a NetWare network.

▶ Microsoft Windows 98 includes an IPX/SPX-compatible protocol that allows integration into existing NetWare LANs and interoperability with NetWare 2.x and 3.x networks, as well as NetWare 4.x networks with servers using bindery emulation or NDS.

continues

Configure a Windows 98 computer for remote access by using various methods in a Microsoft environment or a mixed Microsoft and NetWare environment. Methods include the following:

- **Dial-Up Networking**

- **Proxy Server**

▶ To access the Internet or a WAN across TCP/IP, Windows 98 offers a Dial-Up Networking client and server. To improve performance and security, Microsoft offers a proxy server to which Windows 98 can connect.

CONFIGURE A WINDOWS 98 COMPUTER AS A CLIENT COMPUTER IN A WINDOWS NT NETWORK

1. **Which of the following are valid NetBIOS names? Select two answers.**

   A. Computer One

   B. ComputerOne

   C. Computer 1

   D. Computer1

   E. Computer number 1

2. **You are the administrator of a Windows NT network. A user contacts you and requests help connecting to a printer located on the network. What steps would you use to guide the user? Select one answer.**

   A. Click Start, Run, and then type **//computer_name/printer_name**.

   B. Click Start, Settings, Printers, Add Printer, Network, and then type **//computer_name/share_name**.

   C. Click Start, Control Panel, Printers, Add Printer, Network, and then type **//computer_name/printer_name**.

   D. Click Start, Settings, Printers, Add Printer, Network, and then type **\\computer_name\share_name**.

   E. Click Start, Settings, Printers, Add PrinterNetwork, and then type **\\computer_name\printer_name**.

The following question is scenario-based. Please read all the requirements and proposed solution before answering.

3. **Scenario:**

   A small company is adding a Windows NT domain to the network.

   Required component:
   Log on to a Windows NT domain.

   Optional components:
   Connect to a network shared folder on one of the servers in the domain without having to log on again.

   Share a folder so that members of the domain can read the files it contains without having them use a different password.

   Proposed solution:
   Install and configure Client for Microsoft Networks to log on to Windows NT Domain. Install File and Printer Sharing for NetWare networks.

   A. The proposed solution satisfies the required component and all the optional components.

   B. The proposed solution satisfies the required component but only one of the optional components.

   C. The proposed solution satisfies the required component but none of the optional components.

D. The proposed solution satisfies one of the optional components but does not satisfy the required component.

E. The proposed solution satisfies none of the optional components and does not satisfy the required component.

4. **When installing TCP/IP, it is recommended that a default gateway be configured for the Windows 98 client. What steps must be taken to achieve this?**

   A. Click Start, Programs, Control Panel, Network.

   B. Select TCP/IP, Properties, Gateway tab.

   C. Click Start, Settings, Control Panel, Network.

   D. Select TCP/IP, Properties, IP Properties, Gateway tab.

   E. None of the above.

5. **Susan gets a call at the company help desk. A user finds that each time she logs in to the system, it takes forever to reconnect all the drives she used last time. She wants to know whether she can speed up the process during login.**

   A. She cannot. If the connections are present, Windows 98 must reconnect them each time.

   B. She can disconnect all the drives each time she logs out and then reconnect manually each time she needs them again.

   C. Use the Network Client properties and select Quick logon.

   D. Use the Logon icon in the Control Panel and select Quick Logon.

6. **A user installs a network adapter card on a computer running Windows 98. When he does this, Windows 98 automatically installs two protocols for this card. Which two protocols are installed by default when the first network adapter driver is installed?**

   A. AppleTalk

   B. NetBEUI

   C. TCP/IP

   D. IPX/SPX-compatible

   E. Fast Infrared

7. **Susan prepares for a presentation describing the Windows 98 network architecture. One of the bullet points is this: A _____ maps network names used by an application to a physical network device name. Choose the appropriate answer to fill in the blank.**

   A. Device driver

   B. Redirector

   C. Requestor

   D. Transport interface

   E. NDIS Collector

8. **Which three of the following are layers in the Windows 98 networking architecture?**

   A. Transport Programming Interface

   B. Internal File System Manager

   C. Device Driver Interface

   D. Network Providers

   E. Device Manager

9. **Windows 98's modular architecture includes the Installable File Service (IFS) Manager. The IFS Manager manages communication between three of the following. Choose the three best answers.**

    A. The miniport driver

    B. The various installable file systems

    C. The network provider

    D. The network redirectors and services

    E. The NetBIOS interface

10. **What command-line utility enables you to connect to a network shared folder using a drive letter? Select the best answer.**

    A. MAP

    B. NET

    C. Redirect

    D. Connect

    E. Network connect

11. **A user's Windows 98 machine is a member of a peer-to-peer workgroup. What security-level options are available?**

    A. Domain-level

    B. Share-level

    C. Group-level

    D. Workgroup-level

    E. Admin-level

12. **A Windows 98 system can be in a workgroup and a member of a domain at the same time. Is this true or false?**

    A. True

    B. False

The following two questions are based on the same scenario, required components, and optional components. Please read all the requirements and proposed solution before answering.

13. **Scenario:**

    A small network administrator is having a hard time with clients trying to browse the network using Network Neighborhood. All the clients are Windows 98 with the Client for Microsoft enabled.

    Required component:
    Browse the network using the Network Neighborhood.

    Optional components:
    You do not want to enable File and Printer Sharing.

    All Windows 98 systems should remain part of the same domain.

    Proposed solution:
    Set up all the clients to be a master browser by enabling Maintain master browse list in the Microsoft Client.

    A. The proposed solution satisfies the required component and all the optional components.

    B. The proposed solution satisfies the required component but only one of the optional components.

    C. The proposed solution satisfies the required component but none of the optional components.

    D. The proposed solution satisfies only one of the optional components and does not satisfy the required component.

    E. The proposed solution satisfies none of the optional components and does not satisfy the required component.

14. Scenario:

A small network administrator is having a hard time with clients trying to browse the network using Network Neighborhood. All the clients are Windows 98 with the Client for Microsoft enabled.

Required component:
Browse the network using the Network Neighborhood.

Optional components:
You do not want to enable File and Printer Sharing.

All Windows 98 systems should remain part of the same domain.

Proposed solution:
Set up all the clients to have the domain name as their workgroup name as well.

A. The proposed solution satisfies the required component and all the optional components.

B. The proposed solution satisfies the required component but only one of the optional components.

C. The proposed solution satisfies the required component but none of the optional components.

D. The proposed solution satisfies only one of the optional components and does not satisfy the required component.

E. The proposed solution satisfies none of the optional components and does not satisfy the required component.

15. What are the methods used by the Microsoft Client to connect to a network share? Select all that apply.

A. Map

B. UNC

C. Network Neighborhood

D. NET USE from the command prompt

E. Connect

ANSWER KEY

1. B-D	6. B-D	11. B
2. D	7. B	12. A
3. B	8. A-C-D	13. E
4. B-C	9. B-C-D	14. A
5. C	10. B	15. A-B-C-D

CONFIGURE A WINDOWS 98 COMPUTER AS A CLIENT COMPUTER IN A WINDOWS NT NETWORK

1. Which of the following are valid NetBIOS names?

B. ComputerOne

D. Computer1

1. CORRECT ANSWER: B-D

NetBIOS names are limited to 15 characters and cannot contain spaces. For more information, see "Microsoft Network Provider."

2. You are the administrator of a Windows NT network. A user contacts you and requests help connecting to a printer located on the network. What steps would you use to guide the user?

D. Click Start, Settings, Printers, Add Printer, Network, and then type \\computer_name\share_name.

2. CORRECT ANSWER: D

You can use the Add Printer Wizard and follow the prompts. You will need to know the print server name and the print queue. The wizard will offer a browse button to help. A UNC name for NetBIOS shares will use the \\ (backslash characters). For more information, see "Microsoft Network Provider."

3. Proposed solution:

Install and configure Client for Microsoft Networks to log on to Windows NT Domain. Install File and Printer Sharing for NetWare Networks.

B. The proposed solution satisfies the required component but only one of the optional components.

3. CORRECT ANSWER: B

You need to install File and Printer Sharing for Microsoft Networks and have user-level security in place in order to fulfill the other options. For more information, see "Microsoft Network Provider."

4. When installing TCP/IP, it is recommended that a default gateway be configured for the Windows 98 client. What steps must be taken to achieve this?

B. Select TCP/IP, Properties, Gateway tab.

C. Click Start, Settings, Control Panel, Network.

4. CORRECT ANSWER: B-C

You must add an IP address in the Gateway properties of the TCP/IP protocol. For more information, see "Microsoft Network Provider."

5. Susan gets a call at the company help desk. A user finds that each time she logs onto the system, it takes forever to reconnect all the drives she used last time. She wants to know how to speed up the process during login.

   C. Use the Network Client properties and select Quick Logon.

5. CORRECT ANSWER: C

With a quick logon, Windows 98 will only reconnect drives when they are requested. For more information, see "Microsoft Network Provider."

6. A user installs a network adapter card on a computer running Windows 98. When he does this, Windows 98 automatically installs two protocols for this card. Which two protocols are installed by default when the first network adapter driver is installed?

   B. NetBEUI

   D. IPX/SPX-compatible

6. CORRECT ANSWER: B-D

NetBEUI and IPX/SPX-compatible protocols are installed as defaults. For more information, see "Microsoft Network Provider."

7. Susan prepares for a presentation describing the Windows 98 network architecture. One of the bullet points is this: A _____ maps network names used by an application to a physical network device name. Choose the appropriate answer to fill in the blank.

   B. Redirector

7. CORRECT ANSWER: B

The redirector in Windows 98 architecture provides this capability for the Workstation service. For more information, see "Microsoft Network Provider."

8. Which three of the following are layers in the Windows 98 networking architecture?

   A. Transport Programming Interface

   C. Device Driver Interface

   D. Network Providers

8. CORRECT ANSWER: A-C-D

Windows 98 network architecture closely matches the seven layers of the OSI model. For more information, see "Microsoft Network Provider."

9. Windows 98's modular architecture includes the Installable File Service (IFS) Manager. The IFS Manager manages communication between three of the following. Choose the three best answers.

   B. The various installable file systems

   C. The network provider

   D. The network redirectors and services

The IFS Manager acts as a mediator between other various IFS, the network provider, and the network redirector and services. For more information, see "Microsoft Network Provider."

10. What command-line utility enables you to connect to a network shared folder using a drive letter? Select the best answer.

    B. NET

The NET command provides several command line capabilities. For a listing of NET commands, type **NET /?** at the command line. For more information, see "Microsoft Network Provider."

11. A user's Windows 98 machine is a member of a peer-to-peer workgroup. What security-level options are available?

    B. Share-level

User-level security is available only when a system is authenticated in a Windows NT domain or a NetWare environment. For more information, see "Microsoft Network Provider."

12. A windows 98 system can be in a workgroup and a member of a domain at the same time. Is this true or false?

    A. True

A Windows 98 system can be a member of one workgroup and log on to a different domain simultaneously. For more information, see "Microsoft Network Provider."

13. Proposed solution:

    Set up all the clients to be a master browser by enabling Maintain master browse list in the Microsoft Client.

    E. The proposed solution satisfies none of the optional components and does not satisfy the required component.

A Windows 98 system without File and Printer Sharing cannot maintain a browse list. All workgroups must have a master browser. The client component does not have any setting to maintain the master browse list. For more information, see "Microsoft Network Provider."

14. **Proposed solution:**

    Set up all the clients to have the domain name as their workgroup name as well.

    A. The proposed solution satisfies the required component and all of the optional components.

Windows 98 system without File and Printer Sharing cannot maintain a browse list. All workgroups must have a master browser. By having the domain name as the workgroup name, all Windows 98 systems will use the PDC as the master browser. For more information, see "Microsoft Network Provider."

15. **What are the methods used by the Microsoft Client to connect to a network share? Select all that apply.**

    A. Map

    B. UNC

    C. Network Neighborhood

    D. NET USE from the command prompt

Windows 98 can use all methods to connect to a network share. The map drive is probably the best solution for commonly used shares. For more information, see "Microsoft Network Provider."

Microsoft Network Provider

This explanation supports questions 1 through 15.

Windows 98 uses a modular network provider interface to allow multiple simultaneous networks. Each network provider interface uses the service provider interface to access the multiple provider router, where features common to all networks are located. The Windows 98 Client for Microsoft can be found in the Network icon of the Control Panel (see Figure 6.1).

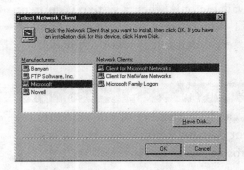

FIGURE 6.1
The Client for Microsoft Networks is one of many clients that can be installed simultaneously in Windows 98.

The network provider interface allows users to access shared disk resources using the particular network's native server name syntax. If you want to access a Microsoft Networks (SMB) compatible shared resource, the UNC format *computer_name**share_name* is recognized. In addition, Windows 98 can correctly interpret the NetWare server syntax *server_name*/*volume name:directory*. The Windows 98 user interface and NET command also support UNC names for connecting to NetWare resources.

If you're installing Windows 98 in a Windows NT environment, one of the first decisions to make is whether to join an existing domain or to establish or join a workgroup. Windows 98 offers the user the unique capability to be a member of a separate workgroup in the browse list yet still log on and be a member of a domain. It is important to remember that Windows 98, unlike a Windows NT machine, does not create a computer account in the Windows NT domain.

The two main administrative architecture types of Windows NT network are workgroups and domains.

Workgroups are used for small groups in which there is no centralized security or server. In a workgroup, each user is in full control of shared network resources on her workstation. The lack of centralized resources makes enforcement of security regulations very difficult (see Figure 6.2).

Domains are used in complex environments to centralize security and administration. A domain requires at least one central server running Windows NT Server that serves as the primary domain controller and manages the security database. The domain model allows relatively easy, centralized administration by a few specialists. Security regulations can be set from the central server to force users to operate within policy constraints (see Figure 6.3).

Microsoft's Universal Naming Convention (UNC) is a standardized nomenclature for specifying a share name on a particular computer. The NetBIOS computer name is limited to 15 characters, and the share name is usually limited to 12 characters in Windows 98. Share names can be given to a print queue or a shared directory of files.

The UNC uniquely specifies the path to the share name on a network. The UNC path takes the form of *computer_name*\ *share_name [\optional path]*. For example, the UNC path of the printer share LaserJet created on the server Server1 would be \\Server1\LaserJet.

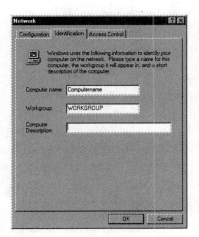

FIGURE 6.2
To configure the workgroup, select the Identification tab from the Network icon in the Control Panel.

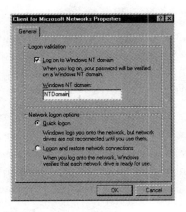

FIGURE 6.3
Log on to a domain and a preferred domain name is configured in the properties of the Client for Microsoft.

▼ NOTE

A UNC name does not require a drive-letter assignment. Windows 98 takes full advantage of network connectivity using UNC names so that you can connect to a remote directory or printer share without having to map a drive letter to it.

The UNC also can specify the full path to a file in a subdirectory of a file share. For example, a file named directions.txt located in the Sample folder on the computer named Simon is represented as \\Simon\Sample\directions.txt.

All Windows 98 functions support using a UNC name, including the Run option on the Start menu and the command prompt. NetWare servers, like Windows NT servers, can be accessed through a UNC name. Instead of a share name, however, substitute a volume name to access a NetWare server.

An alternate connection method is that the drive can be permanently mapped to a drive letter. A drive letter makes it easier for a user to access information since the network drive letter appears in the My Computer icon. When the system restarts, it can be set up to reconnect all drives at logon in a quick logon or to reconnect as needed. For faster logons, use the quick logon. This can be set from the properties of the Microsoft Client (refer to Figure 6.3).

The Windows 98 browsing service reduces network traffic by maintaining a central list of all active servers in a workgroup. This list is kept current by having all active servers send a status message to a single computer, the master browser, on a regular basis. The master browser server updates the list as servers join and leave the local network section.

In a Windows NT network, the Primary Domain Controller (PDC) serves as the Domain Master Browser, collecting browse lists from the local master browsers. This centralized collection of browse lists enables an enterprise-wide browsable network.

If no master browser is present for a workgroup, the first workstation that attempts to access a browse list sends out an election request to the remaining servers in the workgroup. This election request invokes a comparison of all the remaining servers to determine which is most suitable to be the new master browser.

To qualify as a browse master, the system must have File and Printer Sharing turned on. If the Browse Master parameter is set to Automatic (the default), the Windows 98 computer can participate as a master browser. If the Browse Master parameter is set to Enable, the workstation will attempt to become a master browser. This might be desirable for a little-used computer that is always left on. If the Browse Master parameter is set to Disable, the Windows 98 computer will never serve as master or backup browser. Remember that at least one computer in the workgroup must serve as master browser.

When both clients are installed on Windows 98, you must select one to be the primary logon. A primary logon will offer the username, password, and domain or server dialog box. At this time you would be able to change any information. The subsequent logon will assume the username and password type in the primary logon and will use the default domain or server name. If the username and password combination does not exist, a second logon dialog box will appear.

The primary logon also determines where the Windows 98 system will look for policies or profiles.

CONFIGURE A WINDOWS 98 COMPUTER AS A CLIENT COMPUTER IN A NETWARE NETWORK

1. You configure a Windows 98 workstation to connect to a NetWare network. When you install Client for NetWare Networks, which protocol is installed?

   A. TCP/IP

   B. NetBEUI

   C. IPX/SPX-compatible

   D. DLC

   E. Fast Infrared

2. Steve is connecting his Windows 98 computer to a network running Novell NetWare. He wants to share files and a printer with other users. What type of security must he use?

   A. NetWare-level

   B. Share-level

   C. User-level

   D. Group-level

   E. Admin-level

3. You want to install a Windows 98 client on a Novell NetWare network that includes NetWare 4.x servers. Which two of the following network components might you need?

   A. Microsoft Client for NetWare Networks

   B. Microsoft NDS service

   C. File and Printer Sharing for Microsoft Networks

   D. NetBEUI

   E. DLC

4. You are asked to connect 10 Windows 98 computers to a Novell NetWare network. From the following list, pick the two components or features that Windows 98 has for NetWare Networks.

   A. Capability to run File and Printer Sharing for NetWare with File and Printer Sharing with Microsoft Networks at the same time

   B. Share-level security support of File and Printer Sharing for NetWare Networks

   C. IPX/SPX-compatible protocol

   D. 32-bit Client for NetWare Networks

   E. None of the above

5. Susan has been told that she can run multiple network clients under Windows 98, but she is having problems getting this feature to work on her system. She calls you and asks for help. From the following list, what would be the best question to ask her to start diagnosing her problem? Select all that apply.

   A. Does she have protocols for IPX/SPX set up?

   B. Is Windows 98 set up to handle user profiles?

C. Is there a Primary Domain Controller (PDC) established on a Windows 98 Server?

D. Are all the network clients 32-bit clients?

E. Is Windows 98's Service Pack 1 installed?

6. **What is the full UNC path required to access the SYSCON utility located on the "Sales" NetWare server in a share named PUBLIC on a NetWare volume named SYS?**

   A. `\\PUBLIC\Syscon`

   B. `\\Sales\Syscon`

   C. `\\Sys\PUBLIC\Syscon`

   D. `//Sys/public/syscon`

   E. None of the above

7. **You are the administrator of a NetWare network environment. A user contacts you and requests help connecting her Windows 98 client to a printer located on the NetWare server. What steps would you use to guide the user?**

   A. From the Start menu, choose Run and then type **//server/printer_name**.

   B. From the Start menu, choose Settings, and then Printers. Then choose Add Printer, Network, and then type **//server/share_name**.

   C. From the Start menu, choose Control Panel, and click on the Printers icon. Choose Add Printer, Network, and then type **//server/printer_name**.

D. From the Start menu, choose Settings, Printers, Add Printer, Network, and then type **\\server\share_name**.

E. From the Start menu, choose Settings, Printers, Add Printer, Network, and then type **\\server\print_queue**.

8. **A user contacts you and states that he can log on to the Microsoft network, but his system is unable to access files from the NetWare server. You check his permissions and they are in order. What other option would you check? Select the best answer.**

   A. IPX/SPX-compatible protocol

   B. Client for Microsoft Networks

   C. Client for NetWare Networks

   D. File and Printer Sharing for NetWare Networks

   E. Novell network drivers

9. **You are connecting a Windows 98 client to a NetWare 4.x NDS tree. What settings have you configured for Microsoft NDS Service? Select all that apply.**

   A. Preferred Login

   B. Preferred Tree

   C. Preferred Logon

   D. Preferred Server

   E. Preferred Context

10. **You upgrade a Windows 98 client on a NetWare network. The user contacts you and says he can log in, but he cannot see drive M: as he did before. What configuration setting is missing?**

A. Client for NetWare Networks

B. Enable Login Script Processing

C. Preferred Server

D. Client for Microsoft Networks

E. Drive M: no longer exists. You must choose a new letter.

11. **Which files are necessary in order to connect a Windows 98 client to a NetWare network with Client for NetWare Networks? Select all that apply.**

A. LSL

B. IPXODI

C. VLM

D. MLID

E. IPX/SPX-compatible protocol

12. **Which two components can be installed at the same time?**

A. Client for Microsoft Networks

B. File and Printer Sharing for NetWare Networks

C. Client for NetWare Networks

D. File and Printer Sharing for Microsoft Networks

E. File and Printer Sharing for Windows 98

The following question is scenario-based. Please read all the requirements and proposed solution before answering.

13. **Scenario:**

The network administrator would like to connect a Windows 98 system in a Novell environment.

Required component:
Connect a Windows 98 system as a client on a NetWare network.

Optional components:
Provide automated drive mappings for shared resources.

Define Preferred Server and Default Context properties.

Proposed solution:
Install and configure Client for NetWare Networks to log onto an NDS tree. Install File and Printer Sharing for NetWare Networks. Install NetWare Directory Services (NDS) service. Enable Login Script Processing.

A. The proposed solution satisfies the required component and all the optional components.

B. The proposed solution satisfies the required component and only one of the optional components.

C. The proposed solution satisfies the required component and none of the optional components.

D. The proposed solution satisfies only one of the optional components and does not satisfy the required component.

E. The proposed solution satisfies none of the optional components and does not satisfy the required component.

14. **On top of Microsoft clients for NetWare, what other solutions are available? Select all that apply.**

A. Novell's Windows 98 File and Printer Sharing

B. Novell's Windows 98 NDIS drivers

C. Novell's Windows 32-bit client

D. Novell's Windows 16-bit client

E. Novell's Windows 8-bit client

15. **A Windows 98 system runs software that requires support for NetBIOS over IPX. Where can this be configured? Select the best answer.**

A. From the Network icon in the Control Panel

B. From the IPX properties

C. Installing NetBIOS in the Network icon of the Control Panel as a separate protocol

D. IPX does not support NetBIOS

E. From the NetBIOS properties

ANSWER KEY

1. C	6. E	11. E
2. C	7. D	12. A-C
3. A-B	8. C	13. A
4. C-D	9. B-D	14. C
5. D	10. B	15. B

CONFIGURE A WINDOWS 98 COMPUTER AS A CLIENT COMPUTER IN A NETWARE NETWORK

1. You configure a Windows 98 workstation to connect to a NetWare network. When you install Client for NetWare Networks, which protocol is installed?

   C. IPX/SPX-compatible

---

1. CORRECT ANSWER: C

IPX/SPX-compatible protocol is installed automatically when Client for NetWare Networks is installed. For more information, see "Novell NetWare Client."

---

2. Steve is connecting his Windows 98 computer to a network running Novell NetWare. He wants to share files and a printer with other users. What type of security must he use?

   C. User-level

---

2. CORRECT ANSWER: C

User-level access is required when connecting and sharing files and printers on a NetWare network. For more information, see "Novell NetWare Client."

---

3. You want to install a Windows 98 client on a Novell NetWare network that includes NetWare 4.x servers. Which two of the following network components might you need?

   A. Microsoft Client for NetWare Networks

   B. Microsoft NDS service

---

3. CORRECT ANSWER: A-B

Client for NetWare Networks is mandatory to connect to a NetWare 4.x server. If you want to connect to a 4.x server's NDS, Microsoft NDS service can be used. For more information, see "Novell NetWare Client."

---

4. You are asked to connect 10 Windows 98 computers to a Novell NetWare network. From the following list, choose the two components or features that Windows 98 has for NetWare Networks.

   C. IPX/SPX-compatible protocol

   D. 32-bit Client for NetWare Networks

---

4. CORRECT ANSWER: C-D

Client for NetWare Networks is necessary, along with the IPX/SPX-compatible protocol, for communication. For more information, see "Novell NetWare Client."

5. Susan has been told that she can run multiple network clients under Windows 98, but she is having problems getting this feature to work on her system. She asks you for help. From the following list, what would be the best question to ask her to start diagnosing her problem? Select all that apply.

D. Are all the network clients 32-bit clients?

5. CORRECT ANSWER: D

Using Novell's 16-bit network client can cause problems when combining multiple network clients. IPX is not needed if the Novell server and the Windows 98 client are using TCP/IP. For more information, see "Novell NetWare Client."

6. What is the full UNC path required to access the SYSCON utility located on the "Sales" NetWare server in a share named PUBLIC on a NetWare volume named SYS?

E. None of the above

6. CORRECT ANSWER: E

The correct UNC path to a NetWare volume follows the format `\\Server\Volume:\path`. In this case, it would be `\\sales\sys:\public\syscon`. For more information, see "Novell NetWare Client."

7. You are the administrator of a NetWare network environment. A user contacts you and requests help connecting her Windows 98 client to a printer located on the NetWare server. What steps would you use to guide the user?

D. From the Start menu, choose Settings, Printers, Add Printer, Network, and then type `\\server\share_name`.

7. CORRECT ANSWER: D

You can use the Add Printer wizard and reference the printer with the UNC path referencing the print queue. For more information, see "Novell NetWare Client."

8. A user contacts you and states that he can log on to the Microsoft network, but his system is unable to access files from the NetWare server. You check his permissions, and they are in order. What other option would you check? Select the best answer.

C. Client for NetWare Networks

8. CORRECT ANSWER: C

The term "logon" indicates that the user has been authenticated by a Windows NT domain. Check Client for NetWare Networks to verify a connection to a NetWare server. For more information, see "Novell NetWare Client."

9. You are connecting a Windows 98 client to a NetWare 4.x NDS tree. What settings have you configured for Microsoft NDS Service? Select all that apply.

B. Preferred Tree

9. CORRECT ANSWER: B-D

The Microsoft NDS service allows you to configure a preferred tree, preferred server, default context, and first network drive letter. For more information, see "Novell NetWare Client."

10. You upgrade a Windows 98 client on a NetWare network. The user contacts you and says he can log in, but he cannot see drive M: as he did before. What configuration setting is missing?

    B. Enable Login Script Processing

The user most likely had a login script on the NetWare server that mapped drive M:. Enabling Login Script Processing should correct the problem. For more information, see "Novell NetWare Client."

11. Which files are necessary in order to connect a Windows 98 client to a NetWare network with Client for NetWare Networks? Select all that apply.

    E. IPX/SPX-compatible protocol

Client for NetWare Networks installs the Microsoft 32-bit IPX/SPX-compatible protocol. The other options will install the real-mode 16-bit client. For more information, see "Novell NetWare Client."

12. Which two components can be installed at the same time?

    A. Client for Microsoft Networks

    C. Client for NetWare Networks

You can install both Client for Microsoft and NetWare Networks. Because File Sharing services cannot be installed at the same time as any other, you must select between File and Printer Sharing for NetWare Networks or File and Printer Sharing for Microsoft Networks. There is no such service as File and Printer Sharing for Windows 98. For more information, see "Novell NetWare Client."

13. Proposed solution:

Install and configure Client for NetWare Networks to log on to an NDS tree. Install File and Printer Sharing for NetWare Networks. Install NetWare Directory Services (NDS) service. Enable Login Script Processing.

    A. The proposed solution satisfies the required component and all the optional components.

Windows 98 will use a client for NetWare and NDS to connect to a Novell 4.x server. For more information, see "Novell NetWare Client."

14. On top of Microsoft clients for NetWare, what other solutions are available? Select all that apply.

    C. Novell's Windows 32-bit client

Novell has a separate 32-bit client for Windows 95/98 with full NDS support. For more information, see "Novell NetWare Client."

15. A Windows 98 systems runs software that requires support for NetBIOS over IPX. Where can this be configured? Select the best answer.

    B. From the IPX properties

---

15. CORRECT ANSWER: B

From the properties of the IPX protocol in the Network icon, a check box enables NetBIOS over IPX support for applications. For more information, see "Novell NetWare Client."

Novell NetWare Client

This explanation supports questions 1 through 15.

Microsoft Windows 98 includes an IPX/SPX-compatible protocol that allows integration into existing NetWare LANs. For interoperability with NetWare 2.x and 3.x networks, and NetWare 4.x networks with servers using bindery emulation or NDS, Windows 98 includes the following:

- The 32-bit Client for NetWare Networks, using the NWREDIR.VXD driver

- Support for older 16-bit NetWare clients

- A NetWare logon script processor

- The IPX/SPX-compatible protocol

- The IPX ODI protocol for compatibility with older NetWare Networks

- NetWare Directory Services (NDS) service

- File and Printer Sharing for NetWare Networks service

The File and Printer Sharing for NetWare Networks service allows Windows 98 to act as a peer-to-peer server on a NetWare network. This allows sharing of resources such as printers that may be attached to the Windows 98 computer.

Windows 98's capability to use multiple network providers allows Windows 98 workstations to be integrated into mixed NetWare and Windows NT networks.

To take advantage of the IPX/SPX-compatible protocol and allow connections to NetWare servers with binderies, your Windows 98 workstation can be configured with the Client for NetWare Networks (see Figure 6.4).

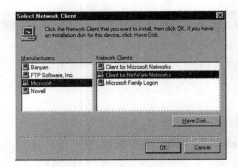

FIGURE 6.4
The Client for NetWare Networks provided by Microsoft.

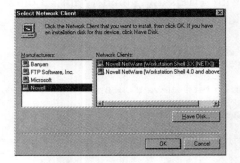

FIGURE 6.5
The Client for NetWare provided by Novell for 16-bit compatibility on the Windows 98 CD.

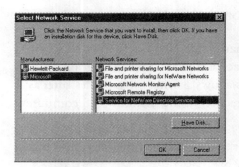

FIGURE 6.6
The NDS server services will help manage NDS servers.

Windows 98 also offers a choice of two NetWare clients provided by Novell. These are 16-bit compatible options. A last option for NetWare would be Novell 32-bit client that is provided by Novell itself and not listed in Windows 98 (see Figure 6.5).

Windows 98 supports a NetWare Directory Services (NDS) service to allow access to NetWare 4.x NDS "trees." Earlier versions of Windows could run the NDS service only if the version had been upgraded to at least Service Pack 1 (Windows 95).

The options on the Directory Services property sheet are described in the following list:

- **Preferred Tree**. This is the NDS tree where the user will want to access shared resources.

- **Workstation Default Context**. The default context where the user's NDS user object can be found.

▼ **NOTE**

This service can be configured on only Windows 98 workstations that *already* have the IPX/SPX-compatible protocol and the Client for NetWare Networks installed.

Microsoft with Windows 98 has included support for NDS management from the Windows 98 desktop. It is installed as a network service (see Figure 6.6).

File and Printer Sharing for NetWare Networks allows directories and printers to be shared with other NetWare users. Following are two very important points to keep in mind if you're considering using File and Printer Sharing for NetWare:

- You cannot simultaneously have File and Printer Sharing for NetWare Networks and File and Printer Sharing for Microsoft Networks installed. Only one can be configured on a particular Windows 98 workstation.

- File and Printer Sharing for NetWare Networks must use the user-level security model. The account list must be on a NetWare server bindery or in the bindery context of a NetWare 4.x server using bindery emulation.

User-level security with NetWare Networks is similar to user-level security for Microsoft networks. A server is queried anytime a shared resource access is attempted. The username or group membership must be on the NetWare server's account list and must have the necessary rights to gain access to the resource.

Windows 98 doesn't normally make a distinction between Microsoft shares and Novell volumes: Both appear as directories, also called folders, on the network to a Windows 98 computer.

You can use the NET command from a command prompt to control connections to either type of network resource, using either Microsoft networking UNC paths or NetWare *server/ volume* paths. This could be useful in the creation of batch files or login scripts. At the command prompt, type **Net /?** for a listing of net commands.

The IPX/SPX-compatible protocol is installed automatically when the Client for NetWare Networks is installed. You can also install this protocol to support different network clients, including the built-in Client for Microsoft Networks.

NetBIOS over IPX is also included with Windows 98 and can be enabled by selecting the I Want to Enable NetBIOS over IPX/SPX check box in the IPX/SPX-compatible properties sheet. After you enable that option, name resolution can be obtained over an IPX network.

The IPX/SPX-compatible protocol usually is self-configuring. By default, when a Windows 98 computer with IPX/SPX-compatible protocol is started, it determines by responses from routers which frame type is most prevalent on the local network. Network addresses are also determined automatically.

In a mixed Windows NT and NetWare network, client to transport protocol bindings may need to be changed. This can improve your networking performance and can eliminate problems with older 16-bit network applications that may require a certain client-protocol configuration.

PRACTICE QUESTIONS

CONFIGURE A WINDOWS 98 COMPUTER TO ACCESS THE INTERNET BY USING VARIOUS METHODS IN A MICROSOFT ENVIRONMENT AND A MIXED MICROSOFT AND NETWARE ENVIRONMENT

1. With Windows 98, what methods can you use to resolve Fully Qualified Domain Names?

   A. DNS

   B. LMHOSTS file

   C. HOSTS file

   D. WINS

   E. Name cache

2. While setting up Windows 98 to access the Internet, you find that connections over TCP/IP by host don't work but connections by IP number do. What could be wrong?

   A. No WINS server is available.

   B. IPX/SPX-compatible protocol is not installed.

   C. No DNS server is available.

   D. No TCP/IP server is available.

   E. No entry in the name cache.

3. You're installing TCP/IP to configure a subnet mask for the Windows 98 client. What steps must you take to achieve this?

   A. Click Start, Programs, Control Panel, Network.

   B. Select TCP/IP, Properties, IP Address.

   C. Click Start, Settings, Control Panel, Network.

   D. Select TCP/IP, Programs, IP Properties.

   E. None of the above.

   The following question is scenario-based. Please read all the requirements and proposed solution before answering.

4. **Scenario:**

   As a member of the corporate MIS team, it is your responsibility to fulfill the needs of the Help Desk department. The Help Desk department has requested access to resources available on the Internet. Your company currently has Internet access, but only the Sales department is properly configured.

   Required component:
   Provide the Help Desk department with access to the Internet.

   Optional components:
   Download support files from the Internet.

   Order books from www.mcp.com using Internet Explorer.

Proposed solution:
Install and configure TCP/IP protocol with a static IP address and subnet mask. Install Client for Microsoft Networks. Configure an external DNS server to resolve IP addresses.

A. The proposed solution satisfies the required component and all the optional components.

B. The proposed solution satisfies the required component and only one of the optional components.

C. The proposed solution satisfies the required component and none of the optional components.

D. The proposed solution satisfies only one of the optional components and does not satisfy the required component.

E. The proposed solution satisfies none of the optional components and does not satisfy the required component.

5. You have Windows 98 installed on a computer connected to an intranet. You receive a message stating an IP address conflict has occurred. What could be causing this error?

A. Two DHCP servers with overlapping scopes

B. Internet Explorer

C. A static IP configured incorrectly

D. A cached IP address from a different subnet

E. A WINS server's database is corrupted

6. You have just loaded Personal Web Server on your Windows 98 client and created a Web site. You tell a colleague to connect to your FQDN of www.company.com. You also tell him your IP address is 131.107.2.200. He cannot connect to your computer. What file can be modified quickly to enable such a connection?

A. User.dat

B. HOSTS

C. LMHOSTS

D. System.dat

E. Name cache

7. To access the Internet, you need to use Windows 98 Dial-Up Adapter and associated software. Choose two items from the following list that you must have in order to set up Windows 98 to access the Internet via Dial-Up Networking.

A. ISP account

B. Modem

C. Network card

D. DNS name

E. WINS server address

8. You want to configure a Dial-Up connection to a server that allows simultaneous applications to be run using multiple network protocols. Assuming that the server is capable, what line protocol do you have to use to connect?

A. SLIP

B. NRN

C. PPP

D. RAS (Asynchronous NetBEUI)

E. FTP

9. **Which of the following password authentication protocols protect against a playback-type attack and are supported by DUN?**

A. PAP

B. CHAP

C. MS CHAP

D. DUN terminal pop-up windows

E. MS APPS

10. **Jenny wants to gain access to the Internet, but her company does not have Internet connectivity. Using Windows 98, how can she connect to the Internet with her phone line?**

A. Install File and Printer Sharing for Microsoft Networks.

B. Install Dial-Up Networking.

C. Configure her Web browser to access a proxy server.

D. Install a modem.

E. None of the above.

11. **You are working the help desk at your company. A user calls and tells you he has set up Dial-Up Networking. What protocols are available to the user?**

A. TCP/IP

B. NetBEUI

C. IPX/SPX-compatible

D. AppleTalk

E. DLC

The following question is scenario-based. Please read all the requirements and proposed solution before answering.

12. **Scenario:**

Your company CEO has just received his new laptop computer. He is enjoying his newfound mobility, but he has one request. He would like to get to the same files he has access to while he is at his desk in the office.

Required component:
Give your CEO access to the company network from home.

Optional components:
Access a shared printer and print a document.

Copy a file from the user's directory on the server to his home computer.

Proposed solution:
Install and configure Dial-Up Networking to call and log in to the company RAS server. Install File and Printer Sharing for Microsoft Networks. Select user-level access control.

A. The proposed solution satisfies the required component and all the optional components.

B. The proposed solution satisfies the required component and only one of the optional components.

C. The proposed solution satisfies the required component and none of the optional components.

D. The proposed solution satisfies only one of the optional components and does not satisfy the required component.

E. The proposed solution satisfies none of the optional components and does not satisfy the required component.

13. **You are the administrator of a NetWare network with Windows 98 clients. Sara, from accounting, calls and needs help installing Dial-Up Networking. She has already installed a modem. How would you walk her through? Select all that apply.**

A. Click Start, Programs, Accessories, and then Dial-Up Networking.

B. Double-click Network Neighborhood and click Dial-Up Networking.

C. Use the Dial-Up Connection Wizard.

D. Use the Make New Connection Wizard.

E. Use the Modem Wizard.

14. **What is the name of the Microsoft solution to access the Internet from a secured network?**

A. Internet Explorer

B. Proxy client

C. Proxy server

D. Internet server

E. None of the above

15. **What are the two implementations of the proxy client?**

A. Proxy server configuration

B. Proxy client

C. Internet Explorer's configuration to use proxy server

D. Internet Explorer's configuration to use proxy client

E. Microsoft RAS configuration to use proxy server during dial-up

16. **What is required of TCP/IP from a client that connects to a proxy server on their local subnet? Select all that apply.**

A. An IP address

B. A subnet mask entry

C. A default gateway entry

D. A DNS server entry

E. A WINS server entry

17. **What type of Internet traffic can MS Proxy Server restrict? Select the best answer.**

A. Inbound

B. Outbound

C. Both

D. None

18. **When an administrator changes the IP address or server name of the proxy server, what must the client do to continue to have access to the Internet? Select all that apply.**

A. Do nothing since the proxy client will update automatically.

B. Change the name of the proxy client in the Control Panel.

C. Change the name of the proxy server in the Proxy Client icon of the Control Panel.

D. Change the name of the proxy server in the configuration of the Web browser.

E. Change the location of the proxy server to be remote.

The following question is scenario-based. Please read all the requirements and proposed solution before answering.

19. **Scenario:**

Sara would like to connect her office to the Internet. She has heard stories about companies being attacked over the Internet and is very cautious.

Required component:
Allow all users to have access to the Internet from their desktops.

Optional components:
Restrict unauthorized access from the Internet.

Allow each client to use any TCP/IP application without any additional configuration on her part.

Proposed solution:
Set up a proxy server in the office. Configure the proxy server for outbound connection only. From the client system, configure the Web browsers to use the proxy server with the appropriate IP address and port number.

A. The proposed solution satisfies the required component and all the optional components.

B. The proposed solution satisfies the required component and only one of the optional components.

C. The proposed solution satisfies the required component and none of the optional components.

D. The proposed solution satisfies only one of the optional components and does not satisfy the required component.

E. The proposed solution satisfies none of the optional components and does not satisfy the required component.

The following question is scenario-based. Please read all the requirements and proposed solution before answering.

20. **Scenario:**

Sara is still concerned about potential attacks and needs an additional security feature put in place.

Required component:
Eliminate the potential for client computers from being accessed by outside systems.

Optional components:
Still be able to connect to the Internet for Web browsing.

Maintain the use of Microsoft's proxy server. No additional software can be purchased at this time.

Proposed solution:
Install the proxy client for Microsoft's Proxy Server on each client and configure the client to use IPX instead of TCP/IP. Install IPX protocol on the client and remove TCP/IP. Make sure the proxy server is also running IPX.

A. The proposed solution satisfies the required component and all the optional components.

B. The proposed solution satisfies the required component and only one of the optional components.

C. The proposed solution satisfies the
required component and none of the
optional components.

D. The proposed solution satisfies only one
of the optional components and does
not satisfy the required component.

E. The proposed solution satisfies none
of the optional components and does
not satisfy the required component.

ANSWER KEY

1. A-C	6. B	11. A-B-C	16. A-B
2. C	7. A-B	12. A	17. C
3. B-C	8. C	13. A-C	18. C-D
4. E	9. B-C	14. C	19. B
5. A-C	10. B-D	15. B-C	20. A

ANSWERS & EXPLANATIONS

CONFIGURE A WINDOWS 98 COMPUTER TO ACCESS THE INTERNET BY USING VARIOUS METHODS IN A MICROSOFT ENVIRONMENT AND A MIXED MICROSOFT AND NETWARE ENVIRONMENT

1. With Windows 98, what methods can you use to resolve Fully Qualified Domain Names?

   A. DNS

   C. HOSTS file

1. CORRECT ANSWER: A-C

The HOSTS file, located in the Windows 98 directory, resolves host names to IP addresses. A Domain Name Server (DNS) located on a Windows NT server also resolves host names when they are registered in the database. For more information, see "TCP/IP."

2. While setting up Windows 98 to access the Internet, you find that connections over TCP/IP by host don't work but connections by IP number do. What could be wrong?

   C. No DNS server is available.

2. CORRECT ANSWER: C

Although you have Internet connectivity, there is no Domain Name Server (DNS) available to resolve the host name with an IP address. For more information, see "TCP/IP."

3. You're installing TCP/IP to configure a subnet mask for the Windows 98 client. What steps must you take to achieve this?

   B. Select TCP/IP, Properties, IP Address.

   C. Click Start, Settings, Control Panel, Network.

3. CORRECT ANSWER: B-C

You must modify the Subnet Mask entry on the IP Address tab of the TCP/IP properties sheet in order to specify and complete an IP address. For more information, see "TCP/IP."

4. Proposed solution:

   Install and configure TCP/IP protocol with a static IP address and subnet mask. Install Client for Microsoft Networks. Configure an external DNS server to resolve IP addresses.

   E. The proposed solution satisfies none of the optional components and does not satisfy the required component.

4. CORRECT ANSWER: E

The system will not be able to reach the DNS or any other external system without a default gateway address. For more information, see "TCP/IP."

5. You have Windows 98 installed on a computer connected to an intranet. You receive a message stating an IP address conflict has occurred. What could be causing this error?

  A. Two DHCP servers with overlapping scopes

  C. A static IP configured incorrectly

6. You have just loaded Personal Web Server on your Windows 98 client and created a Web site. You tell a colleague to connect to your FQDN of www.company.com. You also tell him your IP address is 131.107.2.200. He cannot connect to your computer. What file can be modified quickly to enable such a connection?

  B. HOSTS

---

5. CORRECT ANSWER: A-C

It is possible that two DHCP servers have overlapping scopes and the same IP address has been handed out to two systems or possibly a system has been manually configured with the same address. For more information, see "TCP/IP."

6. CORRECT ANSWER: B

The HOSTS file can be modified to resolve the FQDN to an IP address. Your friend must type **131.107.2.200**, press the Tab key, and then type **www.company.com**. For more information, see "TCP/IP."

TCP/IP

This explanation supports questions 1 through 6.

Windows 98 comes with the Microsoft 32-bit TCP/IP protocol, related utilities, and an SNMP client. TCP/IP gives Windows 98 an industry standard routable enterprise-level networking protocol. TCP/IP is the transport protocol of the Internet, and with the included TCP/IP utilities, Windows 98 can access its rapidly growing resources.

After you install TCP/IP, the TCP/IP properties sheet appears. It offers the following tabs of options:

- IP Address
- Gateway
- DNS Configuration
- WINS Configuration
- Advanced
- Bindings

The IP Address tab of the TCP/IP properties sheet contains the following two radio buttons from which to choose:

- Obtain an IP Address Automatically
- Specify an IP Address

Dynamic Host Control Protocol (DHCP) allows automatic IP address assignments. When Windows 98 is configured as a DHCP client and then restarted, it broadcasts a message looking for a DHCP server. The DHCP server provides the client with an IP address to use for a predetermined length of time.

A DHCP server can be configured to pass all the necessary IP address information to a DHCP client. This includes the IP address leased to the client, as well as the IP addresses of the default gateway, subnet mask, DNS servers, and WINS servers.

Along with the IP address, a subnet mask is required for every TCP/IP device. A subnet mask is used to determine whether a destination address is located on the local subnet or on a remote network. Subnet masks can be configured manually, along with the IP address, by network administrators. A DHCP server can also assign a subnet mask automatically.

When you have an IP address and subnet mask, your Windows 98 computer is ready to talk to other workstations on the local network, but it still has no way to reach a wide area network or the Internet. A default gateway provides that connectivity to the rest of the networked world.

Name resolution is the process of turning a host or computer name into an IP address. You can configure Windows 98 to attempt name resolution using any of the following methods:

- Domain Name Service (DNS)
- Windows Internet Name Service (WINS)
- LMHOSTS file
- HOSTS file
- Broadcasts

DNS provides a static, centrally administrated database for resolving domain names to IP addresses. A fully qualified DNS name consists of a host name appended to an Internet or intranet domain name. Keep in mind that this is different from a Windows NT domain name. For example, the host www could be appended to microsoft.com to give the fully qualified domain name www.microsoft.com.

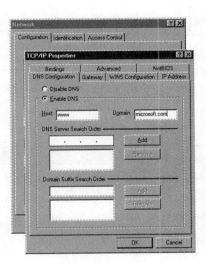

FIGURE 6.7
Enabling DNS through the TCP/IP properties sheet.

You configure Windows 98 to use DNS by using the options on the DNS Configuration tab of the TCP/IP properties sheet (see Figure 6.7).

The Enable DNS fields on the DNS Configuration tab allows Windows 98 to take advantage of several DNS services. Configure the following options:

- Host is the local computer's registered DNS name.

- Domain is the organization's InterNIC registered domain name.

- DNS Server Search Order allows backup DNS servers to be configured in case the primary fails.

- Domain Suffix Search Order tells TCP/IP utilities what domains to append and search if only a host name is given to the utility.

If DNS is unavailable, the HOSTS file provides local and remote static lists that allow name resolution. The HOSTS file is a text file that contains the IP address and host name for the system you need to reach. The filename cannot have any extensions.

7. To access the Internet, you need to use Windows 98 Dial-Up Adapter and associated software. Choose two items from the following list that you must have in order to set up Windows 98 to access the Internet via Dial-Up Networking.

   A. ISP account

   B. Modem

7. CORRECT ANSWER: A-B

You must have an ISP account and a modem. For more information, see "Setting Up Dial-Up Networking."

8. You want to configure a Dial-Up connection to a server that allows simultaneous applications to be run using multiple network protocols. Assuming that the server is capable, what line protocol do you have to use to connect?

   C. PPP

8. CORRECT ANSWER: C

Point-to-Point Protocol (PPP) allows you to run simultaneous applications on multiple protocols through your Dial-Up connection. For more information, see "Setting Up Dial-Up Networking."

9. Which of the following password authentication protocols protect against a playback-type attack and are supported by DUN?

   B. CHAP

   C. MS CHAP

9. CORRECT ANSWER: B-C

Challenge-Handshake Authentication Protocol (CHAP) and MS CHAP provide protection against playback attack because the challenge value changes in every message. For more information, see "Setting Up Dial-Up Networking."

10. Jenny wants to gain access to the Internet, but her company does not have Internet connectivity. Using Windows 98, how can she connect to the Internet with her phone line?

   B. Install Dial-Up Networking.

   D. Install a modem.

10. CORRECT ANSWER: B-D

Along with having an Internet account, she must install a modem and Dial-Up Networking. For more information, see "Setting Up Dial-Up Networking."

11. You are working the help desk at your company. A user calls and tells you he has set up Dial-Up Networking. What protocols are available to the user?

   A. TCP/IP

   B. NetBEUI

   C. IPX/SPX-compatible

11. CORRECT ANSWER: A-B-C

TCP/IP, NetBEUI, and IPX/SPX-compatible protocols are available to use with Dial-Up Networking. For more information, see "Setting Up Dial-Up Networking."

12. Proposed solution:

   Install and configure Dial-Up Networking to call and log in to the company RAS server. Install File and Printer Sharing for Microsoft Networks. Select user-level access control.

   A. The proposed solution satisfies the required component and all the optional components.

12. CORRECT ANSWER: A

File and Printer Sharing with user-level access will not affect how the CEO can access the office network from home. As long as the CEO used DUN to access the office network and has all the protocols that are used at the office, he or she will be able to access shared printers and folders. For more information, see "Setting Up Dial-Up Networking."

13. You are the administrator of a NetWare network with Windows 98 clients. Sara, from accounting, calls and needs help installing Dial-Up Networking. She has already installed a modem. How would you walk her through? Select all that apply.

   A. Click Start, Programs, Accessories, and then Dial-Up Networking.

   C. Use the Dial-Up Connection Wizard.

13. CORRECT ANSWER: A-C

You can get started by method A. After you activate Dial-Up Networking (assuming no previous connection exists), the Make New Connection Wizard appears. For more information, see "Setting Up Dial-Up Networking."

Setting Up Dial-Up Networking

This explanation supports 7 through 13.

Windows 98 includes the Dial-Up Adapter, which you can set up to connect to not only an Internet service provider (ISP), but also a Windows NT server configured as a Remote Access Server (RAS). After the adapter is installed, Windows 98 will automatically bind any previously installed protocols to your new adapter. You might want to confirm the installation of the TCP/IP protocol, dial into your ISP (using the Dial-Up Networking (DUN) feature), and communicate over the Internet.

To access the Internet using Dial-up Networking, a system requires a modem, the Dial-Up Networking software, and an ISP.

Dial-Up Networking supports many configuration options and can be a client for several different dial-up servers. This flexibility allows Windows 98 to connect into most dial-up environments.

Windows 98 can be a client for a Windows NT RAS server, can use the Serial Line Internet Protocol (SLIP) or PPP line protocol, and can function with Novell NetWare Connect. Windows 98 can authenticate passwords using Password Authentication Protocol (PAP), Shiva Password Authentication Protocol (SPAP), and Microsoft's version of Challenge Handshake Authentication Protocol (CHAP). It also provides a terminal dial-up window and scripting capabilities if none of the standard password authentication schemes are being used. DUN can use the following three network protocols:

- NetBEUI
- IPX/SPX-compatible
- TCP/IP

▼ **NOTE**

NetBEUI, IPX/SPX-compatible, and TCP/IP are supported by DUN only in their 32-bit implementations (as provided with Windows 98). Therefore, you cannot use DUN with a real-mode IPX protocol, such as that provided by Novell and installed through a batch file.

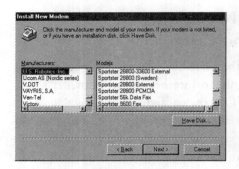

FIGURE 6.8
The modem must be installed and configured before DUN.

FIGURE 6.9
Dial-Up Networking ships as part of Windows 98.

FIGURE 6.10
Dial-Up Networking first selects the modem and offers a name to identify ISP information.

Installing the modem should be done first. Using the Modem icon in the Control Panel, you can install the modem that will be used by DUN (see Figure 6.8).

The Dial-Up Networking software can be found in the Control Panel in Windows 98 Setup, Communications under Add/Remove Programs (see Figure 6.9).

The final step is to configure Dial-Up Networking to use a modem and connect to an ISP (see Figures 6.10 and 6.11).

After the entry to the IPS is configured, it can be accessed from the Dial-Up Networking icon in My Computer. A valid user name and password must also be supplied for the connection to be successful (see Figure 6.12).

Password Authentication Schemes

PPP supports several password authentication schemes, which are used by different servers and have different features. The DUN connection automatically negotiates which of the following authentication protocol schemes to use.

- *Password Authentication Protocol (PAP)* uses a two-way handshake to establish identity. This handshake occurs only when the link is originally established. Passwords are sent over the media in text format, which offers no protection from playback attacks.

- *Challenge-Handshake Authentication Protocol (CHAP)* periodically verifies the identity of the peer by using a three-way handshake. CHAP provides protection from playback attack, and the password is never sent over the media, which also prevents illicit snooping. Windows 98 and Windows NT don't support ongoing challenges with CHAP, but they do implement Microsoft's version of CHAP, called MS CHAP.

- *Shiva Password Authentication Protocol (SPAP)* offers encryption of PAP passwords and Novell NetWare bindery access for user account information.

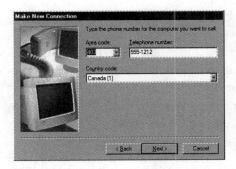

FIGURE 6.11
The ISP phone number information must be entered and will be stored for all future connections.

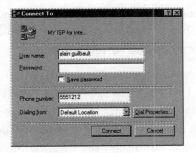

FIGURE 6.12
A username and password is entered to connect to the ISP.

Choosing Line Protocols

Line protocols provide the means by which network protocols are transported over communication media for which they were not originally intended. The line protocol provides a "wrapping" for the network protocol packet, which allows it to be transmitted over the unfamiliar media. When the line protocol packet reaches the dial-up server, the packet is "unwrapped," and the normal network protocol packet is sent on to the network.

The most common line protocol—and the default protocol that Windows 98 installs—is PPP. PPP was originally designed for the TCP/IP environment, but it is capable of transporting all three network protocols DUN supports and connecting to a wide variety of dial-up servers. PPP supports the following features:

- Multiplexing of sessions across a single serial link, allowing multiple network applications to appear to communicate simultaneously.

- Transportation of multiple network protocols simultaneously over a single link.

- Software compression to increase throughput.

- Automatic negotiation of addressing, which allows DHCP to assign a dynamic IP address to Windows 98.

- Error detection.

SLIP, an older line protocol, is not installed by default with Windows 98. Rather, it must be installed separately from the Windows 98 CD. Unfortunately, SLIP has the following limitations:

- Does not support dynamic IP addressing

- Does not support multiple protocols

- Provides no error detection or correction

- Lacks data compression support (although you can compress the IP header information)

Configuring Network Protocols Through DUN

Three networks are protocols supported by Windows 98 DUN: NetBEUI, IPX/SPX-compatible, and TCP/IP. These three protocols are configured through the Server Types properties sheet. To enable or disable NetBEUI and IPX/SPX-compatible, you simply select the appropriate check boxes. In order to increase the speed of your connection, having only the necessary protocols enabled is a good idea.

For TCP/IP, however, you must also configure the IP address the ISP assigns, DNS information, and WINS information, in the TCP/IP Settings properties sheet. This allows you to have multiple sets of IP address information—one for each DUN connection icon you create. There are also two other check boxes on the TCP/IP Settings properties sheet. One allows higher throughput by enabling IP header compression, and the other uses the default gateway on the remote network.

The Microsoft Dial-Up Networking client supports Point-to-Point Tunneling Protocol (PPTP). PPTP allows the Windows 98 user to establish a Virtual Private Network (VPN) over the Internet. Your VPN connection allows PPTP to encapsulate its data stream in the PPP protocol and send the information over the public Internet. PPTP can encrypt the data, preventing others from easily accessing your sensitive information.

14. What is the name of Microsoft solution to access the Internet from a secured network?

   C. Proxy server

14. CORRECT ANSWER: C

The proxy server can restrict inbound and outbound communication on a secured network. For more information, see "Getting to the Internet through Proxy Server."

15. What are the two implementations of the proxy client?

   B. Proxy client

   C. Internet Explorer's configuration to use proxy server

15. CORRECT ANSWER: B-C

The proxy client can be installed and used to intercept all Winsock requests or the Internet Explorer can be configured to use the proxy server. For more information, see "Getting to the Internet through Proxy Server."

16. **What is required of TCP/IP from a client that connects to a proxy server on their local subnet? Select all that apply.**

    A. An IP address

    B. A subnet mask entry

An IP address and subnet mask is all that is required to connect to a local proxy server. The server will need a default gateway and a DNS entry to connect to the Internet on behalf of the client. For more information, see "Getting to the Internet through Proxy Server."

17. **What type of Internet traffic can MS Proxy Server restrict? Select the best answer.**

    C. Both

The proxy client can be configured to use a different port and thus restrict inbound and outbound traffic. Proxy servers can also filter inbound requests. For more information, see "Getting to the Internet through Proxy Server."

18. **When an administrator changes the IP address or server name of the proxy server, what must the client do to continue to have access to the Internet? Select all that apply.**

    C. Change the name of the proxy server in the Proxy Client icon in the Control Panel.

    D. Change the name of the proxy server in the configuration of the Web browser.

The proxy client contains the proxy server name or IP address. When a change occurs, the client needs to be updated. If the Web browser has been configured separately, it must also be updated manually. For more information, see "Getting to the Internet through Proxy Server."

19. **Proposed solution:**

    Set up a proxy server in the office. Configure the proxy server for outbound connection only. From the client system, configure the Web browsers to use the proxy server with the appropriate IP address and port number.

    B. The proposed solution satisfies the required component and only one of the optional components.

The proxy server will allow Internet access for Web browsing. Each additional application will need to be configured as well because the proxy client was not installed. For more information, see "Getting to the Internet through Proxy Server."

20. Proposed solution:

Install the proxy client for Microsoft's Proxy Server on each client and configure the client to use IPX instead of TCP/IP. Install IPX protocol on the client and remove TCP/IP. Make sure the proxy server is also running IPX.

A. The proposed solution satisfies the required component and all the optional components.

Now with the proxy client in place, all Internet requests can be transferred to the proxy server. As long as the proxy server and clients are both running IPX, the clients can be configured to use IPX only. For more information, see "Getting to the Internet through Proxy Server."

Getting to the Internet through Proxy Server

This explanation supports questions 14 through 20.

Accessing the Internet from any network will usually involve the use of a proxy server. A proxy server will accept requests from clients and perform the tasks of getting the information from the Internet on their behalf.

Proxy servers can be configured to improve performance by caching web page information on a local hard drive and handing out such information to clients without the delays normally associated with the Internet.

And finally a proxy server can be used to protect local networks by filtering out any request from systems that have not been authorized. Each client connecting out is not usually restricted. The incoming requests are more susceptible to attacks and therefore can be restricted. Microsoft Proxy Server can enable filters based on IP addresses or domain names. Furthermore, logs can be activated to monitor activity and track down culprits.

The advantage of using a proxy client is that client systems do not need to be configured for full Internet access. All they need is to be able to connect to the proxy server. In a small network, the proxy server may be a local system and a default gateway, and DNS servers are not required for the clients.

There are two implementations of proxy server on the client. The first is to install a proxy client that will capture all Winsock requests and pass them along to the proxy server. This installation is simple and does not need to be repeated for each Internet application that might be installed on a system. The proxy client, once installed, will have an icon in the Control Panel that can be used to change the proxy servers to which the client is connected (see Figure 6.13).

FIGURE 6.13

The proxy client, once installed, has an icon in the Control Panel for configuration.

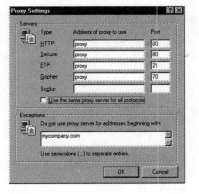

FIGURE 6.14

Applications can be configured separately to use a proxy server without the need for a proxy client.

The second implementation does not require the proxy client to be installed; the application that will need access to the Internet is configured to use a proxy server. This method must be repeated if more than one application needs access and may not even be available on some applications. Using Microsoft's Internet Explorer with a proxy server will require the proxy server name or IP address to be placed in the configuration settings. The Internet Explorer will be able to use the proxy server to gain access to the Internet (see Figure 6.14).

Each implementation of proxy server will be slightly different. The proxy server may implement security features like port assignment. Each Winsock application connects using a Port number. When all default port numbers are used, there is no extra security in place. An administrator can change the port number on the proxy server and force all clients to do the same if they wish to connect. This extra security will prevent unauthorized clients from gaining access to the Internet. Each service that the proxy server provides uses its own port, and they can be controlled separately.

Proxy client can also set up to allow the client to use the IPX/SPX protocol instead of TCP/IP. From the proxy client icon in the Control Panel, you need to use the force IPX. This will remove the need to have TCP/IP at all on the clients, thus reducing exposure to the Internet.

CHAPTER SUMMARY

Windows 98 supports Novell 3.x and 4.x servers. With NDS components, preferred trees and context can also be configured. Windows 98 provide the IPX/SPX protocol for Novell compatibility.

Windows 98 systems can have multiple clients installed simultaneously using multiple network protocols. The Microsoft Client will be used to log on to a domain.

All systems that will be connected to the Internet will require the TCP/IP protocol to be installed. TCP/IP uses a unique IP address and a subnet mask to locate other systems on the network. A DNS server or HOSTS file can be used to resolve host names to IP addresses, making Internet access easier for the user.

Internet access can be done through a Dial-Up client or a proxy server. The dial-up requires a modem while the proxy is mostly across a network.

CHAPTER 7

Monitoring and Optimization

Monitoring a computer system, which can prevent errors from occurring, is an important part of administration. This chapter presents questions about the tools that will help you monitor, optimize, and troubleshoot problems in a Windows 98 environment. Some of these tools, such as the Disk Defragmenter, ScanDisk, Updating drivers and services packs, should be run on a regular basis (that is, weekly for a heavily used computer) to provide a proactive approach to problems. The Maintenance Wizard can help with scheduling regular maintenance activities. Other tools, such as the Net Watcher and the System Monitor, will be used when you make changes to your environment, or when you suspect trouble.

OBJECTIVES

This chapter will help you prepare for the exam by covering the following objectives:

Monitor system performance by using Net Watcher, System Monitor, and Resource Meter.

▶ The Net Watcher will monitor network connection to your Windows 98 system and display the resources being used. The System Monitor will offer information on the system's current performance and reveal possible bottlenecks.

Tune and optimize the system in a Microsoft environment and a mixed Microsoft and NetWare environment, including the following tasks:

- **Optimizing the hard disk by using Disk Defragmenter and ScanDisk**

- **Compressing data by using DriveSpace3 and the Compression Agent**

- **Updating drivers and applying service packs by using Windows Update and the Signature Verification Tool**

- **Automating tasks by using the Maintenance Wizard**

continues

- **Scheduling tasks by using Task Scheduler**

- **Checking for corrupt files and extracting files from the installation media by using System File Checker**

▶ Overall system performance can be improved by performing regular maintenance such as ScanDisk and Disk Defragmenter—all of which can be automated for ease of implementation.

MONITOR SYSTEM PERFORMANCE

1. **Which of the following can you do with Net Watcher? Choose one answer.**

    A. Show all connected users

    B. Connect to a remote computer

    C. Disconnect a user

    D. Close files users have opened

    E. All of the above

2. **To connect to a remote computer using the Net Watcher utility, you must enter a password for the remote computer. What are the two types of security that can be used?**

    A. Share-level

    B. Group-level

    C. User-level

    D. Resource-level

    E. Admin-level

3. **Your computer is using share-level security. What types of computers can you connect to for remote administration?**

    A. Any computer

    B. Any computer that uses File and Printer Sharing

    C. Computers that use user-level security and File and Printer Sharing

    D. Computers that use share-level security and File and Printer Sharing

    E. Computers that run NT server

4. **Patrick wants to use Net Watcher to view connections to his local computer. He wants to see the users connected to your computer. Which toolbar button do you click to allow this?**

    A. View Users

    B. Show Connected Users

    C. View Connected Users

    D. Show Users

    E. Show share activity

5. **Using Net Watcher, you discover that your users are sharing a large number of resources, including sensitive data. Can you alter these shares and reduce the number of shares on your network by using Net Watcher?**

    A. No. The shares can only be changed at the local computer by the user who created the share.

    B. No. You must alter the shares at the local computer.

    C. Yes. You may control and remove the shares of remote computers.

    D. No. After the resource is shared, users have that level of access until the shared resource is removed and then re-added with the appropriate share permissions.

    E. Yes. You can share the folders using the Administer button on the Edit menu.

6. **Where would Michael find the installation files for Net Watcher on the Windows 98 CD?**

   A. `ADMIN\RESKIT\NETWATCH`

   B. `RESKIT\ADMIN\NETWATCH`

   C. `NETTOOLS\REMOTE\NETWATCH`

   D. `NETTOOLS\RESKET\ADMIN\NETWATCH`

   E. None of the above

7. **To create a shared folder on a remote computer using the Net Watcher administration tool, you would select which one of the following choices to initiate the process of creating the shared resource?**

   A. Select the Administer menu and then select Add Shared Folder.

   B. Select Administer menu and then select Add Shared Local Resource.

   C. You must connect to the computer prior to creating shares on the remote computer.

   D. After connecting to the remote computer, you should select the Administer menu and then select Add Shared Folder.

   E. None of the above.

8. **You may only use the remote Net Watcher administration tool to administer remote computers if you are a member of the Domain Admins group on an NT domain or a Supervisory equivalent on a NetWare server. When is this true or false?**

   A. This is only true if you are using user-level security.

   B. This is only true if the user's computer you want to monitor has user-level security enabled.

   C. This is not true in a Windows NT domain, but is true in a NetWare environment.

   D. This is not true in a NetWare environment, but is true in an NT domain.

   E. None of the above is accurate.

9. **You are unable to connect to the ADMIN$ share on several computers using the Net Watcher administration tool. Which of the following choices best indicates what the problem might be? Select the best answer.**

   A. The computer to which you are attempting to connect is not sharing resources.

   B. The remote computer does not have Remote Administration enabled.

   C. You do not have access to the special share. You are not a remote administrator.

   D. You are not a domain administrator.

   E. None of the above.

10. **Before you can use the System Monitor to monitor a remote computer, which tool must be installed on your computer and the remote computer?**

   A. Net Watcher

   B. System Policy Editor

   C. Microsoft Remote Registry

D. Registry Editor

E. Performance Monitor

11. **System Monitor can be used to do which of the following? Choose three of the following answers.**

    A. Determine hardware performance

    B. View connected users

    C. Find performance bottlenecks

    D. Measure the effects of system configuration changes

    E. Monitor remote users

12. **Which one of the following is a category of the System Monitor?**

    A. Kernel

    B. User

    C. GDI

    D. Usage

    E. NDIS

13. **Which System Monitor category is used to view items such as bytes read per second, the amount of dirty data in cache, and the number of write operations per second?**

    A. Memory Manager

    B. File System

C. IPX/SPX-compatible Protocol

D. Kernel

E. Hard Disk

14. **Which of the following categories of the System Monitor allow you to see performance over a network? Choose three of the following answers.**

    A. Microsoft Client for NetWare Networks

    B. Microsoft Network Client

    C. Microsoft Network Server

    D. Net Watcher

    E. Network Manager

15. **When connecting to a remote computer in System Monitor, what must you specify?**

    A. The MAC address of the remote computer's network card

    B. The name of the user currently using the remote computer

    C. The NetBIOS name of the remote computer

    D. The name of the domain in which the remote computer is a member

    E. The word Remote followed by the computer name

ANSWER KEY

1. E	6. E	11. A-C-D
2. A-C	7. D	12. A
3. D	8. E	13. B
4. D	9. C	14. A-B-C
5. C	10. C	15. C

ANSWERS & EXPLANATIONS

MONITOR SYSTEM PERFORMANCE

1. Which of the following can you do with Net Watcher?

    E. All of the above

1. CORRECT ANSWER: E

Net Watcher can be used to show all users connected to a computer, to connect to a remote computer, to disconnect a user, and to close files and resources that another user has open. For more information, see "Net Watcher."

2. To connect to a remote computer using the Net Watcher utility, you must enter a password for the remote computer. What are the two types of security that can be used?

    A. Share-level

    C. User-level

2. CORRECT ANSWER: A-C

The two types of security that Windows 98 uses are share-level and user-level security. For more information, see "Net Watcher."

3. Your computer is using share-level security. What types of computers can you connect to for remote administration?

    D. Computers that use share-level security and File and Printer Sharing.

3. CORRECT ANSWER: D

If you are using share-level security, you can only connect to other computers that also are using share-level security, and which have File and Printer Sharing enabled. For more information, see "Net Watcher."

4. Patrick wants to use Net Watcher to view connections to his local computer. He wants to see the users connected to your computer. Which toolbar button do you click to allow this?

    D. Show Users

4. CORRECT ANSWER: D

Show Users will show the username, computer name, connection time, open files, idle time, and number of shares he is using. For more information, see "Net Watcher."

5. Using Net Watcher, you discover that your users are sharing a large number of resources, including sensitive data. Can you alter these shares and reduce the number of shares on your network by using Net Watcher?

    C. Yes. You may control and remove the shares of remote computers.

5. CORRECT ANSWER: C

Net Watcher enables you to create new shares and stop existing shares. For more information, see "Net Watcher."

6. Where would Michael find the installation files for Net Watcher on the Windows 98 CD?

    E. None of the above

Net Watcher is contained in the .cab files and can be installed from Add/Remove, Windows Setup, Accessories. For more information, see "Net Watcher."

7. To create a shared folder on a remote computer using the Net Watcher administration tool, you would select which of the following choices to initiate the process of creating the shared resource?

    D. After connecting to the remote computer, you should select the Administer menu and then select Add Shared Folder.

You must be connected to the remote computer before you can add shared folders. For more information, see "Net Watcher."

8. You may only use the remote Net Watcher administration tool to administer remote computers if you are a member of the Domain Admins group on an NT domain or a Supervisory equivalent on a NetWare server.

    E. None of the above is accurate.

You may use Net Watcher to administer remote computers as long as you are granted Remote Administration privileges. For more information, see "Net Watcher."

9. You are unable to connect to the ADMIN$ share on several computers using the Net Watcher administration tool. Which of the following choices best indicates what the problem might be? Select the best answer.

    C. You do not have access to the special share. You are not a remote administrator.

This is a special share created when Net Watcher is installed and it is not accessible. For more information, see "Net Watcher."

Net Watcher

This explanation supports questions 1 through 9.

Net Watcher enables a user to manage shared resources on a local or remote computer. A user can create or delete a shared resource on a remote computer and monitor access to the shared resources (see Figure 7.1).

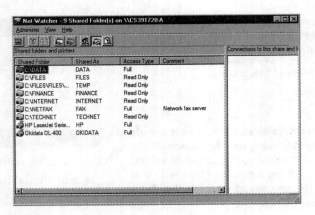

FIGURE 7.1
A list of all shares can be viewed and users connected to each share can be monitored.

FIGURE 7.2
The Administer menu will offer management items if the share view is active.

The Net Watcher is included in the Accessories group and can be used to view connections to the local computer or to remote computers if Remote Administration is enabled on the remote computer. Net Watcher can also be used to create new shares, stop existing shares, or modify existing shares (see Figure 7.2).

Net Watcher is primarily used to display the status of connections to shared folders. The features of Net Watcher enable an administrator to remotely perform the following tasks:

- Create a new shared folder
- List the shared folders on a server
- Stop the sharing of a folder
- Show which users are connected to a shared folder
- Show how long a user has been connected to a shared folder and how long the user has been idle
- Close files a user has opened (only on Microsoft networks)
- Disconnect a user from a shared resource

Net Watcher also can be accessed through the Network Neighborhood by right-clicking on a computer and selecting Properties from the context-sensitive menu. Choose Net

FIGURE 7.3
For remote administration, use the properties of the remote server from the Network Neighborhood.

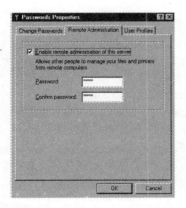

FIGURE 7.4
A password is needed if Remote Administration uses share-level security. A valid logon will be needed if user-level security is in place.

10. **Before you can use the System Monitor to monitor a remote computer, which tool must be installed on your computer and the remote computer?**

    C. Microsoft Remote Registry

Watcher from the Tools tab to view the shared folders and the users accessing those folders on the selected computer (see Figure 7.3).

To use Net Watcher, the following characteristics must apply:

- File and Printer Sharing must be enabled on the remote computer.

- You can only access remote systems that use the same access control that you are using on your computer; that is, both computers must be set to user-level access control or share-level access control.

- You can only access remote systems using the same type of file and printer sharing (Microsoft or NetWare).

Net Watcher is useful as an administration tool in a peer-to-peer network because it allows one administrator to manage the resources on all computers in the workgroup.

When connecting to a remote computer using share-level access control, the password used is the one specified in the Remote Administration dialog box (see Figure 7.4).

When connecting to a remote computer using user-level access control, the password is that of any administrator's account in the domain admin group or any other user listed.

10. CORRECT ANSWER: C

To use the System Monitor to monitor a remote computer, you must first install Microsoft Remote Registry. For more information, see "Using the System Monitor."

11. System Monitor can be used to do which of the following?

A. Determine hardware performance

C. Find performance bottlenecks

D. Measure the effects of system configuration changes

The System Monitor can be used to view hardware performance, look for bottlenecks, and measure the changes to a system configuration. It cannot be used to view connected users. That is a job of the Net Watcher. For more information, see "Using the System Monitor."

12. Which of the following is a category of the System Monitor?

A. Kernel

Kernel is a category of the System Monitor that provides a view into processor usage, threads, and virtual machines. For more information, see "Using the System Monitor."

13. Which System Monitor category is used to view items such as bytes read per second, the amount of dirty data in cache, and the number of write operations per second?

B. File System

The File System category can be used to view information about disk activity. For more information, see "Using the System Monitor."

14. Which of the following categories of the System Monitor allow you to see performance over a network?

A. Microsoft Client for NetWare Networks

B. Microsoft Network Client

C. Microsoft Network Server

Three categories of the System Monitor allow you to view performance in relation to a network. They are Microsoft Client for NetWare Networks, Microsoft Network Client, and Microsoft Network Server. For more information, see "Using the System Monitor."

15. When connecting to a remote computer in System Monitor, what must you specify?

C. The NetBIOS name of the remote computer

When connecting to a remote computer through Net Watcher, the NetBIOS name of the remote computer is entered. For more information, see "Using the System Monitor."

Using the System Monitor

This explanation supports questions 10 through 15.

The System Monitor is a Windows 98 accessory used to display data on various performance counters in Windows 98.

With System Monitor and Remote Administration enabled, you can connect to remote computers to view their system performance through the System Monitor.

You also can quickly enable monitoring of a remote computer by right-clicking on that computer in Network Neighborhood and selecting Properties from the context-sensitive menu. Choose System Monitor to start the applet and connect to the selected computer.

System Monitor can be used to monitor the performance of a Windows 98 computer. System Monitor can be used to provide realtime tracking of system activities on local or remote computers.

System Monitor is useful for viewing the effects of configuration or hardware changes on the computer's performance. It can also be used to identify bottlenecks that can affect the computer's performance.

The system monitor can display information in different type of graphs (see Figures 7.5, 7.6, and 7.7).

Performance information including processor usage, the number of reads per second, or the amount of dirty data can be viewed over time as a line chart, bar chart, or as values.

The following system activities can be monitored:

- Dial-Up Adapter
- Cache
- File System
- IPX/SPX-compatible protocol
- Kernel
- Memory Manager
- Microsoft Client for NetWare Networks
- Microsoft Network Client
- Microsoft Network Server

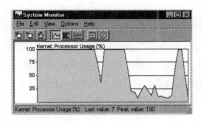

FIGURE 7.5
One of the graph types is a line graph.

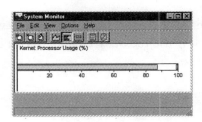

FIGURE 7.6
One of the graph types is a bar graph.

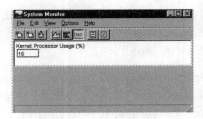

FIGURE 7.7
One of the graph types is a numerical value.

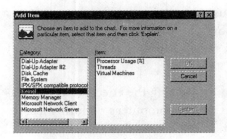

FIGURE 7.8
Windows 98 offers a list of items that can be monitored. Each item is then made up of counters.

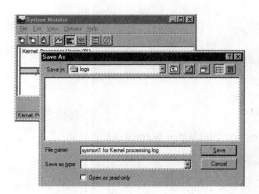

FIGURE 7.9
Windows 98 can log the activities that are being monitored for long-term record keeping or comparisons.

This list is dependent on the items that are installed on the specific Windows 98 system. Each item is broken down into individual counters (see Figure 7.8).

To view the effect of a configuration or hardware change on a Windows 98 computer:

- Determine which items in System Monitor are to be tracked.

- Run System Monitor before the change is made to establish the baseline and record the information.

- Make the desired configuration change.

- Run System Monitor after the change and view the results of the change.

The results of the change can then be compared to the baseline to see whether the change has had a positive or negative effect on system performance.

When establishing the baseline, make sure you run System Monitor during "average or normal" usage. Monitoring the computer's performance while performing abnormal system-intensive tasks will affect System Monitor's values and may not give a true baseline.

In order to monitor a remote computer, Remote Administration must be enabled on the other computer and the password must be known.

System Monitor results can be saved to a log file. This is new to Windows 98. To start a log, use the Start Logging menu in the File menu (see Figure 7.9).

TUNE AND OPTIMIZE THE SYSTEM IN A MICROSOFT ENVIRONMENT AND A MIXED MICROSOFT AND NETWARE ENVIRONMENT

1. **Which of the following is a benefit of using the Disk Defragmenter?**

   A. Fixing corrupt files

   B. Increasing memory

   C. Repairing bad sectors

   D. Improving file access time

   E. Deleting old temp files

2. **Disk Defragmenter allows you to defragment which types of drives?**

   A. Uncompressed drives

   B. Drives compressed with DriveSpace

   C. Drives compressed with DoubleSpace

   D. Network drives

   E. CD-ROM drives

3. **Disk Defragmenter allows you to do which of the following?**

   A. Defragment files

   B. Defragment free space

   C. Both of the above

   D. None of the above

4. **Which of the following will improve the performance of the Disk Defragmenter?**

   A. Defragmenting files and free space at the same time

   B. Showing details while running

   C. Minimizing the Defragmenter while running

   D. Checking the drive for errors while defragmenting

   E. Defragmenting RAM

5. **Which types of files will the Disk Defragmenter move during operation?**

   A. Files marked as Hidden and System

   B. Files marked as Hidden and non-System

   C. Files marked as non-Hidden and System

   D. Files marked as both non-Hidden and non-System

   E. All files that were not defragmented last time Defrag was run

6. **Carol has never run Disk Defragmenter on her PC. Which two advanced options should she choose?**

   A. Full defragmentation

   B. Check drive for errors

   C. Defragment files only

D. Consolidate free space only

E. Defragment temp files only

7. **When running ScanDisk, what are the two options for handling lost file fragments?**

   A. Free

   B. Ignore

   C. Make Copies

   D. Convert to files

   E. Delete

8. **Which option do you use when running ScanDisk from a command prompt to check all local non-removable drives?**

   A. `/n`

   B. `/a`

   C. `/p`

   D. `/x`

   E. `/w`

9. **Two files, File A and File B, can erroneously reference the same cluster. This problem is referred to as what?**

   A. Lost clustering

   B. Fragmented data

   C. Cross-linking

   D. Reference error

   E. None of the above as it can't happen in Windows 98

10. **Where would you look for the results of a ScanDisk operation after running ScanDisk on drive C?**

   A. In the file `C:\SCAN.LOG`

   B. In the file `C:\Windows\SCANDISK.LOG`

   C. In the file `C:\SCANDISK.LOG`

   D. In the file `C:\SCANLOG.TXT`

   E. In the file `C:\SCANDISKLOG.TXT`

11. **Which of the following is a property of a compressed volume file?**

   A. Read-only

   B. Hidden

   C. System

   D. All of the above

   E. None of the above

12. **Which of the following relationships is true?**

   A. A compressed drive is a file on a host drive.

   B. A host drive is a file on a compressed drive.

   C. A compressed drive is a partition of a host drive.

   D. Compressed and host drives are separate, unrelated items.

   E. A compressed drive is host of a file.

13. **What is the maximum size of a compressed drive that can be created using DriveSpace included with Windows 98?**

   A. 256MB

   B. 512MB

   C. 1GB

   D. 2GB

   E. 16GB

14. **What will the `dir /c` command do on a disk drive?**

    A. Compress the drive

    B. Display CVFs on a host drive

    C. Display the compression ratio for files

    D. Give a syntax error

    E. Display only the C drive

15. **When Patrick runs Disk Compression under Windows 98, he asks you how files are compressed. You tell him which two of the following are ways in which disk compression maximizes disk space.**

    A. Cluster conversion

    B. Token conversion

    C. ASCII collapse

    D. Sector allocation granularity

    E. Deleting old temp files

16. **Windows 98 implements which form of disk compression?**

    A. On-the-fly compression

    B. Read/write compression

    C. Token conversion

    D. LZ compression

    E. ZIP compression

17. **What is the smallest measure of disk allocation under Windows 98 compression?**

    A. One byte

    B. One cluster

    C. One sector

    D. One cylinder

    E. One partition

The following question is scenario-based. Please read all the requirements and proposed solution before answering.

18. **Scenario:**

    Several Windows 98 users are running out of drive space. The company does not want to invest in new equipment this year.

    Required component:
    Provide more storage for Windows 98 users on their local systems.

    Optional components:
    Keep FAT on all the systems.

    Keep the access times about the same as they are now.

    Proposed solution:
    Install DriveSpace 3.0 on all systems and compress the drives with HiPack and UltraPack where needed.

    A. The proposed solution satisfies the required component and all the optional components.

    B. The proposed solution satisfies the required component and only one of the optional components.

    C. The proposed solution satisfies the required component and none of the optional components.

    D. The proposed solution satisfies only one of the optional components but does not satisfy the required component.

    E. The proposed solution satisfies none of the optional components and does not satisfy the required component.

19. **What is the purpose of Windows Update? Select all that apply.**

A. To update device drivers

B. To update Windows components

C. To download fixes and service packs

D. To scan the system for illegal software

E. To update the Registry

20. What is required to download all the updates and extras using Windows Update? Select all that apply.

A. Internet access

B. Any Web browser

C. A registered copy of Windows 98

D. A security signature tool

E. The Registry Editor

21. How can you list only the updates that you currently do not have?

A. You will always get a full list. If you download an update you already have, it will simply overwrite it.

B. You can use the Web site to scan your system and only list the items you need. You must be registered for this to work.

C. From the Updates tool, agree to a scan of the system. All items listed after the scan will be only the new items.

D. This can only be done for device drivers.

E. You can scan for devices first, then connect to the Update site and load only what is needed.

22. Who can use the Windows 98 Update tool? Select the best answer.

A. Only registered owners of Windows 98

B. Only administrators in the network

C. All Windows 98 users

D. Any user with access to the Internet

E. Only users with a full version on Windows 98

The following question is scenario-based. Please read all the requirements and proposed solution before answering.

23. Scenario:

A home user is having problems with some of the Windows 98 features. What can be done to help?

Required component:
Have Windows 98 run the latest device drivers and updates.

Optional components:
Do not buy any extra software.

Keep track of devices already installed.

Proposed solution:
Register your copy of Windows 98. Connect to the Windows Update and let the active setup scan the system. After the scan is complete, add all the required components and latest drivers.

A. The proposed solution satisfies the required component and all the optional components.

B. The proposed solution satisfies the required component and only one of the optional components.

C. The proposed solution satisfies the required component and none of the optional components.

D. The proposed solution satisfies only one of the optional components but does not satisfy the required component.

E. The proposed solution satisfies none of the optional components and does not satisfy the required component.

24. **Which tasks does the Maintenance Wizard perform? Select all that apply.**

A. ScanDisk

B. Compression

C. Defragmentation

D. Backups

E. Windows Update

25. **How can you control the settings on the different utilities run by the Maintenance Wizard?**

A. By setting up default configurations in the separate utilities before running the Maintenance Wizard.

B. You cannot control the settings.

C. By using the Custom setup in each of the utilities before running the Maintenance Wizard.

D. By using the Custom setup in the Maintenance Wizard.

E. By using the minimal setup in the Maintenance Wizard.

The following question is scenario-based. Please read all the requirements and proposed solution before answering.

26. **Scenario:**

A new administrator has decided to be proactive in maintaining the new Windows 98 systems in the office.

Required component:
Make sure the hard drives are error-free and run as efficiently as possible.

Optional components:
Do not interrupt users' work with maintenance issues.

Perform ScanDisk and Defragmenter, Disk Clean Up, and Backups each night.

Proposed solution:
Set up the Maintenance Wizard with a Custom setup to run each night between midnight and 3 a.m. Add the Backup command in with the three basic tasks. Inform all users to leave their systems on when they leave at the end of the day.

A. The proposed solution satisfies the required component and all the optional components.

B. The proposed solution satisfies the required component and only one of the optional components.

C. The proposed solution satisfies the required component and none of the optional components.

D. The proposed solution satisfies only one of the optional components but does not satisfy the required component.

E. The proposed solution satisfies none of the optional components and does not satisfy the required component.

27. **Where do you find the Task Scheduler?**

A. In the Control Panel

B. In the My Computer icon

C. In System tools of the Start menu

D. In the Network applet of the Control Panel

E. In the Taskbar properties

28. What application can be added to the Task Scheduler?

A. ScanDisk, Defragmenter, Disk Cleanup

B. Only disk management tools installed on the system

C. Any application currently installed on the system

D. Only applications currently installed that can be automated

E. Only applications that are common to all users on the system

29. What is the purpose of the Task Scheduler? Select the best answer.

A. To automate programs to run at startup

B. To run applications in the background

C. To perform regular maintenance on a system after hours

D. To control tasks that are currently running

E. To run applications the user cannot

The following question is scenario-based. Please read all the requirements and proposed solution before answering.

30. Scenario:

An administrator would like to manage the automation of all the systems in the office and wants to run a batch file every night from a central location.

Required component:
Remotely manage the Task Scheduler.

Optional components:
Users must not be involved in the backup.

The batch file must exist on all systems.

Proposed solution:
Create a batch file and copy it to all systems by placing a command in the Login script for all users. Enable Remote Administration and File and Printer Sharing on all systems. From the Tasks Scheduler on the administrator's system, create tasks for all systems.

A. The proposed solution satisfies the required component and all the optional components.

B. The proposed solution satisfies the required component and only one of the optional components.

C. The proposed solution satisfies the required component and none of the optional components.

D. The proposed solution satisfies only one of the optional components but does not satisfy the required component.

E. The proposed solution satisfies none of the optional components and does not satisfy the required component.

31. What is the name of the command-line utility used to reload files from the source CAB files?

A. Reload

B. Install

C. Setup

D. Extract

E. Update

32. How can you reload system files if Windows 98 is running?

A. Using the Extract utility.

B. Using the System File Checker.

C. Using Setup to overwrite system files.

D. You cannot; you must reboot in DOS.

E. Using the Update program.

The following question is scenario-based. Please read all the requirements and proposed solution before answering.

33. Scenario:

An administrator is having difficulties with a Windows 98 system. One of the problems might be related to critical system files.

Required component:
Verify the integrity of system files.

Optional components:
Use existing tools.

Replace any corrupted file without leaving Windows 98.

Proposed solution:
Boot up the system using a startup disk and run the System Files Checker.

A. The proposed solution satisfies the required component and all the optional components.

B. The proposed solution satisfies the required component and only one of the optional components.

C. The proposed solution satisfies the required component and none of the optional components.

D. The proposed solution satisfies only one of the optional components but does not satisfy the required component.

E. The proposed solution satisfies none of the optional components and does not satisfy the required component.

ANSWER KEY

1. D	10. C	19. A-B-C	28. C
2. A-B-C	11. D	20. A-B-C	29. C
3. C	12. A	21. C	30. A
4. C	13. D	22. D	31. D
5. B-C-D	14. C	23. A	32. B
6. A-B	15. B-D	24. A-C	33. E
7. A-D	16. A	25. D	
8. B	17. C	26. B	
9. C	18. B	27. B	

TUNE AND OPTIMIZE THE SYSTEM IN A MICROSOFT ENVIRONMENT AND A MIXED MICROSOFT AND NETWARE ENVIRONMENT

1. Which of the following is a benefit of using the Disk Defragmenter?

D. Improving file access time

1. CORRECT ANSWER: D

The Disk Defragmenter can be used to improve file access time. Fixing corrupt files and repairing bad sectors are functions of ScanDisk. For more information, see "Disk Defragmenter."

2. Disk Defragmenter allows you to defragment which types of drives?

A. Uncompressed drives

B. Drives compressed with DriveSpace

C. Drives compressed with DoubleSpace

2. CORRECT ANSWER: A-B-C

Disk Defragmenter cannot be used on network drives. For more information, see "Disk Defragmenter."

3. Disk Defragmenter allows you to do which of the following?

C. Both of the above

3. CORRECT ANSWER: C

Disk Defragmenter options allow you to defragment files, free space, or both. For more information, see "Disk Defragmenter."

4. Which of the following will improve the performance of the Disk Defragmenter?

C. Minimizing the Defragmenter while running

4. CORRECT ANSWER: C

The performance of the Disk Defragmenter can be increased slightly if it is minimized while running. For more information, see "Disk Defragmenter."

5. Which types of files will the Disk Defragmenter move during operation?

B. Files marked as Hidden and non-System

C. Files marked as non-Hidden and System

D. Files marked as both non-Hidden and non-System

5. CORRECT ANSWER: B-C-D

The Disk Defragmenter will not move files that are marked as both Hidden and System files. For more information, see "Disk Defragmenter."

6. Carol has never run Disk Defragmenter on her PC. Which two advanced options should she choose?

A. Full defragmentation

B. Check drive for errors

If Disk Defragmenter has never been run on a machine, having it check the disk for errors before starting the defragmentation process is a good idea. The first time you run Disk Defragmenter, the disk probably is badly fragmented and a full defragmentation should be run. For more information, see "Disk Defragmenter."

Disk Defragmenter

This explanation supports questions 1 through 6.

Three key disk-management utilities are included with Windows 98. Each is intended to address particular file system issues or problems. Table 7.1 provides a summary of the disk-management utilities and the issues they address.

TABLE 7.1   WINDOWS 98 UTILITIES FOR VARIOUS FILE SYSTEM ISSUES

Utility	Issue
Disk Defragmenter	Prevention of file system performance degradation due to inefficient hard disk access.
ScanDisk	Correction of cross-linked files, lost clusters, and other hard disk errors.
Disk Compression	Maximization of available hard disk space.

To select the appropriate disk-management tool, you must examine the symptoms displayed in a given situation. Table 7.2 matches symptoms to the appropriate disk-management tool to be used to correct them.

TABLE 7.2   SELECTING THE APPROPRIATE TOOL FOR VARIOUS FILE SYSTEM SYMPTOMS

Utility	Symptom
Disk Defragmenter	Applications open, read, or write to files slowly.
ScanDisk	Applications report corruption of data or are unable to open files.
Disk Compression	Applications report insufficient available hard disk space.

The use of one utility often leads to the use of another. For example, while you're correcting slow hard disk access by running Disk Defragmenter, the utility may report an error. In this case, you should run ScanDisk and specify a physical surface scan.

One of the most common performance issues related to the FAT file system, which is native to both MS-DOS and Windows 98, is disk fragmentation. When a hard drive is new and contains no information, it is possible for the file system to write all the data for a new file to a contiguous area of the hard drive. As the hard drive fills up and files are deleted and copied numerous times, the space available to new files no longer is contiguous. The file system is forced to put part of the new file in one location, part at another location, and so on. When a request is made to read the file, the hard disk must access all these different locations to reconstitute the file. This requires much more mechanical activity and takes longer than reading the whole file from one location on the hard disk.

Windows 98 includes a utility called *Disk Defragmenter* that is designed to address this issue. It does so by rewriting all the files on the hard drive to contiguous locations, thus enhancing file system performance for that drive. This procedure can be time-consuming because, as the drive becomes full, there is less room to temporarily store the different parts of a file before it is rewritten to a new location.

The defragmenter can also place files in an order more prone to quicker loading. This is an option that can be set each time you run ScanDisk or permanently (see Figure 7.10).

FIGURE 7.10
An option to the Defragmenter is to rearrange program files so they may start faster.

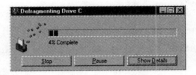

FIGURE 7.11
The defragmenter will display progress. For more detailed information, select the Show Details button.

The Disk Defragmenter can be run against compressed and uncompressed drives. If you want to use it against compressed drives, those drives must have been compressed in a format recognizable by Windows 98. These formats include drives compressed with the MS-DOS utilities DoubleSpace and DriveSpace, programs which came with version of MS-DOS 6.x, and later DriveSpace 3.0 with Windows 95 and 98. The status window will show progress and may return to 0 percent if the system notices new or modified files on the system (see Figure 7.11).

Although the Disk Defragmenter existed in MS-DOS 6.2 and is still a 16-bit application, the Windows 98 Disk Defragmenter utility has the following enhancements:

- It is much faster at optimizing drives compressed in MS-DOS 6.x using DoubleSpace or DriveSpace.

- The utility no longer requires any .INI files because all settings are stored in the Registry.

- The utility now has a Windows 98 GUI interface.

- The Windows 98 Disk Defragmenter is capable of running as a background application, freeing the user to perform other tasks.

The following types of files are not handled by Disk Defragmenter in the normal fashion:

- Files with both Hidden and System attributes are not moved.

- Files with either Hidden or System attributes are moved.

- Mounted DriveSpace or DoubleSpace volumes are not moved.

The following points should also be noted when using the Disk Defragmenter:

- If Disk Defragmenter reports errors (usually at the beginning of the process), you should run ScanDisk (including a surface scan).

• This utility should not be run on Stacker drives because the compression scheme on such drives is different from that of DriveSpace and DoubleSpace. Stacker is a third-party disk compression utility.

When running Disk Defragmenter, the user can select three defragment options:

• Full defragmentation

• Defragment files only

• Consolidate free space only

7. **When running ScanDisk, what are the two options for handling lost file fragments?**

A. Free

D. Convert to files

7. CORRECT ANSWER: A-D

When ScanDisk detects lost file fragments (fragments not associated with a file), they can either be freed (removed) or converted to files. For more information, see "ScanDisk."

8. **Which option do you use when running ScanDisk from a command prompt, to check all local non-removable drives?**

B. /a

8. CORRECT ANSWER: B

Using the /a parameter will cause ScanDisk to check all non-removable drives. For more information, see "ScanDisk."

9. **Two files, File A and File B, can erroneously reference the same cluster. This problem is referred to as what?**

C. Cross-linking

9. CORRECT ANSWER: C

Cross-linking occurs when two files are linked to the same cluster on a drive. For more information, see "ScanDisk."

10. **Where would you look for the results of a ScanDisk operation after running ScanDisk on drive C?**

C. In the file C:\SCANDISK.LOG

10. CORRECT ANSWER: C

ScanDisk writes a SCANDISK.LOG file in the root directory of the disk being analyzed. For more information, see "ScanDisk."

ScanDisk

This explanation supports questions 7 through 10.

ScanDisk is used to check a disk for physical errors (such as bad sectors) and logical errors (such as cross-linked files), and to repair the problem areas. ScanDisk also checks and repairs DMF-formatted floppy disks (see Figure 7.12).

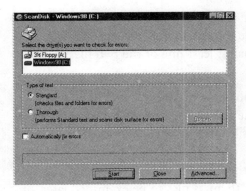

FIGURE 7.12
ScanDisk can perform a Standard or Thorough test.

Any time a disk is shut down improperly, or physical problems exist with the media, ScanDisk should be run.

ScanDisk can be configured to run in the background while other applications are running. ScanDisk can also be run from a command prompt by using the following parameters:

- /a: Checks all local, nonremovable drives
- /n: Starts and closes ScanDisk when complete
- /p: Does not correct errors encountered

When you run the Windows 98 Setup program to install Windows 98, ScanDisk runs automatically. The following are areas on which ScanDisk checks and fixes errors:

- File system structure, including lost clusters and cross-linked files
- Long Filenames
- File Allocation Table
- Physical surface of the drive
- Directory tree structure
- DriveSpace or DoubleSpace volumes

Under a FAT file system, the clusters for a specific file are often scattered throughout the drive. Each cluster for a file contains both data and a pointer to the location of the next cluster in the chain. When a file is requested, the file system looks up the name of the file in the directory tree (which tells where the first cluster for the file is located) and begins to read through the various clusters, collecting the file's data.

Problems can occur when the pointer to the next cluster becomes corrupted. If, for example, file A has a cluster with some data and a pointer to cluster 12, and file B has a cluster that also points to cluster 12, these files are said to be *cross-linked*. The data at cluster 12 cannot belong to both files; therefore, there is a logical inconsistency in the file structure of the drive. ScanDisk is able to detect such inconsistencies, but it cannot determine to which file the cluster truly belongs.

ScanDisk defaults to making a copy of the cluster so that each file can make use of the information in the cluster. This increases the chance that at least one of the two files in question can be salvaged.

Another associated problem is that now the clusters that should have been in the chain after the corrupted cluster are not referenced by any file, and are thus "orphaned" or lost. These clusters may still contain valid data, but they no longer are part of any file on the drive. ScanDisk is able to find these clusters and either save them as files to be examined later, or mark the clusters as available to the file system, thus freeing up space on the drive.

ScanDisk can perform two levels of testing on hard drives: standard and thorough. Standard mode is best used on a daily basis, whereas thorough mode is best used when you suspect a problem with the hard drive.

In *standard* mode, ScanDisk performs logical tests against the file allocation table (FAT) of the file system, checking for the logical inconsistencies outlined earlier. In addition, the standard scan checks for various other potential problems, such as invalid filenames and invalid date and time stamps.

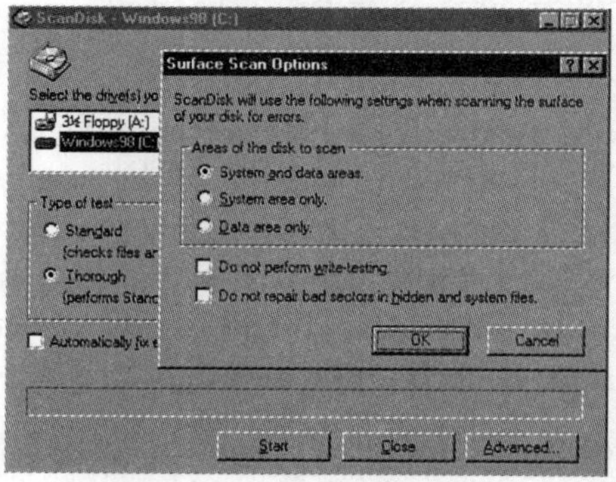

In *thorough* mode, ScanDisk not only performs all the tests included in standard mode, but also performs a surface scan. Each cluster on the drive is checked for physical defects that would make the cluster in question unsafe for data storage. A surface scan is performed by reading the information from the cluster and rewriting it back to the same cluster. If the information matches what ScanDisk read the first time, the cluster is likely to be safe. If the data is different, a media problem might exist, in which case ScanDisk marks the cluster as bad. To select the option for the thorough scan, select the option button (see Figure 7.13).

FIGURE 7.13
The option box will list the areas of the hard drive to scan during a thorough scan.

▼ NOTE

ScanDisk does not test clusters that have been marked as bad in the FAT by other programs. You must use other programs to fix those clusters.

ScanDisk contains a number of additional features, such as the following:

- ScanDisk can be run from the command line, with parameters to specify how it will run, or from the Windows 98 graphical interface.

- ScanDisk can fix problems on hard drives, floppy disk drives, RAM drives, and removable media (such as PCMCIA hard cards and Bernoulli drives).

- ScanDisk can detect and repair errors in Long Filenames (see Figure 7.14).

- ScanDisk can be used to test and maintain the integrity of DoubleSpace and DriveSpace volumes.

- ScanDisk can log its activities. The results of the scan are stored in the file SCANDISK.LOG in the root of the drive that has been examined.

- ScanDisk cannot fix errors on CD-ROMs, network drives, drives created by the DOS command INTERLNK, or drives referenced via MS-DOS commands (such as ASSIGN, JOIN, or SUBST).

- As with the Disk Defragmenter, it is possible to multi-task with ScanDisk, but if any disk write activity occurs, ScanDisk may be forced to restart the testing process.

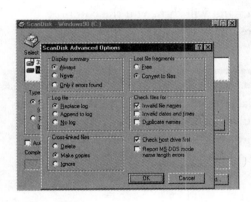

FIGURE 7.14
The log parameters are set in the Advanced button on the main ScanDisk dialog box.

11. Which of the following is a property of a compressed volume file?

    D. All of the above

11. CORRECT ANSWER: D

A compressed volume file (CVF) is marked as Read-Only, System, and Hidden. For more information, see "DriveSpace."

12. Which of the following relationships is true?

    A. A compressed drive is a file on a host drive.

12. CORRECT ANSWER: A

A CVF is simply a file that resides on a host (physical) drive. For more information, see "DriveSpace."

13. **What is the maximum size of a compressed drive that can be created using DriveSpace included with Windows 98?**

    D. 2GB

The maximum size of a compressed file using the version of DriveSpace packaged with Windows 98 is 2GB. DriveSpace 2.0 could only be used on drives less than 512MB. For more information, see "DriveSpace."

14. **What will the** `dir /c` **command do on a disk drive?**

    C. Display the compression ratio for files

Using the `dir /c` command will show you the compression ratio for files. For more information, see "DriveSpace."

15. **When Patrick runs Disk Compression under Windows 98, he asks you how files are compressed. You tell him which two of the following are ways in which disk compression maximizes disk space.**

    B. Token conversion

    D. Sector allocation granularity

Token conversion replaces repetitive data patterns with tokens. Sector allocation granularity allocates file space by sector, not by cluster, reducing wasted disk space. For more information, see "DriveSpace."

16. **Windows 98 implements which form of disk compression?**

    A. On-the-fly compression

DriveSpace performs compression on-the-fly, transparently, and in the background. For more information, see "DriveSpace."

17. **What is the smallest measure of disk allocation under Windows 98 compression?**

    C. One sector

Sector allocation granularity enables file space to be allocated sector-by-sector instead of cluster-by-cluster. For more information, see "DriveSpace."

18. **Proposed solution:**

Install DriveSpace 3.0 on all systems and compress the drives with HiPack and UltraPack where needed.

    B. The proposed solution satisfies the required component and only one of the optional components.

Each system will be able to store more information on its FAT hard drives, but the access time will be reduced with the use of HiPack and UltraPack. For more information, see "DriveSpace."

DriveSpace

This explanation supports questions 11 through 18.

Windows 98 implements a form of disk compression known as *on-the-fly compression*. On-the-fly compression is so named because the compression/decompression process occurs automatically in the background and is transparent to the user. On-the-fly compression is the process of intercepting normal MS-DOS read/write calls and compressing the data before writing it to the hard disk, so that the data consumes less space. Similarly, when the data is read back, it is automatically uncompressed before being transferred to the application or process that requested it.

Disk compression, as implemented in Windows 98 (and in the versions released with Windows 95 and MS-DOS 6.x), consists of two processes:

- **Token Conversion**: A token, which takes up less space, replaces repetitive patterns that occur in a given piece of data.

- **Sector Allocation Granularity**: By circumventing the often large amounts of wasted space created under a normal FAT file system, changes the way data is stored on a hard drive.

Any FAT file system operates based on a cluster being the smallest traceable unit of measure. Therefore, if the cluster size is 4KB, for example, and a 2KB file is stored in that cluster, 2KB can be wasted. If 1,000 such files exist on a hard drive, 1,000 × 2KB is wasted. With disk compression in place, the smallest allocation unit shrinks to one sector, or 512 bytes, which can greatly reduce the amount of wasted space on a drive.

Disk compression (called *DoubleSpace*) was first introduced in version 6.0 of MS-DOS. It was later re-released as *DriveSpace* in version 6.2, with some changes to the compression routines and with a new feature: the capability to uncompress a drive. The compression structure has remained fairly consistent. The latest version is now DriveSpace 3.0.

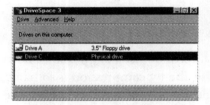

FIGURE 7.15
DriveSpace 3.0 will show all physical drives on the system, even if the drive cannot be compressed.

After disk compression is installed and the files initially compressed, the files are stored in the *Compressed Volume File* (CVF), a large hidden file that sits on the physical drive C. When the system boots up, however, the CVF is assigned the drive letter C and is known as the Compressed drive. The physical C drive, which now contains only a few files because everything else is in a compressed state inside the CVF, is assigned a higher drive letter, typically H, and is known as the *host drive*. The process of switching the drive letters and making the CVF available for viewing in MS-DOS and Windows is called *mounting*. From this point on, any file operation is handled through the disk compression routines, which are responsible for compressing and uncompressing files as disk I/O requests are made by the operating system (see Figure 7.15).

Windows 98's DriveSpace 3.0 contains many features that have been specifically optimized. The main advantages to using Windows 98's DriveSpace 3.0 are as follows:

- Disk compression is implemented with 32-bit code for better performance.

- It does not use conventional memory.

- It is integrated with the operating system for ease of use and better performance.

▼ NOTE

When a floppy is compressed, the DriveSpace drivers load only when the floppy is in the drive. In general, the DriveSpace drivers load only when compressed media (hard drive or floppy) is detected.

The following information should be noted whenever a user is considering Windows 98's DriveSpace 3.0:

- Windows 98 is compatible with third-party compression software such as Stacker versions 2.x, 3.x, and 4.x, and with all versions of SuperStor, but these use real-mode compression and thus take up conventional memory and usually are slower.

- DriveSpace 3.0 cannot be used to compress a hard drive that uses FAT32.

- The maximum size of a compressed volume is 2GB when you are using DriveSpace 3.0, which comes with Windows 98.

- The best compression ratio of a compressed volume is 2.4:1 with DriveSpace 3.0. If the Compression Agent is used, UltraPack compression can be implemented on a file-by-file basis for even higher ratio.

- Using compression slows down system performance because of the processing required by the operating system to interpret compressed data. With the continuing drop in prices for storage devices, disk compression is less important today than in the past, and should be avoided.

- A compressed drive, or CVF, is just a file stored on a hard drive or floppy. It is just as susceptible to disk errors as any other file, but any error in the CVF can cause the loss of all data in the CVF.

DriveSpace 3.0 has been improved over DriveSpace 2.0 in the area of compression type and ratio. A drive may be compressed in four ways using DriveSpace 3.0 and a fifth using Compression Agent. To access the compression methods, use the Settings item in the Advanced menu. See Figure 7.16 for a list of compression types.

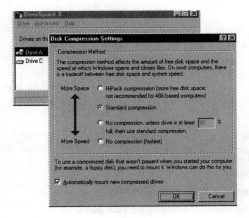

FIGURE 7.16
Four methods of compression can allow a better compression ratio but at slower speeds. Lower compression ratio will yield faster speeds.

Even the option of No Compression will create a CVF file and allow for more storage on the drive. Each file type will compress at different ratios. A text file will compress much more than a program file. Microsoft Word files can compress at a ratio of 16:1.

Compression Agent is a separate utility that works with DriveSpace 3.0 to enhance compression ratio on certain files. Compression Agent will only work with a drive that has been compressed with DriveSpace 3.0 (see Figure 7.17).

This method is called UltraPack and provides the highest compression possible, but it takes longer to access these files. A drive cannot be set to UltraPack. Once the drive is compressed, then the compression agent can be used to further compress the drive (see Figure 7.18).

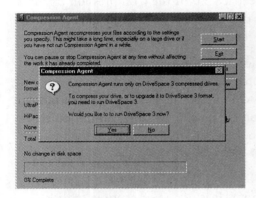

FIGURE 7.17
A warning appears if DriveSpace 3.0 is not present.

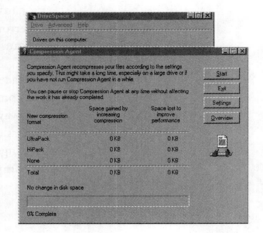

FIGURE 7.18
The compression agent will show a before-and-after table to help determine if the compression is worthwhile.

19. **What is the purpose of Windows Update? Select all that apply.**

   A. **To update device drivers**
   B. **To update Windows components**
   C. **To download fixes and service packs**

19. CORRECT ANSWER: A-B-C

Windows 98 Update will scan your system and recommend updates or devices drivers. Service Pack will be available. The system does not scan for unregistered software. For more information, see "Updating Drivers and Service Pack."

20. What is required to download all the updates and extras using Windows Update? Select all that apply.

  A. Internet access

  B. Any Web browser

  C. A registered copy of Windows 98

The Windows Update is a Web-based service. Only some items can be downloaded by non-registered software users. For more information, see "Updating Drivers and Service Pack."

21. How can you list only the updates that you currently do not have?

  C. From the Updates tool, agree to a scan of the system. All items listed after the scan will be only the new items.

The Update tool will always prompt for a system scan. This is true for software updates and device drivers. After the scan is complete, the Web site will only list items you do not already have. For more information, see "Updating Drivers and Service Pack."

22. Who can use the Windows 98 Update tool? Select the best answer.

  D. Any user with access to the Internet

All users that have access to the Internet can use the Windows Update. Only registered users will have access to everything on the site. For more information, see "Updating Drivers and Service Pack."

23. Proposed solution:

  Register your copy of Windows 98. Connect to the Windows Update and let the active setup scan the system. After the scan is complete, add all the required components and latest drivers.

  A. The proposed solution satisfies the required component and all the optional components.

With the software registered, all updates and new drivers are available free of charge. With a scan, the active setup can keep a history folder to track the updates. For more information, see "Updating Drivers and Service Pack."

Updating Drivers and Service Pack

This explanation supports questions 19 through 23.

Windows 98 provide users with a new online Web-based software and drivers update tool. Windows Update is shipped with Windows 98 and can be accessed from the main screen of the Start menu (see Figure 7.19).

FIGURE 7.19
The Windows Update tools can be found on the Start menu.

This new tool requires that the system be able to connect to the Internet. The tool will launch the Internet Explorer and connect to one of Microsoft's Web sites.

There are three main sections of the Web site: Windows Update, Device Drivers, and Member Services. Windows components and new Device Drivers are found in the products update section (see Figure 7.20).

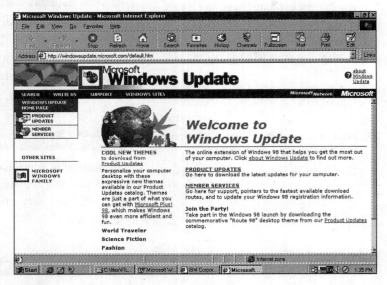

FIGURE 7.20
The main welcoming screen for Windows Update will explain the process and guide the user.

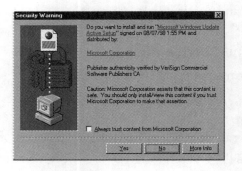

FIGURE 7.21
Before Active Setup is enabled, you must trust that this is a valid Microsoft site.

Microsoft will be actively scanning the system locally but will not be sending any of your information over the Internet. Each time the system is about to initiate such a scan, a confirmation of authenticity appears. Microsoft uses a Signature Verification tool that validates the authenticity of the Web site. This is to ensure that no one else can pass himself off as Microsoft and potentially damage your system. To accept the claim of authenticity and continue on, select Yes (see Figure 7.21).

FIGURE 7.22
You can have the Update program scan your system and only recommend an item you do not already have.

After you agree to the active setup, the update program will offer to scan the local system and recommend updates. If you answer No, the catalog of items will appear but there may well be an item you already have. The prompt will appear as soon as you agree to the authentication screen (see Figure 7.22).

When the list of items from the catalog is displayed, you can select any or all and start a download. You will notice that the items are categorized; there is a Recommended section as well as one just of fun. The list will also include items you simply did not install yourself from the CD (see Figure 7.23).

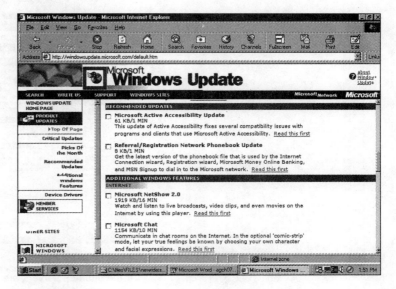

FIGURE 7.23
You can select any item on the list, but Microsoft has a recommended list that should be downloaded on all systems.

Device drivers will download in the same way as Windows Updates. You will be asked to accept the validation and to scan your local system. The only difference is that only one driver can be downloaded at a time. Each driver once installed may prompt to restart the system. You should follow any direction given and return to Windows Update if additional drivers are to be loaded.

The member services area will keep you informed on the status of all the Windows Update servers. If several servers are shut down for maintenance, you are advised to try at another time.

FIGURE 7.24
The results page will use an icon to quickly identify the type of update. Look for Registered items only if you have registered your copy of Windows 98.

The member services also includes a section on registration. Some components of the Windows Update cannot be downloaded unless you have a registered copy of Windows 98. A legend appears at the beginning of the Catalog screen, indicating which components are Cool, New, for power users, or registered users (see Figure 7.24).

To find out whether the servers are running properly, visit the Member Services pages (see Figure 7.25).

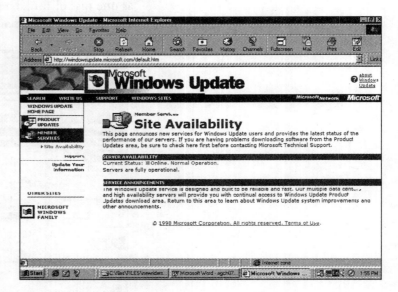

FIGURE 7.25
If the updates servers are unavailable, the Member Services page will keep you informed.

24. What tasks does the Maintenance Wizard perform? Select all that apply.

A. ScanDisk

C. Defragmentation

24. CORRECT ANSWER: A-C

The Maintenance Wizard will perform ScanDisks, defragment the hard drive, and run Disk Clean Up. For more information, see "Automating Tasks by Using the Maintenance Wizard."

25. How can you control the settings on the different utilities run by the Maintenance Wizard?

D. By using the Custom setup in the Maintenance Wizard

25. CORRECT ANSWER: D

The Maintenance Wizard will use the default setting unless a custom setup is used when the Maintenance Wizard is used. For more information, see "Automating Tasks by Using the Maintenance Wizard."

26. Proposed solution:

> **Set up the Maintenance Wizard with a Custom setup to run each night between midnight and 3 a.m. Add the Backup command in with the three basic tasks. Inform all users to leave their systems on when they leave at the end of the day.**
>
> B. The proposed solution satisfies the required component and only one of the optional components.

The systems will run each night and not interfere with users' work. They will be checked for errors and run more efficiently. The Custom setup, however, will not permit you to add a task to the list. For more information, see "Automating Tasks by Using the Maintenance Wizard."

Automating Tasks by Using the Maintenance Wizard

This explanation supports questions 24 through 26.

Windows 98 provides a Maintenance Wizard to help keep track of system maintenance. The wizard will help you set up a schedule and a list of activities.

There are three basic tools that are called by the wizard: Disk Defragmenter, ScanDisk, and Disk Clean Up. Disk Defragmenter and ScanDisk were mentioned earlier in this chapter.

Disk Clean Up can be used to delete old or temporary files on the system. Internet access created larger folders with history files that can be deleted to free up space. Disk Clean Up can also be set up to empty the Recycle Bin, but it will not be the default setting (see Figure 7.26).

The wizard will first ask for an Express or Custom configuration (see Figure 7.27). Select Express to run all components without make any changes to the default setting. Select Custom to select and configure each tool independently.

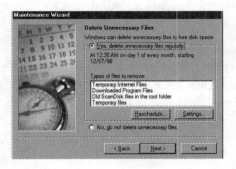

FIGURE 7.26
Disk Clean Up will delete any old temporary files or Internet history and caches.

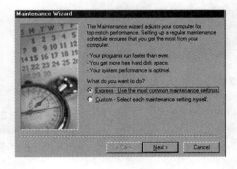

FIGURE 7.27
Express and Custom can be used to set up the Maintenance schedule.

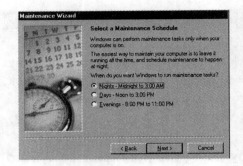

FIGURE 7.28
Three basic schedules can be selected from
the Maintenance Wizard.

In both cases, Express or Custom, you get to select the time of
day to perform the tasks. Three basic times are midnight to
3:00 a.m., noon to 3 p.m., or 8 a.m. to 11 a.m. Depending on
the system (home or office), you will want to select a time
when the system is not being used (see Figure 7.28). The only
way to perform the tasks immediately is to complete an initial
configuration, choosing any time and rerunning the wizard
(see Figure 7.29).

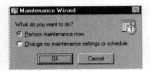

FIGURE 7.29
In order to perform the maintenance, immediately rerun the Maintenance
Wizard.

All three program can be found separately on the System Tools
menu under Start, Programs, Accessories. All three can be run
independently or through the Maintenance Wizard.

The custom setup will also specify dates and times for each
task. A task could be performed only twice a week or monthly.
You can also combine schedule once a week and every third
day. Figure 7.30 and Figure 7.31 display the custom setup and
Reschedule button.

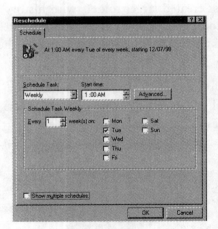

FIGURE 7.30
A basic reschedule will offer weekly or daily as
well as several times in a week.

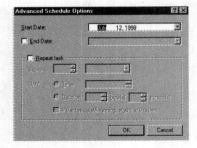

FIGURE 7.31
The advanced reschedule option can perform a task for a period of time
and then stop or return to a normal routine.

27. Where do you find the Task Scheduler?

    B. In the My Computer icon

From the My Computer icon, you can access the Tasks Scheduler. For more information, see "Scheduling Tasks by Using the Task Scheduler."

28. What application can be added to the Task Scheduler?

    C. Any application currently installed on the system

Any application that is on the system can be added to the list of tasks. Only tasks that can be automated should be added to the list because they can be configured to run without user intervention. For more information, see "Scheduling Tasks by Using the Task Scheduler."

29. What is the purpose of the Task Scheduler? Select the best answer.

    C. To perform regular maintenance on a system after hours

The Task Scheduler was intended to work with or instead of the Maintenance Wizard to automate routine functions. These functions can take place when the user is not using the system. For more information, see "Scheduling Tasks by Using the Task Scheduler."

30. Proposed solution:

Create a batch file and copy it to all systems by placing a command in the Login script for all users. Enable Remote Administration and File and Printer Sharing on all systems. From the Tasks Scheduler on the administrator's system, create tasks for all systems.

    A. The proposed solution satisfies the required component and all the optional components.

The Task Scheduler cannot be used to manage scheduling of tasks remotely. For more information, see "Scheduling Tasks by Using the Task Scheduler."

Scheduling Tasks by Using the Task Scheduler

This explanation supports questions 27 through 30.

The Tasks Scheduler is simply an extension of the Maintenance Wizard. When you open the Scheduled Tasks item in My Computer, you will notice the three basic Maintenance items if your ran the Maintenance Wizard (see Figure 7.32).

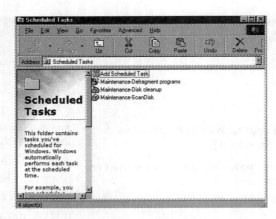

FIGURE 7.32
Because the Maintenance Wizard has already been run on the system, three tasks are in the Scheduled Tasks area.

The Scheduled Tasks window is the only way to delete tasks set up through the Maintenance Wizard.

Unlike the Maintenance Wizard, any application can be set up to run at a given time. As long as an application can be set up to run automatically (without user interaction), it can be added to the list.

There is also a Task Scheduler Wizard that will guide you through the steps. Adding a task will begin by listing all the applications on the systems (see Figure 7.33).

The second step is to determine the time, day, and frequency the task is going to run (see Figure 7.34).

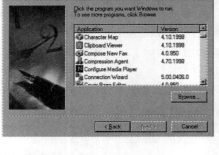

FIGURE 7.33
All applications on the local hard drive will be listed. This does not mean they can all be automated to run without user intervention.

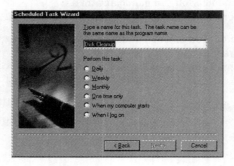

FIGURE 7.34
Depending on the frequency chosen, the following screen will allow for further clarification.

Each task, once it is added to the list, can be deleted or even detailed further. Each program has a full path, settings, and detail schedule that will appear when you double-click on the task name or user in the Properties item of the File menu (see Figure 7.35).

FIGURE 7.35
Selecting the properties of the task will reveal even more configuration settings.

All tasks are added to the list. If they are added manually through the Task Scheduler wizard or the Maintenance wizard, they are controlled and treated the same way.

31. What is the name of the command-line utility used to reload files from the source CAB files?

    D. Extract

31. CORRECT ANSWER: D

Extract is a command-line utility to extract and reload files from the source files. For more information, see "Checking for Corrupt Files."

32. How can you reload system files if Windows 98 is running?

    B. Using the System File Checker.

32. CORRECT ANSWER: B

The System File Checker can be run from within Windows 98. For more information, see "Checking for Corrupt Files."

33. Proposed solution:

Boot up the system using a startup disk and run the System Files Checker.

E. The proposed solution satisfies none of the optional components and does not satisfy the required component.

The System File Checker cannot run from a system disk. Rebooting the computer from a disk will only allow for the Extract command to work. You may not be aware of which file is corrupted. For more information, see "Checking for Corrupt Files."

Checking for Corrupt Files

This explanation supports questions 31 through 33.

Windows 98 provides two tools to deal with corrupted files. The first is using the Extract command to reload a file or files from the original CAB source files. The second is the System File Checker to verify the corrupted files.

The Extract command is a command-line utility that works best if the system is booted from a Windows 98 startup disk or at least in the command prompt.

To create a startup disk, use the Start Up Disk tab in the Add/Remove program icon of the Control Panel. The disk can be used to boot the system in a basic Windows 98 command line environment. Booting the system this way ensures that none of the files on the hard drive are opened and can be updated.

Following is the syntax to reload a file from a CAB file to the local hard drive:

```
- extract /a drive:\file.cab <filename> /l <destination>
```

The Extract command will use the switches from Table 7.3. For a complete list and description, use Extract /? at any command prompt.

TABLE 7.3 SWITCHES USED BY THE EXTRACT COMMAND

Switch	Function
/a	The Extract command looks into the CAB file mentioned and will continue to look in the other CAB files, if the file is not found.
/`	Copies the CAB file to a local destination.
/e	Extracts all files from a CAB file.

Switch	Function
/l	Indicates that the next location is the destination.
/y	Answers yes for any overwrite prompts.
/d	Displays the content of a CAB file without extracting any files.

You can use wildcards with the Extract command to access several files. The Extract command also can be set up to search through many CAB files. Windows 98 has `precopy1.cab`, `precopy2.cab`, and `mini.cab`, as well as the full program cabs that can be searched.

The System File Checker allows you to pinpoint which file(s) are corrupted before extracting any replacements for the CAB files. The tool can verify integrity, restore, or extract if needed.

The System File Checker is part of the System Information item in the System tools. Using the Tools menu, select System File Checker (see Figures 7.36 and 7.37).

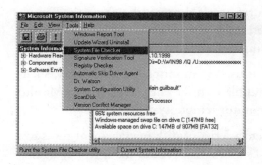

FIGURE 7.36
The System File Checker is part of the tools in the System Information program.

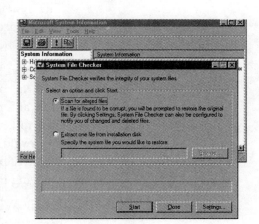

FIGURE 7.37
System File Checker can be used to scan the hard drive for corrupted files or extract files from the CAB files.

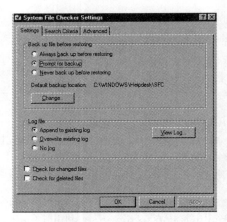

FIGURE 7.38
Additional settings can be configured prior to checking system files. File types may be added or removed from the list.

The System File Checker scans the system and verifies the integrity of all files. If a file is corrupt, it will be identified and then can be restored. The System File Checker can also be used to extract files in a GUI environment rather than using the Extract command-line utility. The System File Checker can be used in an active search or configured to notify the user when a problem does occur. Additional settings can be configured by clicking on the Setting button from the main System File Checker tool (see Figure 7.38).

CHAPTER SUMMARY

Windows 98 offers remote administration tools that can be used to monitor resource access through the network. The Net Watcher is used to determine who is accessing data and what shares they are accessing.

The System Monitor is used to monitor system activity, such as hard drive usage and file transfer rates. The System Monitor can also be used to monitor remote systems.

Windows 98 also offers a series of disk management tools to perform routine checks. ScanDisk verifies the integrity of the drive and tries to correct any data errors. Disk Defragmenter is used to keep all the clusters of a file in a contiguous stream to improve disk access times. DriveSpace improves the usage of the drive by compressing all the data into one large file, thus reducing the number of clusters with empty space.

Finally, Windows 98 offers a series of utilities to clean up the hard drive and maintain a proper working environment. To assist you in performing these tasks, Maintenance Wizard and Tasks Scheduler are used to perform routine checks. In the event of a corrupted file, the System File Checker and the Extract command are used to reload files from source CAB files.

CHAPTER 8

Troubleshooting

This troubleshooting chapter will pull together most topics in the book. Windows 98 ships with several tools used to help troubleshoot installation and configuration issues as well as user usage errors.

This chapter helps you prepare for the exam by covering the following objectives:

Diagnose and resolve installation failures. Tasks include the following:

- **Resolve file and driver version conflicts by using Version Conflict Manager and the Microsoft System Information utility.**

▶ Windows 98 can be installed as an upgrade and as such will overwrite certain files. As a precaution, the driver version manager can restore overwritten files if the need arises.

Diagnose and resolve boot process failures. Tasks include the following:

- **Editing configuration files by using System Configuration utility.**

▶ The System Configuration utility offers central tools to maintain and troubleshoot Windows 98.

continues

Diagnose and resolve connectivity problems in a Microsoft environment and a mixed Microsoft and NetWare environment. Tools include the following:

- **WinIPCfg**
- **Net Watcher**
- **PING**
- **TRACERT**

▶ WinIPCfg, among other TCP/IP troubleshooting tools, will help pinpoint communication setting errors. NetWatcher can be used to monitor remote user access to a given Windows 98 systems shared resources.

Diagnose and resolve printing problems in a Microsoft environment and a mixed Microsoft and NetWare environment.

▶ Windows 98 offers a few tips and a troubleshooting wizard in the help system to identify and correct print errors.

Diagnose and resolve file system problems.

▶ Each hard drive on a system needs to be properly maintained to eliminate file system errors and possible lost data.

Diagnose and resolve resource access problems in a Microsoft environment and a mixed Microsoft and NetWare environment.

▶ As more and more users share resources, they are confronted with access errors. Windows 98 tools can monitor access and permission of folders.

Diagnose and resolve hardware device and device driver problems. Tasks include the following:

- **Checking for corrupt Registry files by using ScanReg and ScanRegW**

▶ The Registry in Windows 98 is critical to the proper operation of the system and requires proper maintenance through the ScanReg and ScanRegW utilities.

DIAGNOSE AND RESOLVE INSTALLATION FAILURES

1. **Installation fails while Setup is detecting hardware devices. Which file can you check to help determine the cause of the failure?**

   A. `SYSTEM.INI`

   B. `SETUP.LOG`

   C. `DETLOG.LOG`

   D. `HARDWARE.INI`

   E. `DETCRASH.LOG`

2. **Which file does Windows 98 use if installation is interrupted (that is, by a failure) before hardware detection and then restart?**

   A. `STARTUP.LOG`

   B. `SETUP.LOG`

   C. `SETUPLOG.TXT`

   D. `DETLOG.LOG`

   E. `DETCRASH.LOG`

3. **What is the purpose of the `NETLOG.TXT` file?**

   A. Logging all invalid logon attempts

   B. Maintaining a list of all users that have made a network connection from the machine

   C. Keeping an encrypted list of Windows user IDs and passwords

   D. Tracking network component detection and installation

   E. None of the above

4. **Which file does Windows 98 Setup use to bypass devices that previously caused a hardware detection failure?**

   A. `DETCRASH.LOG`

   B. `DETLOG.LOG`

   C. `BYPASS.LOG`

   D. `SETUPLOG.TXT`

   E. `SETUP.LOG`

   The following question is scenario-based. Please read all the requirements and proposed solution before answering.

5. **Scenario:**

   A Windows 95 system is being upgraded to Windows 98. The installation seems to be successful.

   Required component:
   You need to verify that all resources are functioning correctly.

   Optional components:
   Verify that no hardware conflicts exist.

   Produce a printout of the current configuration settings.

   Proposed solution:
   After Windows 98 is installed, use the System Information utility and view the hardware category. From the File menu, select Print.

   A. The proposed solution satisfies the required component and all the optional components.

B. The proposed solution satisfies the required component and only one of the optional components.

C. The proposed solution satisfies the required component and none of the optional components.

D. The proposed solution satisfies only one of the optional components and does not satisfy the required component.

E. The proposed solution satisfies none of the optional components and does not satisfy the required component.

6. **If Setup fails during hardware detection, what should you do?**

A. Remove the hardware that is causing the failure.

B. Uninstall Windows 98, remove all log files, and restart the process.

C. Run Setup again, repeating the process until detection is completed.

D. Buy new hardware.

E. Windows 98 does not install devices that are incompatible and will not detect them.

ANSWER KEY

1. C	3. D	5. A
2. C	4. A	6. C

ANSWERS & EXPLANATIONS

DIAGNOSE AND RESOLVE INSTALLATION FAILURES

1. Installation fails while Setup is detecting hardware devices. Which file can you check to help determine the cause of the failure?

   C. DETLOG.TXT

1. CORRECT ANSWER: C

DETLOG.TXT is an ASCII file created by the Setup process that contains information about hardware detection. For more information, see "Resolving Installation Failures."

2. Which file does Windows 98 use if installation is interrupted (that is, by a failure) before hardware detection and then restart?

   C. SETUPLOG.TXT

2. CORRECT ANSWER: C

If the Setup process is interrupted, the SETUPLOG.TXT file will be used to restart from the point of interruption. For more information, see "Resolving Installation Failures."

3. What is the purpose of the NETLOG.TXT file?

   D. Tracking network component detection and installation

3. CORRECT ANSWER: D

NETLOG.TXT contains information about network detection and installation. For more information, see "Resolving Installation Failures."

4. Which file does Windows 98 Setup use to bypass devices that previously caused a hardware detection failure.

   A. DETCRASH.LOG

4. CORRECT ANSWER: A

If the hardware detection process fails, Setup uses DETCRASH.LOG to determine which device failed and bypass that device during the next Setup attempt. For more information, see "Resolving Installation Failures."

5. Proposed solution:

After Windows 98 is installed, use the System Information utility and view the hardware category. From the File menu, select Print.

   A. The proposed solution satisfies the required component and all the optional components.

5. CORRECT ANSWER: A

The System Information utility will be able to display the hardware configuration and system resource usage. For more information, see "Resolving Installation Failures."

6. If Setup fails during hardware detection, what should you do?

C. Run Setup again, repeating the process until detection is completed.

If Setup fails during hardware detection, rerun Setup. The hardware that caused the failure will be bypassed the second time. For more information, see "Resolving Installation Failures."

Resolving Installation Failures

This explanation supports questions 1 through 6.

Although Windows 98 has been designed to install without problems, hardware and software can cause problems during a Windows 98 installation. Microsoft has built-in mechanisms for the Windows 98 Setup program to detect failure and to recover automatically.

The Windows 98 Setup program maintains a setup log (SETUPLOG.TXT) during the installation and can determine where failures have occurred. The most likely place for failure is during hardware detection. A detection log (DETLOG.TXT) keeps track of what the Windows 98 Setup program discovers during the hardware detection phase. The following are basic Safe Recovery rules for you to know in case you have a failure:

- Before hardware detection begins, the Windows 98 Setup program uses SETUPLOG.TXT to determine the point of failure when you restart.

- The DETCRASH.LOG file is only created if there is a hardware failure during installation. This file contains information about the detection module that was running during the installation of 98. It also tracks the I/O and memory resources it was accessing during the failure. When the system reboots, the Safe Recovery mode knows to skip all detected modules up to the failed one. It will then bypass the problem module and go on to the next one. The DETCRASH.LOG file can be read only by the system setup. The DETLOG.TXT is the text equivalent of DETCRASH.LOG.

▼ **NOTE**

The DETLOG.TXT file is updated every time a new hardware device is added or the hardware detection process is run. The old file is renamed DETLOG.OLD and stored in the root directory of the startup drive.

- After completion of the hardware detection phase, the Windows 98 Setup program recognizes that hardware detection was successfully completed and skips past this point.

If Windows 98 Setup stops during hardware detection, execute the following steps:

1. Press F3 or click the Cancel button to quit Setup.

   If the computer does not respond to clicking the Cancel button, restart the computer by turning it off and then back on again. Do not just warm-boot using the Ctrl+Alt+Del key sequence.

2. Run Setup again. The Windows 98 Setup program prompts you to use Safe Recovery to recover the failed Windows 98 installation.

3. Choose Use Safe Recovery (should be the default) and then click on the Next button.

4. Repeat your installation choices. Hardware detection then runs again, but the Windows 98 Setup program skips the portion that caused the initial failure.

5. If the computer stops again during the hardware detection process, repeat this procedure until the hardware detection portion of Setup completes successfully.

DIAGNOSE AND RESOLVE BOOT PROCESS FAILURES

1. **You have just upgraded to Windows 98 and find that your network card is not working anymore. What can be done to restore the previous version of the driver?**

   A. Remove the network card and reinstall.

   B. Use the Restore command in the Backup utility recover the old driver.

   C. Use the Restore command in the System Configuration utility.

   D. Use the Restore command in the Version Conflict Manager.

   E. Delete all references to the card and install a new compatible card.

2. **Windows 98 can keep track of older files that have been overwritten if the system files are saved during an installation. What tool allows you to view the file-names and version numbers? Select the best answer.**

   A. The System Configuration Manager

   B. The System Information utility

   C. The Device Manager

   D. The Driver list in the System icon

   E. The Restore command

3. **If you have already installed Windows 98 successfully and you try to run Setup again, what happens?**

   A. The installed version is removed, and Windows 98 is reinstalled.

   B. Setup fails.

   C. You are prompted to either reinstall Windows or verify install components.

   D. Windows is uninstalled and the computer reverts to the previous operating system.

   E. Windows 98 will be reinstalled over the existing software.

4. **You need to control the way Windows 98 starts up in order to test a hypothesis. Which tool can be used? Select the best answer.**

   A. Using a Safe Mode boot with the F4 key

   B. Using the System Information utility

   C. Using the System Configuration utility

   D. Using the Version Conflict Manager and selecting the Boot sequence tab

   E. Using the System Boot Manager

5. **Windows 98 does not require the AUTOEXEC.BAT and CONFIG.SYS FILESbut they are still present for 16-bit applications and realmode drivers. How can Windows 98 edit the two files simultaneously? Select all that apply.**

   A. Using Sysedit from the Run command

   B. Using EDIT.COM from the Run command

C. Using the System Configuration Manager

D. Using the System Configuration utility

E. Using the Syscon utility

6. **How can you restart the system in Safe Mode? Select all that apply.**

A. Reboot by using the F8 key and select Safe Mode.

B. Reboot by using the F4 key and select Safe Mode.

C. Change the startup setting in the System Icon to default to Safe Mode.

D. Change the Selective Startup in the System Configuration utility.

E. In Safe Mode, select the Restart menu from the Start menu.

The following question is scenario-based. Please read all the requirements and proposed solution before answering.

7. **Scenario:**

A Windows 98 user would like to understand which settings are in place for various hardware.

Required component:
Display the information about various hardware on the system.

Optional components:
View the content of the AUTOEXEC.BAT and CONFIG.SYS files.

Disable Plug and Play on a card to avoid detection and configure the card manually.

Proposed solution:
Use the System Information utility to view the hardware settings and the System Configuration utility to view the AUTOEXEC.BAT and CONFIG.SYS. In the hardware category, disable Plug and Play for any card.

A. The proposed solution satisfies the required component and all the optional components.

B. The proposed solution satisfies the required component and only one of the optional components.

C. The proposed solution satisfies the required component and none of the optional components.

D. The proposed solution satisfies only one of the optional components and does not satisfy the required component.

E. The proposed solution satisfies none of the optional components and does not satisfy the required component.

8. **How can you get a list of 16-bit and 32-bit modules loaded in Windows 98?**

A. Use the System icon in the Control Panel.

B. Use the software component in the System Configuration utility.

C. Use the software component of the System Information utility.

D. Use the software component of the Version Conflict Manager.

E. None of the above.

9. **You have installed Windows 98 but continually receive error messages reporting
bad or missing files. What should you do?**

   A. Reinstall Windows 98.

   B. Always use Safe Mode.

   C. Run Setup's verification of installed components option.

   D. Use the Emergency Repair Disk.

   E. Use the Rebuild command to restore missing files.

ANSWER KEY

1. D	4. C	7. B
2. B	5. A-D	8. C
3. C	6. A-D	9. C

ANSWERS & EXPLANATIONS

DIAGNOSE AND RESOLVE BOOT PROCESS FAILURES

1. You have just upgraded to Windows 98 and find that your network card is not working any more. What can be done to restore the previous version of the driver?

   D. Use the Restore command in the Version Conflict Manager.

1. CORRECT ANSWER: D

The Version Conflict Manager will list new drivers and compare the version numbers. A Restore command is used to recover files. For more information, see "Resolving Boot Failures."

2. Windows 98 can keep track of older files that have been overwritten if the system files are saved during an installation. What tool allows you to view the filenames and version numbers? Select the best answer.

   B. The System Information utility

2. CORRECT ANSWER: B

The System Information utility will provide the Version Conflict Manager to view the files. For more information, see "Resolving Boot Failures."

3. If you have already installed Windows 98 successfully and you try to run Setup again, what happens?

   C. You are prompted to either reinstall Windows or verify install components

3. CORRECT ANSWER: C

If you run Setup on a machine that already has Windows 98 installed, Setup verifies the installed components. For more information, see "Resolving Boot Failures."

4. You need to control the way Windows 98 starts up in order to test a hypothesis. Which tool can be used? Select the best answer.

   C. Using the System Configuration utility

4. CORRECT ANSWER: C

The System Configuration utility offers a startup section to list all components. You can select which components to load. For more information, see "Resolving Boot Failures."

5. Windows 98 does not require the Autoexec.bat and Config.sys but they are still present for 16-bit applications and real-mode drivers. How can Windows 98 edit the two files simultaneously? Select all that apply.

   A. Using Sysedit from the Run command
   D. Using the System Configuration utility

5. CORRECT ANSWER: A-D

Sysedit is a basic editor that will list all specific configuration files. Sysedit must be run from the Start, Run menu. The System Configuration utility will offer CONFIG.SYS and AUTOEXEC.BAT file content. It offers a GUI environment to enable/disable, reorder content, edit, or add to AUTOEXEC.BAT and CONFIG.SYS files. The System Configuration utility can be found in the tools menu of the System Information utility. Sysedit also displays the content of MSMAIL.INI, SYSTEM.INI, WIN.INI, and PROTOCOL.INI. For more information, see "Resolving Boot Failures."

6. How can you restart the system in Safe Mode? Select all that apply.

    A. Reboot by using the F8 key and select Safe Mode.

    D. Change the Selective Startup in the System Configuration utility.

6. CORRECT ANSWER: A-D

Pressing the F8 key during boot-up will list startup options. Selecting Safe Mode will bypass most drivers. The Configuration utility can be changed to skip certain files during startup as well. For more information, see "Resolving Boot Failures."

7. Proposed solution:

Use the System Information utility to view the hardware settings and the System Configuration utility to view the Autoexec.bat and Config.sys. In the hardware category, disable Plug and Play for any card.

    B. The proposed solution satisfies the required component and only one of the optional components.

7. CORRECT ANSWER: B

The Configuration Manager can view the AUTOEXEC.BAT and CONFIG.SYS files. The Hardware category can be used to view information about hardware devices, but not disable Plug and Play. For more information, see "Resolving Boot Failures."

8. How can you get a list of 16-bit and 32-bit modules loaded in Windows 98?

    C. Use the software component of the System Information utility

8. CORRECT ANSWER: C

The software component will show the 16-bit and 32-bit modules that are currently loaded. For more information, see "Resolving Boot Failures."

9. You have installed Windows 98, but continually receive error messages reporting bad or missing files. What should you do?

    C. Run Setup's verification of installed components option.

9. CORRECT ANSWER: C

Run Setup's verification of installed components option. Through Setup, you can run a verification that will ensure that 98's system files are in working order. If they are found to be damaged or missing, Setup reinstalls the appropriate files. For more information, see "Resolving Boot Failures."

Resolving Boot Failures

This explanation supports questions 1 through 9.

Windows 98 provides a System Information utility that replaces the old version's Microsoft Windows Diagnostic. The new tool, however, will not only display system information but also offer tools to manage or repair the system. The system information can be found in the System Tools from the Accessories menu (see Figure 8.1). The System Information utility contains the following categories:

- **Hardware Resources**. This category will list all system resources in use by different hardware, as well as any conflicts or shared resources.

- **Components**. This category will list all the hardware present and show all information about the devices, including Registry entries.

- **Software environment**. This category will show which applications run in a 16- or 32-bit environment and will display all the settings.

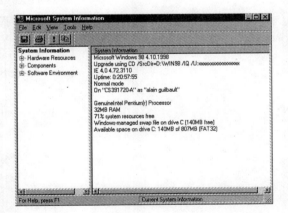

FIGURE 8.1
The System Information utility is used to view and edit configuration changes.

The System Information utility will connect to several additional tools to help in managing and editing the environment. Some of the tools can be accessed in other areas of Windows 98 (see Figure 8.2).

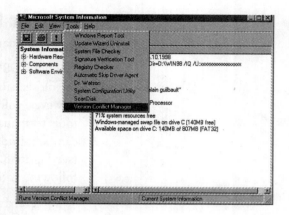

FIGURE 8.2
The Tools menu lists applications that will help in monitoring and actively altering system configuration.

One tool that can assist in installation troubleshooting is the Version Conflict Manager. It is found in the Tools menu of the Information Configuration utility. For some users, Windows 98 will be an upgrade. In such cases, there will be software and hardware drivers already installed. Windows 98 will upgrade to newer files if they are present. Windows 98 will also keep a backup copy if the installer requested it. Some newer drivers may not function properly, for whatever reason. The Version Conflict Manager can be used to revert back to an older driver (see Figure 8.3).

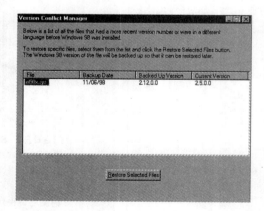

FIGURE 8.3
An older version of the network card driver can be restored over the new Windows 98 version, if the need arises.

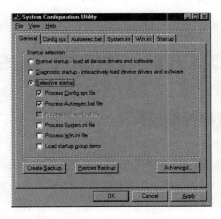

FIGURE 8.4

The startup routine can be altered while the system is being diagnosed.

The System Configuration utility is used instead of a text editor to edit the content of critical configuration files. This tool offers a central management concept.

As Windows 98 boots, several files are read into memory as well as into the Registry. Each of these files controls devices or software. During troubleshooting, it may be necessary to alter the normal startup procedure to isolate a specific device or component. The AUTOEXEC.BAT, CONFIG.SYS, PROTOCOL.INI, MSMAIL.INI, WIN.INI, and SYSTEM.INI can all be viewed and modified from the System Configuration utility. The entire settings can be backed up prior to making changes and can be restored in the event of a mistake (see Figure 8.4).

PRACTICE QUESTIONS

DIAGNOSE AND RESOLVE CONNECTIVITY PROBLEMS IN A MICROSOFT ENVIRONMENT AND A MIXED MICROSOFT AND NETWARE ENVIRONMENT

1. Which utility enables you to examine the IP address assigned to your computer?

   A. Net Watcher

   B. System Monitor

   C. WinIPCfg

   D. TCP/IP

   E. IPCONFIG

2. WinIPCfg enables you to view configuration values for computers running which protocol?

   A. TCP/IP

   B. NetBEUI

   C. IPX/SPX

   D. NetWare

   E. DLC

3. WinIPCfg helps you determine which values have been configured by DHCP.

   A. True.

   B. False. The answer should be TCPconfig.

   C. True if you configure TCP/IP to use DHCP only.

   D. False. The answer should be WINCFGIP.

   E. True if you install it separately.

4. Which of the following can explain why you are having problems connecting a client machine to a server?

   A. The two machines are running different operating systems.

   B. The two machines are running different protocols.

   C. The client user doesn't have sufficient rights.

   D. The server is running NT 3.51.

   E. None of the above.

5. In which situations can Dial-Up Networking be used?

   A. To connect to a Banyan VINES server running SLIP

   B. To connect a remote laptop to a Windows 98 computer using an ISDN line

   C. To connect to the Internet

   D. To connect to a Windows NT server using DLC

   E. To connect to OS/2 using DLC

6. Dial-Up Networking supports which two protocols to connect to a Windows NT server?

A. PPP

B. SLIP

C. CSLIP

D. RAS

E. DLC

7. **Which network transport protocols does PPP support?**

A. NetBEUI

B. IPX/SPX

C. TCP/IP

D. DLC

E. NDIS

8. **Which protocol must be used to connect to the Internet?**

A. NetBEUI

B. IPX/SPX

C. TCP/IP

D. Infrared

E. None of the above

9. **The files stored on the startup disk can be used only on the system from which the disk was created. Is this true or false?**

A. True if you copy exact files

B. False because the boot files are generic

C. True if you enable create unique disk

D. False because Windows 98's Registry files are generic

E. True if you copy the WINDOWS.INI file

10. **Which system cannot be used to connect to Windows 98 Dial-Up Networking?**

A. Windows NT

B. Windows for Workgroups

C. NetWare Connect

D. OS/2

E. Windows 98

11. **In which file are dialing properties for a modem stored?**

A. The Registry in HKEY_LOCAL_MACHINE

B. In a file named TELEPHON.INI

C. In a file named DIALUP.INI

D. In a file named TELEPHONY.INI

E. In the Registry under HKEY_MODEMS

12. **As an administrator, how can you make sure users are not sharing folders without appropriate permissions while maintaining remote administration? Select the best answer.**

A. Disable File Sharing

B. Monitor their systems with System Monitor and look for server traffic

C. Monitor their systems with Net Watcher

D. Monitor their systems with Share Manager

E. Disable printer sharing

13. **If enabled, a log file of all modem AT commands sent to the modem is stored in which file?**

A. `MODEM.LOG`.

B. `MODEMLOG.TXT`.

C. `AT.TXT`.

D. SYSTEM.LOG.

E. No such file exists.

14. **In a network situation, what can the startup disk *not* be?**

A. An image file on a network drive.

B. A floppy disk.

C. A hard disk.

D. A CD-ROM drive.

E. None of the above. The image can be any one of the list.

The following question is scenario-based. Please read all the requirements and proposed solution before answering.

15. **Scenario:**

One of your users is going to be connecting to various servers using Dial-Up Networking. You have to install the various networking protocols so that the computer can connect to each of the desired servers.

Required components:
Use Dial-Up Networking to connect to remote servers.

Connect to Windows NT servers.

Connect to NetWare servers.

Optional components:
Connect to the Internet.

Connect to UNIX servers.

Proposed solution:
You install TCP/IP with PPP and RAS protocols for your user so that he or she can remotely connect to servers using Dial-Up Networking.

A. The proposed solution satisfies all the required components and all the optional components.

B. The proposed solution satisfies all the required components but only one of the optional components.

C. The proposed solution satisfies all the required components but none of the optional components.

D. The proposed solution satisfies none of the required components but only one of the optional components.

E. The proposed solution satisfies none of the required components and none of the optional components.

ANSWER KEY

1. C	6. A-D	11. B
2. A	7. A-C	12. C
3. A	8. C	13. B
4. B-C	9. B	14. D
5. A-B-C	10. D	15. B

DIAGNOSE AND RESOLVE CONNECTIVITY PROBLEMS IN A MICROSOFT ENVIRONMENT AND A MIXED MICROSOFT AND NETWARE ENVIRONMENT

1. Which utility enables you to examine the IP address assigned to your computer?

C. WinIPCfg

1. CORRECT ANSWER: C

WinIPCfg is a utility that enables you to examine IP addresses. For more information, see "Connectivity Problems."

2. WinIPCfg enables you to view configuration values for computers running which protocol?

A. TCP/IP

2. CORRECT ANSWER: A

WinIPCfg lets you view computers running TCP/IP. For more information, see "Connectivity Problems."

3. WinIPCfg helps you determine which values have been configured by DHCP?

A. True.

3. CORRECT ANSWER: A

WinIPCfg can be used to determine which values have been set by DHCP. For more information, see "Connectivity Problems."

4. Which of the following can explain why you are having problems connecting a client machine to a server?

B. The two machines are running different protocols.

C. The client user doesn't have sufficient rights.

4. CORRECT ANSWER: B-C

If you cannot connect to a server, it might mean that the client and server are using different network protocols or that the client doesn't have the required privileges. For more information, see "Connectivity Problems."

5. In which situations can Dial-Up Networking be used?

A. To connect to a Banyan VINES server running SLIP

B. To connect a remote laptop to a Windows 98 computer using an ISDN line

C. To connect to the Internet

5. CORRECT ANSWER: A-B-C

Dial-Up Networking is most often used to connect to a network from offsite or to connect to the Internet by using a modem or IDSN line. DUN can connect to any server that supports SLIP. In all cases, the modem acts as a network card to provide connectivity. For more information, see "Connectivity Problems."

6. **Dial-Up Networking supports which two protocols to connect to a Windows NT server?**

    A. PPP

    D. RAS

6. CORRECT ANSWER: A-D

SLIP and CSLIP are used to connect to UNIX servers. For more information, see "Connectivity Problems."

7. **Which network transport protocols does PPP support?**

    A. NetBEUI

    C. TCP/IP

7. CORRECT ANSWER: A-C

NetBEUI and TCP/IP are supported by PPP. For more information, see "Connectivity Problems."

8. **Which protocol must be used to connect to the Internet?**

    C. TCP/IP

8. CORRECT ANSWER: C

TCP/IP is the only protocol that provides Internet access. For more information, see "Connectivity Problems."

9. **The files stored on the startup disk can be used only on the system from which the disk was created. Is this true or false?**

    B. False because the boot files are generic

9. CORRECT ANSWER: B

The startup disk is generic and can be used to start up any Windows 98 system. For more information, see "Connectivity Problems."

10. **Which system cannot be used to connect to Windows 98 Dial-Up Networking?**

    D. OS/2

10. CORRECT ANSWER: D

Windows 98 can use Dial-Up Networking to connect only to Windows 98 and 95, Windows NT, Windows for Workgroups, and NetWare connect systems. For more information, see "Connectivity Problems."

11. **In which file are dialing properties for a modem stored?**

    B. In a file named TELEPHON.INI

11. CORRECT ANSWER: B

Modem properties are stored in the TELEPHON.INI text file in the \WINDOWS folder. For more information, see "Connectivity Problems."

12. **As an administrator, how can you make sure users are not sharing folders without appropriate permissions while maintaining remote administration? Select the best answer.**

    C. Monitor their systems with Net Watcher

12. CORRECT ANSWER: C

Each system can be monitored with Net Watcher. Shares can be created or stopped and the permissions viewed. For more information, see "Connectivity Problems."

13. If enabled, a log file of all modem AT commands sent to the modem is stored in which file?

    B. MODEMLOG.TXT.

MODEMLOG.TXT stores all AT commands sent by the modem. This file is used for troubleshooting purposes and can be viewed in the Advance box of the Modem properties. For more information, see "Connectivity Problems."

14. In a network situation, what can the startup disk *not* be?

    D. A CD-ROM drive.

CD-ROMs are not supported in a network environment as a startup disk. For more information, see "Connectivity Problems."

15. Proposed solution:

You install TCP/IP with PPP and RAS protocols for your user so that she can remotely connect to servers using Dial-Up Networking.

    B. The proposed solution satisfies all the required components but only one of the optional components.

Using PPP and RAS, the user can connect to NT servers but not UNIX servers. You must install SLIP or CSLIP to use Dial-Up Networking to connect to UNIX servers. For more information, see "Connectivity Problems."

Connectivity Problems

This explanation supports questions 1 through 15.

In Windows 98, there are several methods available to connect to Microsoft network or Mixed Microsoft and Novell network environments. Some tools will apply to all methods while others are specific to the connection type.

Dial-Up Networking

Various problems can occur when you use Dial-Up Networking to connect to remote computers. It is increasingly important these days to be aware of where problems can occur and how to fix them. Because of the growing popularity of the Internet, more and more people are using Dial-Up Networking.

The majority of the problems described in this section are common the first time a user attempts to establish a connection to a remote server. Problems such as using the wrong phone number or not having the proper protocol installed usually occur once. These are typically easy to fix if you know what to look for and how to go about correcting the problem.

Dial-Up Networking problems can be divided into six categories:

- **Modem problems:** Ensure that the modem is installed properly. Check to see that the phone line is plugged into the modem and that the modem is turned on (if it is an external modem). Also check to see that the phone line is plugged into the modem.

- **Phone numbers:** Ensure that the phone number being dialed is the correct number. If you share your modem with the phone line, disable call waiting. When dialing a long-distance number, ensure that the entire number, including 1 + area code, is being used.

- **Protocol:** Ensure that the same protocol (such as NetBEUI or IPX/SPX) is installed on the client and server. If TCP/IP is used, ensure that it is configured.

- **Access rights:** Ensure that you have the appropriate rights to connect to the remote server. If a password is used, check to see that the correct password is being typed.

- **Server problems:** If the client computer is configured properly, the problem might be with the server computer. Ensure that the server is configured to allow client to dial in. Check the modem and the phone line as well.

- **Application problems:** If the problem occurs when connected to the remote server, the connection might be bad or the application might not support remote access.

During installation of a modem, or when troubleshooting problems with a modem, you need to use the Modems Properties sheet and the Diagnostic tab of this sheet. The Modems Properties sheet tab is available by clicking the Modem icon in the Control Panel.

The Diagnostics tab on the Modems Properties sheet displays information about your modem, including the port it uses, resources, highest speed, and command set configured for it. You cannot run this utility while you are using the modem (see Figure 8.5).

FIGURE 8.5
All ports are listed and each modem will be shown. The Diagnostic tab can also be used to test a connection.

FIGURE 8.6
To record a log, use the Append to log check box. To view the log, select the View button.

Modem command logging is available only when you use Windows 98 TAPI-compliant communication software. Because Windows 3.1 communication software does not use the same software layers to communicate with the modem, Windows 98 cannot trap the AT commands that these applications send to the modem.

To diagnose connection problems when using Dial-Up Networking, Windows 98 provides two log files:

- PPPLOG.TXT
- MODEMLOG.TXT

The PPPLOG.TXT file contains information on how the software layers of PPP have processed a Dial-Up Networking call. This logging feature is disabled by default.

Although the MODEMLOG.TXT log file is not specific to Dial-Up Networking, it is nonetheless useful in troubleshooting connection difficulties. It records all AT-type commands sent to the modem and logs responses from the modem. This logging feature is disabled by default.

To enable modem command logging, select the modem in the Modems Control Panel applet, select the Connection tab of the Properties sheet, choose Advanced, and then choose Append to log. To view the log, the same dialog box offers View log button (see Figure 8.6).

A log file can be used to troubleshoot connection problems, such as modem initialization problems and slow baud rate connections, and to determine which computer (the host or the guest) is dropping the connection.

Using the Startup Disk to Repair a Faulty Network Setup
During the installation of Windows 98, the user is prompted to create a startup disk. This startup disk can also be created at a later time using the Add/Remove Program option in the Control Panel (see Figure 8.7).

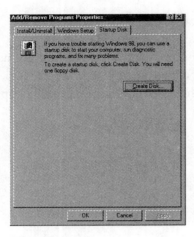

FIGURE 8.7
A startup disk is generic. It can be used on any Windows 98 system. After additional files are added, it may become specific to the system.

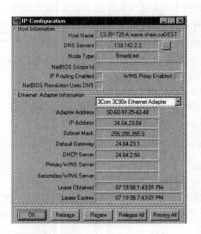

FIGURE 8.8
The WinIPCfg displays current TCP/IP address settings. Incorrect addressing will prevent connections.

The startup disk serves two primary functions:

- It functions as an emergency boot disk for Windows 98.
- It contains useful Windows 98/MS-DOS–based commands and utilities for troubleshooting purposes.

In addition, other files should be copied to the startup disk for troubleshooting purposes. These include the following:

- A copy of SYSTEM.DAT
- A copy of the computer's AUTOEXEC.BAT and CONFIG.SYS
- Any CD-ROM drivers

The startup disk also serves an additional function in a shared network installation. It contains real-mode software that is required to boot the computer and attach to the shared Windows folder located on the server. A copy of the mini-Registry used to start the computer is also stored on the startup disk. In a network situation, the startup disk can be a local drive or a disk image on the server.

WinIPCfg

WinIPCfg is a utility that comes with Windows 98 that lets you view information about your IP configuration. You can use this tool to view information about the following:

- Installed adapters
- The IP address assigned to your computer
- Subnet mask
- Default gateway
- Hostname
- DNS information
- Lease Information for an IP address

WINIPCFG.EXE is available in the \WINDOWS directory. To use WinIPCfg, choose Run from the Start menu, type it from an MS-DOS prompt, or find the application in the Windows directory (see Figure 8.8).

Net Watcher

Another tool for troubleshooting, available with Windows 98, is the Net Watcher. Net Watcher enables a user to manage shared resources on a local or remote computer. A user can create or delete a shared resource on a remote computer and monitor access to the shared resources.

The following characteristics must apply to use Net Watcher:

- File and Printer Sharing must be enabled on the remote computer.

- You can access only remote systems that use the same access control that you use on your computer; that is, both computers must be set to user-level access control or share-level access control.

- You can access only remote systems using the same type of File and Printer Sharing (Microsoft or NetWare).

Using Net Watcher, a user might perform the following tasks on the local or remote computer:

- List all shared resources and connected users.

- Create a new shared resource.

- Close files a user has opened (only on Microsoft networks).

- Disconnect a user from a shared resource.

Net Watcher is useful as an administration tool in a peer-to-peer network because it enables one administrator to manage the resources on all computers in the workgroup.

When connecting to a remote computer using share-level access control, the password used is the one specified in the Remote Administration dialog box.

When connecting to a remote computer using user-level access control, the password is the Administrator's account password.

Troubleshooting Wizards

Windows provides numerous troubleshooting wizards that can help you to resolve problems in Windows 98. These wizards are available as part of the help system. Simply click on Start and Help, and from the Windows 98 Help dialog box, click on the Contents tab. One of the books in the Contents is the Troubleshooting book (see Figure 8.9). From here, you can get help for the following items:

- Printing

- Hardware conflicts

- Networking

- Modem and dial-up problems

These wizards walk you through a series of questions to help you determine the cause of problems you are having with Windows 98.

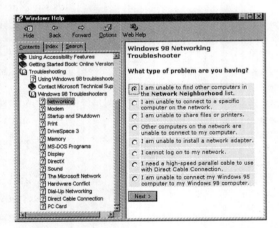

FIGURE 8.9

The wizard will ask questions and try to narrow down the scope of the search. Some areas of the wizard will offer links to the appropriate configuration tools in Windows 98.

DIAGNOSE AND RESOLVE PRINTING PROBLEMS IN A MICROSOFT ENVIRONMENT AND A MIXED MICROSOFT AND NETWARE ENVIRONMENT

1. **Which file is a built-in list of printer models and manufacturers?**

   A. PRINTERS.DAT

   B. PRTUPD.DAT

   C. PRTUPD.INF

   D. PRINTERS.INF

   E. PRINTS.DAT

2. **How can you start a Printer Wizard to help you troubleshoot printing problems?**

   A. Click on Start, Help, and then open the Troubleshooting book.

   B. Right-click on the Printer icon in the Control Panel and select Wizard.

   C. Click on Start, Programs, Accessories, and Troubleshooters.

   D. Run the Enhanced Print troubleshooter from the Windows 98 CD.

   E. Run the wizard from the Start Menu

3. **If you have print problems due to the spooler, how do you disable the spooler?**

   A. From the Device Manager.

   B. From the printer's properties.

   C. From the printer itself.

   D. The spooler cannot be disabled.

   E. From the Spooler's properties.

4. **You have installed a printer on a network, and you have shared it so that your users can print remotely to that printer. One of the users tells you that he's trying to print but isn't receiving any output and isn't getting any error messages. What is the most likely cause of the problem? Choose two correct answers.**

   A. The user isn't logged onto the network.

   B. The user is printing to a different printer.

   C. The printer is paused.

   D. The user's machine doesn't have File and Printer Sharing.

   E. The printer is not configured to use Windows 98.

5. **How can you clear the print buffer?**

   A. Right-click the Printer icon and select the Clear Buffer option.

   B. Reinstall the print drivers.

   C. Turn the printer off and on.

   D. Disconnect the printer from the PC and then reconnect it.

   E. Use the Clear Buffer button in the Printer properties.

6. **Where do you control the printing format of RAW or EMF?**

    A. From the Printer Wizard in the Help system.

    B. From the Properties of the Add Printer icon in the Control Panel.

    C. This cannot be done. Some printers do not support EMF spooling.

    D. From the properties of the printer.

    E. From the EMF icon in the Control Panel.

7. **What are possible causes for slow printing?**

    A. Low hard-disk space.

    B. Low system resources.

    C. A clogged print head.

    D. A loose connection to the printer.

    E. The printer is full.

8. **The Print Troubleshooter is a wizard that helps you fix printer problems. How do you run the Troubleshooter?**

    A. From the Windows 98 CD-ROM

    B. By right-clicking the Printer icon and selecting Print Wizard

    C. From the Programs, Accessories, System Tools menu

    D. By opening the Troubleshooting book from Windows Help

    E. From the Wizard in the Start menu

9. **Which of the following improves printer performance? Select all that apply.**

    A. Adding more RAM to the computer

    B. Increasing printer memory

    C. Running the Disk Defragmenter

    D. Printing with lower resolutions

    E. All of the above

10. **Your computer is running Windows 98 and you want to share your printer on the Windows NT network. You want only valid NT users to access the printer. Which access control should you select in the network properties?**

    A. Share-level

    B. User-level

    C. Domain-level

    D. Admin-level

    E. Group-level

11. **You are printing many documents to your local printer. You need to send a financial report to the printer but are worried that it will not print in time for the meeting in 10 minutes. What is the best method to ensure that the financial budget prints next?**

    A. Purge the printer and then send the financial budget.

    B. Delete all print jobs from the print queue that came before the financial budget.

    C. Pause all individual print jobs except the financial budget.

    D. Reorder the print jobs by dragging the financial budget print job to the top of the list after the currently printing print job.

    E. Nothing can be done about print jobs.

12. **A user calls informing you that she cannot print to a network printer. What should you check? Select all that apply.**

    A. Check the user permissions for the shared printer.

    B. Check whether the user has logged on to the network properly.

    C. Check to see whether the printer is shared.

    D. Check to see whether the printer is online.

    E. All of the above.

13. **A user can print from a Windows 32-bit application but cannot print from an MS-DOS application. What should you do to enable printing?**

    A. Reinstall the print driver.

    B. Capture the printer port in the printer's Properties dialog box.

    C. Enable spooling for MS-DOS applications.

    D. Redirect the print job to a network printer by using a UNC.

    E. Use the DOS properties tab.

14. **When printing many files to a printer, it takes too long for the print jobs to spool** and return control to the application. **What should you enable to speed up the processing of the print jobs by the printer?**

    A. Set the spool option to use Virtual Memory.

    B. Set the jobs to print directly to the printer.

    C. Set the spool option to print after the last page is spooled.

    D. Set the spool option to print after the first page is spooled.

    E. Disable the spool option.

15. **A user printed a memo but the print job does not reach the desired printer. No print errors were displayed and the job is not listed in the print queue. What is the most likely cause?**

    A. The wrong print driver was installed.

    B. The user is not logged on to the network.

    C. The print job was sent to another printer.

    D. The printer was paused.

    E. The printer that was chosen was turned off and Windows 98 just sent the job to an active printer.

ANSWER KEY

1. C	6. D	11. D
2. A	7. A-B	12. E
3. B	8. D	13. B
4. B-C	9. E	14. D
5. C	10. B	15. C

DIAGNOSE AND RESOLVE PRINTING PROBLEMS IN A MICROSOFT ENVIRONMENT AND A MIXED MICROSOFT AND NETWARE ENVIRONMENT

1. Which file is a built-in list of printer models and manufacturers?

   C. PRTUPD.INF

1. CORRECT ANSWER: C

The PRTUPD.INF file is a list of supported printers and manufacturers. For more information, see "Printing."

2. How can you start a Printer Wizard to help you troubleshoot printing problems?

   A. Click on Start, Help, and then open the Troubleshooting book.

2. CORRECT ANSWER: A

The Printer Troubleshooter is available from the Help window. For more information, see "Printing."

3. If you have print problems due to the spooler, how do you disable the spooler?

   B. From the printer's properties.

3. CORRECT ANSWER: B

The spooler can be disabled from the printer's property page. For more information, see "Printing."

4. You have installed a printer on a network, and you have shared it so that your users can print remotely to that printer. One of the users tells you that he's trying to print but isn't receiving any output and isn't getting any error messages. What is the most likely cause of the problem? Choose two correct answers.

   B. The user is printing to a different printer.

   C. The printer is paused.

4. CORRECT ANSWER: B-C

If the user doesn't receive any error messages, it most likely means that data is being printed, but by a printer other than the one desired. It can also mean that the printer is paused and that the print job is simply waiting in the queue. For more information, see "Printing."

5. How can you clear the print buffer?

   C. Turn the printer off and on.

5. CORRECT ANSWER: C

Turning the printer off and on clears the print buffer. For more information, see "Printing."

6. Where do you control the printing format of RAW or EMF?

    D. From the properties of the printer.

6. CORRECT ANSWER: D

The printer properties will allow you to control where the system is using RAW or EMF. For more information, see "Printing."

7. What are possible causes for slow printing?

    A. Low hard-disk space

    B. Low system resources

7. CORRECT ANSWER: A-B

Slow printing can be caused by low system resources, or low hard-disk space that is required for spooling. For more information, see "Printing."

8. The Print Troubleshooter is a wizard that helps you fix printer problems. How do you run the Troubleshooter?

    D. By opening the Troubleshooting book from Windows Help

8. CORRECT ANSWER: D

The Printer Troubleshooter is run from Windows Help. For more information, see "Printing."

9. Which of the following improves printer performance? Select all that apply.

    E. All of the above

9. CORRECT ANSWER: E

All these options improve printer performance in Windows 98. Adding memory to the computer and the printer reduces the need to access the hard drive. Running the Defragmenter opens more contiguous space for spooling. For more information, see "Printing."

10. Your computer is running Windows 98 and you want to share your printer on the Windows NT network. You only want valid NT users to access the printer. Which access control should you select in the network properties?

    B. User-level

10. CORRECT ANSWER: B

User-level security enables the user to select valid users from the NT domain. The name of the domain from which the users are a member must be provided as the security provider. For more information, see "Printing."

11. You are printing many documents to your local printer. You need to send a financial report to the printer but are worried that it will not print in time for the meeting in 10 minutes. What is the best method to ensure that the financial budget prints next?

    D. Reorder the print jobs by dragging the financial budget print job to the top of the list after the currently printing print job.

11. CORRECT ANSWER: D

Reordering the print job is the simplest and fastest method. Be sure to place the print job in the list after the currently printing print job. For more information, see "Printing."

12. A user calls informing you that she cannot print to a network printer. What should you check? Select all that apply.

    E. All of the above.

12. CORRECT ANSWER: E

All the options affect printing to access to a network shared printer. For more information, see "Printing."

13. A user can print from a Windows 32-bit application but cannot print from an MS-DOS application. What should you do to enable printing?

    B. Capture the printer port in the printer's Properties dialog box.

13. CORRECT ANSWER: B

Most MS-DOS applications require the printer to be physically attached to a printer port. This can be done by capturing the printer port in the Details tab of the printer's Properties dialog box. For more information, see "Printing."

14. When printing many files to a printer, it takes too long for the print jobs to spool and return control to the application. What should you enable to speed the processing of the print jobs by the printer?

    D. Set the spool option to print after the first page is spooled.

14. CORRECT ANSWER: D

Setting the spool option to print after the first page has spooled enables the printer to print while the other pages are spooling. This is enabled by default. For more information, see "Printing."

15. A user printed a memo but the print job does not reach the desired printer. No print errors were displayed and the job is not listed in the print queue. What is the most likely cause?

    C. The print job was sent to another printer.

15. CORRECT ANSWER: C

The most likely cause is that the wrong printer was selected as the default printer. Ensure that the desired printer is selected. For more information, see "Printing."

Printing

This explanation supports questions 1 through 15.

This section addresses the issues of printer optimization and troubleshooting printer problems. To optimize printer performance, you typically adjust spool settings for the printer. When dealing with printer performance, you must also remember "perceived speed"—how does the user perceive the speed of the printer and how quickly does control return to the application? This section also provides recommended steps to use when approaching printer problems.

Each Windows 98 computer's printer spool can be configured for EMF printing or RAW printing.

- EMF uses a proprietary internal page description format called *Enhanced Metafile* for printing. EMF is printer-independent with most of the processing of the print job to RAW format occurring in the background. This returns control back to the application sooner than printing in RAW format.

- RAW printing is printer-dependent format with the processing occurring in the foreground. This results in a long wait for control to return to the application.

On a local Windows 98 computer, both processes occur at the local computer. In a Microsoft networked environment, the process of converting the EMF format to the printer's RAW format occurs on the server (see Figure 8.10).

Each Windows 98 computer can also be configured to return control to the user after the print job is submitted. Print jobs can be configured to start printing after the last page has been spooled or after the first page has been spooled. The printer can also be configured to print directly to the printer on a local computer; however, this method is the slowest.

These options can be configured in the Spool Settings (from the Device Options tab of the Printer Properties dialog box).

FIGURE 8.10

Not all printers can use the new EMF spool. If EMF is available, it will return control to the application much faster than RAW.

Use the following guidelines to solve printing problems:

- Ensure that the printer is turned on, is online, and has paper in the paper tray.

- Ensure that the printer is not paused or does not have a print job that is stuck.

- Ensure that the printer cable is attached to the printer and to the computer. If using a serial cable, ensure that it is plugged into the correct serial port on the Windows 98 computer (if it has multiple serial ports).

- Ensure that the printer properties are correct by right-clicking the printer and selecting Properties. Be sure that the correct print driver is installed and that paper options are set correctly.

- Ensure that the latest driver is being used. Download an upgraded 32-bit driver from the printer manufacturer's Web page if necessary.

- Ensure that print spooling has enough free disk space. If necessary, delete unnecessary files or compress the drive.

- Try printing from another application. If you can print, the original application might have to be reconfigured. If you cannot print, reinstall the printer.

- Print to a file instead of the printer. Copy the file to the printer port in DOS. If the file prints correctly, the spooler might be corrupt.

- Restart Windows 98. Try turning the printer on and off to clear its buffer.

- Document all printing problems and their solutions. Have this information available to all users in the work-group via an intranet or email.

- If it is a shared printer on the network, you can access other shared printers on the same systems.

Novell systems can also provide printer to Windows 98 systems if the Windows 98 systems have a NetWare client. Novell printers are shared through print queues to which the Windows 98 system connects.

Some network printer diagnostics may resolve the problem. These include the following:

- Check to see that the printer has a current connection to the network.

- Try to ping the printer.

- Check to see whether the icon is grayed out in the settings/printer section.

- Check to see whether other users on the network can print to the printer.

- Check to see whether the user is trying to print a PostScript file to a non-PostScript printer.

PRACTICE QUESTIONS

DIAGNOSE AND RESOLVE FILE SYSTEM PROBLEMS

1. Disabling write-behind caching will _____. (Complete the sentence with all that apply.)

   A. Cause data to be saved immediately

   B. Cause files to be stored when the system is idle

   C. Improve disk performance

   D. Degrade disk performance

   E. Improve access time

2. If you suspect that the problems you are having with corrupt files are related to physical problems on your hard drive, which utility should you run?

   A. Disk Defragmenter

   B. ScanDisk

   C. System Monitor

   D. Net Watcher

   E. Troubleshooting Wizard

3. What are the typical roles that can be selected for a computer from the System Performance tab?

   A. Desktop computer

   B. Net PC

   C. Mobile computer

   D. Network Server

   E. Remote system

4. CD-ROM cache is the same cache used for disk and network access.

   A. True if the CD-ROM is synchronized with the disk

   B. False because Windows 98 uses a separate cache for CD-ROMs

   C. True if the disk cache is disabled

   D. False because Windows 98 uses a separate cache for floppy drives, local drives, network drives, and CD-ROMs

   E. True if the CD-ROM cache is disabled

5. Which two features affect Windows 16-bit applications?

   A. Disabling file sharing

   B. Disabling write-behind caching

   C. Disabling Long Filename preservation for old programs

   D. Enabling Windows 98 support for Win 16-bit applications

   E. None of the above

6. Long Filenames are preserved for older applications using which technique?

   A. LFN conversion

   B. Thunking

   C. Tunneling

   D. Thonking

   E. LFNBK

7. **If you have older disk drives that aren't properly reading or writing under Windows 98, which of the following can you do?**

   A. Disable real-mode drivers.

   B. Disable protected-mode drivers.

   C. Disable FAT16 drivers.

   D. Disable FAT32 drivers.

   E. Disable real-mode drivers.

8. **You want to increase the performance of a dual-speed CD-ROM drive by setting the CD-ROM as a quad speed in the CD-ROM Settings tab of the File System Properties dialog box. You notice, however, that the system is even slower than it was before you made the change. Why is the CD-ROM drive slower?**

   A. Changing the setting sets the cache size to 0.

   B. You do not have enough RAM to support the new setting.

   C. Windows 98 detected that the CD-ROM is not a quad speed.

   D. Windows 98 can only use 20X-and-up CD-ROM.

   E. None of the above.

9. **How many directory entries are allowed in the root of a drive using FAT16?**

   A. 128

   B. 256

   C. 512

   D. 1,024

   E. 2,048

10. **You are experiencing intermittent problems with your older 240MB hard disk while running Windows 98. Which feature(s) should you disable?**

    A. File sharing

    B. Long Filename preservation

    C. Protected-mode hard disk interrupt handling

    D. All 32-bit protected-mode disk drivers

    E. Windows 98 support for Large Disks (FAT32)

11. **Long Filenames can be temporarily disabled if you need to run an application that doesn't support them.**

    A. True by using the File System tab

    B. False because Long Filenames are an integral part of Windows 98

    C. True by using the Long Filename switch on Startup

    D. False because Windows 98 supports both short and long names

    E. True by using the Device Manager

12. **Which utility is used to remove and restore Long Filenames?**

    A. LongFN

    B. SwapLFN

    C. LFNBK

    D. BackLFN

    E. Backup

13. **If you back up and delete Long Filenames, how does Windows 98 store the information to restore the names?**

A. In the System Registry.

B. In LFNBK.DAT.

C. In the SYSTEM.INI file.

D. It doesn't. They must be restored manually.

E. In the BACKUP.INI file.

14. **How do you permanently disable Long Filenames?**

A. LFNBK /b

B. From the File System icon in the Control Panel.

C. ScanDskw /o

D. You cannot permanently disable Long Filenames.

E. LFNBK /L

15. **Which applications do not support Long Filenames?**

A. MS-DOS applications

B. Windows 16-bit applications

C. Windows 32-bit applications

D. OS/2-based applications

E. All of the above

ANSWER KEY

1. A-D	6. C	11. A
2. B	7. B	12. C
3. A-C-D	8. B	13. B
4. B	9. C	14. A-C
5. A-C	10. C-D	15. A-B

DIAGNOSE AND RESOLVE FILE SYSTEM PROBLEMS

1. Disabling write-behind caching will _____. Complete the sentence with all that apply.

    A. Cause data to be saved immediately

    D. Degrade disk performance

1. CORRECT ANSWER: A-D

Disabling write-behind caching causes data to be saved immediately instead of being placed in cache. This degrades disk performance because the system must deal with each write immediately instead of when it has free time. For more information, see "File System Problems."

2. If you suspect that problems you are having with corrupt files are related to physical problems on your hard drive, which utility should you run?

    B. ScanDisk

2. CORRECT ANSWER: B

A thorough ScanDisk detects physical problems on a hard drive. For more information, see "File System Problems."

3. What are the typical roles that can be selected for a computer from the system performance tab?

    A. Desktop computer

    C. Mobile computer

    D. Network server

3. CORRECT ANSWER: A-C-D

You can identify your computer as a desktop, mobile, or network server through the System Performance tab. For more information, see "File System Problems."

4. CD-ROM cache is the same cache used for disk and network access.

    B. False because the Windows 98 uses a separate cache for CD-ROMs

4. CORRECT ANSWER: B

CD-ROM and disk access use separate caches. For more information, see "File System Problems."

5. Which two features affect Windows 16-bit applications?

    A. Disabling file sharing

    C. Disabling Long Filename preservation for old programs

5. CORRECT ANSWER: A-C

Disabling file sharing and Long Filename preservation can affect older 16-bit applications. Long Filenames are not supported under most 16-bit applications, and the Windows 98 file sharing might not be compatible with older 16-bit applications. For more information, see "File System Problems."

6. **Long Filenames are preserved for older applications by using which technique?**

   C. Tunneling

6. CORRECT ANSWER: C

Tunneling is used by Windows 98 to preserve Long Filenames with older applications. For more information, see "File System Problems."

7. **If you have older disk drives that aren't properly reading or writing under Windows 98, which of the following can you do?**

   B. Disable protected-mode drivers.

7. CORRECT ANSWER: B

Disabling protected-mode drivers might help you access older disk devices. For more information, see "File System Problems."

8. **You want to increase the performance of a dual-speed CD-ROM drive by setting the CD-ROM as a quad speed in the CD-ROM Settings tab of the File System Properties dialog box. You notice, however, that the system is even slower than it was before you made the change. Why is the CD-ROM drive slower?**

   B. You do not have enough RAM to support the new setting.

8. CORRECT ANSWER: B

Changing the CD-ROM setting increases the amount of cache available to the CD-ROM. This can negatively affect system performance if RAM is limited. For more information, see "File System Problems."

9. **How many directory entries are allowed in the root of a drive using FAT16?**

   C. 512

9. CORRECT ANSWER: C

The limit of directory entries is 512 for the root directory. Each Long Filename will take up one entry for each 13 characters and one entry for the short name. For more information, see "File System Problems."

10. **You are experiencing intermittent problems with your older 240MB hard disk while running Windows 98. Which feature(s) should you disable?**

   C. Protected-mode hard disk interrupt handling

   D. All 32-bit protected-mode disk drivers

10. CORRECT ANSWER: C-D

Older drives might not support the newer 32-bit drivers. Also, Windows 98's protected-mode hard disk interrupt handling might cause problems with older drives for the same reason. For more information, see "File System Problems."

11. Long Filenames can be temporarily disabled if you need to run an application that doesn't support them.

   A. True by using the File System tab

Long Filenames can be disabled if necessary to run older applications. For more information, see "File System Problems."

12. Which utility is used to remove and restore Long Filenames?

   C. LFNBK

LFNBK is the utility that can be used to disable and enable Long Filenames. For more information, see "File System Problems."

13. If you back up and delete Long Filenames, how does Windows 98 store the information to restore the names?

   B. In LFNBK.DAT.

When you disable Long Filenames, the information is stored in LFNBK.DAT and is used when Long Filenames are restored. For more information, see "File System Problems."

14. How do you permanently disable Long Filenames?

   A. LFNBK /b
   C. ScanDskw /o

Both LFNBK and ScanDskw can be used to permanently disable Long Filenames. For more information, see "File System Problems."

15. Which applications do not support Long Filenames?

   A. MS-DOS applications
   B. Windows 16-bit applications

MS-DOS and most Windows 16-bit applications do not support Long Filenames. For more information, see "File System Problems."

File System Problems

This explanation supports questions 1 through 15.

Most applications work under Windows 98 with little, if any, user intervention. Some older MS-DOS and Windows 16-bit applications, however, might not run properly under Windows 98's file system. To solve this problem, some advanced features of Windows 98 can be disabled to provide support for older applications. The following features can be enabled or disabled using the File System box of the Performance tab of the My Computer Properties sheet. The System icon in the Control Panel will take you to the same location (see Figure 8.11).

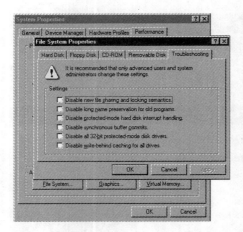

FIGURE 8.11
Microsoft recommends leaving the settings as is unless specific applications are not functioning properly. Disabling items in this dialog box will disable some Windows 98 advancements.

The following options are found in the Troubleshooting tab:

- **Disable New File Sharing and Locking Semantics.** Some older applications do not work properly using Windows 98's file sharing. Disable this option until the application is updated and works properly with Windows 98.

- **Disable Long Name Preservation for Old Programs.** Some older applications, especially Windows 16-bit applications, do not support Long Filenames and will destroy the Long Filenames of files saved with the application. Disable this feature to provide compatibility with short filenames.

- **Disable Protected-Mode Hard Disk Interrupt Handling.** Some applications have disk access problems using Windows 98's 32-bit virtual disk driver. Disable this feature to provide compatibility but note that you will experience a performance penalty.

- **Disable All 32-Bit Protected-Mode Disk Drivers.** Some older disk drives do not work properly with Windows 98's disk drivers when reading or writing to the hard disk. Disable this feature to enable real-mode drivers that are supported. This degrades disk performance, however.

- **Disable Write-Behind Caching for All Drives.** Windows 98 uses write-behind caching to enhance disk performance by storing writes to the hard disk in cache temporarily until the processor can commit the cache to disk. Disabling this feature writes the data immediately to disk. This slows down disk performance but ensures that the data is written to disk in the event of a power failure.

Four key disk-management utilities are included with Windows 98. Each is intended to address particular file system issues or problems. Table 8.1 provides a summary of the disk-management utilities and the issues they address.

TABLE 8.1   WINDOWS 98 UTILITIES FOR VARIOUS FILE SYSTEM ISSUES

Utility	Issue
Disk Defragmenter	Prevention of file system performance degradation due to inefficient hard disk access
ScanDisk	Correction of cross-linked files, lost clusters, and other hard disk errors
Backup	Prevention of data loss due to power failures, corruption, or hard disk failures
Disk Compression	Maximization of available hard disk space

To select the appropriate disk-management tool, you must examine the symptoms displayed in a given situation. Table 8.2 matches symptoms to the appropriate disk-management tool to be used to correct them.

TABLE 8.2   SELECTING THE APPROPRIATE TOOL FOR VARIOUS FILE SYSTEM SYMPTOMS

Utility	Symptom
Disk Defragmenter	Applications open, read, or write to files slowly.
ScanDisk	Applications report corruption of data or are unable to open files.
Backup	Valuable data is considered to be at risk of loss.
Disk Compression	Applications report insufficient available hard disk space.

The use of one utility often leads to the use of another. For example, while you're correcting slow hard disk access by running Disk Defragmenter, the utility might report an error. In this case, run ScanDisk and specify a physical surface scan.

DIAGNOSE AND RESOLVE RESOURCE ACCESS PROBLEMS IN A MICROSOFT ENVIRONMENT AND A MIXED MICROSOFT AND NETWARE ENVIRONMENT

1. **If other users cannot connect to your shared resources, what should you do?**

   A. Verify that File and Printer Sharing is installed.

   B. Make sure you are running TCP/IP.

   C. Check to see whether the other users are running a common protocol.

   D. Be sure to configure your computer as a server.

   E. Make sure you are running IPX.

2. **If File and Printer Sharing for NetWare Networks is installed, which security option must be used?**

   A. Share-level

   B. User-level

   C. Group-level

   D. Admin-level

   E. Password-level

3. **Under which security option are passwords assigned to each resource?**

   A. Share-level

   B. User-level

   C. Group-level

   D. Admin-level

   E. Password-level

4. **What Access option(s) can be assigned to share-level resources?**

   A. Read

   B. Read/Write

   C. Full

   D. Depends on password

   E. Change

5. **If no password is assigned a resource in share-level security, what rights will a remote user have to the directory?**

   A. Full

   B. Read-only

   C. Depends on which option was specified when the shared directory was created

   D. Modify

   E. No Access

6. **When implementing user-level security, where can a Windows 98 machine obtain an accounts list for resources?**

   A. A Windows NT server

   B. A Windows 98 client

   C. A NetWare 3.x server

   D. A NetWare 4.x server

   E. Windows for Workgroups

7. **What happens when you change from share-level security to user-level security or vice versa?**

    A. Access rights are converted when changing from one to the other.

    B. Access rights are converted only when changing to share-level.

    C. Access rights are converted only when changing to user-level.

    D. Access rights are not converted and must be set up again.

    E. Access rights are not converted and must be saved separately before changing and restored afterward.

8. **Which level of security is used by default when Microsoft File and Printer Sharing is installed?**

    A. Group-level

    B. User-level

    C. Share-level

    D. Resource-level

    E. Admin-level

9. **Print queues also can be shared with other network users by using _____. Choose from the following to fill in the blank.**

    A. Group-level

    B. User-level

    C. Share-level

    D. Resource-level

    E. Password-level

10. **With which level of security can specific user accounts or group accounts be granted access to a shared directory or printer?**

    A. Group-level

    B. User-level

    C. Share-level

    D. Resource-level

    E. Password-level

ANSWER KEY

1. A-C
2. B
3. A
4. A-C-D

5. C
6. A-C-D
7. D
8. C

9. C
10. B

ANSWERS & EXPLANATIONS

DIAGNOSE AND RESOLVE RESOURCE ACCESS PROBLEMS IN A MICROSOFT ENVIRONMENT AND A MIXED MICROSOFT AND NETWARE ENVIRONMENT

1. If other users cannot connect to your shared resources, what should you do?

   A. Verify that File and Printer Sharing is installed.

   C. Check to see whether the other users are running a common protocol.

1. CORRECT ANSWER: A-C

File and Printer Sharing must be enabled and common protocols must be used to allow sharing of resources. For more information, see "Resource Access Problems."

2. If File and Printer Sharing for NetWare networks is installed, which security option must be used?

   B. User-level

2. CORRECT ANSWER: B

If you use File and Printer Sharing for NetWare, you must also use user-level security. For more information, see "Resource Access Problems."

3. Under which security option are passwords assigned to each resource?

   A. Share-level

3. CORRECT ANSWER: A

Passwords are assigned to resources under Share-level security. For more information, see "Resource Access Problems."

4. Which access option(s) can be assigned to share-level resources?

   A. Read

   C. Full

   D. Depends on password

4. CORRECT ANSWER: A-C-D

Read/write is not an option of share-level security. For more information, see "Resource Access Problems."

5. If no password is assigned a resource in share-level security, what rights will a remote user have to the directory?

   C. Depends on which option was specified when the shared directory was created

5. CORRECT ANSWER: C

If no password is used, any user will have full or read-only access to the directory, depending on which option was specified when the shared directory was created. For more information, see "Resource Access Problems."

6. **When implementing user-level security, where can a Windows 98 machine obtain an account list for resources?**

   A. A Windows NT server

   C. A NetWare 3.x server

   D. A NetWare 4.x server

6. CORRECT ANSWER: A-C-D

Windows 98 can get an account list of resources from a Windows NT server, or NetWare 3.x and 4.x servers, but not a Windows 98 client. For more information, see "Resource Access Problems."

7. **What happens when you change from share-level security to user-level security or vice versa?**

   D. Access rights are not converted and must be set up again.

7. CORRECT ANSWER: D

Access rights are not converted when security is switched between share-level and user-level. For more information, see "Resource Access Problems."

8. **Which level of security is used by default when Microsoft File and Printer Sharing is installed?**

   C. Share-level

8. CORRECT ANSWER: C

Share-level security is used by default when File and Printer Sharing for Microsoft Networks is installed. For more information, see "Resource Access Problems."

9. **Print queues also can be shared with other network users by using**

   _____.

   C. Share-level

9. CORRECT ANSWER: C

Print queues can be shared with other network users using share-level security. For more information, see "Resource Access Problems."

10. **With which level of security can specific user accounts or group accounts be granted access to a shared directory or printer?**

   B. User-level

10. CORRECT ANSWER: B

With user-level security, specific user accounts or group accounts can be granted access to a shared directory or printer. For more information, see "Resource Access Problems."

Resource Access Problems

This explanation supports questions 1 through 10.

On a network, a user must often share resources (files or printers) with others and decide whether, and how, they will prevent unauthorized access to these resources.

Windows 98 enables you to leverage security access to users by utilizing either share-level or user-level security. Share-level security is used by default when File and Printer Sharing for Microsoft Networks is installed.

▼ **NOTE**

File and Printer Sharing for NetWare Networks must use user-level security. The share-level security option is unavailable if File and Printer Sharing for NetWare Networks is installed.

With share-level security, passwords are assigned to each individual share to permit access. To access the share, a user must supply the correct password. This can become difficult to manage, even in small workgroups. If no password is used, any user will have full or read-only access to the directory, depending on which option was specified when the shared directory was created. When creating a shared directory using share-level security, one of three types of access can be granted: Read, Full, or Depends on Password. Print queues also can be shared with other network users using share-level security. Printers are either shared or not shared in Windows 98.

Because share-level security relies on access passwords, this form of security has the following disadvantages:

- To access different shares, a network user must know numerous passwords.

- Passwords can easily be forgotten. Users must enter a password each time they try to access a share. If the creator of the share forgets the password, however, the password has to be changed to allow another user to access the share.

- Nothing prevents a user from disclosing the password to an unauthorized user.

With user-level security, specific user accounts or group accounts can be granted access to a shared directory or printer. Rather than relying on a password that can be used by anyone, the user account accessing a shared resource must be authenticated to ensure that the account has been granted access.

Windows 98 does not manage user accounts by itself. User-level security must rely on a central server such as NT or Novell. Before a user can gain access to a resource, he or she must log on to the central server or at least have an account on the central server. When a user tries to access a share, his or her name is passed-through for authentication to a Windows NT or NetWare server.

You can use user-level security to provide security for a variety of services beyond network access, such as network management, backup agents, and Dial-Up Networking.

To use user-level security, the Windows 98 computer must obtain a copy of the accounts list from one of the following sources:

- Windows NT server or Workstation 3.5 (or later) computer
- NetWare 3.x or 4.x

With user-level security, when a directory is shared, the users or groups that have access to the share are assigned privileges that allow the appropriate levels of access to the resource. When sharing a printer, users or groups can be added to a list of users with access to that printer.

Although you can change from user-level to share-level security, or from share-level to user-level security, you probably should not. When you switch from one to the other, you lose all the current security settings. You must re-create all security settings on each individual share.

DIAGNOSE AND RESOLVE HARDWARE DEVICE AND DEVICE DRIVER PROBLEMS

1. **You need to manually reallocate resources in your computer. Before you do, you want to look at the current allocations. Where can you display, by resource type, lists of all the devices on your computer? Select the best answer.**

   A. In Device Manager, click on My Computer in the device type list and choose Properties.

   B. In the Registry Editor, click on the plus sign (+) next to HKEY_LOCAL_MACHINE.

   C. The System Information utility in the System tools.

   D. In the Registry Editor, click on the + next to HARDWARE.

   E. From Help, select Resources.

2. **Adding a new card to your computer created a conflict between two devices. A Plug and Play card is using IRQ 5, but a legacy card also needs this same IRQ. Which is the best strategy for you to use to resolve the conflict?**

   A. Use Device Manager to manually change the IRQ settings for each device.

   B. Remove the Plug and Play device from the current configuration, manually change the IRQ setting for the legacy device, add the Plug and Play device back to the configuration, and then let

Windows 98 dynamically assign an available IRQ to the Plug and Play device.

   C. Physically remove the Plug and Play device from the computer, manually change the IRQ setting for the legacy device, insert the Plug and Play device back into the computer, and then let Windows 98 dynamically assign an available IRQ to the Plug and Play device.

   D. Change the jumper switch on the legacy device.

   E. Let Plug and Play deal with the allocation of resources.

3. **How do you gain access to the Device Manager?**

   A. Running it from the Windows 98 CD-ROM

   B. Through the troubleshooting tab in Help

   C. From the System dialog box of the Control Panel

   D. From the Device Manager icon in My Computer

   E. From the Start menu

4. **You just downloaded an updated driver for your display adapter. What are two ways you can install the new driver?**

A. Use the Change Driver button in the Driver tab of the device's properties sheet.

B. Copy the file to the `Drivers` directory.

C. Use the Network applet in the Control Panel.

D. Use the Add New Hardware applet in the Control Panel.

E. Run Setup again.

5. **Through the Device Manager, what information can you obtain from the device's property page? Select all that apply.**

A. Manufacturer

B. Supporting drivers

C. Driver version

D. Hardware version

E. All of the above

6. **You need to manually reconfigure one of your Plug and Play devices. What's the first thing you need to do to change the device's settings in the Resource tab of the device's Properties sheet?**

A. Double-click on the resource type you want to change.

B. Turn on the Allow Manual Settings check box.

C. Click on the resource type you want to change and then choose Change Settings.

D. Turn off the Use Automatic Settings check box.

E. Enable Plug and Play configuration.

7. **What are the two drawbacks of manually configuring a Plug and Play device?**

A. You must set jumpers or switches on the device.

B. The settings become fixed so that Windows 98 will have less flexibility when configuring other devices.

C. Doing so can cause hardware conflicts, making some devices unavailable on the system.

D. To do so, you must install the Configuration Manager from the Windows 98 CD-ROM.

E. The device will run slower.

8. **Which files make up the Windows Registry? Choose two.**

A. `SYSTEM.DAT`

B. `USER.DAT`

C. `WINDOWS.REG`

D. `REG.DAT`

E. `REGISTRY.DAT`

9. **What is the utility that you use to edit the Registry?**

A. `REGSVR.EXE`

B. `REGSVR32.EXE`

C. `REGEDIT.EXE`

D. `REGEDT32.EXE`

E. `SCANREGW.BAT`

10. **Which Registry key can contain multiple hardware configurations?**

A. `HKEY_CLASSES_ROOT`

B. `HKEY_LOCAL_MACHINE`

C. `HKEY_CURRENT_CONFG`

D. `HKEY_DYN_DATA`

E. `HKEY_CURRENT_USER`

11. **How can you make changes to the Registry?**

    A. Using `REGEDIT.EXE`

    B. Changing Control Panel settings

    C. Editing `SYSTEM.DAT` and `USER.DAT` with Notepad

    D. Using the System Policies Editor

    E. Using the `SCANREGW.BAT` utility

12. **Windows 98 contains how many root keys?**

    A. Six

    B. Eight

    C. One

    D. Four

    E. Five

13. **Similar to configuring user profiles, to use system policies, your workstations must have _____ for policy settings to be established. Choose the answer that best completes the statement.**

    A. User profiles enabled

    B. A computer account on the domain

C. Local user profiles

D. Hardware profiles enabled

E. None of the above

14. **Which of the following scenarios would best be suited for system policies?**

    A. An environment in which users require similar settings and use similar workstations

    B. An environment in which users are not connecting to a logon server

    C. An environment in which users require a high degree of variation in the levels of system access required

    D. An environment in which administrators can start and stop Windows 98 services

    E. All of the above

15. **What are the tools that can be used to scan the Registry for errors? Select all that apply.**

    A. ScanDisk

    B. ScanReg

    C. Registry Checker

    D. ScanRegW

    E. Regedt32

ANSWER KEY

1. C	6. D	11. A-B-D
2. B	7. B-C	12. A
3. C	8. A-B	13. A
4. A-D	9. C	14. A
5. E	10. B	15. B-C-D

DIAGNOSE AND RESOLVE HARDWARE DEVICE AND DEVICE DRIVER PROBLEMS

1. You need to manually reallocate resources in your computer. Before you do, you want to look at the current allocations. Where can you display, by resource type, lists of all the devices on your computer? Select the best answer.

   C. The System Information utility in the System tools.

1. CORRECT ANSWER: C

To view system resources, go to System Information utility and select the Hardware category. For more information, see "Hardware/Software Conflicts."

2. Adding a new card to your computer created a conflict between two devices. A Plug and Play card is using IRQ 5, but a legacy card also needs this same IRQ. Which is the best strategy for you to use to resolve the conflict?

   B. Remove the Plug and Play device from the current configuration, manually change the IRQ setting for the legacy device, add the Plug and Play device back to the configuration, and then let Windows 98 dynamically assign an available IRQ to the Plug and Play device.

2. CORRECT ANSWER: B

The best route would be to remove both cards and reboot the system. Insert the legacy card and let it have the settings it wants and then insert the PnP device and let it detect a resource on its own. For more information, see "Hardware/Software Conflicts."

3. How do you gain access to the Device Manager?

   C. From the System dialog box of the Control Panel

3. CORRECT ANSWER: C

The Device Manager can be accessed through the Control Panel's System icon. For more information, see "Hardware/Software Conflicts."

4. **You just downloaded an updated driver for your display adapter. What are two ways you can install the new driver?**

   A. Use the Change Driver button in the Driver tab of the device's Properties sheet.

   D. Use the Add New Hardware applet in the Control Panel.

4. CORRECT ANSWER: A-D

One place to install a new driver is in the Driver tab of the device's Properties sheet. (To display the display adapter's Properties sheet, go to Device Manager, double-click on Display Adapter, and then double-click on the adapter name.) The other way to install a new driver is by using the Add New Hardware applet. For more information, see "Hardware/Software Conflicts."

5. **Through the Device Manager, what information can you obtain from the device's property page? Select all that apply.**

   E. All of the above

5. CORRECT ANSWER: E

The Device Manager shows the manufacturer of a device, the supporting drivers, and the version of the device, but not the version of the drivers. For more information, see "Hardware/Software Conflicts."

6. **You need to manually reconfigure one of your Plug and Play devices. What's the first thing you need to do to change the device's settings in the Resource tab of the device's properties sheet?**

   D. Turn off the Use Automatic Settings check box.

6. CORRECT ANSWER: D

You will be unable to change the settings until the Use Automatic Settings check box is disabled. For more information, see "Hardware/Software Conflicts."

7. **What are the two drawbacks of manually configuring a Plug and Play device?**

   B. The settings become fixed so that Windows 98 will have less flexibility when configuring other devices.

   C. Doing so can cause hardware conflicts, making some devices unavailable on the system.

7. CORRECT ANSWER: B-C

When you manually configure a PnP device, the resource settings become fixed, restricting Windows 98's capability to configure other devices. Also, some settings might actually make one or more devices unavailable. For more information, see "Hardware/Software Conflicts."

Hardware/Software Conflicts

This explanation supports questions 1 through 7.

Microsoft publishes a list of supported hardware and software that have been tested with Windows 98. Items not on the list might work with Windows 98; however, they have not been tested and certified by Microsoft. As such, technical help might not be available from Microsoft. These lists are available on the Windows 98 CD in a file called `driver98.chm` from the `Drivers` folder, from the Microsoft Web site, or from TechNet.

The System Information utility will provide a complete list of hardware and software devices that are loaded and all their current settings. In the hardware section, there is a conflict category to show all system resources that might need attention. Shared resources might not be conflicts (see Figure 8.12).

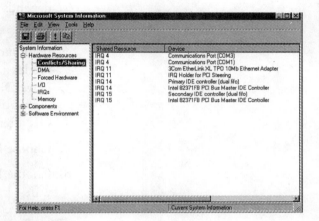

FIGURE 8.12
Hardware conflicts are exposed in the Hardware section of the System Information utility.

The information utility will be used to display all types of information about Windows 98. A print option exists to be used for hard-copy record keeping or comparisons.

With Windows 98, many of the complications with installing hardware are minimized. The key to minimizing hardware installation is the Add New Hardware Wizard. This wizard walks users through the process of detecting the new hardware and then installing the proper device driver for it.

To install new hardware under Windows 98, use the following steps:

1. From the Start menu, choose Settings, Control Panel to open the Control Panel window.

2. Double-click on the Add New Hardware icon to open the Add New Hardware Wizard.

3. Choose the Next button to begin the wizard. A new wizard screen appears.

4. To have Windows search for your new hardware, keep the Yes option clicked. To specify the type and name of the device you are installing, choose No. The following steps assume that you chose the No option.

5. Choose Next. On the next screen, select the type of hardware to install. The next wizard screen that displays depends on the device type you select here.

6. Choose Next. A screen appears, showing you manufacturer and model names. If your manufacturer and model names appear, click on them. If not, click on the Have Disk button and select the path for the hardware installation disk that comes with your device. Choose OK after entering this information.

7. Choose Next. The final wizard screen appears.

8. Choose Finish to have Windows install your new hardware.

After Windows installs the hardware drivers, you might need to shut down and restart Windows for the new device to be active.

8. Which files make up the Windows Registry?

   A. SYSTEM.DAT

   B. USER.DAT

8. CORRECT ANSWER: A-B

The Registry is made up of SYSTEM.DAT and USER.DAT. Sometimes there is also a CONFIG.POL file. For more information, see "Modification of the Registry."

9. What is the utility that you use to edit the Registry?

   C. REGEDIT.EXE

9. CORRECT ANSWER: C

REGEDIT.EXE can be used to change the Registry manually. For more information, see "Modification of the Registry."

10. Which Registry key can contain multiple hardware configurations?

   B. HKEY_LOCAL_MACHINE

10. CORRECT ANSWER: B

Multiple configurations for a machine are stored in the HKEY_LOCAL_MACHINE key. For more information, see "Modification of the Registry."

11. How can you make changes to the Registry?

A. Using REGEDIT.EXE

B. Changing Control Panel settings

D. Using the System Policies Editor

11. CORRECT ANSWER: A-B-D

The Registry can be changed directly with REGEDIT.EXE, or indirectly through the Control Panel or the System Policies Editor. For more information, see "Modification of the Registry."

12. Windows 98 contains how many root keys?

A. Six

12. CORRECT ANSWER: A

There are six root keys. For more information, see "Modification of the Registry."

13. Similar to configuring user profiles, to use system policies, your workstations must have_____for policy settings to be established.

A. User profiles enabled

13. CORRECT ANSWER: A

Profiles must be manually turned on. For more information, see "Modification of the Registry."

14. Which of the following scenarios would best be suited for system policies?

A. An environment in which users require similar settings and use similar workstations

14. CORRECT ANSWER: A

Similar settings and similar workstations provide consistency for administration. For more information, see "Modification of the Registry."

15. What are the tools that can be used to scan the Registry for errors? Select all that apply.

B. ScanReg

C. Registry Checker

D. ScanRegW

15. CORRECT ANSWER: B-C-D

The Registry Checker is the same as ScanRegW—a GUI interface to scan the Registry for errors. Registry Checker is found in the System Information utility. ScanReg is an MS-DOS–based utility. For more information, see "Modification of the Registry."

Modification of the Registry

This explanation supports questions 8 through 15.

The Windows 98 Registry was designed for the following purposes:

- To centralize all the configuration information
- To utilize a tree-structured, hierarchical database structure

- To provide a means to store user, application, and computer-specific information

- To simplify the support burden and allow both local and remote access to configuration information

The Windows 98 Registry is stored in two files. The SYSTEM.DAT file contains the computer hardware configurations, and the USER.DAT file contains user-specific settings. Together, these two files are the central repository of information for the Windows 98 operating system. After each successful boot of Windows 98, copies of both files are saved as SYSTEM.DA0 and USER.DA0.

Some Windows 98 references include a third file, CONFIG.POL, that stores administrative policies that are set up on a network server.

◆ **WARNING**

Microsoft provides the REGEDIT utility to view and change the contents of the Windows 98 Registry. Before you make changes to the Windows 98 Registry, first make a backup copy of the two Registry files, SYSTEM.DAT and USER.DAT. Both of these files are hidden in the Windows folder.

For backward compatibility, the older Windows 3.x configuration files, such as CONFIG.SYS, AUTOEXEC.BAT, WIN.INI, SYSTEM.INI, PROGMAN.INI, CONTROL.INI, and PROTOCOL.INI, still exist. The 16-bit Windows APIs used to update the .INI files also still exist.

The Windows 98 Registry is made up of six root keys. The following sections describe the six root keys.

HKEY_CLASSES_ROOT

This key contains the same type of data as the simple REG.DAT Registry file in Windows 3.x and provides backward-compatibility for OLE and DDE support. It also contains OLE and association-mapping information to support drag-and-drop operations, Windows 98 shortcuts (that are, in fact, OLE links), and core aspects of the Windows 98 user interface.

The association mappings allow Windows 98 to run or print from an application when a specific file type is selected.

HKEY_CURRENT_USER

This key contains user-specific settings for applications, desktop configurations, and user preferences. This key is created at runtime (when the user logs on to Windows 98) from information stored in the user's entry under HKEY_USERS. If the user does not already exist, the DEFAULT information is used.

These user-specific settings are copied back into the HKEY_USERS branch when you shut down Windows 98. There are several different key types: events, schemes, user-specific Control Panel settings, most recently used (MRU) location of installation files, keyboard layout, network, Dial-Up Networking settings, and software settings.

HKEY_LOCAL_MACHINE

This key contains computer-specific information about the type of hardware installed, drivers, and other system settings. It is the same information stored within the SYSTEM.DAT configuration file.

Multiple hardware configurations are listed under the Config key, in the case of a laptop computer with a docking station and both docked and undocked configurations. Much of the Device Manager information can be found under the Enum key, although this information is easier to view through the System icon in the Control Panel.

HKEY_USERS

This key contains information about all users who log on to the computer, including the DEFAULT generic user settings. The generic program and system settings act as a template for any new users on the computer. It is the same information stored within the USER.DAT configuration file and is required to properly run the system.

HKEY_CURRENT_CONFIG

This key contains information about the current running hardware configuration. It is used when multiple hardware configurations are available to the computer. The prime example of multiple hardware configurations is a laptop computer that can be either docked or undocked in a docking station. The information for this key is directly copied from the various configuration information contained in the HKEY_LOCAL_MACHINE key.

HKEY_DYN_DATA

This key contains the dynamic status information for various devices as part of the Plug and Play configuration. It is regenerated every time the system starts up. This information can change as hardware devices are added to or removed from the computer. The information kept for each hardware device includes the associated hardware key, any problems, and current status. This key also contains information on system monitoring being performed using the System Monitor tool. This key is not part of either Registry file and is always dynamically created.

The Windows 98 Registry contains all the Windows 98 system and user information. It is an ASCII database that pulls information from the three files listed in Table 8.3. These files are not in readable form, so you can view or change their contents only by using a Windows application, such as the Windows 98 Registry Editor program, the Control Panel icons, or the System Policies Editor (for the optional CONFIG.POL file). The USER.DAT and SYSTEM.DAT files are stored on the local computer's hard drive. If the CONFIG.POL file exists, it is stored on a network file server to be downloaded when a user logs on to the network.

TABLE 8.3 FILES IN THE WINDOWS 98 REGISTRY

Registry File	Description
SYSTEM.DAT	Contains hardware-related and computer-specific settings.
USER.DAT	Contains user-specific information found in user profiles, such as user rights, desktop settings, and so on.
CONFIG.POL (Optional)	Contains policy information related to the system and user settings. The information in the system policies file can override information in both SYSTEM.DAT and USER.DAT files. This is an optional file.

Most of the configuration information you can modify in the
Windows 98 Registry can be changed using a GUI front-end;
however, some configuration information cannot. Only in
these situations is it appropriate to modify the Registry using
the Registry Editor program.

The following are some of these situations:

- You might need to edit the Registry via the Registry
  Editor because of data not deleted from the Registry
  from an application or device you have removed.

- You might read about a bug fix from Microsoft that you
  need to use the Registry Editor to fix.

- You might want to enhance a feature using the Registry
  Editor.

Windows 98 policies enable an administrator to set various
Registry entries and control whether a user can change such
settings as the following:

- Computer-specific (HKEY_LOCAL_MACHINE) Registry
  entries can be enforced through a computer policy.

- User-specific Registry entries can be enforced through
  User policies.

- Group policies can be created to enforce user-specific
  settings for groups of user accounts defined on a
  Windows NT or NetWare server.

System policies are more inclusive than mandatory user profiles in that they allow an administrator to restrict user-specific
and computer-specific settings. User profiles allow control over
user-specific settings only. The System Policy Editor will use a
GUI interface and will be much safer than the Registry Editor.

Computer, User, and Group System policies are created using
the System Policy Editor, POLEDIT.EXE.

The System Policy Editor uses a template that defines which
keys in the Registry can be affected by the System policy. The
template ADMIN.ADM, which is included with the System Policy
Editor, allows many standard policies to be enforced.

In addition to creating System policies, the System Policy Editor can be used to perform the following functions:

- Access the local Registry settings defined in the System policy template being used

- Access the Registry settings on a remote Windows 98 computer to change the settings defined in the template

Policies created with the System Policy Editor are saved with the filename extension .POL. The System policy to be used should be given the name CONFIG.POL and must be placed in the default location:

- For computers using share-level security, CONFIG.POL should be placed in the <systemroot> directory, for example, C:\WINDOWS.

- For computers using user-level security, CONFIG.POL should be placed in the NETLOGON directory on the Windows NT Server or in the PUBLIC directory on a NetWare server.

The default location for the CONFIG.POL file can be changed later using a specific policy setting.

Registry information in the CONFIG.POL file can overwrite existing information in the computer's Registry. The policy setting also can be configured so that it will not change the Registry setting if it already exists; therefore, even if a Registry on a computer has a certain setting, that setting can be changed to the setting in the CONFIG.POL policy file.

A Group policy might be used to enforce a User policy for a group of users. The group must be defined on the Windows NT or NetWare server, and each computer in the group using the Group policy must have the GROUPPOL.DLL copied to its <systemroot>\system directory.

To create a Group policy, choose Edit, Add Group in the System Policy Editor and enter the name of the group.

A User policy is processed after a Group policy and therefore overrides any policies set by the Group policy. If multiple

Group policies are defined and a user belongs to more than one group, the order in which the Group policies are processed can be defined in the Group Priorities option of the Options menu. Group policies with a higher precedence override policies with a lower precedence.

The final tools in dealing with the Registry are the ScanReg and ScanRegW. Both are used to scan the Registry for errors. ScanReg is command based and can be run from the MS-DOS prompt. ScanRegW is simply the GUI interface and can be run from Start, Run or from the System Information utility's Tool menu (see Figure 8.13).

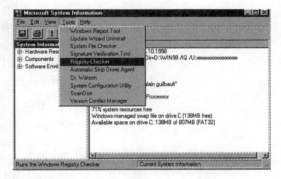

FIGURE 8.13
ScanRegW will also back up the Registry once a check has been made.

CHAPTER SUMMARY

Windows 98 has built in autocorrection tools that are used during installation to make sure the proper hardware and software are installed and that Windows 98 runs properly. Once the installation is complete, additional tools are available to check the integrity of files and control the startup of Windows 98 during a diagnostic session.

Each type of connection will have its own troubleshooting tool. The Dial-Up Networking will offer Modem logs and PPP logs. Network connections will offer Net Watcher and WinIPCfg. One of the best tools is still the Help system. There is a section on troubleshooting that invokes a wizard to guide you through the appropriate questions.

Printing is one of the most common tasks office users will be performing. The steps to print are quite simple. Windows 98 offers a Printer Troubleshooting Wizard to help pinpoint causes of print problems. Two formats exist: RAW, which is the format the printer understands, and EMF, a newer format that the operating system can use to print in the background while the application can return to other tasks. In the end, a printer will receive a RAW format print job.

Windows 98 supports older applications very well. Older applications, however, may not be compatible with all the new file systems implemented in Windows 98. Some of the features can be disabled to accommodate an older application.

Windows 98 will offer basic sharing services. Share-level security can only use passwords to secure a resource. User-level security will use an account database from NT or Novell to authenticate access.

The Registry contains all the configuration settings for Windows 98 and 32-bit applications. A Registry Editor is provided but is not recommended for inexperienced users. The Control Panel and System Policy Editor will provide a safer GUI to make changes. Windows 98 also provides a Registry scanning tool to verify the integrity of the Registry.

EXAM QUESTIONS

1. You have just recently enabled user profiles on your network. You decide to use roving mandatory user profiles and place the appropriate USER.DAT file in the NETLOGON directory of your Windows NT Server. You note, however, that when you log on to a Windows 98 computer that has user profiles enabled, your profile information is not downloaded to the workstation.

   In this scenario, which step must you take to correct this problem and complete your implementation of user profiles?

   A. Rename the USER.DAT file to USER.MAN.

   B. Share the NETLOGON directory as EVERYONE read access.

   C. Rename the USER.DAT file to USER.MAN and place the file in the user's home directory.

   D. Rename the USER.DAT file to USER.MAN and place the file in the user's mail user_id directory.

   E. Share the USER.DAT file for everyone to read only.

2. What is the difference between USB and IEEE 1394 BUS specifications? Select the best answer.

   A. The USB devices support hot swapping; IEEE 1394 does not.

   B. USB supports external devices; IEEE 1394 is for internal devices only.

   C. USB is used for modems and printers; IEEE 1394 is used only for video players.

   D. USB transmits data at rates of 10–12MB/s. IEEE 1394 supports 100–400MB/s transfers.

   E. The USB is for graphics; IEEE is for new hardware devices.

3. The company for which you work is implementing Windows 98. Your job is to configure a user desktop environment that limits access to the configuration of the computer, reduces administration, and provides a more efficient workspace. This environment would best be served by instituting which of the following?

   A. Installing the Remote Registry service to enable centralized administration of Windows 98 computers

   B. Implementing mandatory user profiles

   C. Implementing system policies

   D. Implementing user profiles

   E. Implementing Roaming user profiles

4. **Scenario:**

Sara finds that after setting up her computer, she cannot communicate with the rest of the four-computer workgroup using NetBIOS names. The network uses DHCP. There is no WINS server.

Required component:

Sara must be able to use NetBIOS names to communicate.

Optional component:

This must be done without additional expense; there is no money in the budget to upgrade any hardware or software.

Proposed Solution:

Tell Sara to enable the Use DHCP for WINS Configuration setting in the WINS tab of the TCP/IP Properties in the Network Control Panel of her Windows 98 system.

   A. The proposed solution satisfies the required component and the optional component.

   B. The proposed solution satisfies the required component but does not satisfy the optional component.

   C. The proposed solution satisfies the optional component but does not satisfy the required component.

   D. The proposed solution satisfies neither the required component nor the optional component.

5. **Scenario:**

Sara finds that after setting up her computer, she cannot communicate with the rest of the four-computer workgroup using NetBIOS names. The network uses DHCP. There is no WINS server.

Required component:

Sara must be able to use NetBIOS names to communicate.

Optional component:

This must be done without additional expense; there is no money in the budget to upgrade any hardware or software.

Proposed solution:

Tell Sara to add the WINS service on the DHCP server and to enable the Use DHCP for WINS Configuration setting in the WINS tab of the TCP/IP Properties in the Network Control Panel of her Windows 98 system. From the DCHP server, she can assign the WINS address for all clients.

   A. The proposed solution satisfies the required component and the optional component.

   B. The proposed solution satisfies the required component but does not satisfy the optional component.

   C. The proposed solution satisfies the optional component but does not satisfy the required component.

   D. The proposed solution satisfies neither the required component nor the optional component.

6. **How can Windows 98's Dial-Up Networking make use of multiple ISDN lines to improve connection speeds? Select the best answer.**

   A. Windows 98 cannot use ISDN lines.

   B. Use the Windows 98 ISDN adapter and configure it for dial-up adapters.

   C. Use the Multilink feature in the Control Panel.

D. Use the Multilink feature in the Dial-Up Adapter Configuration dialog box.

E. Using the Modem properties, select ISDN Multilink.

7. **Which Registry key is actually stored in memory and not on the hard disk?**

   A. HKEY_DYN_DATA

   B. HKEY_LOCAL_MACHINE

   C. HKEY_CURRENT_USER

   D. HKEY_USERS

   E. HKEY_CURRENT_CONFIG

8. **Which of the following networks support group policies?**

   A. Windows NT

   B. Novell NetWare

   C. Banyan VINES

   D. LANtastic

   E. OS/2 Warp Server

9. **Patrick is using Windows 98 Dial-Up Networking with PPP. What authentication protocols can Dial-Up Networking use to negotiate with?**

   A. PAP

   B. CHAP

   C. SPAP

   D. TCPAP

   E. MCAP

10. **What are some of the benefits of using USB devices?**

   A. USB connectors are standard one size fits all.

   B. The USB system supports transmission rated up to 400MB/s.

   C. USB devices require only one IRQ for each device.

   D. Most USB devices do not require power connectors.

   E. USB devices are better for high-end video.

11. **Scenario:**

   Donald is setting up Windows 98 on 15 computers in the accounting department. Nine of the computers are currently running Windows for Workgroups 3.11, and the remaining six are running MS-DOS.

   Required components:
   The users need to share files.

   The users need to share the three printers in the department.

   Optional component:
   The managers would like to be able to access the Internet by using modems connected to their computers.

   Proposed solution:
   Upgrade all 15 computers to Windows 98 and configure them as a workgroup called Accounting. Install and configure the IPX/SPX protocol on each computer. Connect the three printers to three users' workstations, and then enable File and Printer Sharing for Microsoft Networks on all computers in the workgroup. Connect a modem to each manager's computer. Install and configure the TCP/IP protocol and Dial-Up Networking on each manager's computer.

A. The proposed solution satisfies all of the required components and satisfies the optional component.

B. The proposed solution satisfies all of the required components and does not satisfy the optional component.

C. The proposed solution satisfies one of the required components and satisfies the optional component.

D. The proposed solution satisfies one of the required components and does not satisfy the optional component.

E. The proposed solution satisfies neither the required components nor the optional component.

12. **A user complains that her profile does not follow her to every Windows 98 system on the network. What could be the problem? Select all that apply.**

A. Not all systems have profiles enabled.

B. Some systems are NDS while others connect as binary emulation to a Novell server acting as the primary logon.

C. Profiles do not work with Novell.

D. The system profiles must have a home directory on a Novell server.

E. The profiles cannot be set up to follow a user from one system to another.

13. **Scenario:**

Michael works in the accounting department on the third floor. You are the administrator of a Windows NT domain, of which he is a member. He wants to save a document to a folder located on a coworker's machine. Both machines are running Windows 98. You instruct the coworker to create a folder and share it with user-level security. After creating the folder and assigning the proper rights to the username Michael, you go on your way. Michael contacts you in a few minutes and explains he cannot find the newly created resource in Network Neighborhood.

Required component:
Connect Michael to the shared folder located on the coworker's Windows 98 system.

Optional components:
Allow Michael to continually connect to the shared folder automatically.

Assign Michael's coworker Full Control over the shared folder.

Proposed solution:
Have Michael right-click on Network Neighborhood, select Map a Network Drive, type //**computer_name**/**share_name** in the Path box, and select the Reconnect option box.

A. The proposed solution satisfies the required component and all of the optional components.

B. The proposed solution satisfies the required component and only one of the optional components.

C. The proposed solution satisfies the required component and none of the optional components.

D. The proposed solution satisfies one of the optional components and does not satisfy the required component.

E. The proposed solution satisfies none of the optional components and does not satisfy the required component.

14. **What happens when an IrDA-equipped laptop enters a room with an IrDA printer?**

    A. The IrDA specification is not implemented on Printers.

    B. The printer's drivers will be loaded on the laptop.

    C. The user must install the drivers for the printer on the laptop before it can be used. After the drivers are present, the laptop will be able to use the printer thought the IrDA port.

    D. The laptop will be sent a test page to the printer.

    E. The printer will prompt you to print.

15. **When new users log on to a Windows 98 computer that has user profiles enabled, a copy of what profile is loaded for the new user?**

    A. DEFAULT

    B. SYSTEM

    C. USER.DAT

    D. USER.MAN

    E. SYSTEM.MAN

16. **As the network administrator of a company, you must sometimes access your network from a remote location. Recently, you decided to set up access to your Windows NT Domain through the Internet. You set up a RAS server and make it accessible over the Internet. To enable a secure channel of communication, you decide to create a Virtual Private Network (VPN). What protocol would you select in your Windows 98**

client machine's Network properties sheet to access the VPN?

    A. TCP/IP

    B. PPTP

    C. NWLink

    D. NetBEUI

    E. Secure TCP/IP

17. **Scenario:**

    A small company has just upgraded some systems to NT and Windows 98. There are still many servers and clients using Novell.

    Required component:
    All clients need to interact with both Novell and NT networks. Shared folders must be available to all types of clients.

    Optional components:
    Windows 98 systems must be able to share resources to both Microsoft and Novell clients.

    All Windows 98 systems need to be able to access resources on NT servers and Novell servers.

    Proposed solution:
    Install Client for Microsoft and Client for Novell on all Windows 98 systems. Install File and Printer Sharing for Microsoft and Novell on all Windows 98 systems.

    A. The proposed solution satisfies the required component and all of the optional components.

    B. The proposed solution satisfies the required component and only one of the optional components.

    C. The proposed solution satisfies the required component and none of the optional components.

D. The proposed solution satisfies one of the optional components and does not satisfy the required component.

E. The proposed solution satisfies none of the optional components and does not satisfy the required component.

18. **To create a shared folder on a remote computer using the Net Watcher administration tool, you would select which one of the following to initiate the process of creating the shared resources?**

A. From the Administer menu, select Add Shared Folder.

B. From the Administer menu, select Add Shared Local Resource.

C. You must connect to the computer prior to creating shares on the remote computer.

D. After connecting to the remote computer, select the Administer menu and then select Add Shared Folder.

E. Select the Connect menu from the Administer button and turn on Sharing.

19. **Scenario:**

Last week, you upgraded one of your users' machines from Windows 3.1 to Windows 98. Before doing so, you created a full backup of the hard drive by using the Windows 3.1 Backup utility. After the installation, the user calls to report that some of the data files that were on the drive before the upgrade are unexplainably gone. Other data files from the same directory are still there, however, and have been modified since the upgrade.

Required components:
Restore the missing files.

Keep the files that aren't missing (don't replace them with backup copies of the files).

Optional components:
Make an incremental backup before doing the restore, just in case something goes wrong.

Check the directory structure of the drive against the backup to ensure that it is the same as it was prior to the upgrade.

Proposed solution:
You run the Windows 98 Backup utility and then do an incremental backup to a new tape. When that is done, you run the Backup utility again, select the files you want to restore from the full backup set, and then restore those files.

A. The proposed solution satisfies all the required components and all of the optional components.

B. The proposed solution satisfies all the required components but only one of the optional components.

C. The proposed solution satisfies all the required components but none of the optional components.

D. The proposed solution satisfies none the required components and none of the optional components.

20. **Scenario:**

You are setting up Windows 98 workstations to be the workgroup clients and servers part of a NetWare 3.1x network. When the users enter their usernames and passwords, in the View Network Neighborhood, they see only an icon for the entire network. When they click this icon, nothing happens.

Required component:
Windows 98 users need to be able to browse the network by using the Network Neighborhood.

Optional components:
Only a few dedicated systems should be responsible for maintaining the list of servers in the Windows 98 workgroup.

Servers should be grouped by department.

Proposed solution:
Assign all systems to a workgroup based on the Novell server name in the NetWare 3.1x network. Set all Windows 98 systems in each workgroup to have potential or preferred master browser status.

   A. The proposed solution satisfies the required component and all of the optional components.

   B. The proposed solution satisfies the required component and only one of the optional components.

   C. The proposed solution satisfies the required component and none of the optional components.

   D. The proposed solution satisfies one of the optional components and does not satisfy the required component.

   E. The proposed solution satisfies none of the optional components and does not satisfy the required component.

21. **You have installed Windows 98 on several computers in your environment. These computers cannot see one another, although they can see the Windows NT servers. What do you suspect is the problem?**

   A. They do not have permission to see one another.

   B. They do not have File and Printer Sharing activated.

   C. System policies restrict them from seeing their workgroup.

   D. The Browse list has not yet been built.

   E. The SAP advertising is not turned on.

22. **You and a colleague are using system policies for your Windows 98 users. The policies do not seem to be working. However, you think they are being saved in the wrong location. Where on a NetWare server are logon scripts saved?**

   A. User's home directories

   B. User's Mail id

   C. SYS:LOGON

   D. SYS:PUBLIC

   E. SYS:PRIVATE

23. **Scenario:**

Connie is an administrator of a large Novell NetWare LAN. She is planning to upgrade the PCs on her network to Windows 98.

Required component:
Each Windows 98 user must be able to log on to any Windows 98 computer and see his or her own personal desktop settings.

Optional component:
Windows 98 users should be able to make the files on their local C: drives available to other users on the network.

Proposed solution:
Upgrade the PCs to Windows 98. Install and configure the IPX/SPX protocol. Install and configure the Client for NetWare Networks.

A. The proposed solution satisfies the required component and the optional component.

B. The proposed solution satisfies the required component but does not satisfy the optional component.

C. The proposed solution satisfies the optional component but does not satisfy the required component.

D. The proposed solution satisfies neither the required component nor the optional component.

24. **Scenario:**

Connie is an administrator of a large Novell NetWare LAN. She is planning to upgrade the PCs on her network to Windows 98.

Required component:
Each Windows 98 user to be able to log on to any Windows 98 computer and see his or her own personal desktop settings.

Optional component:
Windows 98 users to be able to make the files on their local C: drives available to other users on the network.

Proposed solution:
Upgrade the PCs to Windows 98. Install and configure the IPX/SPX protocol. Install and configure the Client for NetWare Networks. Enable profiles on the Windows 98 PCs.

A. The proposed solution satisfies the required component and the optional component.

B. The proposed solution satisfies the required component but does not satisfy the optional component.

C. The proposed solution satisfies the optional component but does not satisfy the required component.

D. The proposed solution satisfies neither the required component nor the optional component.

25. **Scenario:**

Connie is an administrator of a large Novell NetWare LAN. She is planning to upgrade the PCs on her network to Windows 98.

Required component:
Each Windows 98 user to be able to log on to any Windows 98 computer and see his or her own personal desktop settings.

Optional component:
Windows 98 users to be able to make the files on their local C: drives available to other users on the network.

Proposed Solution:
Upgrade the PCs to Windows 98. Install and configure the IPX/SPX protocol. Install and configure the Client for NetWare Networks. Enable profiles on the Windows 98 PCs. Install and configure File and Printer Sharing for Novell Networks.

A. The proposed solution satisfies the required component and the optional component.

B. The proposed solution satisfies the required component but does not satisfy the optional component.

C. The proposed solution satisfies the optional component but does not satisfy the required component.

D. The proposed solution satisfies neither the required component nor the optional component.

26. **How can you register your copy of Windows 98? Select the best answer.**

    A. Use the Windows Update and Registration page.

    B. Use the Windows Update and the Member Services page.

    C. Use the Online Registration item in the Start menu.

    D. Use the Online Registration item in the Control Panel.

    E. Use the Online Registration item in the Welcome screen.

27. **You can reach a remote computer by using its IP address, but not with its hostname. Which setting is most likely the problem?**

    A. IP address of the WINS server

    B. Frame type not the same

    C. IP address of the DNS server

    D. Your subnet mask

28. **Where does Windows 98 Setup store your Windows for Workgroups settings during an installation procedure?**

    A. `c:\temp`

    B. `c:\windows\temp`

    C. Registry

    D. `SYSTEM.INI`

    E. `WIN.INI`

29. **Scenario:**

    As an administrator, you want to use Net Watcher to monitor activity in your network. Your network consists of Windows 98 and Windows NT Workstation clients, and a Windows NT Server.

    Required components:
    Monitor file sharing on all systems in the network from your Windows 98 workstation.

    Monitor printer services in the network.

    Limit file sharing for "classified" data in the network.

    Optional components:
    View users who are connected to your Windows 98 workstation.

    Close resources shared by other users.

    Proposed solution:
    You install share-level security on your Windows 98 workstation, and user-level security on all of the other Windows 98 workstations that you want to monitor. In addition, you install File and Printer Sharing services on all of the machines.

    A. The proposed solution satisfies all the required components and all of the optional components.

    B. The proposed solution satisfies all the required components but only one of the optional components.

    C. The proposed solution satisfies all the required components but none of the optional components.

    D. The proposed solution satisfies one of the required components but none of the optional components.

E. The proposed solution satisfies none the required components and none of the optional components.

30. **You recently installed some new hardware devices in your computer and you suspect that it has something to do with the problems you are having starting Windows 98. What is the first thing you should do to fix any hardware conflicts?**

    A. Start the computer in Safe mode.

    B. Boot in DOS mode from a disk.

    C. Start Windows 98 in Logged mode.

    D. Reinstall Windows 98.

    E. Start Windows 98 in Troubleshooting mode.

31. **Where can the Extract utility be accessed? Select all that apply.**

    A. From the Windows folder

    B. From the Windows\command folder

    C. From the Startup disk

    D. From the Emergency Recovery Disk

    E. From the Windows\System32 folder

32. **What are the five frame types that you can choose from when setting up IPX/SPX? Select all that apply.**

    A. 802.2 and 802.3

    B. 802.4 and 802.5

    C. Ethernet II

    D. Token_Ring and Token_Ring_Snap

    E. Fiber and Fiber_Snap

33. **Which TCP/IP feature automatically assigns an IP address to a computer?**

    A. IPS

    B. DHCP

    C. DNS

    D. WINS

    E. TCPCFG

34. **Scenario:**

    You need to install a tool or tools that will allow you to view and control various aspects of your environment, including system performance, changes to your workstation, and disk and network activity.

    Required components:
    Monitor hardware performance.

    Find performance bottlenecks in the system.

    Determine when other users are connected to your workstation.

    Optional components:
    View and log changes to your system configuration.

    Monitor system page faults to reduce disk activity.

    Proposed solution:
    You install the Windows 98 System Monitor software on your system and use that as the tool to perform the above objectives.

    A. The proposed solution satisfies all the required components and all of the optional components.

    B. The proposed solution satisfies all the required components but only one of the optional components.

C. The proposed solution satisfies all the required components but none of the optional components.

D. The proposed solution satisfies none the required components and none of the optional components.

E. The proposed solution meets some of the primary objectives and some of secondary objectives.

35. Scenario:

Patrick just upgraded his computer, and in a cost-saving effort, he is using the old non–Plug and Play network card from the computer that was replaced. He installed the card in the new computer, and installed the network card in the Network Control Panel with the same settings from the old computer. When he tries to load Windows 98, however, Windows 98 reports an IRQ conflict with the sound card. Patrick must have communication with the network by the end of the day.

Required component:
Patrick's computer must be communicating with the network by the end of the day.

Optional components:
The sound card must work.

No other devices should be disabled.

Proposed solution:
Tell Patrick to change the IRQ in the Network Control Panel, under Properties of the Network Card, to an unused IRQ.

A. The proposed solution satisfies the required component and all of the optional components.

B. The proposed solution satisfies the required component and only one of the optional components.

C. The proposed solution satisfies the required component and none of the optional components.

D. The proposed solution satisfies all of the optional components but does not satisfy the required component.

E. The proposed solution satisfies none of the optional components and does not satisfy the required component.

36. After connecting to a remote computer using the Net Watcher administration tool, you want to view the shares on that computer. What must you do to view the current shares on the target remote computer?

A. Click on the Show Shared Folders button to see the names of the shared folders on the selected computer.

B. Click on the Show Shared Resources button to see the names of the shared folders on the selected computer.

C. Click on the Shared Folders button to see the names of the shared folders on the selected computer.

D. Click on the Shared Files button and select the computer you want to view.

E. None of the above will display the shared resources on the remote computer.

37. As the system administrator, you need to configure Exchange to send and receive mail in Microsoft Mail. Which three of the following actions must you take?

A. Create a Workgroup Post Office on a Windows 98 computer running the Microsoft Mail workstation edition.

B. Create a mailbox for each member of the Workgroup Post Office.

C. Create the requisite Exchange folders: Inbox, Outbox, Sent Items, and Deleted Items.

D. Configure the Exchange Client with the Microsoft Mail service.

E. Configure the Microsoft Mail to handle Windows 98 clients.

38. Scenario:

You are setting up Windows 98 workstations to be the workgroup clients and servers part of a NetWare 3.1x network. When the users enter their usernames and passwords, in the View Network Neighborhood they only see an icon for the entire network. When they click this icon, nothing happens.

Required component

Windows 98 users need to be able to browse the network using Network Neighborhood.

Optional components:

Only a few dedicated systems should be responsible for maintaining the list of servers in the Windows 98 workgroup.

Servers should be grouped by department.

Proposed solution:

Make sure the File and Printer Sharing for Novell is enabled and the properties for SAP advertising are also enabled. Assign all systems to a workgroup based on the Novell server name in the NetWare 3.1x network. Set all Windows 98 systems in each workgroup to have potential or preferred master browser status.

A. The proposed solution satisfies the required component and all of the optional components.

B. The proposed solution satisfies the required component and only one of the optional components.

C. The proposed solution satisfies the required component and none of the optional components.

D. The proposed solution satisfies one of the optional components and does not satisfy the required component.

E. The proposed solution satisfies none of the optional components and does not satisfy the required component.

39. Scenario:

Sara has just brought a few new assistants in to help her administer the network. The new assistants, Patrick and Carol, would like to work from home. They need to access the Internet through the corporate intranet as well as the entire server. Sara decides she wants to maintain good security standards.

Required component:

Allow the assistants to manage the NT and Windows 98 network from home.

Optional components:

Allow the assistants to use the Internet through the corporate Intranet.

Keep the network secured.

Proposed solution:

Install PPTP on the NT server at the office and enable access for the two assistants in the Remote Access Server. Have each assistant install the Proxy client at home to connect to the Internet as well as dial-up connections to the office.

A. The proposed solution satisfies the required component and all of the optional components.

B. The proposed solution satisfies the required component and only one of the optional components.

C. The proposed solution satisfies the required component and none of the optional components.

D. The proposed solution satisfies one of the optional components and does not satisfy the required component.

E. The proposed solution satisfies none of the optional components and does not satisfy the required component.

40. **Carol, one of your users, tells you she has two clients installed and the username and password for both clients is the same. She wants to be able to log on by using two different names but the second logon screen never shows up. What can Carol do the resolve the problem? Select the best answer.**

A. The second logon does not appear because the names are the same and Windows 98 will simply pass on the information. Changing one password will change the scenario and allow both names to appear.

B. The second logon must always be the same as the first. Windows 98 will not support different names or passwords.

C. The Windows 98 primary logon should be changed to Windows logon. All logons are then treated separately.

D. The username for NT should always be different than the username for Novell.

E. The NT server must be used first to allow for a second logon to take place.

41. **Scenario:**

A user tells you that a large number of General Protection Faults are occurring on his system and that Windows frequently fails during start-up. You suspect that Windows DLLs or the Registry is corrupt.

Required components:
Eliminate the frequent occurrence of General Protection Faults.

Have Windows 98 start cleanly each time the user starts the computer.

Optional component:
Create a boot-up log each time the user starts Windows 98.

Log any GPF messages when they occur.

Proposed solution:
You decide to run the Windows 98 Setup program again to replace any corrupt files and repair the system Registry.

A. The proposed solution satisfies all the required components and the optional component.

B. The proposed solution satisfies all the required components but does not satisfy the optional component.

C. The proposed solution satisfies the optional component and one of the required components.

D. The proposed solution satisfies the optional component and does not satisfy the required components.

E. The proposed solution satisfies none of the required components and does not satisfy the optional component.

42. **When setting up PPTP/VPN, what must you specify on the remote workstation? Select the best answer.**

    A. Phone number of the modem on the RAS server

    B. IP address of the network adapter on the RAS server

    C. Computer name of the RAS server

    D. Remote system VPN number

    E. IP address of the DNS server on the remote network

43. **Which of the following are features of FAT32? Select all that apply.**

    A. Can be compressed by using DriveSpace 3.0

    B. Can be converted back to FAT at any time

    C. Can run from a graphical interface and a command prompt

    D. Uses a smaller cluster size

    E. Is used in Windows 98 and NT

44. **Scenario:**

    You are planning to install disk compression on a 750MB hard disk running Windows 98.

    Required component:
    You need to get the most data storage space as possible on the disk.

    Optional components:
    The user must be able to access all the data without the need of a third-party application each time she tries to open a file.

    The average access time of files must not be compromised.

Proposed solution:
Using DriveSpace 3.0 and Ultrapack will enable the most storage space by using on-the-fly decompression.

    A. The proposed solution satisfies the required component and all of the optional components.

    B. The proposed solution satisfies the required component and only one of the optional components.

    C. The proposed solution satisfies the required component and none of the optional components.

    D. The proposed solution satisfies all of the optional components but does not satisfy the required component.

    E. The proposed solution satisfies none of the optional components and does not satisfy the required component.

45. **Scenario:**

    A new administrator has decided to be proactive in maintaining the new Windows 98 systems in the office.

    Required component:
    Make sure the hard drives are error free and run as efficiently as possible.

    Optional components:
    Do not interrupt users' work with maintenance issues.

    Perform only ScanDisk and Defragmenter.

    Proposed solution:
    Set up the Maintenance Wizard with an Express setup to run each night between midnight and 3 a.m. Inform all users to leave their systems on when they leave at the end of the day.

A. The proposed solution satisfies the required component and all of the optional components.

B. The proposed solution satisfies the required component and only one of the optional components.

C. The proposed solution satisfies the required component and none of the optional components.

D. The proposed solution satisfies all of the optional components but does not satisfy the required component.

E. The proposed solution satisfies none of the optional components and does not satisfy the required component.

46. Scenario:

A new administrator has decided to be proactive in maintaining the new Windows 98 systems in the office.

Required component:
Make sure the hard drives are error free and run as efficiently as possible.

Optional components:
Do not interrupt users' work with maintenance issues.

Perform only ScanDisk and Defragmenter.

Proposed solution:
Set up the Maintenance Wizard with a Custom setup to run each night between midnight and 3 a.m. Inform all users to shut down their systems when they leave at the end of the day so the maintenance can be performed.

A. The proposed solution satisfies the required component and all of the optional components.

B. The proposed solution satisfies the required component and only one of the optional components.

C. The proposed solution satisfies the required component and none of the optional components.

D. The proposed solution satisfies only one of the optional components and does not satisfy the required component.

E. The proposed solution satisfies none of the optional components and does not satisfy the required component.

47. **You have implemented roving user profiles on your network, but your users are complaining that when they log on to other Windows 98 computers, they do not get their user profile information. What could be the cause of this problem?**

A. User profiles are not enabled on the computers the users are accessing.

B. The users in question are not members of your Windows NT domain and cannot access information on the Windows NT Server.

C. The network users do not have rights to the NETLOGON directory located on the Windows NT Server.

D. The users have accidentally deleted their profile information.

E. The users have not been given user rights to use profiles on the NT Server.

48. **You are installing Windows 98 on your computer, and Setup stalls during the hardware detection phase. Where can you look to determine why this happened?**

    A. The SETUPLOG.TXT file

    B. The DETCRASH.LOG file

    C. The DETLOG.TXT file

    D. The SETUP.TXT file

    E. The SETUP.LOG file

49. **Windows 98 Setup stalls during the hardware detection phase. You examine the DETCRASH.LOG file to troubleshoot the situation and find that the file is unreadable. Why?**

    A. The DETCRASH.LOG file can only be read by Setup.

    B. The file became damaged during the failed Setup.

    C. The file must be debugged.

    D. The system contains a virus.

    E. The SETUP.TXT file has been deleted.

50. **Scenario:**

    You are installing Windows 98 on your computer, and Windows 98 Setup hangs during the hardware detection phase. You suspect a hardware conflict.

    Required component:
    Resolve setup conflicts issues.

    Optional component:
    Determine which devices are causing the system to hang.

    Proposed solution:
    Turn off the computer, wait a few seconds, and turn it back on. When the operating system begins to load, press F8 and choose Command Prompt. Delete the DETCRASH.LOG file and restart the system. Resume Windows 98 setup.

    A. The proposed solution satisfies the required component and the optional component.

    B. The proposed solution satisfies the required component but does not satisfy the optional component.

    C. The proposed solution satisfies the optional component but does not satisfy the required component.

    D. The proposed solution satisfies neither the required component nor the optional component.

51. **Scenario:**

    You are installing Windows 98 on your computer, and Windows 98 Setup hangs during the hardware detection phase. You suspect a hardware conflict.

    Required component:
    Resolve setup conflicts issues.

    Optional component:
    Determine which devices are causing the system to hang.

    Proposed solution:
    Turn off the computer, wait a few seconds, and turn it back on. Resume Windows 98 Setup. When Setup is complete, examine the DETCRASH.LOG file to determine which device caused Setup to hang.

A. The proposed solution satisfies the required component and the optional component.

B. The proposed solution satisfies the required component but does not satisfy the optional component.

C. The proposed solution satisfies the optional component but does not satisfy the required component.

D. The proposed solution satisfies neither the required component nor the optional component.

52. **Which Registry key contains information about system hardware?**

A. HKEY_DYN_DATA

B. HKEY_LOCAL_MACHINE

C. HKEY_CURRENT_USER

D. HKEY_USERS

The following two questions are scenario-based and all present the same scenario, required results, and optional results. Please read all the requirements and proposed solution before answering.

53. **Scenario:**

Donald is setting up Windows 98 on 15 computers in the accounting department. Nine of the computers are currently running Windows for Workgroups 3.11, and the remaining six are running MS-DOS.

Required components:
The users need to share files.

The users need to share the three printers in the department.

Optional component:
The managers would like to be able to access the Internet by using modems connected to their computers.

Proposed solution:
Upgrade all 15 computers to Windows 98 and configure them as a workgroup called Accounting. Install and configure the IPX/SPX protocol on each computer. Connect the three printers to three users' workstations, and then enable File and Printer Sharing for Microsoft Networks on those computers. Connect a modem to each manager's computer.

A. The proposed solution satisfies all the required components and the optional component.

B. The proposed solution satisfies all the required components but does not satisfy the optional component.

C. The proposed solution satisfies one of the required components and the optional component.

D. The proposed solution satisfies one of the required components and does not satisfy the optional component.

E. The proposed solution satisfies none of the required components and does not satisfy the optional component.

54. **Scenario:**

Donald is setting up Windows 98 on 15 computers in the accounting department. Nine of the computers are currently running Windows for Workgroups 3.11, and the remaining six are running MS-DOS.

Required components:

The users need to share files.

The users need to share the three printers in the department.

Optional component:

The managers would like to be able to access the Internet by using modems connected to their computers.

Proposed solution:

Upgrade all 15 computers to Windows 98 and configure them as a workgroup called Accounting. Install and configure the IPX/SPX protocol on each computer. Connect the three printers to three users' workstations, and then enable File and Printer Sharing for Microsoft Networks on all computers in the workgroup. Connect a modem to each manager's computer.

A. The proposed solution satisfies all the required components and the optional component.

B. The proposed solution satisfies all the required components but does not satisfy the optional component.

C. The proposed solution satisfies one of the required components and the optional component.

D. The proposed solution satisfies one of the required components and does not satisfy the optional component.

E. The proposed solution satisfies none of the required components and does not satisfy the optional component.

55. **Which utility is used to create and modify system policies?**

A. SYSEDIT

B. REGEDIT

C. POLEDIT

D. Notepad

ANSWERS & EXPLANATIONS

1. **C.**   The file must have the .MAN extension and be located in the user's home directory.

2. **D.**   The IEEE 1394 and USB specifications are very similar. IEEE 1394 was designed for high-bandwidth digital devices. These devices run at 100–400MB/s, whereas USB is more widely implemented on devices that run at 10–12MB/s.

3. **C.**   System policies enable the greatest control of the users' environment from the administration side.

4. **C.**   The secondary objective of not spending money is met. However, the proposed solution does not allow for NetBIOS communication. It will automatically set the WINS configuration using DHCP. This will not work unless there is a WINS server to use. This option does not turn the DHCP server into a WINS server, or enable it to act as a WINS server in any way.

5. **A.**   The objective of not spending money is met. The proposed solution allows for NetBIOS communication through WINS. This option does not turn the DHCP server into a WINS server, or enable it to act as a WINS server in any way; it only configures clients to use WINS.

6. **D.**   Multilink allows a system to use multiple analog lines or multiple ISDN lines to make a remote connection and make use of the full bandwidth.

7. **A.**   The HKEY_DYN_DATA Registry key is created and modified dynamically and is stored in system memory for faster access (instead of on the hard disk, which is relatively slow).

8. **A-B.**   Both Windows NT and Novell NetWare support the use of group policies.

9. **A-B-C.**   When using PPP, Dial-Up Networking supports the following authentication protocols: PAP, CHAP, and SPAP.

10. **A-D.**   USB connectors are standard and will connect with each other through a HUB-like device.

11. **A.**   The users can all share their files, and the managers can use their modems to access the Internet via TCP/IP and Dial-Up Networking.

12. **A-B-D.**   All systems must have user profiles enabled and have a primary logon of NT or Novell for a user to have his personal settings follow him. A Novell server cannot be mixed between Binary and NDS.

13. **E.**   Michael should use the correct UNC path of \\computer_name\share_name and check the Reconnect at Logon box.

14. **B.**   The IrDA- or Infrared-enabled laptop will detect the infrared printer and Plug and Play will take over to install the drivers.

15. **A.**   The default is used for new users and any changes made to the settings will remain for that particular user in the future.

16. B. Point-to-Point Tunneling Protocol would allow you to set up a secure communication channel with your RAS server's VPN. The RAS server's VPN would accept PPTP requests from your client machines, unwrap them, and process them on the company network. You can use NetBEUI, IPX/SPX, or TCP/IP with PPTP.

17. D. File and Printer Sharing for Microsoft and Novell cannot be installed at the same time on Windows 98 systems. Novell clients will not be able to connect to NT servers. The only option that will work is that both clients being installed on the Windows 98 systems will allow them to connect to NT and Novell.

18. D. You must be connected to the remote computer before you can manage shared folders.

19. D. This is a bad solution. Because the computer was upgraded after the full backup was made, you can no longer use the Windows 98 Backup utility to restore the files. Backups created with the Windows 3.1 Backup utility are not compatible with the Windows 98 Backup utility. An alternative solution might be to restore the files to a different Windows 3.1 computer and then copy the files to the Window 98 machine manually.

20. E. Each workgroup must have its own master browser. By default, all Windows 98 clients will be potential master browsers. Changing the status of some clients to non-browsers will help maintain control. Windows 98 machines will not be visible to other 98 machines by default.

21. B. Windows 98 computers will not show up in the Network Neighborhood unless File and Printer Sharing has been activated.

22. D. System policies are saved on the NetWare server in SYS:PUBLIC.

23. D. Users can access files but cannot share. Also, there is no information about how users can keep their profiles.

24. B. Profiles and client configuration are in place. There is no information about file sharing, however.

25. A. By logging on to a Novell server with the Novell Client as the primary login and having profiles enabled, the users will have roaming profiles. File and Printer Sharing will allow for sharing their local files.

26. B. Under the Member Services page there is a link to update or register your copy of Windows 98.

27. C. A DNS server is responsible for resolving a TCP/IP hostname to an IP address. Because you can connect using the IP address, you know it is the hostname resolution at fault.

28. C. Settings are stored in the Windows 98 Registry.

29. E. Computers using share-level security can only connect to other computers using share-level security. Windows 98's Net Watcher can only monitor other Windows 98 systems, not NT. If you have chosen user-level security, you will not be able to see the other workstations in the environment. When you switch your workstation to user-level security, you will meet all of the objectives, assuming you have the proper authorization as the network administrator.

30. A. From Safe mode, you can look at hardware devices in the Device Manager or System Information Utility to see which ones have conflicts.

31. B-C. The Startup disk and the Windows\ command folder will contain a copy of the Extract utility.

32. A-C-D. The default setting is Auto and will try to automatically detect the appropriate frame type.

33. B. DHCP is installed on an NT server and distributes IP addresses to clients during the startup procedure.

34. E. System monitor will not be able to tell you if other users are connected to your workstation, and it cannot be used to log changes to your system configuration. To monitor connected users, you will need to use Net Watcher.

35. D. The conflict has rendered the sound card useless, along with the network card. Changing the settings in the Control Panel is necessary; usually this must be done in the Device Manager, but this is not the only step. Patrick must also change the settings on the network card. Usually this is done by using jumpers, dip switches, or software on the older legacy cards.

36. A. The Show Shared Folders button shows the folders and their descriptions, if any.

37. A-B-D. The system administrator must set up the workgroup Post Office and all the mailboxes before configuring Exchange for Microsoft Mail. The Exchange folders are created automatically.

38. C. Each workgroup must have its own master browser. By default, all Windows 98 clients will be potential master browsers. Changing the status of some clients to non-browsers will help maintain control. Each Windows 98 system must have SAP advertising enabled for other Windows 98 and Novell clients to see the shares.

39. B. The assistants will be able to access the network from home and use the intranet's Proxy server to get to the Internet. However, because the PPTP is only installed on the RAS server and not the on the client, a Virtual Private Network cannot be established. The connections are not as secured as they could be.

40. A. The user cannot use two different names to log on to NT and Novell if the primary logon name and password match the second.

41. B. Rerunning the Windows 98 Setup program replaces corrupted Windows files and repairs any errors it finds in the system Registry. You can create a boot-up log during Windows 98 startup, but it is not a setting you can use during Windows 98 installation. Windows 98 doesn't have a utility that logs GPF messages and information.

42. B. PPTP/VPN works by carrying other packets within the data section of the IP packet. This IP packet is sent through a TCP/IP network to the remote RAS server, and therefore requires the IP address of the RAS server.

43. C-D. The convert utility in the command prompt is CVT drive: /cvt and the graphical interface is found in System Tools. Typically the cluster size is smaller for the same size hard drive.

44. C. DriveSpace 3.0 with Ultrapack will compress files, but not on the fly. It will also slow down the read time.

45. B. The system will run each night and not interfere with users' work. The hard drives will be checked for errors and run more efficiently. However, the Express setup will not permit the customization of the list of tasks and the system will run Disk Cleanup.

46. D. The maintenance manager cannot run if the system is off. It will prompt the users in the morning and will interfere with users' work. The hard drives will be checked for errors and run more efficiently. However, the Custom setup will permit you to customize the list of tasks and the system can be set to remove Disk Cleanup.

47. A. Profiles have not been enabled under Control Panel, Passwords, User Profiles.

48. C. The DETLOG.TXT file is an ASCII text file that contains information regarding the hardware detection phase of Windows 95 Setup.

49. A. The DETCRASH.LOG file is a binary file used by the Windows 98 Setup program. It does not contain any human readable information. Instead, look in the DETLOG.TXT file for information regarding the hardware detection phase of Windows 98 Setup.

50. D. Deleting the DETCRASH.LOG file will cause the system to crash again. Each time the system restarts, it opens the DETCRASH.LOG file to read the error messages and will not attempt same tests that caused the crash in the first place. To view the components that might be causing a problem, view the file DETLOG.TXT.

51. B. Each time the system restarts, it opens the DETCRASH.LOG file to read the error messages and will not attempt the same tests that caused the crash in the first place. To view the components that might be causing a problem, view the DETLOG.TXT file.

52. B. The HKEY_LOCAL_MACHINE Registry key contains information about system hardware.

53. D. File and Printer Sharing must be enabled on all the computers because all users need to share files with other users.

54. B. The users can all share their files, but managers cannot use their modems.

55. C. The POLEDIT utility is used to create and edit system policies.

EXAM QUESTIONS

1. When remote administration is enabled on a Windows 98 computer, two special shared directories are created. What are those two special shares?

    A. ADMIN

    B. IPC

    C. ADMIN$

    D. IPC$

    E. PRINTER

    F. PRINTER$

2. Which of the following statements is true about FAT16, FAT32, and NTFS file systems? Choose the best answer.

    A. Windows 98 and Windows NT can both read all the formats.

    B. Windows 98 can read FAT16 drives, and Windows NT can read all the formats.

    C. Windows 98 can read all formats; Windows NT can read only NTFS.

    D. Windows 98 cannot read FAT32.

    E. Windows 98 can read FAT16 and FAT32; Windows NT can read FAT16 and NTFS.

    The following two questions are based on the same scenario, required component, and optional components. Please read all the requirements and proposed solution before answering.

Practice Exam 2

3. **Scenario:**

    The network administrator must be able to have all systems run a backup each night without having to rely on users.

    Required component:
    Back up all data on local hard drives each night to a common network share.

    Optional components:
    Require no user intervention.

    Have backup completed even if the users shut down their computers at the end of the day.

    Proposed solution:
    Create a batch file to run the backup and have all settings pre-selected.

    A. The proposed solution satisfies the required component and all of the optional components.

    B. The proposed solution satisfies the required component and only one of the optional components.

    C. The proposed solution satisfies the required component and none of the optional components.

D. The proposed solution satisfies one of the optional components but does not satisfy the required component.

E. The proposed solution satisfies none of the optional components and does not sastisfy the required component.

4. **Scenario:**

The network administrator must be able to have all systems run a backup each night without having to rely on users.

Required component:
Back up all data on local hard drives each night to a common network share.

Optional components:
Require no user intervention.

Have backup completed even if the users shut down their computers at the end of the day.

Proposed solution:
Create a batch file to run the backup and have all settings pre-selected. Add the batch file to the Scheduler to run after hours.

A. The proposed solution satisfies the required component and all of the optional components.

B. The proposed solution satisfies the required component and only one of the optional components.

C. The proposed solution satisfies the required component and none of the optional components.

D. The proposed solution satisfies one of the optional components but does not satisfy the required component.

E. The proposed solution satisfies none of the optional components and does not satisfy the required component.

5. **Where does Windows 98 look for the CONFIG.POL file in a Windows NT domain?**

A. `%SYSTEMROOT%\SYSTEM32\EXPORT\SCRIPTS\`

B. `%SYSTEMROOT%\SYSTEM32\IMPORT\SCRIPTS\`

C. `%SYSTEMROOT%\SYSTEM\REPL\IMPORT\SCRIPTS\`

D. `%SYSTEMROOT%\SYSTEM23\RPL\IMPORT\SCRIPTS\`

E. `%SYSTEMROOT%\SYSTEM\REPL32\IMPORT\SCRIPTS\`

6. **Workgroups must use which level of security in a Windows 98–only network?**

A. Group-level

B. User-level

C. Share-level

D. Resource-level

E. Workgroup-level

7. **As a network administrator, you choose to implement roving user profiles by using Windows 98 and Novell NetWare. Where should you place the user profiles on the NetWare server?**

A. `SYS:SYSTEM`

B. `SYS:PUBLIC`

C. User's home directory

D. `Mail user_id` directory

E. `SYS:PRIVATE`

The following two questions are based on the same scenario, required components, and optional components. Please read all the requirements and proposed solution before answering.

8. Scenario:

At your corporation, you have been tasked with the job of upgrading 100 computers from Windows 3.1 to Windows 98. The users of these machines have varying needs. Some have local printers; others use network printers. The majority of the computers are desktops, but some are notebooks. To complicate the effort, some of the users still want access to Windows 3.1.

Required components:
Install Windows 98 on all the computers.

Reduce the need for user intervention in the setup process.

Optional components:
Install Windows 98 quickly.

Leave Windows 3.1 installed for the users who still need it, but replace Windows 3.1 for those who don't.

Proposed solution:
You run NETSETUP to place all the installation files on a network server. Then you use BATCH.EXE to create an automated script for installing Windows 98. You send out an email telling your users where to find the SETUP.EXE file and asking them to run it with the batch script.

   A. The proposed solution satisfies all the required components and all of the optional components.

   B. The proposed solution satisfies all the required components but only one of the optional components.

   C. The proposed solution satisfies all the required components but none of the optional components.

   D. The proposed solution satisfies one of the required components but none of the optional components.

   E. The proposed solution satisfies none of the required components and none of the optional components.

9. Scenario:

At your corporation, you have been tasked with the job of upgrading 100 computers from Windows 3.1 to Windows 98. The users of these machines have varying needs. Some have local printers; others use network printers. The majority of the computers are desktops, but some are notebooks. To complicate the effort, some of the users still want access to Windows 3.1.

Required components:
Install Windows 98 on all the computers.

Reduce the need for user intervention in the setup process.

Optional components:
Install Windows 98 quickly.

Leave Windows 3.1 installed for the users who still need it, but replace Windows 3.1 for those who don't.

Proposed solution:
You run NETSETUP to place all the installation files on a network server. Then you use BATCH.EXE to create an automated script for installing Windows 98. In the batch have one question prompt the user: Do you want to upgrade or keep Windows 3.1? You then send out an email telling your users where to find the SETUP.EXE file and asking them to run it with the batch script.

A. The proposed solution satisfies all the required components and all of the optional components.

B. The proposed solution satisfies all the required components but only one of the optional components.

C. The proposed solution satisfies all the required components but none of the optional components.

D. The proposed solution satisfies one of the required components but none of the optional components.

E. The proposed solution satisfies none of the required components and none of the optional components.

10. **How can a PWS administrator keep a section of the Web site separate for the main page without the use of links on the main page?**

A. Create a default home location that includes all the data.

B. Create a shortcut.

C. Create an alias.

D. Create a default alias name.

E. Create a separate Web page.

11. **Why might someone choose to use multiple display adapters? Select all that apply.**

A. To have one application on each monitor and not have to switch between them

B. To display the same information on several monitors for a demo or presentation

C. To split the screen of one application to display a portion on different screens

D. To connect several PCs and display each PC's data on a separate monitor

E. To split the PC between two users, if you also add another mouse and keyboard

The following two questions are based on the same scenario, required components, and optional components. Please read all the requirements and proposed solution before answering.

12. **Scenario:**

You have several users complaining about the performance of their computers. They are saying that it is taking them longer and longer to open and save files, and that files are getting corrupted on a regular basis.

Required components:
Improve disk access to speed performance.

Reduce the occurrences of corrupt files.

Optional components:
Scan hard drives for viruses.

Increase available memory.

Repair corrupt files.

Proposed solution:
You install the ScanDisk and Disk Defragmenter utilities on the users' machines, and then run a thorough ScanDisk before defragmenting their hard drives. After the immediate problem is fixed, you set up the Maintenance Wizard for routine checks and cleaning.

A. The proposed solution satisfies all the required components and all of the optional components.

B. The proposed solution satisfies all the required components but only one of the optional components.

C. The proposed solution satisfies all the required components but none of the optional components.

D. The proposed solution satisfies one of the required components but none of the optional components.

E. The proposed solution satisfies none of the required components and none of the optional components.

13. **Scenario:**

You have several users who are complaining about the performance of their computers. They are saying that it is taking them longer and longer to open and save files, and that files are getting corrupted on a regular basis.

Required components:
Improve disk access to speed performance.

Reduce the occurrences of corrupt files.

Optional components:
Scan hard drives for viruses.

Increase available memory.

Repair corrupt files.

Proposed solution:
You install the ScanDisk and Disk Defragmenter utilities on the users' machines, and then run a thorough ScanDisk before defragmenting their hard drives. After the immediate problem is fixed, you set up the Maintenance Wizard for routine checks and cleaning. Also enable a virus scanning program.

A. The proposed solution satisfies all the required components and all of the optional components.

B. The proposed solution satisfies all the required components but only two of the optional components.

C. The proposed solution satisfies all the required components but none of the optional components.

D. The proposed solution satisfies none of the required components and none of the optional components.

14. **You need to be able to provide user restrictions for both individuals and groups in your network. Which policy will provide the required restrictions to both the users and the groups?**

A. System policies

B. Mandatory user profiles

C. User profiles

D. Mandatory user policies

E. Login scripts

15. **When setting up Dial-Up Networking what devices are used to establish the connection? Select all that apply.**

A. A network card

B. A cable modem

C. The VPN device

D. A modem

E. The PPTP device

16. **Alice asks how she can modify her user profile. She is running a Windows 98 computer that is not connected to a network. What are the general steps needed to modify her user profile?**

Study each scenario carefully and decide which solution would best answer this question.

A. Make sure the Users Can Customize Their Preferences and Desktop Settings option, which can be enabled on the User Profiles tab of the Passwords Properties sheet, is selected.

Next, advise the user to make any changes to the desktop, Start menu, and program groups.

Shut down and reboot the system.

After logging in, your new changes appear and are part of the user profile for that user.

B. Make sure the Users Can Customize Their Preferences and desktop Settings option, which can be enabled on the User Profiles tab of the Security Properties sheet, is selected.

Next, advise the user to make any changes to the desktop, Start menu, and program groups.

Shut down and reboot the system.

After the user logs in, the new changes appear and are part of the user profile for that user.

C. Make sure the Users Cannot Customize Their Preferences and Desktop Settings option, which can be enabled on the User Profiles tab of the Passwords Properties sheet, is selected.

Next, advise the user to make changes to the desktop, Start menu, and program groups.

Shut down and reboot the system.

After athe user logs in, the new changes appear and are part of the user profile for that user.

D. Make sure the Users Can Customize Their Preferences and Desktop Settings option, which can be enabled on the User Profiles tab of the Passwords Properties sheet, is selected.

Next, advise the user to make changes to the desktop, Start menu, and program groups.

Shut down and reboot the system.

After the user logs in, the new changes appear and are part of the user profile for that user.

E. Make sure the Users Cannot Customize Their Preferences and Desktop Settings option, which can be enabled on the User Profiles tab of the Passwords Properties sheet, is selected.

Next, advise the user to make changes to the desktop, Start menu, and program groups.

Shut down and reboot the system.

After logging in, do not save settings. The system is trying to use the default values if you say Yes to save settings.

The following two questions are based on the same scenario, required component, and optional components. Please read all the requirements and proposed solution before answering.

17. **Scenario:**

Sara, Carol, and Jeremy are in a three-user workgroup. Carol can communicate with Sara and Jeremy, but Sara and Jeremy cannot communicate with each other. You examine the network settings and find that Sara and Carol are using NetBEUI, and Jeremy and Carol are using IPX/SPX.

Required component:
Change the network settings so that all three computers can communicate with one another.

Optional components:
Maintain the speed of the network by not creating unnecessary traffic.

Make sure that all the users can view a browse list.

Proposed solution:
Tell Sara to add IPX/SPX protocol.

A. The proposed solution satisfies the required component and all of the optional components.

B. The proposed solution satisfies the required component and only one of the optional components.

C. The proposed solution satisfies the required component and none of the optional components.

D. The proposed solution satisfies all of the optional components but does not satisfy the required component.

E. The proposed solution satisfies none of the optional components and does not satisfy the required component.

18. **Scenario:**

Sara, Carol, and Jeremy are in a three-user workgroup. Carol can communicate with Sara and Jeremy, but Sara and Jeremy cannot communicate with each other. You examine the network settings and find that Sara and Carol are using NetBEUI, and Jeremy and Carol are using IPX/SPX.

Required component:
Change the network settings so that all three computers can communicate with one another.

Optional components:
Maintain the speed of the network by not creating unnecessary traffic.

Make sure that all the users can view a browse list.

Proposed solution:
Tell Sara to add IPX/SPX protocol and Carol to remove NetBEUI. Have all three users enable NetBIOS over IPX.

A. The proposed solution satisfies the required component and all of the optional components.

B. The proposed solution satisfies the required component and only one of the optional components.

C. The proposed solution satisfies the required component and none of the optional components.

D. The proposed solution satisfies all of the optional components but does not satisfy the required component.

E. The proposed solution satisfies none of the optional components and does not satisfy the required component.

19. **In your networked environment, you have sensitive files to which you want to restrict access. You want to allow some users the ability to update these files, enable some to read the files, and prevent other users from accessing the files at all. How should you implement this? Choose two answers.**

A. Implement share-level security with a read/write password and a read password. Give users the appropriate password.

B. Implement user-level security with a read/write password and a read password. Give users the appropriate password.

C. Implement share-level security and set up the user IDs with appropriate rights so that users don't need to know a password.

D. Implement user-level security and set up the user IDs with appropriate rights so that users don't need to know a password.

E. Implement password-level security and set up the user IDs with appropriate rights so that users don't need to know a password.

20. **What condition must be met on a Windows NT network in order for a user profile to follow the user around a network?**

A. The user must be part of a global group.

B. The Windows NT network must be configured as a workgroup.

C. The user must be part of a local group.

D. The Windows NT network must be configured as a domain.

E. The Windows 98 system must have network profiles enabled though the Passwords icon.

21. **Before Margaret can use her modem to send a fax with Exchange, which three of the following items does she need?**

A. Installed Microsoft FAX software

B. The Microsoft FAX Information Service added to her profile

C. A fax profile

D. A fax modem configured for the Windows 98 client

E. A fax machine

The following two questions are based on the same scenario, required component, and optional components. Please read all the requirements and proposed solution before answering.

22. **Scenario:**

You are setting up a Windows 98 network of 25 systems. Four of the systems will be sharing resources with the other systems on the network. One system will be sharing a printer. Two systems will be sharing two applications and printers. One system will be sharing files, applications, printer, and modem.

Ten users will not have access to the last system's files (three DIR) and three applications. Share-level access has been enabled for the resources.

Required component:
Distribute the correct passwords to the correct users and control the number of passwords you will have to configure.

Optional components:
Keep the passwords current in order to reduce inappropriate use of the resources.

Simplify access for all users of the common resources.

Proposed solution:
Thirteen passwords, and distribute email to the groups that have access to their respective resources.

Allow each user to change the password to match his own Windows 98 logon password.

Change the passwords every 30 days to improve security.

A. The proposed solution satisfies the required component and all of the optional components.

B. The proposed solution satisfies the required component and only one of the optional components.

C. The proposed solution satisfies the required component and none of the optional components.

D. The proposed solution satisfies one of the optional components but does not satisfy the required component.

E. The proposed solution satisfies none of the optional components and does not satisfy the required component.

23. Scenario:

You are setting up a Windows 98 network of 25 systems. Four of the systems will be sharing resources with the other systems on the network. One system will be sharing a printer. Two systems will be sharing two applications and printers. One system will be sharing files, applications, printer, and modem.

Ten users will not have access to the last system's files (three DIR) and three applications. Share-level access has been enabled for the resources.

To distribute the correct passwords to the correct users and to control the number of passwords you will have to configure.

Optional components:

Keep the password current in order to reduce inappropriate use of the resources.

Simplify access for all users to the common resources.

Proposed solution:

Change to user-level security with an NT server or Novell server.

Have users change their passwords every 30 days to improve security.

A. The proposed solution satisfies the required component and all of the optional components.

B. The proposed solution satisfies the required component and only one of the optional components.

C. The proposed solution satisfies the required component and none of the optional components.

D. The proposed solution satisfies one of the optional components but does not satisfy the required component.

E. The proposed solution satisfies none of the optional components and does not satisfy the required component.

24. When you are creating a Workgroup Post Office, it is important that you take which two of the following steps?

A. Give all Post Office members full-control access to the Workgroup Post Office directory.

B. Assign the same password to all Post Office members when share-level security is used.

C. Give all Post Office members read-only access to the Workgroup Post Office directory.

D. Have each Post Office member choose a unique password when share-level security is used.

E. Have each user create his own post office and have the post offices shared.

The following two questions are based on the same scenario, required components, and optional components. Please read all the requirements and proposed solution before answering.

25. Scenario:

A user has asked you for help installing both Windows 98 and Windows NT on a computer. The user is fairly advanced, and she needs the Windows 98 online help files and the Resource Kit help files. The computer is currently running Windows for Workgroups, but the user no longer has a need for it.

Required components:
Set up the computer for a Windows 98/Windows NT dual boot.

Provide access in Windows 98 to all the applications that the user currently sees in Windows for Workgroups.

Optional components:
Install the Windows 98 online help and the Resource Kit help.

Install Windows 98 and Windows NT on the same drive.

Proposed solution:
You create a setup on the network by running NETSETUP from the Windows 98 CD-ROM. Then, from the network, you install Windows 98 into the same directory as Windows for Workgroups. Finally, you install Windows NT and allow it to create the dual boot for you.

A. The proposed solution satisfies all the required components and all of the optional components.

B. The proposed solution satisfies all the required components but only one of the optional components.

C. The proposed solution satisfies all the required components but none of the optional components.

D. The proposed solution satisfies none of the required components but one of the optional components.

E. The proposed solution satisfies none of the required components and none of the optional components.

26. Scenario:

A user has asked you for help installing both Windows 98 and Windows NT on a computer. The user is fairly advanced, and she needs the Windows 98 online help files and the Resource Kit help files. The computer is currently running Windows for Workgroups, but the user no longer has a need for it.

Required components:
Set up the computer for a Windows 98/Windows NT dual boot.

Provide access in Windows 98 to all the applications that the user currently sees in Windows for Workgroups.

Optional components:
Install the Windows 98 online help and the Resource Kit help.

Install Windows 98 and Windows NT on the same drive.

Proposed solution:
You create a setup on the network by running NETSETUP from the Windows 98 CD-ROM. Then, from the network, you install Windows 98 into the same directory as Windows for Workgroups. Install Windows NT and allow it to create the dual boot for you. Finally, install the Resource Kit off the Windows 98 CD-ROM.

A. The proposed solution satisfies all the required components and all of the optional components.

B. The proposed solution satisfies all the required components but only one of the optional components.

C. The proposed solution satisfies all the required components but none of the optional components.

D. The proposed solution satisfies none of the required components but one of the optional components.

E. The proposed solution satisfies none of the required components and none of the optional components.

27. **The Task Scheduler and the Maintenance Wizard share the same configuration settings. Is this true or false?**

A. True, initially, because the three basic tasks are the same.

B. False, initially, but Task Scheduler can be configured to look like Maintenance Wizard.

C. True, but only if the Maintenance Wizard is run first.

D. False, because Task Scheduler is used for remote systems and Maintenance Wizard is used for local resources.

E. True, but only if the Task Scheduler is run first.

28. **What must be running on each client to have user-level security working in a Windows NT environment with Windows 98 clients? Select all that apply.**

A. Client for Microsoft

B. Client for NetWare Networks

C. File and Printer Sharing for Microsoft Networks

D. File and Printer Sharing for NetWare Networks

E. Client for Windows 98

29. **For a PowerPoint presentation in front of the help desk staff, you create a slide with a bullet point describing the Windows 98 System Policy feature. What would be the appropriate ending to the sentence: A Windows 98 system policy _____.**

A. Assigns priorities to applications accessing memory

B. Assigns priorities to users

C. Enables an administrator to set various Windows 95 Registry entries

D. Is a summary of configuration details

E. Enables users to set their own restrictions

The following two questions are based on the same scenario, required component, and optional components. Please read all the requirements and proposed solution before answering.

30. **Scenario:**

One of the employees has decided to change the TCP/IP settings of his computer. After having changed most settings, he finds that he cannot communicate with the network, and calls you for help. He tells you that he does not know what the old numbers were.

Required component:
The computer must be able to communicate with the network again.

Optional components:
The computer must be able to use NetBIOS names to communicate.

The computer must be able to communicate with other remote subnets.

Proposed solution:
Provide him with new numbers for him to change his IP address, subnet mask, and the IP address of the default gateway.

A. The proposed solution satisfies the required component and all of the optional components.

B. The proposed solution satisfies the required component and only one of the optional components.

C. The proposed solution satisfies the required component and none of the optional components.

D. The proposed solution satisfies one of the optional components but does not satisfy the required component.

E. The proposed solution satisfies none of the optional components and does not satisfy the required component.

31. **Scenario:**

One of the employees has decided to change the TCP/IP settings of his computer. After having changed most settings, he finds that he cannot communicate with the network, and calls you for help. He tells you that he does not know what the old numbers were.

Required component:
The computer must be able to communicate with the network again.

Optional components:
The computer must be able to use NetBIOS names to communicate.

The computer must be able to communicate with other remote subnets.

Proposed solution:
Provide him with new numbers for him to change his IP address, subnet mask, WINS server address, and the IP address of the default gateway.

A. The proposed solution satisfies the required component and all of the optional components.

B. The proposed solution satisfies the required component and only one of the optional components.

C. The proposed solution satisfies the required component and none of the optional components.

D. The proposed solution satisfies one of the optional components but does not satisfy the required component.

E. The proposed solution satisfies none of the optional components and does not satisfy the required component.

32. **How can errors be monitored and recorded for troubleshooting purposes when setting up Dial-Up Networking by using PPTP and VPN? Select the best answer.**

A. Activate the log file from the Advanced tab of the VPN.

B. Use Network Monitor.

C. Activate a PPTP log from the network icon.

D. Use Performance Monitor.

E. Use the Network Error Log.

33. **Similar to configuring user profiles, to use system policies, your workstation must have which of the following for policy settings to be established?**

    A. User profiles enabled

    B. A computer account on the domain

    C. Local user profiles

    D. User-level security

    E. Part of a domain

34. **Your company has decided to upgrade all user machines from Windows 3.11 and Windows 95 to Windows 98. The powers that be want to allow for Internet access. Your network currently consists of 25 clients accessing a Windows NT Server. You upgrade everyone's system to Windows 98 with the default settings. You then configure a router to access the Internet through your company's Internet service provider.**

    When you test the connection to the Internet, it fails. You can see everyone on the network, as well as the NT servers. You can even access all the same files that you could before. Which of the following is the best solution?

    A. You must first install and configure a modem on all clients, and then enable Dial-Up Networking to access the Internet service provider.

    B. You must install Client for Microsoft Networks and configure user-level security to access the Internet service provider.

    C. You must install TCP/IP on all clients and configure an IP address, subnet mask, and default gateway.

    D. You must run WinIPCfg to configure the IP settings to access the Internet service provider and assign a NetBIOS identification.

    E. You must first install Dial-Up Networking using a VPN.

35. **To reload files from the CAB files you must run the extract command. What is the best environment to run it from?**

    A. From Windows 98 Start menu

    B. From the MS-DOS prompt

    C. From Windows 98 restarted in command prompt only

    D. From a Startup disk

    E. From Windows 98's Maintenance tool

    The following two questions are based on the same scenario, required component, and optional components. Please read all the requirements and proposed solution before answering.

36. **Scenario:**

    Alan, an employee in the shipping department, has a request to share information regarding packages that have been shipped. He wants to make the shipping information located on his computer available to all other employees to reduce the number of phone calls and inquiries he receives. Your network currently consists of 65 Windows 98 clients and 25 DOS/NetWare clients, all connected to a NetWare 4.11 server in bindery emulation.

    Required component:
    Configure Alan's machine to be a file server for all the Windows 98 clients and NetWare clients on the network. On Alan's machine, share the folder that contains the shipping information.

Optional components:
Assign Full Control rights to Henry, Alan's assistant, so that he can update the files and information in Alan's absence.

Assign Read-Only rights to all users.

Proposed solution:
Install File and Printer Sharing for Microsoft Networks on Alan's machine. Configure his machine for user-level security. On the Access Control tab of the Network Properties sheet, type the NetWare server name in the Obtain a List of Users and Groups From box. Share and assign the default permissions to the folder containing the shipping information. Assign user rights to Henry's account on the NetWare server.

A. The proposed solution satisfies the required component and all of the optional components.

B. The proposed solution satisfies the required component and only one of the optional components.

C. The proposed solution satisfies the required component and none of the optional components.

D. The proposed solution satisfies one of the optional components but does not satisfy the required component.

E. The proposed solution satisfies none of the optional components and does not satisfy the required component.

37. **Scenario:**

Alan, an employee in the shipping department, has a request to share information regarding packages that have been shipped. He wants to make the shipping information, located on his computer, available to all other employees to reduce the number of phone calls and inquiries he receives. Your network currently consists of 65 Windows 98 clients and 25 DOS/NetWare clients, all connected to a NetWare 4.11 server in bindery emulation.

Required component:
Configure Alan's machine to be a file server for all the Windows 98 clients and NetWare clients on the network. On Alan's machine, share the folder that contains the shipping information.

Optional components:
Assign Full Control rights to Henry, Alan's assistant, so that he can update the files and information in Alan's absence.

Assign Read-Only rights to all users.

Proposed solution:
Install File and Printer Sharing for Novell Networks on Alan's machine. Configure his machine for user-level security. On the Access Control tab of the Network Properties sheet, type the NetWare server name in the Obtain a List of Users and Groups From box. Share and assign the default permissions to the folder containing the shipping information. Assign user rights to Henry's account on the NetWare server.

A. The proposed solution satisfies the required component and all of the optional components.

B. The proposed solution satisfies the required component and only one of the optional components.

C. The proposed solution satisfies the required component and none of the optional components.

D. The proposed solution satisfies one of the optional components but does not satisfy the required component.

E. The proposed solution satisfies none of the optional components and does not satisfy the required component.

The following two questions are based on the same scenario, required component, and optional components. Please read all the requirements and proposed solution before answering.

38. **Scenario:**

Leonard, a member of the Human Resources group, has been working on an Access database that will include all the company's employees. Each listing will contain the employee's name, address, phone number, email address, title, and some family information. He has been saving the database to his Windows 98 client and saving a copy on his domain's NT server to ensure that a backup is made each night.

Close to finishing the database, he shares the folder on his Windows 98 client with the default settings. He places the database in the newly shared folder. He then posts a note in the company newsgroup, informing people of its location and asking everyone to look at it and provide feedback.

Required component:
Allow the Human Resources group access to the database to provide feedback.

Optional components:
Allow the company employees to view all the information in the database but not change anything in the database directly.

Allow some users to make changes to the database.

Under no circumstances should anyone outside the company have access to the database.

Proposed solution:
Configure Leonard's machine for user-level security.

A. The proposed solution satisfies the required component and all of the optional components.

B. The proposed solution satisfies the required component and only one of the optional components.

C. The proposed solution satisfies the required component and none of the optional components.

D. The proposed solution satisfies one of the optional components but does not satisfy the required component.

E. The proposed solution satisfies none of the optional components and does not satisfy the required component.

39. **Scenario:**

Leonard, a member of the Human Resources group, has been working on an Access database that will include all the company's employees. Each listing will contain the employee's name, address, phone number, email address, title, and some family information. He has been saving the database to his Windows 98 client and saving a copy on his domain's NT server to ensure that a backup is made each night.

Close to finishing the database, he shares the folder on his Windows 98 client with the default settings. He places the database in the newly shared folder. He then posts a note in the company newsgroup, informing people of its location and asking everyone to look at it and provide feedback.

Required component:
Allow the Human Resources group access to the database to provide feedback.

Optional components:
Allow the company employees to view all the information in the database but not change anything in the database directly.

Allow some users to make changes to the database.

Under no circumstances should anyone outside the company have access to the database.

Proposed solution:
Configure Leonard's machine for user-level security. Share the folder as Read-only to some users and as Full to others.

A. The proposed solution satisfies the required component and all of the optional components.

B. The proposed solution satisfies the required component and only one of the optional components.

C. The proposed solution satisfies the required component and none of the optional components.

D. The proposed solution satisfies one of the optional components but does not satisfy the required component.

E. The proposed solution satisfies none of the optional components and does not satisfy the required component.

40. **You have just installed a new modem and the supporting device drivers, and it appears that this has corrupted your system Registry. How can you recover from this problem? Choose the best answer.**

A. Rerun Windows 98 Setup and let it re-create the system Registry.

B. Restore the Registry from the backup you made immediately before installing the modem and drivers.

C. Get a copy of the system Registry files from a friend.

D. Restore the old modem, then upgrade the drivers in the modem properties.

E. Restore the system Registry from backups that Windows created the last time it successfully started.

The following two questions are based on the same scenario, required component, and optional components. Please read all the requirements and proposed solution before answering.

41. **Scenario:**

Susan has been working with Patrick and Michael on an important project for the Sales department. Her machine has been updated to Windows 98 over the weekend. As the administrator of a mixed network environment, she calls you and tells you that although she can see Patrick's and Michael's machines on the network, she can no longer see or access the shared folder to update the sales project files. Your network is connected to a NetWare 4.11 server in bindery emulation.

Required component:
Connect Susan's machine to the shared folder containing the sales project files.

Optional components:
Automatically connect Susan to the shared folder containing the sales project files each time she logs in.

Give Susan the rights to share folders on her machine with other Windows 98 clients.

Proposed solution:
Install File and Printer sharing for Microsoft Networks on Susan's machine. Configure her machine for user-level security. On the Access Control tab of the Network Properties sheet, type the NetWare server name in the Obtain a List of Users and Groups From box. Install Client Services for Microsoft Networks. Install Client Services for NetWare Networks.

A. The proposed solution satisfies the required component and all of the optional components.

B. The proposed solution satisfies the required component and only one of the optional components.

C. The proposed solution satisfies the required component and none of the optional components.

D. The proposed solution satisfies one of the optional components but does not satisfy the required component.

E. The proposed solution satisfies none of the optional components and does not satisfy the required component.

42. **Scenario:**

Susan has been working with Patrick and Michael on an important project for the Sales department. Her machine has been updated to Windows 98 over the weekend. As the administrator of a mixed network environment, she calls you and tells you that although she can see Patrick's and Michael's machines on the network, she can no longer see or access the shared folder to update the sales project files. Your network is connected to a NetWare 4.11 server in bindery emulation.

Required component:
Connect Susan's machine to the shared folder containing the sales project files.

Optional components:
Automatically connect Susan to the shared folder containing the sales project files each time she logs in.

Give Susan the rights to share folders on her machine with other Windows 98 clients.

Proposed solution:
Install File and Printer Sharing for Microsoft Networks on Susan's machine. Configure her machine for user-level security. On the Access Control tab of the Network Properties sheet, type the NT server name in the Obtain a List of Users and Groups From box. Install Client Services for Microsoft Networks. Install Client Services for NetWare Networks. Map a drive to the shared folder and make it reconnect at login.

A. The proposed solution satisfies the required component and all of the optional components.

B. The proposed solution satisfies the required component and only one of the optional components.

C. The proposed solution satisfies the required component and none of the optional components.

D. The proposed solution satisfies one of the optional components but does not satisfy the required component.

E. The proposed solution satisfies none of the optional components and does not satisfy the required component.

The following two questions are based on the same scenario, required component, and optional components. Please read all the requirements and proposed solution before answering.

43. **Scenario:**

You have just purchased a new Windows 98 system but have found that a few files need to be reloaded from the source files. You do not know where the files are found on the CAB files.

Required component:
Display the contents of the CAB files to see where the corrupted files are located.

Optional components:
Use existing utilities.

Reload the files that are corrupted.

Proposed solution:
From a command prompt you decide to use the Extract command with the /d switch to display files. You use the command Extract *.* /d /a.

A. The proposed solution satisfies the required component and all of the optional components.

B. The proposed solution satisfies the required component and only one of the optional components.

C. The proposed solution satisfies the required component and none of the optional components.

D. The proposed solution satisfies one of the optional components but does not satisfy the required component.

E. The proposed solution satisfies none of the optional components and does not satisfy the required component.

44. **Scenario:**

You have just purchased a new Windows 98 system but have found that a few files need to be reloaded from the source files. You do not know where the files are found on the CAB files.

Required component:
Display the content of the CAB files to see where the corrupted files are located.

Optional components:
Use existing utilities.

Reload the files that are corrupted.

Proposed solution:
From a command prompt you decide to use the Extract command with the /d switch to display files. You use the command Extract *.* /d /a. After the corrupted file is determined, use the Extract command followed by the filename to extract.

A. The proposed solution satisfies the required component and all of the optional components.

B. The proposed solution satisfies the required component and only one of the optional components.

C. The proposed solution satisfies the required component and none of the optional components.

D. The proposed solution satisfies one of the optional components but does not satisfy the required component.

E. The proposed solution satisfies none of the optional components and does not satisfy the required component.

The following question is scenario based. Please read all the requirements and proposed solution before answering.

45. **Scenario:**

In your user environment are a number of older computers that the users are saying shut down too slowly. You notice that some of the users don't wait for Windows 98 to shut down before turning the power off because it is taking too long. Some of these users are also complaining about losing data that they have saved.

Required components:
Prevent the problem of lost data.

Improve disk performance.

Optional components:

Speed up Windows Shutdown.

Improve the system response when saving data.

Proposed solution:

Disable write-behind caching on the users' machines.

A. The proposed solution satisfies all the required components and all of the optional components.

B. The proposed solution satisfies all the required components but only one of the optional components.

C. The proposed solution meets only one of the primary objectives and one of the secondary objectives.

D. The proposed solution satisfies all the required components but none of the optional components.

E. The proposed solution satisfies none of the required components and none of the optional components.

46. **Dave is running Windows 98 Disk Defragmenter as a background task. When he saves a file he is working on in his foreground application, Disk Defragmenter does what?**

A. Fails

B. Restarts immediately and defragments the whole hard drive again

C. Stops the defragmentation and asks for user input

D. Defragments the new file after the current defragmentation is complete

E. Does nothing

47. **You get an error message when you try to print to your local printer. What can you do to resolve this problem? Select all that apply.**

A. Verify that there is free space on the hard disk.

B. Reinstall the printer drivers.

C. Verify that the TEMP variable is set correctly.

D. Try to print the document from the command prompt.

E. Turn the printer off, and then back on.

48. **What are the two types of security verification within the PWS security model?**

A. User level

B. Share level

C. Password

D. NT challenge

E. CHAP

49. **Where can you run the Windows Update tool from? Select the best answer.**

A. The Desktop's Windows Update icon

B. The Start, Programs, Accessories, System tools menu

C. The Start menu

D. The Task Bar

E. The System Checker

50. **You are trying to update your system by using Windows Update but are having difficulty downloading files. What should you do? Select the best answer.**

A. Restart Windows 98 and try again.

B. Call MS-Tech support.

C. Visit the Microsoft Web site at www.microsoft.com.

D. Visit the member services page of the Windows Update site to check on the status of server.

E. Run Setup again to fix any corrupted files.

51. **How can you tell which Windows Update items are most important to update?**

A. They are listed under a "must-have" section.

B. They are all important and should all be downloaded.

C. They are listed under a "mandatory" heading.

D. They are listed under a "critical" heading.

E. Microsoft does not recommend any item; it is up to you to decide what you want.

52. **Scott administers a Windows NT network that has several Windows 98 workstations attached to the server. He stores user profiles for all workstations on the server to be downloaded during boot-up time. The user profiles can be updated by the users. To ensure that each profile is available from the server, where are they stored on the server?**

A. In the user's home directory

B. In the user's C:\WINDOWS directory

C. In any directory on the server to which the user has read permissions

D. In the user's mail directory

E. None of the above

53. **Windows 98 ships with the File System Checker utility to verify the integrity of system files. Where can this utility be obtained? Select the best answer.**

A. From the System Information utility

B. From the Control Panel

C. From the System Tools utility

D. From the Windows\command folder

E. From the Tools menu on the toolbar of Explorer

54. **What are the two methods for securing access to the Peer Web Server?**

A. User level

B. Share level

C. File and Printer Sharing for Window 98

D. PWS security

E. PWS sharing

ANSWERS & EXPLANATIONS

1. **C-D.** When remote administration is enabled on a computer, two special shared directories are created: ADMIN$ gives administrators access to the file system on the remote computer. IPC$ provides an interprocess communication (IPC) channel between the two computers.

2. **E.** Windows 98 can read either the FAT16 or FAT32 file systems. Windows NT can read only FAT16 and NTFS.

3. **E.** A batch file can be created, but the users will need to run it. The system cannot perform the backups when the computers are shut down. The next time the users start up their systems, they will be informed of the tasks and asked if they should run it now.

4. **B.** A batch file can be created and added to the scheduler. The backup will run without user intervention. The system cannot perform the backups when the computers are shut down. The next time the users start up their systems, they will be informed of the tasks and asked if they should run it now.

5. **C.** The CONFIG.POL file must be located in the NETLOGON share of all domain controllers. %SYSTEMROOT% is a variable that represents the directory where Windows NT is located. The directory is %SYSTEMROOT%\ SYSTEM32\ REPL\IMPORT\SCRIPTS\.

6. **C.** Workgroups must use share-level security because the clients do not access a central Windows NT or NetWare accounts database.

7. **D.** In NetWare, a user's profile is pulled from his mail user_id directory.

8. **B.** The proposed solution can be used to install Windows 98 on many computers quickly and with little user interaction. Windows 98 will handle the detection of printers for you. Unfortunately, because you're eliminating most of the user interaction, the users won't have the chance to decide where to install Windows 98. If, in your batch script, you decide to install to the same directory containing Windows 3.1, the users will lose access to Windows 3.1 after Windows 98 is installed. If you choose to install Windows 98 to a different directory, all your users will retain access to Windows 3.1 as well as obtain access to Windows 98.

9. **B.** The proposed solution can be used to install Windows 98 on many computers quickly and with little user interaction. Windows 98 will handle the detection of printers for you. The batch file cannot be used to create questions to determine which part of the script to run. Two scripts would need to be created. Each user can choose which script to run. If, in your batch script, you decide to install to the same directory containing Windows 3.1, the users will lose access to Windows 3.1 after Windows 98 is installed. If you choose to install Windows 98 to a different directory, all your users will retain access to Windows 3.1 as well as obtain access to Windows 98.

10. **C.** An alias is a separate directory that can be used when accessing a separate part of the Web page. A link may be present but is not required, and the user would be able to provide the location name.

11. **A-C.** Multiple display support allows you to split the desktop on different monitors. Each application can take up its own display or the same application can be split.

12. **B.** Performing a thorough ScanDisk on a drive will search that drive for physical problems that may be causing slow performance. Disk performance may be slow due to a highly fragmented drive. The Disk Defragmenter can repair this. Neither the ScanDisk nor the Defragmenter utilities will check a drive for viruses, or improve memory on a workstation.

13. **B.** Performing a thorough ScanDisk on a drive will search that drive for physical problems that may be causing slow performance. Disk performance may be slow due to a highly fragmented drive. The Disk Defragmenter can repair this. Neither the ScanDisk nor the Defragmenter utilities will improve memory on a workstation.

14. **A.** System policies enforce computer-specific, user-specific, or group-specific Registry entries.

15. **C-D.** Windows 98 offers a list of installed dial-up devices when setting up a new Dial-Up entry. Modems and VPN are listed. The VPN device will use PPTP to establish a connection.

16. **A.** The user's profile will be stored locally under `<systemroot>\Profiles` and will be available whenever that user logs in to that specific workstation. All user preference changes are retained, but hardware and software settings are not.

17. **C.** The primary objective of communication is met, but the NetBEUI protocols are not removed, and therefore create extra network traffic. The browse list cannot be viewed when solely using IPX/SPX. Browsing requires NetBIOS and must be enabled in the NetBIOS tab of the IPX/SPX properties.

18. **A.** The primary objective of communication is met and only one protocol remains. This will reduce network traffic. The browse list cannot be viewed when solely using IPX/SPX. Browsing requires NetBIOS and must be enabled in the NetBIOS tab of the IPX/SPX properties.

19. **A-D.** If you use share-level security, the users must know a password for a particular resource. For user-level security, you have to give each individual user the appropriate rights to a resource.

20. **D.** The NT network must be configured as a domain. Also, the user account must be assigned a home directory in the User Environment Profile.

21. **A-B-D.** Margaret needs to install Microsoft FAX, add Microsoft FAX to her existing profile, and make sure that her modem is configured.

22. **B.** Even though users have to remember five passwords, this is the most secure answer for the network. Users will not be able to change the passwords to match their own logon password.

23. **A.** The user level will require that users have to remember only a single logon password. Users will not need to change the password to match their own logon password because the share will no longer have a password.

24. **A-B.** Because the Workgroup Post Office directory (`WPGO0000`) is a temporary storage area for all sent messages, it must be shared with full-control access. With share-level security, the same password is assigned to all Post Office members.

25. **B.** The Windows 3.11 directory will contain the upgrade information for Windows 98. NT will install in a different directory, providing for dual boot. There is no mention of installing a Resource Kit.

26. **A.** The Windows 3.11 directory will contain the upgrade information for Windows 98. NT will install in a different directory, providing for dual boot.

27. **A.** All the entries entered through the Maintenance Wizard are in the Tasks Scheduler's list and can be configured.

28. **A-C.** You must have Client for Microsoft Networks enabled to be able to access the account database. File and Printer Sharing is required to set up the permissions.

29. **C.** System policies will automatically edit the Registry on the computers that process the policy.

30. **B.** The user will be able to communicate with the network and remote subnets by using the default gateway, but he will not be able to resolve NetBIOS names to IP addresses without using a WINS server.

31. **A.** The proposed solution will get the computer back to normal. The computer will be able to communicate with the network and remote subnets using the default gateway, and will be able to resolve NetBIOS names to IP addresses by using the WINS server.

32. **A.** A log file can be recorded from the Advanced tab of the Dial-Up Adapter by using VPN.

33. **A.** Profiles must be manually turned on before user system policies for users and groups are enabled.

34. **C.** The original network configuration settings for the Windows 3.11 clients did not include TCP/IP as a protocol. After upgrading the systems, you must add and configure the TCP/IP protocol to access the Internet. The default upgrade does not add TCP/IP automatically.

35. **D.** A startup disk will have `Extract` and will not overwrite opened files.

36. **D.** The proposed solution would allow Alan to share the shipping information with the Windows 98 clients only. You may assign user, level security to an NT domain given the proposed solution. Novell/DOS clients will not be able to access the Windows 98 systems.

37. A. The proposed solution would allow Alan to share the shipping information with the Windows 98 clients only. The DOS/NetWare clients would not gain access to the resource. You may assign user-level security to an NT domain given the proposed solution. To complete Alan's request, you should install File and Printer Sharing for Novell Networks on Alan's client. Then you can configure the Obtain a List of Users and Groups From setting to use the NetWare server as a security authority. This, in turn, would allow Alan to assign the proper permissions.

38. B. The proposed solution would allow only users registered on the domain to access the database. However, the default permission on a share is read only, so some users would not be able to change the database.

39. A. The proposed solution would allow only users registered on the domain to access the database. With the folder shared as read only and adding a few key users with change permissions, you can control who can make changes and who can only view the folder.

40. E. B might also be correct, but most people don't back up the Registry when installing hardware or software. Windows 98 creates backups of the system Registry (SYSTEM.DA0 and USER.DA0) each time it starts successfully.

41. C. Installing Client for NetWare Networks would provide Susan with access to the folder with the sales project files, located on the NetWare server. Installing File and Printer Sharing for Microsoft Networks on Susan's machine would allow her to share resources with other Windows 98 clients. But the list of clients should come from the domain rather than the Novell server. Also, without configuring Enable Login Scripts in the Client for NetWare Networks or mapping a network drive and reconnecting to the sales project folder, her connectivity would not be automated.

42. A. Installing Client for NetWare Networks would provide Susan with access to the folder with the sales project files, located on the NetWare server. Installing File and Printer Sharing for Microsoft Networks on Susan's machine would allow her to share resources with other Windows 98 clients.

43. B. The command will list the content of multiple files if the files are similar, but will not reload the corrupted files.

44. A. The command will list the content of multiple files if the files are similar. The proper syntax would be - "extract /a /d <cabinet>", where <cabinet> would be the name of the first file in the list. For the Preload and mini cab files, you will need to run the command again.

45. C.   Disabling write-behind caching eliminates the problem of lost data, which is caused when the user shuts off the system power before Windows 98 shuts down. Disabling write-behind caching causes data to be written to disk immediately, instead of during idle time or shutdown, thus improving the shutdown response time. Disabling write-behind caching does not improve general system response, however, and causes the saving of information in an application to take longer.

46. B.   Disk Defragmenter will restart if it detects data written to the disk while it is running.

47. A-C.   Windows 98 local printing temporarily writes files to the location on the hard disk specified by the TEMP variable. If this variable is not properly set or if there is no space available on the hard disk, printing will not be successful.

48. C-D.   With password security, users must provide the Web access password each time they access the Web server. With NT challenge, their current username and passwords are used.

49. C.   The Start menu will offer Windows Update in the common section.

50. D.   Windows Update's Member Services page will keep you informed of the status of server that performs the updates.

51. D.   The Update Web site will list all the components and categorize them. The "critical" items will be listed under their own heading.

52. A.   User profiles are stored in the user's home directory on Windows NT networks.

53. A.   System File Checker can be found in the System Information utility's Tool menu.

54. C-D.   Windows 98 offers a basic File and Printer Sharing. After it is in place, each folder can be set up to allow users to gain access to a folder. Alternatively, this option can be turned off and PWS' security features can be used to control the shares intended for Web access.

Exam Strategies

You must pass rigorous certification exams to become a Microsoft Certified Professional. These closed-book exams provide a valid and reliable measure of your technical proficiency and expertise. Developed in consultation with computer industry professionals who have on-the-job experience with Microsoft products in the workplace, the exams are conducted by two independent organizations. Sylvan Prometric offers the exams at more than 1,400 Authorized Prometric Testing Centers around the world. Virtual University Enterprises (VUE) testing centers offer exams as well.

To schedule an exam, call Sylvan Prometric Testing Centers at 800-755-EXAM (3926) or VUE at 888-837-8616.

This appendix is divided into two main sections. First, it describes the different certification options provided by Microsoft, and how you can achieve those certifications. The second portion highlights the different kinds of examinations and the best ways to prepare for those different exam and question styles.

TYPES OF CERTIFICATION

Currently Microsoft offers seven types of certification, based on specific areas of expertise:

- **Microsoft Certified Professional (MCP).** Qualified to provide installation, configuration, and support for users of at least one Microsoft desktop operating system, such as Windows NT Workstation. Candidates can take elective exams to develop areas of specialization. MCP is the base level of expertise.

- **Microsoft Certified Professional+Internet (MCP+Internet).** Qualified to plan security, install and configure server products, manage server resources, extend service to run CGI scripts or ISAPI scripts, monitor and analyze performance, and troubleshoot problems. Expertise is similar to that of an MCP, but with a focus on the Internet.

- **Microsoft Certified Professional+Site Building (MCP+Site Building).** Qualified to plan, build, maintain, and manage Web sites by using Microsoft technologies and products. The credential is appropriate for people who manage sophisticated, interactive Web sites that include database connectivity, multimedia, and searchable content.

- **Microsoft Certified Systems Engineer (MCSE).** Qualified to effectively plan, implement, maintain, and support information systems with Microsoft Windows NT and other Microsoft advanced systems and workgroup products, such as Microsoft Office and Microsoft BackOffice. MCSE is a second level of expertise.

- **Microsoft Certified Systems Engineer+ Internet (MCSE+Internet).** Qualified in the core MCSE areas, and also qualified to enhance, deploy, and manage sophisticated intranet and Internet solutions that include a browser, proxy server, host servers, database, and messaging and commerce components. An MCSE+Internet–certified professional is able to manage and analyze Web sites.

- **Microsoft Certified Solution Developer (MCSD).** Qualified to design and develop custom business solutions by using Microsoft development tools, technologies, and platforms, including Microsoft Office and Microsoft BackOffice. MCSD is a second level of expertise, with a focus on software development.

- **Microsoft Certified Trainer (MCT).** Instructionally and technically qualified by Microsoft to deliver Microsoft Education Courses at Microsoft-authorized sites. An MCT must be employed by a Microsoft Solution Provider Authorized Technical Education Center or a Microsoft Authorized Academic Training site.

▼ **NOTE**

For the most up-to-date information about each type of certification, visit the Microsoft Training and Certification Web site at http://www.microsoft.com/train_cert. You also can call or email the following sources:

- Microsoft Certified Professional Program: 800-636-7544

- mcp@msprograms.com

- Microsoft Online Institute (MOLI): 800-449-9333

Certification Requirements

The requirements for certification in each of the seven areas are detailed below. An asterisk after an exam indicates that the exam is slated for retirement.

How to Become a Microsoft Certified Professional

Passing any Microsoft exam (with the exception of Networking Essentials) is all you need to do to become certified as an MCP.

How to Become a Microsoft Certified Professional+Internet

You must pass the following exams to become an MCP specializing in Internet technology:

- Internetworking Microsoft TCP/IP on Microsoft Windows NT 4.0, #70-059

- Implementing and Supporting Microsoft Windows NT Server 4.0, #70-067

- Implementing and Supporting Microsoft Internet Information Server 3.0 and Microsoft Index Server 1.1, #70-077

  OR Implementing and Supporting Microsoft Internet Information Server 4.0, #70-087

How to Become a Microsoft Certified Professional+Site Building

You need to pass two of the following exams in order to be certified as an MCP+Site Building:

- Designing and Implementing Web Sites with Microsoft FrontPage 98, #70-055

- Designing and Implementing Commerce Solutions with Microsoft Site Server 3.0, Commerce Edition, #70-057

- Designing and Implementing Web Solutions with Microsoft Visual InterDev 6.0, #70-152

How to Become a Microsoft Certified Systems Engineer

You must pass four operating system exams and two elective exams to become an MCSE. The MCSE certification path is divided into two tracks: the Windows NT 3.51 track and the Windows NT 4.0 track.

The following lists show the core requirements (four operating system exams) for both the Windows NT 3.51 and 4.0 tracks, and the elective courses (two exams) you can take for either track.

The four Windows NT 3.51 Track Core Requirements for MCSE certification are as follows:

- Implementing and Supporting Microsoft Windows NT Server 3.51, #70-043*

- Implementing and Supporting Microsoft Windows NT Workstation 3.51, #70-042*

- Microsoft Windows 3.1, #70-030*

  OR Microsoft Windows for Workgroups 3.11, #70-048*

  OR Implementing and Supporting Microsoft Windows 95, #70-064

  OR Implementing and Supporting Microsoft Windows 98, #70-098

- Networking Essentials, #70-058

The four Windows NT 4.0 Track Core Requirements for MCSE certification are as follows:

- Implementing and Supporting Microsoft Windows NT Server 4.0, #70-067

- Implementing and Supporting Microsoft Windows NT Server 4.0 in the Enterprise, #70-068

- Microsoft Windows 3.1, #70-030*

  OR Microsoft Windows for Workgroups 3.11, #70-048*

  OR Implementing and Supporting Microsoft Windows 95, #70-064

  OR Implementing and Supporting Microsoft Windows NT Workstation 4.0, #70-073

  OR Implementing and Supporting Microsoft Windows 98, #70-098

- Networking Essentials, #70-058

For both the Windows NT 3.51 and the 4.0 tracks, you must pass two of the following elective exams for MCSE certification:

- Implementing and Supporting Microsoft SNA Server 3.0, #70-013

  OR Implementing and Supporting Microsoft SNA Server 4.0, #70-085

- Implementing and Supporting Microsoft Systems Management Server 1.0, #70-014*

  OR Implementing and Supporting Microsoft Systems Management Server 1.2, #70-018

  OR Implementing and Supporting Microsoft Systems Management Server 2.0, #70-086

- Microsoft SQL Server 4.2 Database Implementation, #70-021

  OR Implementing a Database Design on Microsoft SQL Server 6.5, #70-027

  OR Implementing a Database Design on Microsoft SQL Server 7.0, #70-029

- Microsoft SQL Server 4.2 Database Administration for Microsoft Windows NT, #70-022

  OR System Administration for Microsoft SQL Server 6.5 (or 6.0), #70-026

  OR System Administration for Microsoft SQL Server 7.0, #70-028

- Microsoft Mail for PC Networks 3.2-Enterprise, #70-037

- Internetworking with Microsoft TCP/IP on Microsoft Windows NT (3.5-3.51), #70-053

  OR Internetworking with Microsoft TCP/IP on Microsoft Windows NT 4.0, #70-059

- Implementing and Supporting Microsoft Exchange Server 4.0, #70-075*

  OR Implementing and Supporting Microsoft Exchange Server 5.0, #70-076

  OR Implementing and Supporting Microsoft Exchange Server 5.5, #70-081

- Implementing and Supporting Microsoft Internet Information Server 3.0 and Microsoft Index Server 1.1, #70-077

  OR Implementing and Supporting Microsoft Internet Information Server 4.0, #70-087

- Implementing and Supporting Microsoft Proxy Server 1.0, #70-078

  OR Implementing and Supporting Microsoft Proxy Server 2.0, #70-088

- Implementing and Supporting Microsoft Internet Explorer 4.0 by Using the Internet Explorer Resource Kit, #70-079

How to Become a Microsoft Certified Systems Engineer+ Internet

You must pass seven operating system exams and two elective exams to become an MCSE specializing in Internet technology.

The seven MCSE+Internet core exams required for certification are as follows:

- Networking Essentials, #70-058

- Internetworking with Microsoft TCP/IP on Microsoft Windows NT 4.0, #70-059

- Implementing and Supporting Microsoft Windows 95, #70-064

  OR Implementing and Supporting Microsoft Windows NT Workstation 4.0, #70-073

  OR Implementing and Supporting Microsoft Windows 98, #70-098

- Implementing and Supporting Microsoft Windows NT Server 4.0, #70-067

- Implementing and Supporting Microsoft Windows NT Server 4.0 in the Enterprise, #70-068

- Implementing and Supporting Microsoft Internet Information Server 3.0 and Microsoft Index Server 1.1, #70-077

  OR Implementing and Supporting Microsoft Internet Information Server 4.0, #70-087

- Implementing and Supporting Microsoft Internet Explorer 4.0 by Using the Internet Explorer Resource Kit, #70-079

You must also pass two of the following elective exams for MCSE+Internet certification:

- System Administration for Microsoft SQL Server 6.5, #70-026

- Implementing a Database Design on Microsoft SQL Server 6.5, #70-027

- Implementing and Supporting Web Sites Using Microsoft Site Server 3.0, # 70-056

- Implementing and Supporting Microsoft Exchange Server 5.0, #70-076

  OR Implementing and Supporting Microsoft Exchange Server 5.5, #70-081

- Implementing and Supporting Microsoft Proxy Server 1.0, #70-078

  OR Implementing and Supporting Microsoft Proxy Server 2.0, #70-088

- Implementing and Supporting Microsoft SNA Server 4.0, #70-085

How to Become a Microsoft Certified Solution Developer

The MCSD certification is undergoing substantial revision. Listed next are the requirements for the new track (available fourth quarter 1998), as well as the old.

For the new track, you must pass three core exams and one elective exam.

The core exams include the following:

Desktop Applications Development (1 required)

- Designing and Implementing Desktop Applications with Microsoft Visual C++ 6.0, #70-016

  OR Designing and Implementing Desktop Applications with Microsoft Visual Basic 6.0, #70-176

Distributed Applications Development (1 required)

- Designing and Implementing Distributed Applications with Microsoft Visual C++ 6.0, #70-015

  OR Designing and Implementing Distributed Applications with Microsoft Visual Basic 6.0, #70-175

Solution Architecture (required)

- Analyzing Requirements and Defining Solution Architectures, #70-100

Elective Exams

You must also pass one of the following elective exams:

- Designing and Implementing Distributed Applications with Microsoft Visual C++ 6.0, #70-015

  OR Designing and Implementing Desktop Applications with Microsoft Visual C++ 6.0, #70-016

  OR Microsoft SQL Server 4.2 Database Implementation, #70-021*

- Implementing a Database Design on Microsoft SQL Server 6.5, #70-027

  OR Implementing a Database Design on Microsoft SQL Server 7.0, #70-029

- Developing Applications with C++ Using the Microsoft Foundation Class Library, #70-024

- Implementing OLE in Microsoft Foundation Class Applications, #70-025

- Designing and Implementing Web Sites with Microsoft FrontPage 98, #70-055

- Designing and Implementing Commerce Solutions with Microsoft Site Server 3.0, Commerce Edition, #70-057

- Programming with Microsoft Visual Basic 4.0, #70-065

  OR Developing Applications with Microsoft Visual Basic 5.0, #70-165

  OR Designing and Implementing Distributed Applications with Microsoft Visual Basic 6.0, #70-175

  OR Designing and Implementing Desktop Applications with Microsoft Visual Basic 6.0, #70-176

- Microsoft Access for Windows 95 and the Microsoft Access Development Toolkit, #70-069

- Designing and Implementing Solutions with Microsoft Office (Code-named Office 9) and Microsoft Visual Basic for Applications, #70-091

- Designing and Implementing Web Solutions with Microsoft Visual InterDev 6.0, #70-152

Former MCSD Track

For the old track, you must pass two core technology exams and two elective exams for MCSD certification. The following lists show the required technology exams and elective exams needed to become an MCSD.

You must pass the following two core technology exams to qualify for MCSD certification:

- Microsoft Windows Architecture I, #70-160*

- Microsoft Windows Architecture II, #70-161*

You must also pass two of the following elective exams to become an MSCD:

- Designing and Implementing Distributed Applications with Microsoft Visual C++ 6.0, #70-015

- Designing and Implementing Desktop Applications with Microsoft Visual C++ 6.0, #70-016

- Microsoft SQL Server 4.2 Database Implementation, #70-021*

  OR Implementing a Database Design on Microsoft SQL Server 6.5, #70-027

  OR Implementing a Database Design on Microsoft SQL Server 7.0, #70-029

- Developing Applications with C++ Using the Microsoft Foundation Class Library, #70-024

- Implementing OLE in Microsoft Foundation Class Applications, #70-025

- Programming with Microsoft Visual Basic 4.0, #70-065

OR Developing Applications with Microsoft Visual Basic 5.0, #70-165

OR Designing and Implementing Distributed Applications with Microsoft Visual Basic 6.0, #70-175

OR Designing and Implementing Desktop Applications with Microsoft Visual Basic 6.0, #70-176

- Microsoft Access 2.0 for Windows-Application Development, #70-051

OR Microsoft Access for Windows 95 and the Microsoft Access Development Toolkit, #70-069

- Developing Applications with Microsoft Excel 5.0 Using Visual Basic for Applications, #70-052

- Programming in Microsoft Visual FoxPro 3.0 for Windows, #70-054

- Designing and Implementing Web Sites with Microsoft FrontPage 98, #70-055

- Designing and Implementing Commerce Solutions with Microsoft Site Server 3.0, Commerce Edition, #70-057

- Designing and Implementing Solutions with Microsoft Office (Code-named Office 9) and Microsoft Visual Basic for Applications, #70-091

- Designing and Implementing Web Solutions with Microsoft Visual InterDev 6.0, #70-152

Becoming a Microsoft Certified Trainer

To understand the requirements and process for becoming an MCT, you need to obtain the Microsoft Certified Trainer Guide document from the following site:

http://www.microsoft.com/train_cert/mct/

At this site, you can read the document as Web pages or display and download it as a Word file. The MCT Guide explains the four-step process of becoming an MCT. The general steps for the MCT certification are as follows:

1. Complete and mail a Microsoft Certified Trainer application to Microsoft. You must include proof of your skills for presenting instructional material. The options for doing so are described in the MCT Guide.

2. Obtain and study the Microsoft Trainer Kit for the Microsoft Official Curricula (MOC) courses for which you want to be certified. Microsoft Trainer Kits can be ordered by calling 800-688-0496 in North America. Interested parties in other regions should review the MCT Guide for information on how to order a Trainer Kit.

3. Take the Microsoft certification exam for the product about which you want to be certified to teach.

4. Attend the MOC course for the course for which you want to be certified. This is done so you can understand how the course is structured, how labs are completed, and how the course flows.

◆ **WARNING**

You should consider the preceding steps a general overview of the MCT certification process. The precise steps that you need to take are described in detail on the Web site mentioned earlier. Do not misinterpret the preceding steps as the exact process you need to undergo.

If you are interested in becoming an MCT, you can receive more information by visiting the Microsoft Certified Training Web site at http://www.microsoft.com/train_cert/mct/ or by calling 800-688-0496.

STUDY AND EXAM PREPARATION TIPS

This part of the appendix provides you with some general guidelines for preparing for the exam. It is organized into three sections. The first section, "Study Tips," addresses your pre-exam preparation activities, covering general study tips. This is followed by "Exam Prep Tips," an extended look at the Microsoft Certification exams, including a number of specific tips that apply to the Microsoft exam formats. Finally, "Putting It All Together" discusses changes in Microsoft's testing policies and how they might affect you.

To better understand the nature of preparation for the test, it is important to understand learning as a process. You probably are aware of how you best learn new material. You may find that outlining works best for you, or you may need to see things as a visual learner. Whatever your learning style, test preparation takes place over time. Although it is obvious that you can't start studying for these exams the night before you take them, it is very important to understand that learning is a devel-

opmental process. Understanding it as a process helps you focus on what you know and what you have yet to learn.

Thinking about how you learn should help you to recognize that learning takes place when you are able to match new information to old. You have some previous experience with computers and networking, and now you are preparing for this certification exam. Using this book, software, and supplementary materials will not just add incrementally to what you know. As you study, you actually change the organization of your knowledge as you integrate this new information into your existing knowledge base. This will lead you to a more comprehensive understanding of the tasks and concepts outlined in the objectives and of computing in general. Again, this happens as an iterative process rather than a singular event. Keep this model of learning in mind as you prepare for the exam, and you will make better decisions about what to study and how much more studying you need to do.

Study Tips

There are many ways to approach studying, just as there are many different types of material to study. However, the tips that follow should prepare you well for the type of material covered on the certification exams.

Study Strategies

Individuals vary in the ways they learn information. Some basic principles of learning apply to everyone, however; you should adopt some study strategies that take advantage of these principles. One of these principles is that learning can be broken into various depths. Recognition (of terms, for example) exemplifies a more surface level of learning—you rely on a prompt of some sort to elicit recall. Comprehension or understanding (of the concepts behind the terms, for instance) represents a deeper level of learning. The ability to analyze a concept and apply your understanding of it in a new way or novel setting represents an even further depth of learning.

Your learning strategy should enable you to understand the material at a level or two deeper than mere recognition. This will help you to do well on the exam(s). You will know the material so thoroughly that you can easily handle the recognition-level types of questions used in multiple-choice testing. You will also be able to apply your knowledge to solve novel problems.

Macro and Micro Study Strategies

One strategy that can lead to this deeper learning includes preparing an outline that covers all the objectives and subobjectives for the particular exam you are working on. You should delve a bit further into the material and include a level or two of detail beyond the stated objectives and subobjectives for the exam. Then flesh out the outline by coming up with a statement of definition or a summary for each point in the outline.

This outline provides two approaches to studying. First, you can study the outline by focusing on the organization of the material. Work your way through the points and subpoints of your outline with the goal of learning how they relate to one another. For example, be sure you understand how each of the main objective areas is similar to and different from another. Then do the same thing with the subobjectives; be sure you know which subobjectives pertain to each objective area and how they relate to one another.

Next, you can work through the outline, focusing on learning the details. Memorize and understand terms and their definitions, facts, rules and strategies, advantages and disadvantages, and so on. In this pass through the outline, attempt to learn detail rather than the big picture (the organizational information that you worked on in the first pass through the outline).

Research has shown that attempting to assimilate both types of information at the same time seems to interfere with the overall learning process. Separate your studying into these two approaches, and you will perform better on the exam than if you attempt to study the material in a more conventional manner.

Active Study Strategies

In addition, the process of writing down and defining the objectives, subobjectives, terms, facts, and definitions promotes a more active learning strategy than merely reading the material. In human information-processing terms, writing forces you to engage in more active encoding of the information. Simply reading over it constitutes more passive processing.

Next, determine whether you can apply the information you have learned by attempting to create examples and scenarios of your own. Think about how or where you could apply the concepts you are learning. Again, write down this information to process the facts and concepts in a more active fashion.

The hands-on nature of the step-by-step tutorials and exercises at the ends of the chapters provide further active learning opportunities that will reinforce concepts as well.

Common-sense Strategies

Finally, you should follow common-sense practices in studying. Study when you are alert, reduce or eliminate distractions, take breaks when you become fatigued, and so on.

Pre-testing Yourself

Pre-testing allows you to assess how well you are learning. One of the most important aspects of learning is what has been called meta-learning. *Meta-learning* has to do with realizing when you know something well or when you need to study more. In other words, you recognize how well or how poorly you have learned the material you are studying. For most people, this can be difficult to assess objectively on their own. Practice tests are useful in that they reveal more objectively what you have learned and what you have not learned. You should use this information to guide review and further studying. Developmental learning takes place as you cycle through studying, assessing how well you have learned, reviewing, assessing again, until you feel you are ready to take the exam.

You may have noticed the practice exams included in this book. Use them as part of this process.

Exam Prep Tips

Having mastered the subject matter, your final preparatory step is to understand how the exam will be presented. Make no mistake about it—a Microsoft Certified Professional (MCP) exam will challenge both your knowledge and test-taking skills! This section starts with the basics of exam design, reviews a new type of exam format, and concludes with hints that are targeted to each of the exam formats.

The MCP Exams

Every MCP exam is released in one of two basic formats. What's being called exam format here is really little more than a combination of the overall exam structure and the presentation method for exam questions.

Each exam format utilizes the same types of questions. These types or styles of questions include multiple-rating (or scenario-based) questions, traditional multiple-choice questions, and simulation-based questions. It's important to understand the types of questions you will be presented with and the actions required to properly answer them.

Understanding the exam formats is key to good preparation because the format determines the number of questions presented, the difficulty of those questions, and the amount of time allowed to complete the exam.

Exam Formats

There are two basic formats for the MCP exams: the traditional fixed-form exam and the adaptive form. As its name implies, the fixed-form exam presents a fixed set of questions during the exam session. The adaptive format, however, uses only a subset of questions drawn from a larger pool during any given exam session.

Fixed-form

A fixed-form, computerized exam is based on a fixed set of exam questions. The individual questions are presented in random order during a test session. If you take the same exam more than once, you won't necessarily see the exact same questions. This is because two to three final forms are typically assembled for every fixed-form exam Microsoft releases. These are usually labeled Forms A, B, and C.

The final forms of a fixed-form exam are identical in terms of content coverage, number of questions, and allotted time, but the questions themselves are different. You may have noticed, however, that some of the same questions appear on, or rather are shared across, different final forms. When questions are shared across multiple final forms of an exam, the percentage of sharing is generally small. Many final forms share no questions, but some older exams may have a ten to fifteen percent duplication of exam questions on the final exam forms.

Fixed-form exams also have a fixed time limit in which you must complete the exam.

Finally, the score you achieve on a fixed-form exam, which is always reported for MCP exams on a scale of 0 to 1000, is based on the number of questions you answer correctly. The exam passing score is the same for all final forms of a given fixed-form exam.

The typical format for the fixed-form exam is as follows:

- 50–60 questions

- 75–90 minute testing time

- Question review allowed, including the opportunity to change your answers

Adaptive Form

An adaptive form exam has the same appearance as a fixed-form exam, but differs in both how questions are selected for presentation and how many questions actually are presented. Although the statistics of adaptive testing are fairly complex, the process is concerned with determining your level of skill or ability with the exam subject matter. This ability assessment begins by presenting questions of varying levels of difficulty and ascertaining at what difficulty level you can reliably answer them. Finally, the ability assessment determines if that ability level is above or below the level required to pass that exam.

Examinees at different levels of ability will then see quite different sets of questions. Those who demonstrate little expertise with the subject matter will continue to be presented with relatively easy questions. Examinees who demonstrate a higher level of expertise will be presented progressively more difficult questions. Both individuals may answer the same number of questions correctly, but because the exam-taker with the higher level of expertise can correctly answer more difficult questions, he or she will receive a higher score, and is more likely to pass the exam.

The typical design for the adaptive form exam is as follows:

- 20–25 questions

- 90-minute testing time, although this is likely to be reduced to 45–60 minutes in the near future

- Question review not allowed, providing no opportunity to change your answers

Your first adaptive exam will be unlike any other testing experience you have had. In fact, many examinees have difficulty accepting the adaptive testing process because they feel that they are not provided the opportunity to adequately demonstrate their full expertise.

You can take consolation in the fact that adaptive exams are painstakingly put together after months of data gathering and analysis and are just as valid as a fixed-form exam. The rigor introduced through the adaptive testing methodology means that there is nothing arbitrary about what you'll see! It is also a more efficient means of testing, requiring less time to conduct and complete.

As you can see from Figure A.1, there are a number of statistical measures that drive the adaptive examination process. The most immediately relevant to you is the ability estimate. Accompanying this test statistic are the standard error of measurement, the item characteristic curve, and the test information curve.

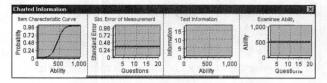

FIGURE A.1
Microsoft's Adaptive Testing Demonstration Program.

The standard error, which is the key factor in determining when an adaptive exam will terminate, reflects the degree of error in the exam ability estimate. The item characteristic curve reflects the probability of a correct response relative to examinee ability. Finally, the test information statistic provides a measure of the information contained in the set of questions the examinee has answered, again relative to the ability level of the individual examinee.

When you begin an adaptive exam, the standard error has already been assigned a target value below which it must drop for the exam to conclude. This target value reflects a particular level of statistical confidence in the process. The examinee ability is initially set to the mean possible exam score: 500 for MCP exams.

As the adaptive exam progresses, questions of varying difficulty are presented. Based on your

pattern of responses to these questions, the ability estimate is recalculated. Simultaneously, the standard error estimate is refined from its first estimated value of one toward the target value. When the standard error reaches its target value, the exam terminates. Thus, the more consistently you answer questions of the same degree of difficulty, the more quickly the standard error estimate drops, and the fewer questions you will end up seeing during the exam session. This situation is depicted in Figure A.2.

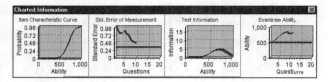

FIGURE A.2
The changing statistics in an adaptive exam.

As you might suspect, one good piece of advice for taking an adaptive exam is to treat every exam question as if it were the most important. The adaptive scoring algorithm is attempting to discover a pattern of responses that reflects some level of proficiency with the subject matter. Incorrect responses almost guarantee that additional questions must be answered (unless, of course, you get every question wrong). This is because the scoring algorithm must adjust to information that is not consistent with the emerging pattern.

New Question Types

A variety of question types can appear on MCP exams. Examples of multiple-choice questions and scenario-based questions appear throughout this book. They appear in the Top Score software as well. Simulation-based questions are new to the MCP exam series.

Simulation Questions

Simulation-based questions reproduce the look and feel of key Microsoft product features for the purpose of testing. The simulation software used in MCP exams has been designed to look and act, as much as possible, just like the actual product. Consequently, answering simulation questions in an MCP exam entails completing one or more tasks just as if you were using the product itself.

The format of a typical Microsoft simulation question is straightforward. It presents a brief scenario or problem statement along with one or more tasks that must be completed to solve the problem. An example of a simulation question for MCP exams is shown in the following section.

A Typical Simulation Question

It sounds obvious, but the first step when you encounter a simulation is to carefully read the question (see Figure A.3). Do not go straight to the simulation application! Assess the problem being presented and identify the conditions that make up the problem scenario. Note the tasks that must be performed or outcomes that must be achieved to answer the question, and review any instructions about how to proceed.

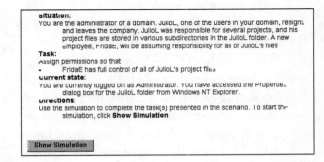

FIGURE A.3
Typical MCP exam simulation question with directions.

The next step is to launch the simulator. Click the Show Simulation button to see a feature of the product, such as the dialog box shown in Figure A.4. The simulation application partially covers the question text on many test center machines. Feel free to reposition the simulation or to move between the question text screen and the simulation using hot keys, point-and-click navigation, or even by clicking the simulation launch button again.

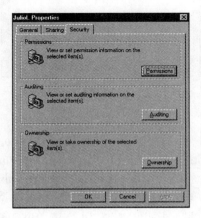

FIGURE A.4
Launching the simulation application.

It is important to understand that your answer to the simulation question is not recorded until you move on to the next exam question. This gives you the added capability to close and reopen the simulation application (using the launch button) on the same question without losing any partial answer you may have made.

The third step is to use the simulator as you would the actual product to solve the problem or perform the defined tasks. Again, the simulation software is designed to function, within reason, just as the product does. But don't expect the simulation to reproduce product behavior perfectly.

Most importantly, do not allow yourself to become flustered if the simulation does not look or act exactly like the product. Figure A.5 shows the solution to the example simulation problem.

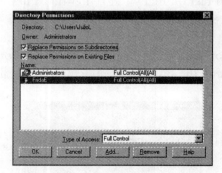

FIGURE A.5
The solution to the simulation example.

There are two final points that will help you tackle simulation questions. First, respond only to what is being asked in the question. Do not solve problems that you are not asked to solve. Second, accept what is being asked of you. You may not entirely agree with conditions in the problem statement, the quality of the desired solution, or the sufficiency of defined tasks to adequately solve the problem. Always remember that you are being tested on your ability to solve the problem as it has been presented.

The solution to the simulation problem shown in Figure A.5 perfectly illustrates both of these points. As you'll recall from the question scenario (refer to Figure A.3), you were asked to assign appropriate permissions to a new user, FridaE. You were not instructed to make any other changes in permissions. Thus, if you had modified or removed Administrators permissions, this item would have been scored as incorrect on an MCP exam.

Putting It All Together

Given all these different pieces of information, the task is now to assemble a set of tips that will help you successfully tackle the different types of MCP exams.

More Pre-exam Preparation Tips

Generic exam preparation advice is always useful. Tips include the following:

- Become familiar with the product. Hands-on experience is one of the keys to success on any MCP exam. Review the exercises and the step-by-step activities in the book.

- Review the current exam preparation guide on the Microsoft MCP Web site. The documentation Microsoft makes publicly available over the Web identifies the skills every exam is intended to test.

- Memorize foundational technical detail as appropriate. Remember that MCP exams are generally heavy on problem solving and application of knowledge rather than just questions that only require rote memorization.

- Take any of the available practice tests. We recommend the ones included in this book and the ones you can create using New Riders' exclusive Top Score Test Simulation software suite, available through your local bookstore or software distributor. Although these are fixed-format exams, they provide practice that is valuable for preparing for an adaptive exam. Because of the interactive nature of adaptive testing, it is not possible to provide examples of the adaptive format in the included practice exams. However, fixed-format exams do provide the same types of questions as found on adaptive exams and are the most effective way to prepare for either type of exam. As a supplement to the material bound with this book, also try the free practice tests available on the Microsoft MCP Web site.

- Look on the Microsoft MCP Web site for samples and demonstration items. These tend to be particularly valuable for one significant reason: They allow you to become familiar with any new testing technologies before you encounter them on an MCP exam.

During the Exam Session

Similarly, the generic exam-taking advice you've heard for years applies when taking an MCP exam:

- Take a deep breath and try to relax when you first sit down for your exam session. It is very important to control the pressure you may (naturally) feel when taking exams.

- You will be provided scratch paper. Take a moment to write down any factual information and technical detail that you've committed to short-term memory.

- Carefully read all information and instruction screens. These displays have been put together to give you information relevant to the exam you are taking.

- Accept the Non-Disclosure Agreement and preliminary survey as part of the examination process. Complete them accurately and quickly move on.

- Read the exam questions carefully. Reread each question to identify all relevant detail.

- Tackle the questions in the order they are presented. Skipping around won't build your confidence; the clock is always counting down.

- Don't rush, but similarly, don't linger on difficult questions. The questions vary in degree of difficulty. Don't let yourself be flustered by a particularly difficult or verbose question.

Fixed-form Exams

Building from this basic preparation and test-taking advice, you also need to consider the challenges presented by the different exam designs. Because a fixed-form exam is composed of a fixed, finite set of questions, add these tips to your strategy for taking a fixed-form exam:

- Note the time allotted and the number of questions appearing on the exam you are taking. Make a rough calculation of how many minutes you can spend on each question and use this to pace yourself through the exam.

- Take advantage of the fact that you can return to and review skipped or previously answered questions. Mark the questions you can't answer confidently, noting the relative difficulty of each question on the scratch paper provided. When you reach the end of the exam, return to the more difficult questions.

- If there is session time remaining after you have completed all questions (and you aren't too fatigued!), review your answers. Pay particular attention to questions that seem to have a lot of detail or that required graphics.

- As for changing your answers, the rule of thumb here is *don't*! If you read the question carefully and completely, and you felt like you knew the right answer, you probably did. Don't second-guess yourself. If, as you check your answers, one stands out as clearly marked incorrectly, however, you should change it in that instance. If you are at all unsure, go with your first impression.

Adaptive Exams

If you are planning to take an adaptive exam, keep these additional tips in mind:

- Read and answer every question with great care. When reading a question, identify every relevant detail, requirement, or task that must be performed and double-check your answer to be sure you have addressed every one of them.

- If you cannot answer a question, use the process of elimination to reduce the set of potential answers, then take your best guess. Stupid mistakes invariably mean additional questions will be presented.

- Forget about reviewing questions and changing your answers. After you leave a question, whether you've answered it or not, you cannot return to it. Do not skip a question, either; if you do, it's counted as incorrect!

Simulation Questions

You may encounter simulation questions on either the fixed-form or adaptive form exam. If you do, keep these tips in mind:

- Avoid changing any simulation settings that don't pertain directly to the problem solution. Solve the problem you are being asked to solve, and nothing more.

- Assume default settings when related information has not been provided. If something has not been mentioned or defined, it is a non-critical detail that does not factor in to the correct solution.

- Be sure your entries are syntactically correct, paying particular attention to your spelling. Enter relevant information just as the product would require it.

- Close all simulation application windows after completing the simulation tasks. The testing system software is designed to trap errors that could result when using the simulation application, but trust yourself over the testing software.

- If simulations are part of a fixed-form exam, you can return to skipped or previously answered questions and review your answers. However, if you choose to change your answer to a simulation question, or even attempt to review the settings you've made in the simulation application, your previous response to that simulation question will be deleted. If simulations are part of an adaptive exam, you cannot return to previous questions.

Final Considerations

There are a number of changes in the MCP program that will impact how frequently you can repeat an exam and what you will see when you do.

- Microsoft has instituted a new exam retake policy. This new rule is "two and two, then one and two." That is, you can attempt any exam two times with no restrictions on the time between attempts. But after the second attempt, you must wait two weeks before you can attempt that exam again. After that, you will be required to wait two weeks between any subsequent attempts. Plan to pass the exam in two attempts, or plan to increase your time horizon for receiving an MCP credential.

- New questions are being seeded into the MCP exams. After performance data has been gathered on new questions, they will replace older questions on all exam forms. This means that the questions appearing on exams are regularly changing.

- Many of the current MCP exams will be republished in adaptive format in the coming months. Prepare yourself for this significant change in testing format; it is entirely likely that this will become the new preferred MCP exam format.

These changes mean that the brute-force strategies for passing MCP exams may soon completely lose their viability. So if you don't pass an exam on the first or second attempt, it is entirely possible that the exam will change significantly in form. It could be updated to adaptive form from fixed-form or have a different set of questions or question types.

The intention of Microsoft is clearly not to make the exams more difficult by introducing unwanted change. Their intent is to create and maintain valid measures of the technical skills and knowledge associated with the different MCP credentials. Preparing for an MCP exam has always involved not only studying the subject matter, but also planning for the testing experience itself. With these changes, this is now more true than ever.

Glossary

A

Adapter   Network Interface Card, also known as NIC. Also, the term is used to describe Dial-Up adapters or SCSI adapters. *See* NIC.

Add/Remove Hardware Wizard   A Windows utility, or Help Wizard, that walks you step by step through the process of adding or removing hardware from a system.

All Selected Files Backup   A backup of all files specified in a file set that changes the archive bit.

Asynchronous Transfer Mode   ATM is a high-speed data transfer protocol.

Automated setup   The process of simplifying the installation of Windows 98 on many machines by creating batch scripts that can control the setup process.

B

Backup   A Windows 98 utility that stores data in a compressed format to be used as a backup.

Backup browser   A computer that receives the browse list from the master browser and responds to browse requests from computers on the network.

Backup set   A backed-up copy of data files along with the preferences that were set up for that backup session.

Backup utility   A Windows 98 program that allows you to back up and restore data.

Batch files   A text-based program used to run several commands consecutively.

Binding   A connection between a protocol and a network adapter.

BOOTLOG.TXT   An ASCII file containing a log of the most recent startup process of Windows 98.

Browser election   Used to determine which computer will become the master browser.

C

CGI   Common Gateway Interface. This interface allows for an application to be written to a certain standard to run when a Web page is accessed. CGI is considered slower and is the predecessor to ISAPI.

CHAP   Challenge Handshake Authentication Protocol is a security protocol used to encrypt authentication between servers and clients during a RAS session.

Class A network address   Category for all IP addresses that start with a particular first octet from 1 to 126 (for example, 107.0.0.0). This means that a class A address might have as many as 16,777,216 IP hosts. 127 is also a class A network address, but is reserved.

Class B network address   Category for the first two octets of an IP address from 128.1 to 191.255 (for example, 145.170.0.0). This allows up to 65,536 hosts.

Class C network address   Category for the first three octets from 192.0.1 to 223.255.254 (for example, 208.192.235.0). This allows a maximum of 256 hosts on a class C network.

Client   A networking functionality built into Windows 98 that allows a Windows 98 computer to be on many different types of networks at the same time.

Cluster   The minimum amount of space on a drive that can be allocated to a file.

COM port   Short for communications port, a port connected to the motherboard that allows data to pass into and out of a computer.

Compressed volume file (CVF)   The CVF contains the contents of a compressed drive.

CONFIG.POL   An optional part of the Registry that contains policy information related to the system and user settings.

Context   Defines your position in relation to the NDS tree. For example, Jim is the Sales Manager for the Eastern Division of the Widget Company.

Cross-linked files   Two or more files that erroneously reference the same cluster on a drive.

CVF   Compressed Volume File. A file that stores data and the structure of a compressed drive.

D

Default Computer   An icon in the System Policy Editor that shows the computer settings applied to the computer regardless of the user who has logged on to the computer. Changes that are implemented are stored in the computer's SYSTEM.DAT file.

Default User   An icon in the System Policy Editor that shows the user settings for each user regardless of the computer that a user logged on to. The changes that are implemented are stored in the user's USER.DAT file.

Defragmenter   A disk utility used to place file clusters into a contiguous chain.

DETCRASH.LOG   A binary file created by Windows 98 if Setup fails during the hardware detection phase. Subsequently used when Setup is rerun.

DETLOG.TXT   An ASCII file containing a list of hardware devices found by Windows 98 during the hardware detection phase of Setup.

Device driver   Program or code written for a specific piece of hardware to allow it to interface with Windows 98.

Device Manager   A Windows 98 utility that enables you to view and change a system's hardware configuration.

DHCP   Dynamic Host Configuration Protocol. Used to dynamically assign IP addresses and other TCP/IP configuration information to computers.

Dial-Up Networking   A Windows feature enabling you to connect to remote servers using a modem and telephone lines. This service is used for remote access to network services such as file and printer sharing, electronic mail, scheduling, SQL database access, and other resources. Increasingly popular for users accessing the Internet.

Dial-Up server   Allows Windows 98 to receive modem calls and allows remote users to access resources.

Disk Cleanup   A disk utility used to remove older temporary files from the hard drive.

Disk compression   The process of increasing available space on a drive by storing data in packed format, reducing the space required by a file.

Disk defragmenter   A utility that moves files and free space to contiguous clusters on a drive.

Distribution Media Format (DMF)   A file format used on Windows 98 setup disks to allow more data on each floppy disk. Such disks cannot be copied with standard methods.

Distribution team   The people you assemble in order to implement Windows 98 on all systems in an organization.

DNS   A domain name server that is used to resolve Host names to IP addresses.

Domain controller   A Windows NT server that stores and authenticates a list of users. Can be primary or backup.

DoubleSpace   A disk compression utility that comes with MS-DOS 6.0.

Driver   A program that allows a piece of hardware to communicate with the operating system.

DriveSpace   A disk compression utility that comes with MS-DOS 6.2, Windows 95, and Windows 98. The latest is DriveSpace 3.0. Compresses the data on the computer's hard disk to make more space on the disk.

E

EMF   Enhanced Metafile. An internal page description format for printing that typically returns control to the user more quickly than RAW format. EMF is printer independent.

Enhanced Metafile (EMF)   A print format using a graphic file that allows control to return to an application more quickly than does RAW print format.

Extended Capabilities Port (ECP)   A feature that allows Windows 98 to use data compression to speed the flow of data to a printer.

Extract   A disk utility that can read the content of source CAB files and extract those files.

F

FAT   File Allocation Table. Maintains the structure of files and folders on a drive. It is used by DOS, Windows 95, Windows 98, and Windows NT.

FAT32   The file system provided by OEMs through Windows 98 and the OSR2 release of Windows 95. Accessible only through Windows 98 and Windows 95 OSR2. FAT32 uses smaller cluster sizes to store data, thus saving disk space.

Fax modem   A device attached to a computer that can send and receive text and images through telephone lines. The fax modem offers the functionality of a fax machine, but all documents are electronic.

FDISK   A utility used to create and delete partitions, mark drives as active, and retrieve disk configuration information.

File and Printer Sharing   A network setting that, when enabled, allows you to share your resources with others, and allows you to use any of their resources that you have authority to access.

File system drivers (FSD)   Enable I/O requests to be sent to and from installed file systems.

File system   The organization of files and folders on a drive. For Windows 98 computers, the file system is either FAT16 or FAT32. For NT, it is either FAT16 or NTFS.

Fragmentation   The scattering of pieces of files across a drive in non-contiguous clusters. Increases the time required to read and write to a disk.

Frame type   Used with the IPX/SPX protocol. Both the workstation and the server must be using the same frame type to communicate.

Free space   Clusters on a drive that have not been assigned to a file, or have not been allocated for system use.

FTP   File Transfer Protocol. File transfer can be controlled by username or can allow anonymous connections.

Full backup   All selected files are backed up.

G

Gateway   A device used to pass packets to remote subnets based on their network IDs.

Graphical user interface (GUI)   A generic term in the context of how an operating system is displayed.

H

Hardware/Software Compatibility List   A list of hardware and software supported by and tested with Windows 98.

Hidden share   A share that has been hidden from view in the browse list by adding a dollar sign to the end of the share name.

Host drive   A drive that contains a compressed volume file (CVF).

HOSTS file   A static file used to resolve TCP/IP host names to IP addresses.

HTTP   Hypertext Transport Protocol. The World Wide Web uses HTTP to create and publish Web pages. *Hypertext* refers to links in the text that, when selected, jump to other locations on the Web.

I

IEEE 1394 Specification The specification that offers a much faster BUS with greater bandwidth for demanding digital video.

IFS Manager The IFS Manager is responsible for analyzing incoming I/O requests from applications and other processors, and then determining which file system driver can fulfill requests most effectively.

IIS Internet Information Server. Microsoft's full Internet Web server. It supports HTTP, FTP, and Gopher.

Image Color Matching (ICM) A color-matching specification that can determine how a screen image will look when printed.

Implementation Model The guidelines you follow when installing and configuring Windows 98.

Incremental backup Only the files that have changed since the last backup are copied.

Installable File System (IFS) A file system with which the operating system may work.

Internet service provider (ISP) Provides users with access to the Internet through a direct line. The ISP is responsible for assigning the IP address, a subnet mask, a default gateway, and, in most cases, a DNS server.

IP address A unique 32-bit, 4-section decimal number to uniquely identify each host on a TCP/IP network.

IPX/SPX (Internetwork Packet Exchange/ Sequenced Packet Exchange) The protocol designed by NetWare for communication in a NetWare network environment. NWLink is the Windows NT–compatible version of the protocol.

IrDA Infrared specification for peripheral communication. The IrDA can be used in a wireless network environment.

ISAPI Internet Server Application programming interface. This is an extension of the Internet server that allows an application to run on the Web server.

J

Job The current configuration of the backup utility with the list of selected files.

K

Kernel The part of the Windows 98 operating system that handles memory management.

L

Legacy Refers to older cards. Usually not Plug and Play. Must be configured manually using jumpers or dip switches.

LMHOSTS file A static file used to resolve NetBIOS names to IP addresses.

Local resources Resources available on your computer.

Logical errors Problems with the data and organization of files stored on a drive.

Long Filename A file or folder that is longer than the 8.3 standard naming convention. Can be up to 255 characters in Windows 98 and 260 characters maximum for both the path and the filename.

M

Master browser A computer system in the network that keeps a list of all computers, shares, servers, and domains on a network.

Minidrivers Printer drivers that are supplied by printer manufacturers (and sometimes Microsoft) and that talk directly to printers.

MODEMLOG.TXT A log file of all modem commands sent and responses received over a phone line.

Multilink Windows 98's ability to utilize two phone lines merged as one for data communication over a modem.

Multiple display support Windows 98's ability to make use of up to nine individual monitors to display information.

N

Name resolution A process used on the network for resolving a computer's address as a computer's name, to support the process of finding and connecting to other computers.

NDIS (Network Driver Interface Specification) The layer that wraps itself around the network device driver to allow communication with the protocol layers and the hardware. NDIS 3.1 adds Plug and Play capabilities.

Net Watcher Windows 98 tool that enables you to see who is currently connected to your shared folders. The Net Watcher provides information about who is currently connected to your computer and to what folder.

NetBEUI NetBios Extended User Interface. A small, fast networking protocol used in LANs.

NetBIOS (Network Basic Input/Output System) An application program interface that provides application programs, such as Windows Explorer, with a set of rules. These rules are used as a guideline to conduct communication between nodes on a network.

NETLOG.TXT An ASCII file containing a list of all network components found during the Windows 98 installation.

NETSETUP A utility that copies Windows 98 files to a network for the purpose of installing to other computers over the network.

NetWare Directory Services (NDS) A user database designed by Novell. It allows a single point of network administration for users, computers, and other objects.

New and Changed Files backup A backup of only those files that have changed since the last All Selected Files backup. Changes the archive bit. Also known as an *incremental backup*.

NIC (Network Interface Card) The peripheral hardware device that provides transport access for network packets.

O

OEM (Original Equipment Manufacturer)
Suppliers or vendors of new computers.

On-the-fly compression   Compression and
expansion of files by the operating system, which
is transparent to the user. The process of disk compression replaces repetitive patterns that take up
space in a given piece of data with a token taking
up less space.

OSR2   The Original Equipment Manufacturer
Service Release 2 version of Windows 95. OSR2
that comes installed on new computers.

P

PAP   Password Authentication Protocol. Uses
clear-text passwords between servers and clients in
a RAS environment.

Physical errors   Problems with the surface of an
actual hardware device or floppy drive.

PING   A command-line utility that is the most
widely used utility for simple troubleshooting. It
sends a network packet to the destination host in
search of a response.

Plug and Play   A technology that allows a piece
of hardware to automatically be detected and configured.

Plug and Play printers   Printers that can be
automatically configured by Windows 98.

Point-to-Point Tunneling Protocol (PPTP)   An
advanced method of networking that allows secure
access, via a Virtual Private Network (VPN), to
remote networks across the Internet. PPTP places
data from one protocol into TCP/IP, thus hiding
or encrypting data over the network. A non-
routable protocol that can be routed through
PPTP over a WAN.

POLEDIT.EXE   The System Policy Editor that
allows an administrator to edit system policies that
are stored in the CONFIG.POL file.

Port   Each Winsock service is uniquely identified
by the port that it uses. There are default ports
that are universally implemented in TCP/IP.

Power Management Scheme   Windows 98's use
of new technology to turn a computer on or off
and not have to wait for a shutdown or power-on
interval.

PPP   Point-to-Point Protocol. This protocol is
widely used on the Internet to connect systems.
Because it is supported by UNIX- and Intel-based
systems, it is very practical.

PPPLOG.TXT   A log file containing information
about how the software layers of PPP have
processed a Dial-Up Networking call.

Printer Spool   Storage of data to be printed. Can
be configured for RAW or EMF format.

Protected mode   An operating system processing
mode in which address spaces are protected from
each other. 32-bit Windows applications run in
protected mode.

Protocol   For two computers to communicate, they both must speak the same language. A protocol is a type of language two or more computers would use to communicate.

Proxy client   The proxy client intercepts any Winsock requests and redirects them to the Proxy Server.

Proxy server   Microsoft's Proxy Server handles Internet requests on behalf of clients.

Pull Model   A broadcast model in which clients request setup or configuration information from servers.

Push Model   A broadcast model in which servers send setup or configuration information to clients.

PWS   Peer Web Server. Designed for small groups that need to share information with HTTP or FTP. PWS also supports ISAPI and CGI.

R

RAS   A service that provides remote networking for telecommuters.

RAW Printing   A printer-dependent print format in which processing occurs in the foreground, keeping control from the user or application.

Real mode   An operating system processing mode in which address spaces of applications are not protected from each other; 16-bit applications run in real `mode.

REGEDIT.EXE   A utility that provides the ability to view and edit the system Registry.

Registry   A database in which Windows 98 stores configuration information for hardware and software. The Registry in Windows 98 is stored in two files: USER.DAT and SYSTEM.DAT.

Remote Administration   The ability of administrators to view and maintain Windows 98 system configurations across a network. The goal of Remote Administration is to give someone on the network full access to the local file system and to allow remote changes to File and Printer Sharing settings.

Remote resources   Resources available to other users through the network.

Restore   A Windows 98 utility that restores to its original format compressed data created by the Backup utility.

S

Safe Recovery   Restart of the Windows 98 Setup program after a failure, allowing Setup to use previous log files to continue installation.

ScanDisk   A utility that checks hard drives and floppy drives for logical and physical errors, and then attempts to repair those errors.

Sector allocation granularity   Process of disk compression that involves changing the way data is stored on a hard drive by circumventing the often large amounts of wasted space created under a normal FAT file system.

Server   Refers to any computer on the network that shares resources. A computer that runs administrative software that controls access to all or part of a network and its resources. Servers can also be peer servers such as Windows 98 systems with File and Printer Sharing turned on, or file servers such as NT.

Server Message Block (SMB)   A file sharing protocol. Its main function is to allow a user, or more specifically a system, to access a remote file transparently.

Server-based   A group of computers that assign rights based on a list of users stored on a central computer.

Service for NetWare directory services   NDS is a NetWare mechanism that allows administrators to group users and servers into more manageable pieces on Novell 4.x servers.

Services   Applications that execute in the background. Services load after Windows 98 boots. They often tend to give additional network functionality in the form of a server application.

SETUPLOG.TXT   An ASCII file containing setup information. Created during Windows 98 installation.

Share   *(verb)* To allow others to access a resource. *(noun)* A resource, such as a directory or print queue, that others can access.

Shared resource   A computer resource, such as a file, folder, or printer, for which you are providing access to other users.

Shared Windows 98   An installation of Windows 98 on a network so that it can be shared by clients to reduce the amount of required hard disk space.

Share-level access control   The user assigns a password to a specific resource in share-level access control. Depending on the password used, a user may have read-only or full control.

Share-level security   A type of security in which a password is assigned to a resource. Anyone that knows the password can access the resource.

Signature Verification tool   A system by which the source of a Web site can be authenticated.

Simple Mail Transfer Protocol (SMTP)   An ASCII message format commonly used for mail sent on the Internet.

SPAP   Shiva Password Authentication Protocol. A two-way (reversible) encryption mechanism employed by Shiva.

Subnet mask   A TCP/IP parameter that distinguishes between the network ID and host ID portions of an IP address.

System Configuration Utility   A tool used to change the startup components and edit system files.

System files   Files that are used to run Windows 98's main components.

System Information Utility   A tool used to view current environment settings. Offers links to additional tools to perform diagnostic tests and configuration changes.

System Monitor   A utility that allows you to view various Windows 98 resources, both on a local machine and on remote computers across a network.

System policies   A single file on a server that is processed when users log on to the network. This file contains a list of settings or restrictions that apply to the users at logon. After the entries are read, they are merged into the Registry.

System Policy Editor   Much of the security that Windows 98 is capable of is implemented through system policies, which are created by the System Policy Editor. Use the System Policy Editor to create system policy users, groups of users, and computers.

SYSTEM.DA0 A backup of the SYSTEM.DAT file created by Windows 98 after the last successful startup.

SYSTEM.DAT One of two files that make up the Registry. This is the Registry file that contains the hardware and computer-specific settings for a workstation. By default, this file is located in the Windows SYSTEM directory. SYSTEM.DAT contains machine-specific data.

T

TAPI Telephony Application Program Interface. A standard set of procedures used for modem communications.

Task An action or application that performs an activity.

TCP/IP Transmission Control Protocol/Internet Protocol. A widely used networking protocol, popular because of the Internet.

Tree In the NDS structure, a tree provides a focal starting point, or *encapsulation*, much like a company name provides recognition for an employee.

Troubleshooting wizards Wizards available through Windows Help that will walk you step by step through the procedures to correct common system problems.

U

UNC Universal Naming Convention. The full name of a resource on the network.

Unidrivers Windows 98 printer drivers that act as an interface between applications and minidrivers. The two unidrivers are PostScript and non-PostScript.

Unified browsing All computers that can be browsed by Windows 98 are displayed together in the Network Neighborhood.

Unimodem Unimodem stands for *universal modem* and refers to the basic modem driver components that Microsoft provides with Windows 98.

Unimodem/V Unimodem/V stands for *Unimodem/Voice*, which is a driver that allows shared FAX servers to operate over your network.

USB Universal Serial Bus. A bi-directional, isochronous, dynamically attachable serial interface for adding peripheral devices. This is a new port and BUS type that removes the limitations of available resources and expansion slots. USBs can handle up to 127 devices.

User profile A profile that enables users to keep personalized settings on a computer. If the computer is used by multiple users, each user can have her own settings.

USER.DA0 A backup of the USER.DAT file created by Windows 98 after the last successful startup.

USER.DAT The file that contains user configuration settings used to implement user profiles either locally or on a network. This is one of the two files that make up the Registry.

User-level access control In user-level access control, specific users are given rights to a specific resource. A network server (NetWare or Microsoft) is required as a security provider, which provides a list of authorized users.

User-level security   A type of security in which rights to resources are granted on a user-by-user basis. No additional passwords are assigned to the resource. Access information is stored in a central account database located on a server.

V

Version Conflict Manager   A tool to verify the version of current driver files with backup copies.

Virtual Private Network (VPN)   Allows communication from a remote client already configured with secure access. It accepts network packets only from its PPTP clients and discards all others.

W

Warm boot   Restarting a computer by pressing the Ctrl+Alt+Del keys.

Windows Update   A utility that connects to a Microsoft Web site to compare and update software components.

WinIPCfg   An IP-configuration utility that displays IP settings and enables a user to change some of those settings.

Winsock   An application interface that TCP/IP utilities and applications use to communicate.

Write-behind caching   A process by which data isn't written immediately to disk but is written when the processor is otherwise idle. Write-behind caching improves disk performance by writing data to cache until the processor can commit the cache to disk.

Fast Facts

INTRODUCTION

By now, you have studied the entire book and are preparing to take the Windows 98 exam. Selecting the correct solution to a given situation often comes down to eliminating the obviously wrong choices, and then choosing the right one from what is left. These exam tips will help you weed out some of the "distracter" answers you will see when you sit for your certification test. Rather than give you a bunch of facts you've read elsewhere in this book, this appendix reflects some of the author's experience in the beta exam—some things you need to know. The information is categorized by objective. Note that this is not a substitution for studying the rest of the book and working on a Windows 98 machine. It is to help you focus your studies.

PLANNING

Develop an appropriate implementation model for specific requirements in a Microsoft environment and a mixed Microsoft and NetWare environment.

Further considerations include choosing the appropriate file system and planning a workgroup.

Choosing the Appropriate File System

See Table C.1 for the file systems Windows 98 supports.

TABLE C.1 **WINDOWS 98–SUPPORTED FILE SYSTEMS**

File System	Operating Systems Supported
FAT	Common to Windows 3.1, 95, 98, and NT, and OS/2. Windows 98 boot disks support only FAT and cannot read FAT32.
FAT32	New to Windows 98 and Windows 95 OSR2. Not compatible with Windows NT or OS/2, thus cannot be used in a dual boot.

Only FAT can be used in a dual boot on the same partition as NT. If FAT32 is present, the partition must be deleted and reformatted.

Planning a Workgroup

Make sure you know the effect of the workgroup name on browsing and joining a domain. It is also important to know the different ways you can log on to an existing domain (that is, quick logon, and logon and restore connections).

Benefits of a Workgroup

- Allows the browsing of computers by workgroup (department).

- One system in each workgroup must use File and Printer Sharing, with Master browser enabled or automatic.

- Just because a Windows 98 system is logged on to a domain does not make it a member of the domain. Only Windows NT computers can be part of the domain.

- If the workgroup matches the domain name, then Domain Master browser is the workgroup master browser.

Logging On to a Domain

- Quick logon does not test the map drives and remote shared. Only when they are needed is a connection established. There is no error if a server is unavailable.

- Logon and Restore Connections check each connection during Startup and report any errors.

Develop a security strategy in a Microsoft environment and a mixed Microsoft and NetWare environment.

Strategies include system policies, user profiles, file and printer sharing, and share-level access control or user-level access control.

System Policies

Make absolutely certain you have installed and configured system policies on a Windows 98 machine. Understanding this topic is crucial for passing this exam. Know what effect checking a box, clearing a box, and leaving a box gray has on the policy. Be very familiar with the kinds of things you can enforce from system policies (such as forcing a logon to a network). Policies are applied only if the Profiles feature is enabled.

Implications of Check Boxes in a Policy File

See Table C.2 for details about check boxes.

TABLE C.2 IMPLICATIONS OF CHECK BOXES IN POLICY FILES

Check Box	Implication
Checked	This option overrides the current settings in the local Registry by enabling the feature.
Unchecked	This option overrides the current settings in the local Registry by disabling the feature.
Grayed	This option does not change the current settings in the local Registry; if the feature was enabled or disabled, it maintains its settings after the policy is run.

Types of Policies

See Table C.3 for system policies.

TABLE C.3 SYSTEM POLICIES

Type of Policy	Application or Use
Specific user	Applies just to that user. That user is not subjected to any other policy in the file. Applies to the users on all Windows 98 systems.
Group	Easier to administer many users, especially when users change groups. If a user is a member of several groups, policy restrictions are applied in the order of the group's priorities. A group member is not subject to the default user policy. Applies to the users on all Windows 98 systems.
Default user	Applies to all users who do not have a specific policy or belong to a group with a policy. Applies to the users on all Windows 98 systems.
Computer	Applies just to that computer name. Any users on the system are affected. The computer is not subjected to the default computer policy in the file.
Default computer	Applies to all computers that do not have a specific policy. Applies to the users on any Windows 98 systems.

Default Location of Policy Files

- **Primary logon for Windows NT**. The file is on the Netlogon share of the PDC. To enable load balancing, copy the policy file to each BDC's Netlogon share and set the load balance option in the location of policy files. The file is named Config.pol for Windows 98 and NTConfig.pol for NT.

- **Primary logon for Novell**. The file is located in the PUBLIC folder on the Logon server. The file is named Config.pol for Windows 98 and NTConfig.pol for NT.

User Profiles

User profiles are stored in the user's mail directory on a NetWare server and in the user's Home folder on an NT server.

File and Printer Sharing

- You can install only one file and printer share per computer. You can install File and Printer Sharing for either Microsoft or NetWare, but not both.

- Additionally, if you do not have File and Printer Sharing installed, your machine cannot share resident files or locally attached printers with other computers in the workgroup or domain.

- File and Printer Sharing must be enabled to perform remote administration commands.

Share-level Access Control or User-level Access Control

- Share-level access control uses passwords—one for read-only and a different one for full access.

- User-level access control depends on a security provider such as NT Domain or Novell server.

- To remotely administer another Windows 98 system, both systems must have the same share type.

- For remote Registry, you must have user-level access control.

▼ **NOTE**

If you change from user-level to share-level access control or vice versa, all current shares are removed.

INSTALLATION AND CONFIGURATION

This objective is one of the main ones covered on the exam. In general, make sure you know how much space Windows 98 requires for a typical installation, a compact installation, and a portable installation. Of course, the Custom Installation option of Setup allows more individualized control.

Install Windows 98.

Installation options include Automated Windows setup, New, Upgrade, Uninstall, and Dual-boot combination with Microsoft Windows NT 4.0.

Automated Windows Setup

- Batch98 is used to create an answer file to set up Windows 98 with little user interaction.

- Windows 98 can be installed on a server share using NETSETUP. This allows network users to connect and run the setup for a local or network copy of 98.

- Use a batch install to select components during an install. This overrides any default settings.

- Use a different batch installation file for each configuration required.

- Leave a specific setting blank if you want the user to provide different information at each system.

New

This is a relatively straightforward topic. Just remember that the hard disk needs an active partition. It also must be formatted with system files placed in it before you can install Windows 98.

Upgrade

- Keeps the basic configuration settings of the old operating system

- Saves the old operating system's settings if you want to uninstall Windows 98

- Can be manual or can use a batch file

You can upgrade over Windows 95, Windows 3.1, Windows for Workgroups 3.11, and various versions of DOS as well as OS/2. You cannot upgrade programs like UNIX. Make sure you understand how to maintain program groups and related issues when upgrading as well.

Uninstall

- If you save the existing operating system files, you can uninstall Windows 98.

- If you do not save the existing operating system file, you cannot uninstall Windows 98. You must reinstall the old operating system.

- Windows 98 using FAT32 cannot be successfully uninstalled because the old operating system cannot read a FAT32 partition.

Dual-Boot Combination with Microsoft Windows NT 4.0

The easiest way to do this is to install Windows 98 first, and then install Windows NT.

- Windows 98 does not work on an NTFS partition.

- Windows NT does not work on FAT32.

- Windows NT does not work if you use Windows 98 disk compression.

Configure Windows 98 server components.

Server components include Microsoft Personal Web Server 4.0 and Dial-Up Networking Server.

Microsoft Personal Web Server 4.0

Remember that Windows 98 ships with a Web server. This is a scaled-down version of IIS 4.0, used primarily for intranet purposes.

- Intranets

- Supports HTTP services

- Supports FTP services

Dial-Up Networking Server

- Only one dial-in at a time.
- Dial-in services can be disabled.
- Can use user-level security with an NT or Novell server.
- Users that dial in can access the Internet by using the remote network's default gateway in TCP/IP. Otherwise, only local network access is provided.

Dial-Up Networking is used for home systems or small networks with less need for security over dial-in systems.

Install and configure the network components of Windows 98 in a Microsoft environment and a mixed Microsoft and NetWare environment.

Network components include Client for Microsoft Networks, Client for NetWare Networks, Network Adapters, File and Printer Sharing for Microsoft Networks, File and Printer Sharing for NetWare Networks, Service for NetWare Directory Services, Asynchronous Transfer Mode, Virtual Private Networking and PPTP, and Browse Master.

Client for Microsoft Networks

- Must be primary login if roaming profiles and policies are to be implemented.
- Logon must be validated if a logon script is to be run.

Client for NetWare Networks

- Preferred servers in Novell are the main logon servers.

- Must be the primary logon server if a logon script is to be run.
- Only keeps Windows 98 common entries in a logon script. Keeps map drives and captures printers.

Just make sure you are comfortable with all the tabs and check boxes when you are configuring the clients. You may want to brush up on things such as selecting the preferred server and logging on to an NT domain. Do you know how to make it process logon scripts?

Network Adapters

Network adapters are listed in the Add Adapter dialog box. You must be able to install adapters not listed and update drivers.

File and Printer Sharing for Microsoft Networks

- This allows other Windows 98, 95, 3.11, and 3.1 clients, as well as DOS clients, to share access.
- Windows 3.1 and 3.11 can only browse up to 8-character share names.
- Windows 98 can only create up to 12-character share names.
- A computer name shows up in the browse list only if File and Printer Sharing is enabled and a common protocol is used.

File and Printer Sharing for NetWare Networks

- For Novell DOS clients to see the Windows 98 system and its shares using SLIST, you must enable SAP advertising.

- All systems must have the same frame type to exchange data over IPX/SPX.

- Novell clients cannot log on to a Windows 98 system. They can only attach to it and access its shares.

Remember that only one File and Printer Sharing service can be running at any time.

Service for NetWare Directory Services (NDS)

- New to Windows 98, this service helps connect to Novell servers running NDS, such as Novell NetWare 4.x.

- NDS uses default context and preferred trees.

Asynchronous Transfer Mode (ATM) Components

To take advantage of ATM technology, Windows 98 includes components in the network icon to connect to an ATM network.

Virtual Private Networking and PPTP

- Using a dial-up adapter, Windows 98 connects with a VPN adapter instead of a modem.

- Communication is done over a secure channel.

- VPN piggybacks over a modem or LAN connection.

- PPTP is Point-to-Point Tunneling Protocol—one protocol inside another.

Browse Master

- All workgroups must have one master browser in order to use the network neighborhood.

- A system running File and Printer Sharing has Master browser set to Automatic. It participates in the master browser elections.

- Enabling Master browser on one system and disabling it on all other systems identifies which system is the master browser.

- Setting the domain name as the workgroup name has Windows 98 system use the same master browser as the domain.

- Browsing does not mean connections. Windows 98 still must perform name resolution for remote systems.

- Only systems using the same protocol show up in your browse list.

- For File and Printer Sharing for Novell, you must enable SAP advertising before server names show up in the browse list.

Install and configure network protocols in a Microsoft environment and a mixed Microsoft and NetWare environment.

Protocols are hit pretty hard on the exam, both directly and indirectly. Most of the questions are about TCP/IP and remote access using a default gateway. In general, make absolutely certain you know what each protocol is used for, and the advantages and disadvantages of each. The following sections address some of the more specific protocol issues on the exam.

NetBEUI

- Not routable; cannot access remote systems
- Can be used on a LAN or with Dial-Up Networking
- No configuration required
- Simple for small, single-segment networks

IPX/SPX-compatible Protocol

- IPX/SPX is used in NetWare environments.
- The NT equivalent is NWLink.
- IPX/SPX is a routable protocol.
- SAP advertising is used to display your server name and is shared to the Novell system and the browse list.
- NetBIOS is not enabled by default with IPX/SPX. In the properties of IPX/SPX there is a check box to enable NetBIOS over IPX/SPX.
- IPX/SPX and Novell use frame types. Two systems must have a common frame type in order to exchange data.

TCP/IP

- TCP/IP is hit really hard on the exam; Microsoft asks all kinds of questions about it. A good background will aid you in the troubleshooting scenario questions.
- TCP/IP is routable.
- A default gateway address is required to access remote systems.
- The default gateway address must be on the same segment.

- DHCP server runs on an NT server and automatically distributes non-conflicting IP addresses and additional settings to clients, such as subnet mask, default gateway, and WINS.
- WINS server runs on an NT server and helps with NetBIOS name resolution. NetBIOS name resolution is used for each remote Microsoft and Novell server. NetBIOS is used for file or printer sharing, Network Neighborhood, and drive mappings. WINS is a dynamic tool.
- LMHOSTS is also used for NetBIOS name resolution or remote NetBIOS server, but this is a file that resides locally on each Windows 98 system in the Windows folder. LMHOSTS has no extension on the filename.
- DNS server runs on an NT or UNIX server and is used for HOSTS name resolution when using TCP/IP utilities such as Web or FTP services. Each computer has a host name and a domain name. A Fully Qualified Domain Name (FQDN) uses the host name and the domain name, such as www.microsoft.com.
- The HOSTS file is used just as DNS is for local and remote hosts' name resolution. This file resides in the Windows folder and has no filename extension.

Microsoft DLC

Basically, all you need to know is what it is used for (that is, some HP printers, and connectivity to mainframes, and, at times, AS-400s).

Fast Infrared

- Fast Infrared is new to Windows 98.

- Fast Infrared is a protocol used by Infrared adapters to connect printers to the network.

Install and configure hardware devices in a Microsoft environment and a mixed Microsoft and NetWare environment.

Hardware devices include modems, printers, Universal Serial Bus, multiple display support, IEEE 1394 Firewire, Infrared Data Association, Multilink, and Power Management Scheme.

Modems

- The Modem Wizard is used to install a new modem.

- A modem is required to use Dial-Up Networking.

- You can set a modem log in the Advanced Configuration tab to record possible errors.

- More recent modems require new drivers from their manufacturers.

Printers

- The Printer Wizard guides you through the installation of local and network printers.

- DOS applications need a local printer port to capture a network location before network printing can take place.

- In Windows 98, a *print device* is the machine that produces paper printed with text or graphics. A *printer* is the software drivers and configuration.

- Postscript printer drivers generate all types of scrambled text on non-Postscript printers.

- Using the EMF format instead of RAW releases the application faster.

- For slow applications, set the spooler to wait for all pages to be spooled before sending to the print device. This prevents print jobs from being mixed up.

- A banner page can be set to print before each print job to identify its origins.

- A separator page prints after each print job to identify the last page of the print job.

- For a PnP printer to be configured automatically, you must have a bidirectional port and an IEEE 1294–compliant cable.

- A network printer's drivers are downloaded to your Windows 98 system if they are compatible. Windows NT servers can have Windows 95/98–compatible drivers loaded and made available for shared printers. Each time a job is sent to a network printer, the print drivers are compared and downloaded if needed.

Universal Serial Bus (USB)

A lot of new devices support USB. Make sure you know the advantages and limits of USB. Contrast USB with conventional devices that require IRQ settings. And you should be able to contrast USB with IEEE 1394 Firewire.

- USB devices do not require unique IRQs, DMAs, IOs, or base addresses.

- Standard connectors are used for all USB devices.

- USB devices can be BUS powered or self powered.
- USB devices can be connected directly to one another or through a USB hub.
- USB can handle up to 127 devices per port.
- USB can communicate at rates up to 12Mbps.
- IEEE1394 Firewire is used for high-demand digital video with transmission rates of 150–400Mbps.
- You can get a USB keyboard, mouse, modem, and scanner, to name just a few.

Multiple Display Support

- PCI (Peripheral Component Interconnect) or AGP (Accelerated Graphics Port) video cards can be used.
- One card is the main device, with additional cards for every other monitor used.
- The slot or IRQ used has no impact on the configuration of the monitors.

IEEE 1394 Firewire

- New technology used for demanding digital video
- Up to 63 devices
- Transmission rates up to 400Mbps

Infrared Data Association (IrDA)

Faster transmission rates than the previous implementation of Infrared in Windows 95.

Multilink

- Two devices connected as one to provide twice the bandwidth.
- Use modem of similar speeds.
- Analog modems or ISDN adapters.
- Multilink and Callback do not work together.

Power Management Scheme

Mostly for laptops, but with the appropriate software, Windows 98 starts up and shuts down instantly. This is not supported by all hardware.

Install and configure the Microsoft Backup.

- Remember that Windows 98 Backup now works with SCSI drives. It also works with QIC 40, 80, and 3010.
- If you have properly installed a compatible tape drive, Windows 98 will automatically detect the drive. If you change drives, you can select Redetect Tape Drive from the Tools menu if needed.
- You can back up your data to tape, floppy, or a networked drive.
- You can back up a networked drive.
- A full backup includes all the files selected and marks the files as being backed up.
- An incremental backup includes only the files that have been added or changed since the last backup and marks the files as being backed up. This method is faster than a full backup. To restore, however, you must use all the backups.

- A differential backup includes only the files that have been added or changed since the last backup, but does not mark the files as being backed up. This method is fastest when you need to restore. To restore you need use only the full backup and the last backup, because it is cumulative.

Configuring and Managing Resource Access

This objective addresses assigning access permissions for shared folders; creating, sharing, and monitoring resources; setting up user environments; backing up data and the Registry; restoring the Registry; and managing hard disks. Although creating hardware profiles is not listed by Microsoft as a subobjective, the Beta exam includes questions about creating hardware profiles.

Assign access permissions for shared folders in a Microsoft environment and a mixed Microsoft and NetWare environment.

Methods include passwords, user permissions, and group permissions.

Passwords

- For Windows NT and 98, use the Password icon in the Control Panel. Passwords are case sensitive.
- For Novell, use the SETPASS utility at a DOS prompt.

User Permissions

- Permission given to a specific username overrides any group permissions.
- For user permission, you must be using user-level security with a security provider such as NT or Novell server.
- Valid permissions are Read-Only, Change, Full Control, and No Access.

Group Permissions

- Group permissions, with the exception of No Access, are cumulative for users in multiple groups.
- For group permissions, you must be using user-level security with a security provider such as NT or Novell server.
- Valid permissions are Read-Only, Change, Full Control, and No Access.

Create, share, and monitor resources.

Resources include remote computers and network computers.

Remote Computers

Remember that you must be running user-level access control to install and configure many of the Remote management tools.

Network Printers

Most of this is already covered in "Printers" earlier in the chapter. Just make sure you remember about RPC Printer, and how you would manage a network printer remotely.

- Everyone can see the list of print jobs.

- Only the owner of a print job and administrators can delete a print job.

- Administrators and owners of the printer can change the priority of a print job.

Set up user environments by using user profiles and system policies.

- User profiles are not automatically enabled in Windows 98.

- Profiles can be changed to Mandatory by renaming User.dat to User.man.

- Roaming profiles are enabled when the user has a home folder on an NT server and Client for Microsoft is the primary logon.

- Roaming profiles are enabled when the user has a mail folder on a Novell server and Client for Novell is the primary logon.

- User profiles must be enabled to use policies.

- The default location for a policy file on an NT Domain is the Netlogon share on the PDC. Only when Load Balancing is turned on does Windows 98 download policies from BDC.

- The default location for a policy on a Novell server is the public directory on the SYS volume.

- Default user and default computer policies are not used if a specific user or computer name has a policy or if a user is a member of a group that has a policy.

- Group policies are not implemented if the Windows 98 system does not have group policies enabled with Groupol.dll.

- Remember that a gray box in the policy file means that policy does not change the current settings of the local Registry.

Back up data and the Registry and restore data and the Registry.

The Registry backup is very important. Understand the difference between exporting a folder and a backup.

- Backing up the Registry includes all the Registry.

- Exporting a Registry file (such as just one key or one subkey) can be used to back up a subsection of the Registry. The Registry file can then be merged back into the Registry.

Configure hard disks.

Tasks include disk compression, partitioning, enabling large disk support, and converting to FAT32.

Disk Compression

- Windows 98 uses DriveSpace 3.0.

- 2GB is the largest partition that can be compressed using DriveSpace.

- A host drive is the location at which data is really stored. Drive C: is where the user accesses information. The host drive is usually hidden.

- NT is not compatible with DriveSpace 3.0.

- A FAT32 partition cannot be compressed using DriveSpace 3.0.

Partitioning

You use FDISK to create and manage partitions on a drive. Make sure you understand about extended DOS partitions, primary DOS partitions, and active partitions. This knowledge will be good for a few extra points on the exam.

- Only primary partitions can be active and bootable.

- Extended partitions can be subdivided into multiple logical drives.

- Windows 98 supports only one primary and one extended partition.

- Windows 98 can support partitions up to 2GB in size.

Enabling Large Disk Support

Know when Windows 98 offers support for FAT32, the FDISK program, and the size of partitions.

- FAT32 uses smaller clusters. 4KB clusters use up less space on the hard drive, allowing for more real storage.

- Windows 98's FDISK offers large disk support when a partition or 540MB or more is created.

- FAT32 is not compatible with NT.

- FAT32 partitions cannot be compressed using DriveSpace.

Converting to FAT32

Understand how to convert from FAT to FAT32. Remember that you cannot dual boot with NT if the main drive is FAT32, and that you cannot convert back from FAT32 to FAT.

- The Convert utility does not re-format the partition and no data is lost. The Convert utility is found in the System Tools.

- Windows 98 can only convert from FAT to FAT32; it cannot convert from FAT32 back to FAT.

Create hardware profiles.

In most cases, an administrator needs to implement two hardware configurations for the same system. An example would be a laptop with one hardware configuration for office use and one for out-of-the-office use.

- Hardware profiles are created in the System icon of the Control Panel.

- After a profile is created, you must reboot into that profile to make changes to it.

- Disable a device under a profile rather than removing it. This way, it can be re-enabled faster if necessary.

INTEGRATION AND INTEROPERABILITY

Some information pertaining to this objective is presented in "Configure Windows 98 server components."

Configure a Windows 98 computer as a client computer in a network that contains a Windows NT 4.0 domain.

See the notes under "Install and configure the network components of Windows 98 in a Microsoft environment and a mixed Microsoft and NetWare environment." Also note that users of Windows 98 can log on to an NT server, but that the Windows 98 system is not part of the domain.

Configure a Windows 98 computer as a client computer in a NetWare network.

See the earlier notes under "Install and configure hardware devices in a Microsoft environment and a mixed Microsoft and NetWare environment." Remember that a Windows 98 system can be a client to NT and Novell at the same time. As long as passwords and user names are identical, the user will not notice a dual logon.

Configure a Windows 98 computer for remote access by using various methods in a Microsoft environment or a mixed Microsoft and NetWare environment.

Methods include Dial-Up Networking and Proxy Server.

Dial-Up Networking

Understand the Dial-Up Networking tool in this case is only the client. Make sure you can integrate Multilink, as well as the VPN device and PPTP with Dial-Up Networking, into this section. This is basically a combination of configuring Dial-Up Networking and TCP/IP.

- Dial-Up Networking can be used to connect to a corporate network or the Internet.

- A pair of modems or ISDN adapters can be used in a multilink session to increase bandwidth.

- Connecting over TCP/IP allows access to the local area network.

- Selecting Use Remote Default Gateway allows access to the LAN and the Internet.

- A VPN (virtual private network) allows a secure connection over the Internet through a modem or network connection.

Here again, it is mostly a matter of getting Dial-Up Networking installed properly, setting up the modem properly, and binding the appropriate protocols. It can get complicated, but mercifully is not hit too hard on the exam. Remember, if you do not have a modem installed, and you try to configure Dial-Up Networking, it will take you through the Add Modem Wizard first. Also, remember that in Windows NT, Dial-Up Networking is called RAS (Remote Access Service).

Proxy Server

The proxy server is not part of Windows 98. Here you need to know how to configure the proxy client in Windows 98 and the purpose of implementing Proxy for security and access reasons.

- A proxy server can be set up to allow a Windows 98 system access to the Internet.

- The proxy client is installed on each Windows 98 system. The client can be configured manually, or you can have the proxy server configure it automatically, which updates each time the client connects.

- A proxy server can restrict connections based on Internet protocol (HTTP, FTP, Gopher, and so on), IP address, or Internet domain name.

MONITORING AND OPTIMIZATION

This area features several important concepts for you to consider.

Monitor system performance by using Net Watcher, System Monitor, and Resource Meter.

Make sure you know the requirements to install and use Net Watcher. You should have a good feel for the kind of information you can obtain here.

- Net Watcher allows administrators to remotely monitor who is connected to a system and which folders are being accessed.

- Net Watcher can also be used to create or stop shares on a remote Windows 98 system.

- Both systems must be running the same access control: user level or share level.

- Remote administration must be enabled, and the user trying to monitor must have permission.

You do not need to know what every single counter is in System Monitor, but you do need to experiment with it, and have a solid feel for the kinds of information you can get from it.

- System Monitor is used to evaluate the system's performance.

- System Monitor can be used to detect possible bottlenecks.

- Remote monitoring can be done if remote administration is enabled and the user has permission.

- Only objects for the components that are installed are displayed.

- For network monitoring, you must install the service for Network Monitor Agent.

- The kernel object and its usage are pivotal to Windows 98's performance. This is the counter to evaluate the processor's usage.

Tune and optimize the system in a Microsoft environment and a mixed Microsoft and NetWare environment.

Tasks include using Disk Defragmenter and ScanDisk to optimize the hard disk, updating drivers, applying service packs, using the Maintenance Wizard to automate tasks, using the Task Scheduler, and checking for corrupt files with System File Checker.

Optimizing the Hard Disk by Using Disk Defragmenter and ScanDisk

Know when you would run the Disk Defragmenter, and why. You also need to remember that there are different ways to run the Disk Defragmenter, such as Full Defragmentation, Defragment Files, and Consolidate Free Space Only. Make sure you have a good feel for when you would use each option.

- Run the Defragmenter utility to collect all the files into a contiguous section of the hard drive, freeing up more space for storage.

- Run the Defragmenter utility to reorganize files so the application can start up faster.

- You should defragment the drive after moving or deleting a lot of files.

- Defragment the drive when file access and storage seem sluggish.

- Defragmenting just free space does not make access any faster, but provides better storage for new files.

You should know what kinds of errors ScanDisk can detect and correct. You should also know the difference between a standard and thorough scan.

- Run ScanDisk to check for errors in files or surface errors on the hard drive.

- ScanDisk can find lost clusters and delete them.

- ScanDisk can fix cross-linked files.

- ScanDisk can mark bad sectors and prevent their future use as data storage.

- A thorough scan checks the surface of the drive.

Compressing Data by Using DriveSpace3 and the Compression Agent

- DriveSpace 3.0 can be used to compress drives up to 2GB in size.

- DriveSpace 3.0 cannot be used with NTFS or FAT32 partitions.

- DriveSpace can use different compression ratios to improve access time (less compression) or improve storage capacity (more compression).

- Not all files compress to the same ratio. Text files compress at higher ratios than program files.

Updating Drivers and Applying Service Packs by Using Windows Update and the Signature Verification Tool

Understand the system requirements to use Windows Update. Namely, access the Internet and registered software to get all updates. Have a basic understanding of the risk of Internet downloads and how the Signature Verification tool helps.

- New drivers for existing hardware.

- New components and fixes for Windows 98 system files.

- Internet connectivity is required to use System Update.

- System Update can scan your system and recommend which updates are necessary and which ones are optional.

- Your copy of Windows 98 must be registered with Microsoft for you to have access to all updates.

- The Signature Verification tool is used to make sure the update has not been tampered with and the source is legitimate.

Automating Tasks by Using Maintenance Wizard

Be familiar with the tool and the difference between a custom and standard install. Also remember that you cannot add other applications in this wizard.

- Disk Defragmenter, ScanDisk, and DiskCleanup can be set up with the Maintenance Wizard.

- A custom install allows you to select which components to load and what time of day to run them.

- No other utilities can be automated with this wizard.

Scheduling Tasks by Using Task Scheduler

You must be able to add other applications to run without user intervention.

- Same basic maintenance tools as provided by the Maintenance Wizard.

- Any other applications can be set up to start at a given time.

- Fully automated applications are preferred because no user interaction is required.

Checking for Corrupt Files and Extracting Files from the Installation Media by Using the System File Checker

Understand how the CAB (cabinet) files are structured. Know the syntax and switches used to extract and view files inside CAB files.

- Windows 98 has CAB files, which contain compressed files used for installation and additional configuration.

- The System File Checker utility can be used to restore damaged files as well as view CAB file content.

TROUBLESHOOTING

Most of the Troubleshooting items have already been covered. On the exam, questions seem to fall into multiple objectives. This is particularly true of the scenario questions.

Diagnose and resolve installation failures.

Tasks include resolving file and driver version conflicts with Version Conflict Manager and the Microsoft System Information utility.

Resolving File and Driver Version Conflicts by Using Version Conflict Manager and the Microsoft System Information Utility

- Usually when a system is upgraded, there are difficulties with drivers. The Conflict Manager keeps a list of replaced files.

- Conflict Manager can restore older files.

- Conflict Manager can verify and compare driver revision numbers and dates.

- The Microsoft System Information utility lists all 16- and 32-bit applications that are currently on the system.

- System Information can also be used to produce reports about the system, assisting administrators and support personnel.

Diagnose and resolve boot process failures.

Tasks include using the System Configuration utility.

Editing Configuration Files by Using the System Configuration Utility

You'll see only a few basic types of boot-up issues with a Windows 98 machine. These include viruses, hardware problems, and Registry problems. Make sure you know the symptoms of each. In addition to these items, if you know how to use Safe Mode to get the machine back up and running, then you have this objective well in hand. You also need to know the files that are used to start up Windows 98 and how to create a boot disk.

- A Windows Startup disk contains the necessary files to start Windows 98 at a command prompt. You can create a startup disk from the Password icon in the Control Panel.

- Using SYS from the Startup disk, you can restore the boot sector on drive C:.

- Command.com, IO.SYS, and MSDOS.SYS are the three boot files needed to start up Windows 98.

- MSDOS.SYS is a text file that is used to configure how Windows 98 starts up.

- The Startup disk is not unique to any computer; it can be used to troubleshoot several systems.

- Using Safe Mode, Windows 98 starts up without any extra device drivers and without network connectivity unless Safe Mode with Network Support is selected.

Diagnose and resolve connectivity problems in a Microsoft environment and a mixed Microsoft and NetWare environment.

Tools include WinIPCfg, Net Watcher, PING, and TRACERT.

WinIPCfg

Make sure you are familiar with the information you obtain from WinIPCfg. Couple this with the information from the TCP/IP section and you will do well here.

- WinIPCfg displays current IP addresses and subnet masks for each network card and modem.

- Using the More Info button in the WinIPCfg dialog box, you will see the default gateway and other configuration settings for TCP/IP.

- WinIPCfg's Release and Renew are used with client machines that are configured by a DHCP server.

Net Watcher

It is important to know what you can do with Net Watcher, and what you cannot do with it. Make sure you understand the requirements for running Net Watcher. Refer to the Net Watcher explanation earlier in this chapter.

PING

PING is a command-line tool that allows you to troubleshoot network connections. You can use PING to send a test packet to a specified address and then, if things are working properly, the packet is returned. Choosing what to ping is the key to using it for successful troubleshooting.

TRACERT

Using TRACERT, you will be able to determine the path that your packets take to the remote host. Execute TRACERT *hostname*, where *hostname* is the computer name or IP address of the computer whose route you want to trace. TRACERT will return the different IP addresses the packet was routed through to reach the final destination. The results also include the number of hops needed to reach the destination. Execute TRACERT without any options to see a help file that describes all the TRACERT switches.

Diagnose and resolve printing problems in a Microsoft environment and a mixed Microsoft and NetWare environment.

See the earlier discussion on printing under "Printers."

Diagnose and resolve file system problems.

Refer to the discussion on ScanDisk and Disk Defragmenter.

Diagnose and resolve resource access problems in a Microsoft environment and a mixed Microsoft and NetWare environment.

This topic was covered in the section "Configuring Windows 98 server components."

Diagnose and resolve hardware device and device driver problems.

Tasks include using ScanReg and ScanRegW to check for corrupt Registry files.

Checking for Corrupt Registry Files by Using ScanReg and ScanRegW

ScanReg and ScanRegW perform the same functions:

- ScanReg is the command-line utility.
- ScanRegW is the graphical utility.

SUMMARY

The exam consists of several types of questions. The most popular is a multiple-choice question that will describe a short scenario in which a typical user or administrator could be involved. There are typically four answers listed. Be very careful to read the full question and all of the answer options before answering. If the question requests the best answer, do not be surprised if *your* best answer is not listed. Think about the question in terms of the situation and how *Microsoft* would expect you to answer.

There is also a new type of question on the Windows 98 exam. It displays a dialog box with selections already made. The question prompts you to identify which box to check or uncheck in order to satisfy the requirements. Using the mouse, click on the check box as you would if it were a real dialog box.

If you are unsure about one of your answers, do not spend too much time on it. Simply mark that question and come back to it at the end of the exam. Keep your eye on the timer and be sure to complete the exam before the time runs out.

Here's hoping you do well on the exam. Hopefully, your exam preparation and the review you've undertaken using this book, as well as your experience actually working with Windows 98 (a must), have appropriately prepared you. If you feel you need more exam-type practice, you are encouraged to take the practice exams in this book and to pick up a copy of Macmillan Publishing's *MCSE Training Guide: Windows 98* for exam 70-098. Study hard and good luck!

Index

SYMBOLS

16-bit clients, 104
32-bit clients, 104

A

ability estimate, adaptive form exams, 424
access rights, troubleshooting, 347-349
accessing Internet through proxy servers, 254-255
activating
    remote administration, 38-40
    user profiles, 24-26
active learning, study strategy, 421
adapters, legacy cards, 110
adaptive form exams, 423-424
    ability estimate, 424
    statistics
        item characteristic curve, 424
        standard error, 424
        test information, 424
    tips for taking, 424, 428
Add Printer Wizard
    local printer installation, 67-68
    network printer installation, 69-70
adding
    clients to networks, 104-105
    entries to policy files, 35-36
    printers, 160-161

administrators
    Final Implementation Model, 15
    sharing services, security concerns, 29-31
AGP video cards, 71
answering simulation questions, 425-428
applications
    dual-booting, creating, 54
    Tasks Scheduler, 295
applying system policies, 190
ATM (Asynchronous Transfer Mode), 114
authentication of passwords, 249-250
automated Windows setup
    installation summary, 446
    planning summary, 445
automating system tasks (Disk Clean Up), 293

B

backup browsers, 117-121
    elections, 119-121
    updates from master, 117-121
Backup utility
    backup sets, 172
    data backup
        destinations, 171
        full, 171-172
        incremental, 171-172
        methods, 171
        selection, 81-82

file restoration, 173
full backups, 79-80
inclusion/exclusion, 82
incremental backups, 79-80
installing, 80-82, 170-171
jobs, 172
tape drives, QIC specifications, 83
Banyan VINES, 103
batch scripting, 53
BATCH.EXE utility, Windows 98 installation, 52-53
boot failures, resolving, 313-315
browse lists, 226
browsers
backup, 117-121
configuration options, 119-121
elections, 119-121
master, 117-121
buffers (printers), clearing, 330

C

Call Back (Remote Access Server), 73
CD-ROM, installation files, 52
certification requirements
Microsoft Certified Professional (MCP), 413-414
Microsoft Certified Professional+Internet (MCP+Internet), 413-414
Microsoft Certified Professional+Site Building (MCP+Site Building), 413-414
Microsoft Certified Solution Developer (MCSD), 414, 417-419

Microsoft Certified Systems Engineer (MCSE), 413-415
Windows NT 3.51, 415-416
Windows NT 4.0, 415
Microsoft Certified Systems Engineer+Internet (MCSE+Internet), 414, 416-417
Microsoft Certified Trainer (MCT), 414, 419-420
Challenge Handshake Authentication Protocol (CHAP), 249-250
characters, filenames, 9-10
clearing print buffer, 330
Client for Microsoft Networks, 105
configuration summary, 447
Client for NetWare Networks, configuration summary, 447-448
clients
16-bit, 104
file sharing
NetWare, 122-123
Windows, 122-123
NetWare
directory services tree, 236
file sharing, 122-123, 236
IPX/SPX protocol, 235-236
network requirements, 113
user-level security, 237
Windows 98 support features, 235-236
networks, adding, 104-105
clusters
partition sizes, 208-209
ScanDisk checks, 281-282

COM ports
Control Panel icon, 75
device connections
modems, 75
other PCs, 75
printers, 75
manual configuration, 75
modem locations, 66
comprehensive learning, 421
compressed volume file (CVF), 283, 286
compressing hard disks (DriveSpace 3.0), 202-204
Compression Agent 3.0 (DriveSpace 3.0), 288
computers
names, changing, 100
policy files, adding, 35-36
Configuration Manager, 312
configuration summary (Fast Facts section)
Client for Microsoft Networks, 447
Client for NetWare Networks, 447-448
Dial-Up Networking Server, 447
Fast Infrared, 450
IEEE 1394 Firewire, 451
IPX/SPX, 449
master browsers, 448
Microsoft Backup, 451-452
Microsoft DLC, 449
modems, 450
mulitple display support, 451
multilink, 451
NetBEUI, 449
Personal Web Server, 446
printers, 450
Service for NetWare Directory Services (NDS), 448

TCP/IP, 449
USB (Universal Serial Bus), 450-451
virtual private networking, 448
configuring
browsers, 120
COM ports, 75
Dial-Up Networking, 249-250
Domain Name Server (DNS), 247
modems, 66
network printers, 69-70
PPTP, 116
Task Scheduler, 296-297
TCP/IP, 134
WINS for TCP/IP clients, 136
Conflict Manager, troubleshooting summary, 458
connectivity
printers, 221
troubleshooting, 325
Dial-Up Networking, 321-324
Windows 98 wizards, 326
WinIPCfg utility, 324
Control Panel
display settings, 193
File and Printer Sharing, 156
network settings, 100
password settings, 193-194
printer settings, 194
converting to FAT32, 208-209
corrupted files, monitoring, 298-300
creating
dual-booting to Windows NT, 56-57
folders, 157-158
hardware profiles, 212-214
policy files (System Policy Editor), 34

startup disks, 53-54

system policies (System Policy Editor), 32

cross-linked files, remedying (ScanDisk), 281

D

data

full backups (Backup utility), 79-80

incremental backups (Backup utility), 79-80

DEC Pathworks, 103

delete permissions (User Profiles), 25-28

Demanding Digital Devices (IEEE 1394), 72-73

demodulation, 65

deploying Windows 98 on networks, 14-17

DETCRASH.LOG file, hardware detection failures, 58-59

DETCRASH.TXT log, installation failures, 305-307

DETLOG.TXT log, installation failures, 305-307

device drivers, troubleshooting, 353-354

Device Manager

hardware profiles, 214

network components, viewing, 110

devices, infrared communication, 76

DHCP (Dynamic Host Configuration Protocol),

IP address assignment, 246

diagnosing, *see* **troubleshooting**

Dial-Up Networking

configuration options, 249-250, 447

connectivity situations, 319

hardware/software requirements, 249-250

integration summary, 455

log files, 323

PPTP, 252

problem categories, 322-323

security

share-level, 91

user-level, 91

server emulation, 90

server installation, 90

supported protocols, 252, 320

troubleshooting, 321-323

dialog boxes

Install New Modem, 65

Remote Administration, 265

Safe Recovery, 58

Select Network Component, 104

disabling

long filenames, 341

print spoolers, 330

Disk Clean Up utility, 293

disk compression

compressed volume file (CVF), 286

Extract command line, 297

resource management summary, 453

sector allocation, 203-204, 284-285

token conversion, 203-204, 284-285

versus system speed, 287

when to use, 277

Disk Defragmentor, 343

compatible drives, 279

drive types, 276-279

files

hidden, 276

system, 276

monitoring/optimization summary, 456

options
  files only, 280
  full, 280
  space consolidation only, 280
primary function, 276
report of errors, 279
when to use, 277-278
Disk Images
installation guidelines, 10
Microsoft White Paper, 11
Plug and Play, 12
versus pull installations, 12
versus push installations, 12
disk space, minimum system requirements, 50
DLC (Data Link Protocol), 128, 138
Domain Name Server (DNS)
configuring, 247
enabling, 247
names
  accessing over TCP/IP, 137
  structure, 137
domains
joining, 224
logging on, 444
name same as workgroups, 12
planning summary, 444
downloading
drivers, 10
Hardware Compatibility List (HCL), 7
system updates (Windows Update), 291
drivers
adapter types, 108
downloading, 10

DriveSpace 3.0, 202-204
Compression Agent, 288
compression methods (UltraPack), 288
compression ratios, 287
maximum file size, 284, 287
monitoring/optimization summary, 457
use guidelines, 286-287
dual-booting, 8
creating, 54-57

E

emergency startup disks, creating, 53-54
EMF (enhanced metafile) printing, 333
enabling
group permissions, 150-151
remote administration, 38-40
user profiles, 24-26
user-level security, 149-150
enhanced-mode NDIS adapter drivers, 108
exams
formats
  adaptive form, 423-424
  fixed form, 422-423
preparation, 420
retaking, 428-429
simulation questions, answering, 425
tips for taking, 422-427
  adaptive exams, 428
  answering simulation questions, 425-426
  fixed-form exams, 427-428
execute permissions (User Profiles), 26-28
explicit permissions, 145
Extract command-line switches, 297-300

F

Fast Facts section
  configuration summary
    Client for Microsoft Networks, 447
    Client for NetWare Networks, 447-448
    Dial-Up Networking Web Server, 447
    Fast Infrared, 450
    IEEE 1394 Firewire, 451
    IPX/SPX, 449
    master browsers, 448
    Microsoft Backup, 451-452
    Microsoft DLC, 449
    modems, 450
    multilink, 451
    multiple display support, 451
    NetBEUI, 449
    Personal Web Server, 446
    printers, 450
    Service for NetWare Directory Services
      (NDS), 448
    TCP/IP, 449
    USB (Universal Serial Bus), 450-451
    virtual private networking, 448
  installation summary
    automated setup, 446
    new setup, 446
    uninstall option, 446
    upgrade setup, 446
  integration summary
    Dial-Up Networking, 455
    Proxy Server, 455
  monitoring/optimization summary
    DiskDefragmenter, 456
    DriveSpace 3.0, 457

    Maintenance Wizard, 457
    Net Watcher, 456
    ScanDisk, 457
    System File Checker utility, 458
    System Monitor, 456
    Task Scheduler, 458
    Windows Update, 457
  planning summary
    access controls, 445
    automated setup, 445
    domains, 444
    file sharing, 445
    file systems, 443
    printer sharing, 445
    system policies, 444-445
    workgroups, 443
  resource management summary
    disk compression, 453
    disk partitioning, 454
    FAT32 conversion, 454
    group permissions, 452
    hardware profiles, 454
    network printers, 452
    passwords, 452
    Registry backup, 453
    remote computers, 452
    user permissions, 452
    user profiles, 453
  troubleshooting summary
    Conflict Manager, 458
    Ping, 459
    System Configuration Utility, 458-459
    Tracert, 459
    WinIPCfg, 459

Fast Infrared, configuration summary, 450

FAT16 (File Allocation Table/16-bit)

cluster size, 208-209

partitions, 206-207

dual-booting, 56-57

FAT32 (File Allocation Table/32-bit)

cluster size, 208-209

converting to, 208-209

dual-booting, 8

hard drive paritions, 7

operating systems, supported, 8

partitions, 206-207

dual-booting, 56-57

resource management summary, 454

versus FAT16, 208-209

FDISK utility, 205-207

File and Printer Sharing for Microsoft Networks, 98-99

File and Printer Sharing for NetWare Networks, 99

File menu commands, Sharing, 157-158

file sharing

administrator concerns, 29-31

clients

NetWare, 122-123, 236

Windows, 122-123

planning summary, 445

restrictions (Policy Editor), 189

status, monitoring, 264

troubleshooting, 347-349

file systems

planning summary, 443

selecting FAT16 versus FAT32, 8-9

files

automatic deletion (Disk Clean Up), 293

corrupted, monitoring, 298-300

disk management utilities, 343

Extract command line, 297

hard disk fragmentation, 278

long names

disabling, 341

LFNBK utility, 341

support, 9-10

management tools

Disk Compression, 277

Disk Defragmentor, 277

ScanDisk, 277

performance settings, 341-342

restoring (Backup utility), 173

troubleshooting, 339

tunneling, 340

write-behind caching, 339

Final Implementation Model, 15

fixed-form exams, 422-423, 427-428

floppy disks, installation files, 52

folders, creating, 157-158

fragmented hard disks (Disk Defragmenter), 278

full backups, 171-172

Backup utility, 79-80

G - H

group permissions

enabling, 150-151

resource management summary, 452

group policy files, adding, 35-36

hard disks

compressing (DriveSpace 3.0), 202-204

fragmentation (Disk Defragmentor), 278

minimum requirements for installation, 50

testing (ScanDisk), 57, 280-282

hardware
boot failures, resolving, 313-315
conflicts, identifying, 355-356
detection phase failures
causes, 59
DETCRASH.LOG file, 58-59
Hardware Compatibility List (HCL), 7
installing, 355-356
minimum Windows requirements, xxi-xxii, 50
profiles
creating, 212-214
laptops, 213-214
resource management summary, 454
system troubleshooting, 213-214
Registry settings, 356-363
System Configuration utility, 312
System Information utility, 355-356
troubleshooting, 353-354
Version Conflict Manager, 314
Hardware Compatibility List (HCL), downloading, 7
HKEY_CLASSES_ROOT, 358
HKEY_CURRENT_CONFIG, 359
HKEY_CURRENT_USER, 359
HKEY_DYN_DATA, 360
HKEY_LOCAL_MACHINE, 359
HKEY_USERS, 359
hot swapping, 71

I

IEEE 802.3 standard, frame type, 127
IEEE 1394 Firewire, 451
Demanding Digital Devices, 72-73
digital video bandwidths, 74
transfer rates, 73

Implementation Models
documentation, 16-17
final, 15
test stage, 16-17
implicit permissions, 151
incremental backups, 171-172
Backup utility, 79-80
.INF extension (Setup Information Files), 10
batch scripting, 53
Information Configuration utility, 314
infrared communication, 76
inherited permissions, 151
Install New Modem dialog box, 65
Installable File Service (IFS) Manager, 223
installation/configuration summary (Fast Facts section)
automated setup, 445-446
new setup, 446
uninstall option, 446
upgrade setup, 446
installing
Backup utility, 80-82, 170-171
failures, troubleshooting, 305-307
hardware, 355-356
modems, 66
Net Watcher from Windows 98 CD-ROM, 263
network services, 98-99
Policy Editor, 187-188
printers, 160-161
local, 67-68
network, 69-70
protocols, 130-131
System Policy Editor, 33-34
TCP/IP, 133-134

Windows 98
  across network method, 51-52
  batch setup scripts, 52-53
  CD-ROM method, 51-52
  floppy disk method, 51-52
  hardware detection failure, 58-59
  logical phases, 51-52
  pull installations, 11
  push installations, 11
  Setup program, 51-52
  upgrade effects, 54-55
integration summary (Fast Facts section)
  Dial-Up Networking, 455
  Proxy Server, 455
Internet, accessing proxy servers, 254-255
IntranetWare Client 2.2 for Windows, 113
IP (Internet Protocol) addresses
  DHCP server, 246
  name resolution, 246
  number of bits, 127
  subnet masks, 135
IPX/SPX, 237
  Client for NetWare Networks, 128, 132-133
  configurable settings, 132-133
  configuration summary, 449
  Dial-Up Networking, 252
  frame types, 132-133
  IEEE 802.3 standard, 127
  NetBIOS, 133

J - L

jobs (Backup utility), 172
joining
  domains, 224
  workgroups, 224

launching
  Policy Editor, 188
  Windows Update, 289-291
  WinIPCfg utility, 324
Legacy cards, 105, 110
LFNBK utility, long filenames, 341
line protocols
  PPP, 251
  SLIP, 251
local printers, 158
  installing, 67-68

M

Maintenance Wizard
  custom configuration, 293
  express configuration, 293
  monitoring/optimization summary, 457
  tools, 293
master browsers
  backup responsibilities, 117-121
  configuration summary, 448
  elections, 119-121, 226
  improper computer shutdowns, 118-121
  qualifying, 13-14, 226
  updates to backup browser, 117-121
MCP+Internet, *see* **Microsoft Certified
  Professional+Internet**
MCP+Site Building, *see* **Microsoft Certified
  Professional+Site Building**
MCP, *see* **Microsoft Certified Professional**
MCSD, *see* **Microsoft Certified Solution
  Developer**
MCSE+Internet, *see* **Microsoft Certified
  Systems Engineer+Internet**

MCSE, *see* Microsoft Certified Systems Engineer

MCT, *see* Microsoft Certified Trainer

MD command, 156

memory, minimum requirements, 50

meta-learning, 422

Microsoft Backup, configuration summary, 451-452

Microsoft Certified Professional (MCP) certification requirements, 413-414

Microsoft Certified Professional+Internet (MCP+Internet) certification requirements, 413-414

Microsoft Certified Professional+Site Building (MCP+Site Building) certification requirements, 413-414

Microsoft Certified Solution Developer (MCSD) certification requirements
  new track, 417-418
  old track, 418-419

Microsoft Certified Systems Engineer (MCSE), 413
  Windows 3.1 requirement, 415-416
  Windows NT 3.51 requirement, 415
  Windows NT 4.0 requirement, 415

Microsoft Certified Systems Engineer+Internet (MCSE+Internet) certification requirements, 414-417

Microsoft Certified Trainer (MCT) certification requirements, 414, 419-420

Microsoft Certified Training Web site, 419-420

Microsoft DLC (Data Link Control) protocol, 138
  configuration summary, 449

Microsoft Web site
  drivers, downloading, 10
  Hardware Compatibility List (HCL), 7
  Windows Update, 289-291

MKDIR command, 156

MODEMLOG.TXT log, 321-323

modems (modulation/demodulation)
  COM ports, 66
  command logging, 323
  configuration summary, 450
  dialing properties, 320
  external, 65
  installing, 66
  internal, 65
  MODEMLOG.TXT, 321
  portable, 65
  properties, modifying, 66
  troubleshooting, 322-323
  Windows 98 support, 65

modulation, 65

monitoring
  corrupted files, 298-300
  file sharing (Net Watcher), 264

monitoring/optimization summary (Fast Facts section)
  Disk Defragmenter, 456
  DriveSpace 3.0, 457
  Maintenance Wizard, 457
  Net Watcher, 456
  ScanDisk, 457
  System File Checker utility, 458
  System Monitor, 456
  task Scheduler, 458
  Windows Update, 457

monitors, multiple display support, 72

multilinking
configuration summary, 451
RAS client, 73
multiple display support
configuration summary, 451
number of monitors, 72

N - O

naming
computers, changing, 100
files, long file support, 9-10
workgroup guidelines, 13-14
Net Watcher, 156
connections, viewing, 262
file sharing, monitoring, 264
functions, 40
installing from Windows 98 CD-ROM, 263
monitoring/optimization summary, 456
peer-to-peer applications, 325
remote administration, 264-265
remote connections, 325
security levels, 262
shares, modifying, 264
when to use, 325
NetBEUI
advantages/disadvantages, 131
bindings, 131
configurable settings, 127, 449
Dial-Up Networking, 252
NetBIOS, 133
IP address resolution, 136
names, character length, 221
NETSETUP program, 57

NetWare
clients
directory services tree, 236
file sharing, 236
IPX/SPX protocol, 235-236
printer sharing, 236
user-level security, 237
networks
client types, 112-113
file sharing, 110-111
long filename support, 110
Microsoft 32-bit Client for NetWare
Networks, 111
NetWare Workstation Shell, 111
printer sharing, 110-111
user-level security, 111
Windows 98 limitations, 112
Workstation Shell, 111
Network Neighborhood, workgroups, 13-14
network printers, 158
installation/configuration, 69-70
print jobs, removing, 159
resource management summary, 452
share configurations, 69-70
network providers, 224
network services, installing, 98-99
networks
backup browsers, 117-121
clients, adding, 104-105
components
adapters, 102-103
clients, 102-103
protocols, 102-103
services, 102-103
configuration settings (Control Panel), 100

initial Windows 98 installation, 102-103

master browsers, 117-121

Net Watcher connections, viewing, 262

types supported by Windows 98, 100, 103

unified logons, 123

User Profiles, enabling, 24-26

Windows 98 deployment, 14-17, 52

NTFS partitions, dual-booting, 56-57

on-the-fly compression, 203-204, 284-285

operating systems

effects of Windows 98 upgrade, 54-55

FAT32 support, 8

NT domains, 12

P

partitions

cluster size, 208-209

dual-booting, 56-57

FAT16, 206-207

FAT32, 7, 206-207

FDISK utility, 205

resource management summary, 454

Password Authentication Protocol (PAP), 249-250

password list file (PWL), 123

passwords

access permissions, 145

authentication methods

Challenge Handshake Authentication Protocol (CHAP), 249-250

Password Authentication Protocol (PAP), 249-250

Shiva Password Authentication Protocol (SPAP), 249-250

blanks, 101

Control Panel settings, 193-194

password list file (PWL), 123

primary logons, 101

resource management summary, 452

security providers, 145

share-level security, 28-31, 148-149

user-level access control, 29-31

PCI video cards, 71

Peer Web Server

Internet protocols

FTP, 89-90

HTTP, 89-90

operating system support, 89-90

small workgroups, 89-90

permissions

explicit, 145

groups, 150-151

inherited, 151

security, share-level versus user-level, 146-149

user profiles, 146-150

delete, 26-28

execute, 26-28

read, 26-28

write, 26-28

Personal Web Server, 446

Ping utility, troubleshooting summary, 459

planning summary (Fast Facts section)

access controls, 445

domains, 444

file sharing, 445

printer sharing, 445

system policies, 444-445

workgroups, 443

Plug and Play
  local printer installation, 67-68
  non-support of legacy cards, 105
Point and Print, network printer installation,
  69-70
Policy Editor
  installing, 187-188
  launching, 188
  policy states
    neutral, 189
    off, 189
    on, 189
  security features
    custom folders, 191-197
    shell restrictions, 191-197
policy files
  creating (System Policy Editor), 34
  directory location (System Policy Editor),
    33-34
  entries, adding, 35-36
  icons
    groups, 35-36
    users, 35-36
PPP (Point-to-Point Protocol), 251
PPPLOG.TXT log, 323
PPTP (Point-to-Point Tunneling Protocol)
  client configuration components, 116
  configuring, 116
  Dial-Up Networking, 252
  filtering, 90
  functions, 115
  required components, 115
  virtual private networks, 114-115
pre-exam preparation tips, 426-427
pre-tests, strategies for studying, 422

Primary Domain Controller (PDC), 226
print jobs
  prioritizing, 68
  removing, 159
  reordering, 332
printer sharing
  administrator concerns, 29-31
  NetWare clients, 236
  planning summary, 445
  restrictions (Policy Editor), 189
  troubleshooting, 347-349
  Windows clients, 122-123
printers
  buffer, clearing, 330
  configuration summary, 450
  Control Panel settings, 194
  drivers
    compatibility, 68
    source files, 158
  EMF (enhanced metafile) print option, 333
  installation options
    Add Printer Wizard, 67-68
    Plug and Play, 67-68
  installing, 160-161
  jobs, reordering, 332
  local, 158
    installing, 67-68
  management of, 161
  network, 158
    connecting, 69-70
  print jobs, prioritizing, 68
  properties, viewing, 162
  RAW print option, 333
  share assignments, 161
  sharing, *see* printer sharing

slow, troubleshooting, 331
spool settings, 159, 162
spoolers, disabling, 330
supported models, 330
troubleshooting, 334-335
user connections, 221
user-level security, 331
prioritizing print jobs, 68
protocols
default setting under Windows 98, 129
Dial-Up Networking support, 320
installing, 130-131
IPX/SPX
Client for NetWare Networks, 132-133
configurable settings, 132-133
NetBEUI
advantages, 131
disadvantages, 131
NetBIOS, 133
routable, 127
supported by Windows 98, 129
TCP/IP
configuring, 134
installing, 133-134
Windows 98 support, 128
Proxy Server
integration summary, 455
Internet access, 254-255
pull installations, 11
push installations, 11

Q - R

QIC (quarter inch cartridge) specifications, 83
quick logon feature, 222

RAW printing, 333
read permissions (User Profiles), 26-28
real-mode NDIS adapter drivers, 108
real-mode ODI adapter drivers, 108
Redirector, 222
Registry
backup, resource management summary, 453
hardware settings, 356-363
modifications, 357-363
policies, creating, 362-363
remote editing, 37
root keys
HKEY_CLASSES_ROOT, 358
HKEY_CURRENT_USER, 359
HKEY_CUURENT_CONFIG, 359
HKEY_DYN_DATA, 360
HKEY_LOCAL_MACHINE, 359
HKEY__USERS, 359
ScanReg utility, 363
ScanRegW utility, 363
system files, 360
System Policy Editor, 361
Remote Access Server, 73
remote administration
directory privileges, 40
enabling, 38-40
Registry editing, 37
system monitoring, 38
Remote Administration dialog box, 265
remote computers, resource management summary, 452
remote file sharing, 157-158
remote servers, push installations, 11
removing Windows 98 from computers, 59
reordering print jobs, 332

resolving, *see* troubleshooting

resource management summary
(Fast Facts section)
disk compression, 453
disk partitioning, 454
FAT32 conversion, 454
group permissions, 452
hardware profiles, 454
network printers, 452
passwords, 452
Registry backup, 453
remote computers, 452
user permissions, 452
user profiles, 453

restoring files (Backup utility), 173

retaking exams, 428-429

roaming user profiles, 183-184

root directories, maximum number of files, 340

routable protocols, 127

roving profiles, 26-28

S

Safe Recovery dialog box, 58

ScanDisk, 57, 343
clusters, 281-282
command prompts, 281-283
cross-linked files, 280
log files, 280, 283
monitoring/optimization summary, 457
multitaskable, 283
primary checkpoints, 280-281
standard mode, 282
throrough mode, 282
typical repairs, 283
when to use, 277

scheduling system maintenance, 294

scripts, BATCH.EXE utility, 52-53

sector allocation, disk compression, 285

security
share-level, 28-31, 348-349
user-level, 29-31, 348-349

Select Network Component dialog box, 104

selecting file systems, FAT16 versus FAT32, 8-9

Service for NetWare Directory Services
(NDS), 448

SETUPLOG.TXT log, troubleshooting
installation failures, 305-307

share-level security, 28-31, 39-40, 348-349
access types
full, 147-149
password-dependent, 147-149
read, 147-149
passwords, 149
permissions, 146-149
planning summary, 445

shared installations, disadvantages, 50

sharing
NetWare clients, 122-123
printers, *see* printer sharing

Sharing command (File menu), 157-158

shell restrictions, 191-197

Shiva Password Authentication Protocol
(SPAP), 249-250

simulation questions, answering, 425-428

SLIP (Serial Line Interface Protocol), 251

software, minimum system requirements, xxi-xxii

spoolers (printers), 159, 162
disabling, 330

standard error statisitcs, adaptive form exams,
424

startup disks
creating, 53-54
troubleshooting functions, 323-324
statistics (adaptive form exams)
item characteristic curve, 424
standard error, 424
test information, 424
study strategies (exams), 420
active learning, 421
outlines, 421
pre-tests, 422
subnet masks (IP addresses), 135
SunSoft PC-NFS, 103
Sysedit, 311
System Configuration utility, 311-312, 315
troubleshooting summary, 458-459
System File Checker utility
monitoring/optimization summary, 458
primary function, 298-300
System Information utility, 312
components, 313
hardware conflicts, 355-356
hardware resources, 313
software environment, 313
system maintenance, scheduling, 294
System Management Server (SMS)
network installation functions, 10
push installations, 11
System Monitor
baseline performance, 268
bottlenecks, 266-267
categories, 266-267
counters, 267
effects of configuration changes, 266-268
functions, 40

graph types, 267
hardware performance, 266-267
log files, 268
monitoring/optimization summary, 456
performance counters, 267
remote administration, 38
system policies, 184-186
applying to
computers, 190
groups, 190
users, 190
check box options, 444
creating, 32
default file locations, 445
defined, 31-32
directory locations, 188
file sharing, restricting, 189
implementing, 187-188
planning summary, 445
Policy Editor, installing, 187-188
printer sharing, restricting, 189
states, setting, 189
type review, 444
User Profiles, 31-32
System Policy Editor
CD-ROM directory location, 32-34
default options, 35
installing, 33-34
system policies, creating, 32
template files, 36-37

T

tape drives, QIC (quarter-inch cartridge)
specifications, 83

Task Scheduler
  accessing, 295
  configuring, 296-297
  monitoring/optimization summary, 458
  primary function, 295
TCP/IP (Transmission Control Protocol/Internet Protocol)
  32-bit addressing, 135
  bindings options, 137
  configuring, 134, 449
  default versus preferred setting, 137
  Dial-Up Networking, 252
  DNS names, 137
  installing, 133-134
  IP addresses, 127, 135
  properties
    bindings, 245-246
    DNS configuration, 245-246
    Gateway, 245-246
    IP address, 245-246
    WINS configuration, 245-246
  WinIPCfg utility, 319
  WINS configuration, 136
templates (System Policy Editor), 36-37
testing Windows 98 deployment, 15-17
tests, *see* exams
third-party protocols, installing, 130-131
tips for taking exams, 422-428
token conversion, disk compression, 285
Tracert utility, troubleshooting summary, 459
troubleshooting
  access rights, 347-349
  boot failures, 313-315
  computers with hardware profiles, 213-214
  connectivity
    Net Watcher, 325
    Windows 98 wizards, 326
  device drivers, 353-354
  Dial-Up Networking, 321-323
  Fast Facts section
    Conflict Manager, 458
    Ping, 459
    System Configuration Utility, 458-459
    Tracert, 459
    WinIPCfg, 459
  files, 339
    disk management utilities, 343
    performance settings, 342
    sharing, 347-349
  hardware, 353-354
  installation failures
    DETCRASH.TXT, 305-307
    DETLOG.TXT, 305-307
    SETUPLOG.TXT, 305-307
  missing installation files, 312
  modems, 322-323
  print sharing, 347-349
  printers, 334-335
    EMF option, 333
    RAW option, 333
    slow, 331
  startup disk functions, 323-324

U - V

unified browsing, 118-121
unified logons, 123
uninstalling Windows 98, 59
updating new drivers, 10

upgrading to Windows 98, 54
  effects on operating systems, 55
USB (Universal Serial Bus)
  configuration summary, 450-451
  device support, 71
  hot swapping, 71
  improvements in Windows 98, 71
user permissions, 149-150
  resource management summary, 452
user profiles
  activating, 24-26
  copies of, 184
  corrupt, 25-26
  customized settings, 25-26, 183
  deleting, 25-26
  permissions, 26-28
  resource management summary, 453
  roaming, 183
  roving, 26-28
  settings, 183
  system policies, 31-32
user-level security, 348-349
  enabling, 149-150
  NetWare clients, 237
  NetWare environment, 122-123
  permissions, 146-149
  printers, 331
  remote administration, 39-40
  Windows environment, 122-123

Version Conflict Manager, 311, 314
video adapter cards
  AGP, 71
  PCI, 71

viewing
  network connections (Net Watcher), 262
  printer properties, 162
Virtual Private Networks, 448
  adapters, 115
  required components, 115
  support for, 114-115

W - Z

Web sites
  Microsoft Certified Training, 419-420
  Microsoft Windows Update, 289-291
Windows 98
  dual-booting, 8
  hardware, xxi-xxii
  installation
    phases, 51-52
    scripts, 52-53
  minimum system requirements, 50
  NetWare clients, 235-236
  networks
    architecture model, 222
    initial installation settings, 102-103
    supported types, 100, 103
  protocols
    default setting, 129
    supported types, 128-129
  shared installations, 50
  software, i-ii
  uninstalling, 59
Windows NT 3.51, Microsoft Certified Systems Engineer (MCSE) certification requirements, 415

Windows NT 4.0
  domains, 12
  dual-booting, creating, 55-57
  Microsoft Certified Systems Engineer
    (MCSE)
    certification requirements, 415
Windows Update
  accessing, 289-291
  device drivers, 290-291
  mandatory registration requirements, 292
  signing in, 290-291
WinIPCfg utility, 319
  launching, 324
  troubleshooting summary, 459
  viewable information, 324
WINS (Windows Internet Naming Service),
  128
  configuration for TCP/IP clients, 136
  IP address resolution, 135
wizards, troubleshooting, 326
workgroups
  benefits, 443
  file sharing, 13-14
  joining, 224
  master browser, electing, 226
  name of, 12-14
  planning summary, 443
  printer sharing, 13-14
workstations, push installations, 11
write permissions, 26-28
write-behind caching, 339

TRAINING GUIDES

Complete, Innovative, Accurate, Thorough

Our next generation *Training Guides* have been developed to help you study and retain the essential knowledge that you need to pass the MCSE exams. We know your study time is valuable, and we have made every effort to make the most of it by presenting clear, accurate, and thorough information.

In creating this series, our goal was to raise the bar on how MCSE content is written, developed, and presented. From the two-color design that gives you easy access to content, to the new software simulator that allows you to perform tasks in a simulated operating system environment, we are confident that you will be well-prepared for exam success.

Our New Riders Top Score Software Suite is a custom-developed set of full-functioning software applications that work in conjunction with the Training Guide by providing you with the following:

Exam Simulator tests your hands-on knowledge with over 150 fact-based and situational-based questions.
Electronic Study Cards really test your knowledge with explanations that are linked to an electronic version of the Training Guide.
Electronic Flash Cards help you retain the facts in a time-tested method.
An Electronic Version of the Book provides quick searches and compact, mobile study.
Customizable Software adapts to the way you want to learn.

MCSE Training Guide: Networking Essentials, Second Edition

1-56205-919-X, $49.99, 9/98

MCSE Training Guide: Windows NT Server 4, Second Edition

1-56205-916-5, $49.99, 9/98

MCSE Training Guide: Windows NT Server 4 Enterprise, Second Edition

1-56205-917-3, $49.99, 9/98

MCSE Training Guide: Windows NT Workstation 4, Second Edition

1-56205-918-1, $49.99, 9/98

MCSE Training Guide: Windows 98

1-56205-890-8, $49.99, Q4/98

MCSE Training Guide: TCP/IP, Second Edition

1-56205-920-3, $49.99, 10/98

MCSE Training Guide: SQL Server 7 Administration

0-7357-0003-6, $49.99, Q1/99

MCSE Training Guide: SQL Server 7 Design and Implementation

0-7357-0004-4, $49.99, Q1/99

MCSD Training Guide: Solution Architectures

0-7357-0026-5, $49.99, Q1/99

MCSD Training Guide: Visual Basic 6, Exam 70-175

0-7357-0002-8, $49.99, Q1/99

MCSD Training
Guide: Microsoft
Visual Basic 6,
Exam 70-176

0-7357-0031-1,
$49.99, Q1/99

TRAINING GUIDES

FIRST EDITIONS

Your Quality Elective Solution

MCSE Training Guide: Systems Management
Server 1.2, 1-56205-748-0

MCSE Training Guide: SQL Server 6.5
Administration, 1-56205-726-X

MCSE Training Guide: SQL Server 6.5
Design and Implementation, 1-56205-830-4

MCSE Training Guide: Windows 95, 70-064
Exam, 1-56205-880-0

MCSE Training Guide: Exchange Server 5,
1-56205-824-X

MCSE Training Guide: Internet Explorer 4,
1-56205-889-4

MCSE Training Guide: Microsoft Exchange
Server 5.5, 1-56205-899-1

MCSE Training Guide: IIS 4, 1-56205-823-1

MCSD Training Guide: Visual Basic 5,
1-56205-850-9

MCSD Training Guide: Microsoft Access,
1-56205-771-5

TESTPREPS

MCSE TestPrep:
Networking Essentials,
Second Edition

0-7357-0010-9,
$19.99, 11/98

MCSE TestPrep:
Windows 95, Second
Edition

0-7357-0011-7,
$19.99, 11/98

MCSE TestPrep:
Windows NT Server 4,
Second Edition

0-7357-0012-5,
$19.99, 12/98

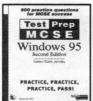

MCSE TestPrep:
Windows NT Server 4
Enterprise, Second
Edition

0-7357-0009-5,
$19.99, 11/98

MCSE TestPrep:
Windows NT
Workstation 4,
Second Edition

0-7357-0008-7,
$19.99, 11/98

MCSE TestPrep:
TCP/IP, Second
Edition

0-7357-0025-7,
$19.99, 12/98

MCSE TestPrep:
Windows 98

1-56205-922-X,
$19.99, Q4/98

TESTPREPS

FIRST EDITIONS

Your Quality Elective Solution

MCSE TestPrep: SQL Server 6.5
Administration, 0-7897-1597-X

MCSE TestPrep: SQL Server 6.5 Design and
Implementation, 1-56205-915-7

MCSE TestPrep: Windows 95 70-64 Exam,
0-7897-1609-7

MCSE TestPrep: Internet Explorer 4,
0-7897-1654-2

MCSE TestPrep: Exchange Server 5.5,
0-7897-1611-9

MCSE TestPrep: IIS 4.0, 0-7897-1610-0

Fast Track Series

The Accelerated Path to Certification Success

Fast Tracks provide an easy way to review the key elements of each certification technology without being bogged down with elementary-level information.

These guides are perfect for when you already have real-world, hands-on experience. They're the ideal enhancement to training courses, test simulators, and comprehensive training guides. *No fluff, simply what you really need to pass the exam!*

LEARN IT FAST

Part I contains only the essential information you need to pass the test. With over 200 pages of information, it is a concise review for the more experienced MCSE candidate.

REVIEW IT EVEN FASTER

Part II averages 50–75 pages, and takes you through the test and into the real-world use of the technology, with chapters on:

1) Fast Facts Review Section
2) The Insider's Spin (on taking the exam)
3) Sample Test Questions
4) Hotlists of Exam-Critical Concepts
5) Did You Know? (real-world applications for the technology covered in the exam)

MCSE Fast Track:
Networking Essentials

1-56205-939-4,
$19.99, 9/98

MCSE Fast Track:
Windows 98

0-7357-0016-8,
$19.99, Q4/98

MCSE Fast Track:
Windows NT Server 4

1-56205-935-1,
$19.99, 9/98

MCSE Fast Track:
Windows NT Server 4
Enterprise

1-56205-940-8,
$19.99, 9/98

MCSE Fast Track:
Windows NT
Workstation 4

1-56205-938-6,
$19.99, 9/98

MCSE Fast Track:
TCP/IP

1-56205-937-8,
$19.99, 9/98

MCSE Fast Track:
Internet Information
Server 4

1-56205-936-X,
$19.99, 9/98

MCSD Fast Track:
Solution Architectures

0-7357-0029-X,
$19.99, Q1/99

MCSD Fast Track:
Visual Basic 6,
Exam 70-175

0-7357-0018-4,
$19.99, Q4/98

MCSD Fast Track:
Visual Basic 6,
Exam 70-176

0-7357-0019-2,
$19.99, Q4/98

How to Contact Us

IF YOU NEED THE LATEST UPDATES ON A TITLE THAT YOU'VE PURCHASED:

1) Visit our Web site at www.newriders.com.

2) Click on the DOWNLOADS link, and enter your book's ISBN number, which is located on the back cover in the bottom right-hand corner.

3) In the DOWNLOADS section, you'll find available updates that are linked to the book page.

IF YOU ARE HAVING TECHNICAL PROBLEMS WITH THE BOOK OR THE CD THAT IS INCLUDED:

1) Check the book's information page on our Web site according to the instructions listed above, or

2) Email us at support@mcp.com, or

3) Fax us at (317) 817-7488 attn: Tech Support.

IF YOU HAVE COMMENTS ABOUT ANY OF OUR CERTIFICATION PRODUCTS THAT ARE NON-SUPPORT RELATED:

1) Email us at certification@mcp.com, or

2) Write to us at New Riders, 201 W. 103rd St., Indianapolis, IN 46290-1097, or

3) Fax us at (317) 581-4663.

IF YOU ARE OUTSIDE THE UNITED STATES AND NEED TO FIND A DISTRIBUTOR IN YOUR AREA:

Please contact our international department at international@mcp.com.

IF YOU WISH TO PREVIEW ANY OF OUR CERTIFICATION BOOKS FOR CLASSROOM USE:

Email us at pr@mcp.com. Your message should include your name, title, training company or school, department, address, phone number, office days/hours, text in use, and enrollment. Send these details along with your request for desk/examination copies and/or additional information.

WE WANT TO KNOW WHAT YOU THINK

To better serve you, we would like your opinion on the content and quality of this book. Please complete this card and mail it to us or fax it to 317-581-4663.

Name _____

Address _____

City _____ State _____ Zip _____

Phone_____ Email Address _____

Occupation _____

Which certification exams have you already passed? _____

_____

_____

_____

Which certification exams do you plan to take? _____

_____

_____

_____

What influenced your purchase of this book?
❑ Recommendation   ❑ Cover Design
❑ Table of Contents   ❑ Index
❑ Magazine Review   ❑ Advertisement
❑ Reputation of New Riders ❑ Author Name

How would you rate the contents of this book?
❑ Excellent   ❑ Very Good
❑ Good   ❑ Fair
❑ Below Average   ❑ Poor

What other types of certification products will you buy/have you bought to help you prepare for the exam?
❑ Quick reference books   ❑ Testing software
❑ Study guides   ❑ Other

What do you like most about this book? Check all that apply.
❑ Content   ❑ Writing Style
❑ Accuracy   ❑ Examples
❑ Listings   ❑ Design
❑ Index   ❑ Page Count
❑ Price   ❑ Illustrations

What do you like least about this book? Check all that apply.
❑ Content   ❑ Writing Style
❑ Accuracy   ❑ Examples
❑ Listings   ❑ Design
❑ Index   ❑ Page Count
❑ Price   ❑ Illustrations

What would be a useful follow-up book to this one for you?_____

Where did you purchase this book? _____

Can you name a similar book that you like better than this one, or one that is as good? Why?_____

_____

_____

How many New Riders books do you own? _____

What are your favorite certification or general computer book titles? _____

_____

What other titles would you like to see New Riders develop? _____

Any comments? _____

_____

_____

Fold here and Scotch tape to mail

- -

New Riders
201 W. 103rd St.
Indianapolis, IN 46290